Internationalists in European History

Internationalists in European History

Rethinking the Twentieth Century

Edited by
David Brydan and Jessica Reinisch

BLOOMSBURY ACADEMIC
LONDON • NEW YORK • OXFORD • NEW DELHI • SYDNEY

BLOOMSBURY ACADEMIC
Bloomsbury Publishing Plc
50 Bedford Square, London, WC1B 3DP, UK
1385 Broadway, New York, NY 10018, USA
29 Earlsfort Terrace, Dublin 2, Ireland

BLOOMSBURY, BLOOMSBURY ACADEMIC and the Diana logo are trademarks of
Bloomsbury Publishing Plc

First published in Great Britain 2021
This paperback edition published in 2022

Copyright © David Brydan and Jessica Reinisch, 2021

David Brydan and Jessica Reinisch have asserted their right under the Copyright, Designs and Patents Act, 1988, to be identified as Author of this work.

Cover Image © Air France: De nuit et de jour dans tous les ciels
(David Rumsey Historical Map Collection. All Rights Reserved)

All rights reserved. No part of this publication may be reproduced or transmitted in any form or by any means, electronic or mechanical, including photocopying, recording, or any information storage or retrieval system, without prior permission in writing from the publishers.

Bloomsbury Publishing Plc does not have any control over, or responsibility for, any third-party websites referred to or in this book. All internet addresses given in this book were correct at the time of going to press. The author and publisher regret any inconvenience caused if addresses have changed or sites have ceased to exist, but can accept no responsibility for any such changes.

Every effort has been made to trace copyright holders and to obtain their permissions for the use of copyright material. The publisher apologizes for any errors or omissions and would be grateful if notified of any corrections that should be incorporated in future reprints or editions of this book.

A catalogue record for this book is available from the British Library.

Library of Congress Cataloging-in-Publication Data
Names: Reinisch, Jessica, editor. | Brydan, David, editor.
Title: Internationalists in european history: rethinking the history of internationalism / edited by Jessica Reinisch and David Brydan.
Description: London; New York: Bloomsbury Academic, 2021. | Series: Histories of internationalism | Includes bibliographical references and index.
Identifiers: LCCN 2020035915 (print) | LCCN 2020035916 (ebook) |
ISBN 9781350107359 (hardback) | ISBN 9781472986986 (paperback) |
ISBN 9781350107366 (ebook) | ISBN 9781350107373 (epub)
Subjects: LCSH: Internationalism–History–20th century. |
Europe–Foreign relations–20th century. | World politics–20th century.
Classification: LCC JZ1308 .E97 2021 (print) | LCC JZ1308 (ebook) | DDC 327.4009/04–dc23
LC record available at https://lccn.loc.gov/2020035915
LC ebook record available at https://lccn.loc.gov/2020035916

ISBN: HB: 978-1-3501-0735-9
PB: 978-1-4729-8698-6
ePDF: 978-1-3501-0736-6
eBook: 978-1-3501-0737-3

Typeset by Deanta Global Publishing Services, Chennai, India

To find out more about our authors and books visit www.bloomsbury.com
and sign up for our newsletters.

Contents

List of contributors vii
List of illustrations xi
Abbreviations xii

Introduction: Internationalists in European History *David Brydan and Jessica Reinisch* 1

Part I   Communication and infrastructure

1   Building a communist Tower of Babel: Esperanto and the language politics of internationalism in revolutionary Russia *Brigid O'Keeffe* 17
2   Coded internationalism and telegraphic language *Heidi Tworek* 33
3   An international language for all: Basic English and the limits of a global communication experiment *Valeska Huber* 51
4   Radio and revolution: Tirana via Bari, from Moscow to Beijing *Elidor Mëhilli* 68

Part II   Local encounters

5   Speaking the language of humanitarianism or 'Speaking Bolshevik': Visions and vocabularies of relief in Soviet Armenia, 1920–8 *Jo Laycock* 89
6   Yugoslav refugees and British relief workers in Italian and Egyptian refugee camps, 1944–6 *Kornelija Ajlec* 105
7   Local and global: Religious institutes, Catholic internationalism and the Peru mission *Carmen M. Mangion* 124
8   Knowledge as aid: Locals experts, international health organizations and building the first Czechoslovak penicillin factory, 1944–9 *Sławomir Łotysz* 140

Part III   Internationalism as activism

9   Student activists and international cooperation in a changing world, 1919–60 *Daniel Laqua* 161
10   Vegetables of the world unite!: Grassroots internationalization of disabled citizens in the post-war period *Monika Baár* 182

11 'A writer deserves to be paid for his work': American progressive writers, foreign royalties and the limits of Soviet internationalism in the mid-to-late 1950s *Kristy Ironside*   198
12 Antagonistic internationalists: Catholic activists and the UN system after 1945 *David Brydan*   215

Part IV   Europe in a global context

13 Internationalists in flight?: Tourism, propaganda and the making of Air France's global empire *Jessica Lynne Pearson*   231
14 Even better than the real thing?: The United States, the TVA and the development of the Mekong *Vincent Lagendijk*   247
Afterword: On the chances and challenges of populating internationalism *Kiran Klaus Patel*   263

Select bibliography   281
Index   283

Contributors

Kornelija Ajlec is Associate Professor of Contemporary History at the Faculty of Arts, University of Ljubljana. She is a member of a national research programme, Slovene History (P6-0235), the Joint History Project at the Center for Democracy and Reconciliation in Southeast Europe and editor-in-chief of the *Retrospektive: Academic Journal for Historiography and Related Fields*. In 2016, she was a Fulbright visiting scholar at Rollins College in Winter Park, the UN Archives in New York and the US National Archives, College Park. Her research focuses on diplomatic relations of post–Second World War Yugoslavia with the United States and international organizations.

Monika Baár is Professor by Special Appointment in Central European Studies at the Institute for History at Leiden University. Her current research revolves around the history of disability and disability movements paying special attention to intersections with class, race, gender and displacement. She is principal investigator of the ERC Consolidator Grant Rethinking Disability: the Global Impact of the International Year of Disabled Persons (1981) in Historical Perspective. She is co-editor with Paul van Trigt of the special issue of *Diplomatica: A Journal of Diplomacy and Society* (2019) on 'Scripts for a New Stage: The United Nations' Global Observances' and the edited volume *Marginalized Groups and the post-War Welfare State in Historical Perspective: Whose Welfare?* (2019).

David Brydan is Lecturer in the History of Modern International Relations at King's College London. He works on the history of international cooperation and exchange in the twentieth century, and on modern Spanish history. His book, *Franco's Internationalists: Social Experts and Spain's Search for Legitimacy* (2019), is available as an open access book with Oxford University Press.

Valeska Huber is Head of the Emmy Noether Research Group 'Reaching the People: Communication and Global Orders in the Twentieth Century' at the Department of History, Free University of Berlin. In her research, she focuses on communication in various forms, from migration and mobility to epidemics and international health regimes, and, more recently, the politics of mass communication in the twentieth century, with a specific interest in education and language. She is the author of *Channelling Mobilities: Migration and Globalisation in the Suez Canal Region and Beyond, 1869-1914* (2013) and co-editor (with Jürgen Osterhammel) of *Global Publics: Their Power and Their Limits 1870-1990* (2020).

Kristy Ironside is Assistant Professor of Russian History at McGill University. Her first monograph, *A Full-Value Ruble: The Promise of Prosperity in the Postwar Soviet*

Union, is forthcoming with Harvard University Press in the spring of 2021. She is in the early stages of a second project on the Soviet Union and international copyright.

Vincent Lagendijk is Assistant Professor in the history department at Maastricht University. Vincent holds a PhD in the History of Technology from Eindhoven University of Technology, and was named postdoctoral fellow at the German Historical Institute in Washington, DC, for 2017–18. He is primarily interested in the history of international organizations, the role of experts and technology, the history of infrastructure, and transnational connections. He has worked on the notion of 'Europe' in relation to the construction of electricity networks, and is currently preparing a monograph on a global history of the Tennessee Valley Authority (TVA). His most recent research focuses on the intersection of road-building and racism in the city of Baltimore.

Daniel Laqua is Associate Professor of European History at Northumbria University in Newcastle upon Tyne, UK. His work is concerned with the dynamics and tensions of transnational activism, covering a variety of international movements and organizations. He has explored these themes in his monograph *The Age of Internationalism and Belgium, 1880–1930: Peace, Progress and Prestige* (2013). He is the editor of *Internationalism Reconfigured: Transnational Ideas and Movements between the World Wars* (2011) and has co-edited *International Organizations and Global Civil Society: Histories of the Union of International Associations* (2019) and *Imagined Cosmopolis: Internationalism and Cultural Exchange, 1870s–1920s* (2019). His current research addresses the role of internationalism within university settings between the 1920s and the 1960s.

Jo Laycock is Senior Lecturer in Migration and Diaspora History at the University of Manchester. She is the author of *Imagining Armenia: Orientalism, Ambiguity and Intervention* (2009). Her current research focuses on refugee relief and resettlement in Soviet Armenia.

Sławomir Łotysz is Professor at the Institute for the History of Science in the Polish Academy of Sciences in Warsaw, Poland. He has conducted research and published on themes in history of technology more generally, including inventiveness and technology transfer. He is also engaged in studying the environmental history. Recently, he has written a book on UNRRA penicillin plant programme in East-Central Europe, *Fabryka z darów. Penicylina za żelazną kurtyną 1945-1954* (*Donated Factory: Penicillin beyond the Iron Curtain 1945-1954*). He has been the president of ICOHTEC, the International Committee for the History of Technology, during 2017–21.

Carmen M. Mangion is Senior Lecturer in the Department of History, Classics and Archaeology at Birkbeck, University of London. Her research examines the cultural and social history of gender and religion in the nineteenth- and twentieth-century

Britain. She is the author of *Catholic Nuns and Sisters in a Secular Age, Britain 1945-1990* (2020) and *Contested Identities: Catholic Women Religious in nineteenth-century England and Wales* (2008), and other publications on gender and religion in Britain's nineteenth-century medical marketplace. Her current research examines the gendered nature of the Catholic medical missionary movement of the early twentieth century in both Britain and Ireland.

Elidor Mëhilli is Associate Professor of History and Public Policy at Hunter College of the City University of New York. He holds a PhD from Princeton University, and has been a visiting scholar at Columbia University, the University of Pennsylvania, New York University, Birkbeck, University of London, and the Zentrum für Zeithistorische Forschung in Potsdam, Germany. His book *From Stalin to Mao: Albania and the Socialist World* (2017) received the Marshall D. Shulman Book Prize, the Davis Center Book Prize and the Stavro Skendi Book Prize.

Brigid O'Keeffe is Associate Professor of history at Brooklyn College of the City University of New York. She is the author of *New Soviet Gypsies: Nationality, Performance, and Selfhood in the Early Soviet Union* (2013) and *Esperanto and Languages of Internationalism in Revolutionary Russia* (forthcoming). She is also preparing a manuscript for Bloomsbury's 'Russian Shorts' book series that will present in compact and accessible format the history of the Soviet Union as a multi-ethnic empire.

Kiran Klaus Patel holds the chair of European history at Ludwig Maximilian University Munich (LMU). Before joining LMU, he held chairs at Maastricht University in the Netherlands (2011–19) and the European University Institute in Florence, Italy (2007–11), and an Assistant Professorship at Humboldt University in Berlin (2002–7). His publications include *Project Europe: A History* (2020), *Nazism across Borders: The Social Policies of the Third Reich and their Global Appeal* (2018, edited with Sandrine Kott) and *The New Deal: A Global History* (2016).

Jessica Lynne Pearson is a historian of internationalism, decolonization and the French empire in the twentieth century. Her first book, *The Colonial Politics of Global Health: France and the United Nations in Postwar Africa*, was published by Harvard University Press in 2018. She is the co-editor of the volume *The United Nations and Decolonization* (Routledge, 2020). Presently, she is working on a book manuscript entitled *Traveling to the End of Empire: Leisure Tourism in the Era of Decolonization*, which explores the global entanglements between travel and the collapse of the French and British Empires in the twentieth century. She is currently Assistant Professor of History at Macalester College in Saint Paul, Minnesota.

Jessica Reinisch is Professor in Modern European History at Birkbeck, University of London. Her publications include *The Perils of Peace: Public Health in Occupied Germany* (2013, available as a free e-book from OUP), *The Disentanglements of*

Populations: Migration, Expulsion and Displacement in postwar Europe, 1944-1949 (edited with Elizabeth White), *Post-War Reconstruction in Europe: International Perspectives, 1945-1949* (edited with Mark Mazower and David Feldman) and *Refugees in Europe, 1919-1959* (2018, edited with Matthew Frank). She was awarded a Wellcome Investigator Award for her project 'The Reluctant Internationalists'. She is the director of the Centre for the Study of Internationalism at Birkbeck.

Heidi Tworek is Associate Professor of International History and Public Policy at the University of British Columbia, Vancouver, Canada. She is a non-resident fellow at the German Marshall Fund of the United States and the Canadian Global Affairs Institute. Her book, *News from Germany: The Competition to Control World Communications* (2019), received the Wiener Holocaust Library Fraenkel Prize and the Ralph Gomory Prize from the Business History Conference. She has co-edited two volumes: *Exorbitant Expectations: International Organizations and the Media in the Nineteenth and Twentieth Centuries* (2018) and *The Routledge Companion to the Makers of Global Business* (2019). She has published widely on the history of communications, international relations and business.

Illustrations

3.1	Basic English Chart	61
4.1	Peasants hear the clandestine radio blaring 'Death to Communism, Freedom to Albania' in the early 1950s	74
13.1	1948 Air France poster	240

Abbreviations

AGBU	Armenian General Benevolent Union
AND	Armenian National Delegation
ARA	American Relief Administration
BBC	British Broadcasting Corporation
CCNR	Central Commission for the Navigation of the Rhine
CELAM	Conference of Latin American Bishops
CHRUSP	Center for the Human Rights of Users and Survivors of Psychiatry
CIA	Central Intelligence Agency
CICIAMS	*Comité International Catholique des Infirmières et Assistantes Médico-Sociales*
CPUSA	Communist Party of the United States of America
CPY	Yugoslav Communist Party
CRB	Central Refugees Board
ČSL	Czechoslovak People's Party (*Československá Strana Lidová*)
DPI	Disabled Peoples' International
ECAFE	UN Economic Commission for Asia and the Far East
EU	European Union
FIDES	Investment Fund for Economic and Social Development
FIMITIC	*Fédération Internationale des Mutiles, des Invalids du Travail et des Invalides Civics*
FLN	National Liberation Front, Algeria
GDR	German Democratic Republic
HUAC	House Un-American Activities Committee
IALA	International Auxiliary Language Association
IASSIDD	International Association for the Scientific Study of Intellectual and Developmental Disabilities
ICN	International Council of Nurses
ICOs	International Catholic Organizations
IFB	International Federation of the Blind

ILO	International Labour Organization
INGOs	International Non-Governmental Organisations
IOs	International Organizations
IRN	International Rivers Network
IRO	International Refugee Organization
ISC	International Student Conference
ISOD	International Sports Organization for the Disabled
ITU	International Telegraph Union (from 1932 the International Telecommunication Union)
IUS	International Union of Students
JECI	International Young Catholic Students (*Jeunnesse Étudiante Catholique Internationale*)
KUTV	Communist University for the Toilers of the East
LMF	Lord Mayor's Fund for Armenian Refugees
MERRA	Middle East Relief and Refugee Administration
NATO	North Atlantic Treaty Organization
NCWC	National Catholic Welfare Conference
NGOs	Non-Governmental Organizations
NEP	New Economic Policy
NER	Near East Relief
OSS	Office of Strategic Services
RFE	Radio Free Europe
RME	World Student Association (*Rassemblement Mondial des Étudiants*)
RL	Radio Liberty
TVA	Tennessee Valley Authority
UCC	Universal Copyright Convention
UGEMA	*Union Générale des Étudiants Musulmans Algériens*
UIA	Union of International Organizations
UN	United Nations
UNCRPD	United Nations Convention on the Rights of Persons with Disabilities
UNESCO	United Nations Educational, Scientific and Cultural Organization
UNRRA	United Nations Relief and Rehabilitation Administration
UNSCCUR	United Nations Scientific Conference on the Conservation and Utilization of Resources

VOKS	All-Union Society for Cultural Relations with Foreign Countries (*Vsesoiuznoe obshchestvo kul'turnoi sviazi s zagranitsei*)
WCD	World Commission on Dams
WHO	World Health Organization
WPA	World Program of Action Concerning Disabled Persons
WSCF	World Student Christian Federation
YNLA	Yugoslav National Liberation Army

Introduction

Internationalists in European History

David Brydan and Jessica Reinisch

Today, thinking about 'internationalism' is no longer a minority interest. After at least a decade of challenges to many international organizations, questions about the nature of the international 'glue' that has held societies and institutions together have become commonplace. Whereas the timelessness of the international system in the post–Cold War world had been widely taken for granted, we are now forced to consider a world that looks very different and less predictable. In the wake of the 2007–8 financial crisis, and again during the refugee crisis in 2015, voters in many parts of the world expressed their nostalgia for a less-connected, less-global age and their resentment towards the apparently unstoppable globalization that seemed to have left many of them behind. Organizations such as the United Nations (UN) and the North Atlantic Treaty Organization (NATO) were forced into a process of self-examination and justification, often with rather mixed results. The European Union, as one of the products of a post-war desire for regional and international cooperation to secure peace and prosperity, faced criticism from a variety of quarters for undermining national sovereignty, national borders and national interests or, alternatively, for not being able to forge compromises and act in the collective interests of its member states.

Writing about the history of internationalism in this context took on a new significance: it was no longer possible to assume that international arrangements were fixed indefinitely in their post-1945 shape or rationale, that the Western liberal take on internationalism had outlived other forms, or even that collaboration to prevent war and conflict was a universally desired good. It was not the end of history, after all.[1] This much was already clear by late 2019, when the first draft of this book was written, and had motivated its contributors to rethink internationalism in its past and present forms. Many of the ideas and themes explored in this volume first emerged from the research and discussions developed during a four-year collaborative research project at Birkbeck, University of London ('The Reluctant Internationalists', 2013–18), which was led by Jessica Reinisch and brought together a network of historians of Europe and beyond.[2]

---

[1] Compare with Francis Fukuyama's *The End of History and the Last Man* (1991), who had argued that the supposed victory of Western liberal capitalism that brought the Cold War to an end made up the 'final form of human government' and marked the end point of evolution and change.

[2] See the archived project website, including its final report, on http://www.bbk.ac.uk/reluctantinternationalists/

After the economic, political and social uncertainties of the late 2000s and 2010s, the relevance of the history of internationalism was then further highlighted by the unfolding of the COVID-19 crisis in early 2020. Writing this introduction in April 2020, it is impossible to say what longer-term patterns of international cooperation will ultimately emerge from the crisis. But already it has thrown into sharp relief how little multilateral action has been pursued by states across the world. At the same time, we have seen how much the successful management of border-crossing hazards such as the coronavirus required a global strategy and degree of international cooperation to arbitrate between competing national interests (in matters such as travel bans and border closures, for example), to mitigate broken global supply chains and to coordinate different research projects in the search for a vaccine. What we are currently witnessing is far removed from the popular sanitized version of internationalism, with its apparently universal values and timeproof institutions, and rather a much more complex and contested process. It is this often fraught history of internationalism which we seek to explore in this volume, and which seems more pertinent now than ever.

What is internationalism?

This volume presents new research on a series of case studies and contexts in which ideas about internationalism were debated, with the aim of presenting a much fuller account of the modern history of internationalism in and beyond Europe. In this volume and in the histories it narrates, 'internationalism' can refer to a number of very different ideas and practices: the search for intergovernmental agreements and conventions; the practice of international assembly; the projection of national agendas across the globe; or the transfer of ideas, objects or people across national boundaries. It can also refer to the shared agendas of particular international movements or organizations – both as an aspiration to universalism and as a much more limited, less ambitious attempts at cooperation.

Academic approaches to these histories have varied significantly over time and across disciplines. Among historians, questions about international political constellations and agreements traditionally fell within the remit of diplomatic history, with a focus on states' foreign policy and international diplomacy. Political historians interested in international relations, in particular, long tended to contrast (at least implicitly) 'internationalism' with 'nationalism'. Both facets were clearly connected, but in a century dominated by bloody world wars and intensifying nationalism and protectionism, to many scholars they seemed to be increasingly pitted against each other. This notion was boosted by a growing focus on internationalism as a liberal and progressive pursuit that was fundamentally anti-nationalist in orientation. Here it is worth bearing in mind that the political clothes of nationalism had changed significantly since the national liberation movements of the mid-nineteenth century, for whom nationalism was an aspiration and ideology largely of left and liberal thinkers who wanted their 'nation' to achieve self-government. However, by the end of the nineteenth and start of the twentieth centuries, nationalism had widely become an ideology of the conservative establishments. In this context, many of the self-declared 'internationalists' of the era wrote about their internationalism as a moral force for good: as a way to correct the evils of war and the hyper-nationalism of the war-mongering states around them, or as a means to imagine a world without borders or states. Scholars often took them at their word and similarly understood internationalism as a liberal, anti-nationalist project. According to this approach, other endeavours may have taken place internationally and brought together individuals or groups of various nationalities, but were not genuinely *international* if they did not fit into this particular political mould.

Since then we have come a long way. A growing, diverse and diversifying body of scholarship has presented a much more complex and nuanced picture.[3] Particularly useful for defining and redefining the emerging fields of research have been a number of edited volumes and special journal issues published in the last two decades. One of the first was Paul Weindling's collection *International Health Organisations and Movements, 1918-1939*, which presented research on a variety of international organizations active in the fields of health, welfare, eugenics and social policy in the decades between the First and the Second World Wars. The volume established international organizations as crucial tools for, or sites of, the promotion of social and political reforms, and, as a result, as important objects of study for historians working beyond the realms of diplomacy and foreign affairs. As Weindling explained, 'International bodies may remedy local deficiencies, set optimal standards and improve the quality of the systems of care and the training of personnel.'[4] A few years later, Martin Geyer and Johannes Paulmann's edited volume *The Mechanics of Internationalism* took a broad look at a rich variety of mid- to late nineteenth-century international movements and organizations, ranging from governmental bodies to informal networks, so as to show 'how national rivalries over forms of representation at an international level were worked out in terms of organization and ideology'.[5] In the process, they made a strong case for the use of the term 'internationalism' rather than 'transnationalism', a term that had grown in popularity in some academic subject areas.[6] As their collection demonstrated, 'internationalism' was the historically more accurate term, used in the nineteenth and well into the twentieth century, and with renewed vigour in the aftermath of the Second World War, by many of those people who were advocating for new international structures and organizations. It applied to both particular political and social movements, and to the process of internationalizing spaces and practices. However, it is worth adding that while 'internationalism' was widely used in English and other languages, it lacked obvious counterparts in other languages.

---

[3] For an overview, see Ana Antic, Johanna Conterio and Dora Vargha, eds, 'Conclusion: Beyond Liberal Internationalism', *Contemporary European History* 25, no. 2 (2016): 359–71.
[4] Paul Weindling, *International Health Organisations and Movements, 1918-1939* (Cambridge: Cambridge University Press, 1995), 1.
[5] Martin H. Geyer and Johannes Paulmann, *The Mechanics of Internationalism* (Oxford: Oxford University Press, 2001), v.
[6] On historians' use of the term 'transnationalism', which was first popularized among the social sciences, see, for example, the *Contemporary European History* special issue edited by Patricia Clavin 14, no. 4 (November 2005), or Pierre-Yves Saunier, *Transnational History* (London: Red Globe Press, 2013).

In 'The Reluctant Internationalists' project, a snapshot of which was published as a *Contemporary European History* special issue in 2016, we set out to think about 'internationalisms' in the plural, avoiding the temptation to identify the one and only true version and simply dismiss the rest.[7] What was needed, we argued, was a more systematic stocktaking of the different internationalist models and perspectives, in an attempt to understand them as different answers to similar questions about the nature of the modern world. This involves incorporating a range of international activities and networks from across the political spectrum into the internationalism canon, including those that had in the Anglo-American literature long been excluded as 'too extreme' or anti-liberal, on both the left and the right.

Kiran Patel and Sven Reichardt's *Journal of Contemporary History* special issue on 'The Dark Side of Transnationalism', published in the same year, similarly took seriously the idea that international and transnational networks of Nazi experts in social engineering in the 1930s and 1940s need to be understood as a version of internationalism in practice.[8] They joined a growing body of scholarship that illustrated the long history of far-right, conservative and nationalist movements cooperating across borders. Recent research has drawn attention to the history of a wide range of right-wing and conservative transnational movements, to international cooperation among anti-communist campaigners and fighters, and to the global networks and ambitions of neoliberal thinkers.[9] Perhaps the most significant strand of this research has focused on international cooperation between fascist states and movements, including the international projects of Mussolini's Italy in the late 1920s and early 1930s, the diplomatic alliances between Italy, Germany, Japan and other states before and during the Second World War, and the pan-Europeanism of many Nazi thinkers and SS volunteers. As the historian of international war veterans' movements, Ángel Alcalde, has recently argued, the transnational turn represents a new 'consensus' in fascism studies, helping the field to move beyond debates over 'generic' fascism to explore questions of transfer, interaction, hybridization and exchange.[10]

At the other end of the political spectrum, the international dimensions of the history of communism and socialism have also been explored in recent and not-so-recent research, drawing attention to both the extent of popular engagement with it and to its different manifestations around the world at different points in time. The First

---

[7] See the special issue on 'Agents of Internationalism' and Jessica Reinisch's introduction, *Contemporary European History*, 25, no. 2 (May 2016): 195–205.

[8] Special issue on 'The Dark Side of Transnationalism', *Journal of Contemporary History* 51, no. 1 (January 2016).

[9] Luc van Dongen, Stéphanie Roulin and Giles Scott-Smith, eds, *Transnational Anti-Communism and the Cold War: Agents, Activities and Networks* (London: Palgrave Macmillan, 2014); Kyle Burke, *Revolutionaries for the Right: Anticommunist Internationalism and Paramilitary Warfare in the Cold War* (Chapel Hill, NC: University of North Carolina Press, 2018); Quinn Slobodian, *Globalists, The End of Empire and the Birth of Neoliberalism* (Cambridge, MA: Harvard University Press, 2018); Giuliana Chamedes, *A Twentieth-Century Crusade: The Vatican's Battle to Remake Christian Europe* (Cambridge, MA: Harvard University Press, 2019). Most recently, see Glenda Sluga and Philippa Hetherington's special issue of the *Journal of World History* on 'Liberal and Illiberal Internationalisms', February 2020.

[10] Ángel Alcalde, 'The Transnational Consensus: Fascism and Nazism in Current Research', *Contemporary European History* 29, no. 2 (May 2020): 243–52.

and Second Socialist Internationals, and the Communist International (Comintern), received periodic (if limited) scholarly attention in the English-speaking literature, but it took much longer for the internationalisms of the Left to be studied in the Cold War years.[11] However, as recent work has shown, throughout the Cold War era sustained international exchanges took place between officials, workers, students and various experts, both within and beyond the socialist bloc.[12] While many of these networks were centred in Eastern Europe and the Soviet Union, others connected Europe and Europeans with socialists in other parts of the world.[13] The 'Socialism Goes Global' research group has helped to uncover the vibrant web of contacts which linked the 'second' and 'third' worlds during the Cold War.[14] Others have highlighted the efforts of countries like China to promote their own model of socialist internationalism, building ties with Asia, Africa and beyond.[15]

In 2017, Glenda Sluga and Patricia Clavin's *Internationalisms: A Twentieth-Century History* brought together many of these strands of research, presenting familiar histories of liberal international activists and institutions alongside work on socialist, fascist, religious and indigenous internationalism, and exploring the role of gender, human rights, law and health in the history of twentieth-century international movements.[16] Thanks to these and many other publications, it is no longer possible to categorize internationalism simply as the antithesis of nationalism, nor as a straightforwardly or solely liberal phenomenon. Instead, scholars have recognized it as an ideologically, politically and practically diverse set of activities and ideas, embraced by actors across the political spectrum for a variety of ends. We now understand the period since the mid-nineteenth century as one of intensive cooperation between nation states, expanding global trade networks, interlinked economic systems, exchanges across borders and encounters between different individuals and cultures.[17] In this context, different models and versions of internationalism fed on each other, were defined against each other and presented at times directly competing views of the world. The Anglo-American liberal version of 'internationalism' itself was the product of

---

[11] On the First, Second and Third Internationals, see, for example, R. Craig Nation, *War on War: Lenin, the Zimmerwald Left and the Origins of Communist Internationalism* (London: Duke University Press, 1989); David Blaazer, *The Popular Front and the Progressive Tradition: Socialists, Liberals and the Quest for Unity, 1884-1939* (Cambridge: Cambridge University Press, 1992); Moira Donald, 'Workers of the World Unite? Exploring the Enigma of the Second International', in Martin H. Geyer and Johannes Paulmann, *The Mechanics of Internationalism* (op. cit.); Kevin McDermott and Jeremy Agnew, *The Comintern: A History of International Communism from Lenin to Stalin* (New York: St Martin's, 1997); Norman LaPorte, Kevin Morgan and Matthew Worley, eds, *Bolshevism, Stalinism and the Comintern: Perspectives on Stalinization, 1917-1953* (Basingstoke: Palgrave, 2008).

[12] Rachel Applebaum, *Empire of Friends: Soviet Power and Socialist Internationalism in Cold War Czechoslovakia* (Ithaca, NY: Cornell University Press, 2019).

[13] Elidor Mëhilli, *From Stalin to Mao: Albania and the Socialist World* (Ithaca, NY: Cornell University Press, 2017).

[14] Socialism Goes Global, http://socialismgoesglobal.exeter.ac.uk/ (accessed 16 December 2019).

[15] Julia Lovell, *Maoism: A Global History* (London: Bodley Head, 2019).

[16] Glenda Sluga and Patricia Clavin, eds, *Internationalisms: A Twentieth-Century History* (Cambridge: Cambridge University Press, 2017).

[17] See esp. Mark Mazower, *Governing the World: The Rise and Fall of an Idea* (London: Penguin, 2012) and Jürgen Osterhammel, *The Transformation of the World: A Global History of the Nineteenth Century* (Princeton, NJ: Princeton University Press, 2014).

competition and clashes with some of these other paradigms, and intersected with a range of local, national and imperial agendas. The nineteenth and twentieth centuries saw the enormous expansion of international professional networks, and witnessed the growth of many international and regional organizations, ranging from voluntary or philanthropic initiatives and NGOs, to state institutions. We also know that the nineteenth and twentieth centuries were shaped by the mass movement of people across borders, and with them the travel of ideas and objects. All of these developments were marked by recurrent controversies about the precise relationship between local, national and international actors and priorities.

Internationalism from below, and internationalism in Europe

In this volume we want to put internationalism at the heart of modern European history, to show how ideas about internationalism were shaped by, and in turn shaped, the lives of millions of people in Europe and beyond. The chapters showcase a diverse set of actors who turned to the international sphere and championed certain forms of international cooperation or international solutions at specific moments, on specific subjects, and to specific ends. These actors and their ideas about the world they lived in drew on different intellectual and political traditions, and in practice were shaped by different constellations of foreign policy objectives, economic policies, humanitarian concerns and professional identities. Necessarily, then, in this volume we think about 'internationalism' in the broadest possible sense, and have avoided adopting a narrow definition which might limit our scope or approach. All of our case studies analyse how the historical actors in questions defined and thought about 'internationalism', some of whom (such as groups of Soviet and Eastern European actors) did not necessarily use that term.

Foregrounding the variety and diversity of twentieth-century internationalisms also involves challenging some of the traditional chronologies of the period, which have often been linked to the rise and fall of major international organizations such as the League of Nations or the UN. The chapters in this volume fit into the frame of the 'short twentieth century' (beginning with the First World War and ending with the end of the Cold War), and foreground certain moments of the century which were particularly conducive to debates about international exchange and cooperation.[18] The aftermaths of the two world wars played an important role in the history of internationalism and feature in several of the case studies here. A number of chapters show that the post-war eras witnessed the widespread (albeit often short-lived) popularity of pragmatic, functionalist solutions to transborder problems such as epidemics or refugees, which were a catalyst for the creation of some of the international organizations and mechanisms that have lasted until today.

In addition to emphasizing the roles played by different models of internationalism at different points in time, the chapters in this volume seek to make two particular contributions to the field:

---

[18] For the thesis of the 'short twentieth century', see Eric Hobsbawm's *Age of Extremes* (1994).

(i) Internationalism as a lived experience

Much of the scholarship on international movements and organizations has traditionally focused on the question of their impact or causal significance. The omnipresence of international organizations and networks in the twenty-first century is often taken as evidence of their institutional and intellectual successes. But international movements collapsed, failed or disappeared from the historical record just as often as they succeeded, survived or solved the problems for which they were created. Even where they didn't explicitly fail, many international projects were restricted to relatively small groups of people in limited areas, or in practice did not influence ideas or institutions beyond their narrowly defined fields. Rather than emphasizing the 'success' or 'impact' of such movements, this volume argues that we need to appreciate the ubiquity and heterogeneity of internationalist endeavours if we are to understand their true significance. Internationalism – in the form of an enormous range of organizations, movements, projects, networks and ideas with international ambitions – was present in almost every aspect of Europeans' lives in the twentieth century, from political movements and religious faith, to disability activism and copyright law (to name but a few examples explored in this volume). Regardless of their area of study or field of interest, our histories are likely to be incomplete if they don't take these international dimensions into account in some way.

This becomes particularly obvious when we shift focus away from the top-down histories of institutions that have tended to dominate past accounts. The chapters in this volume pay close attention to how people have been 'doing internationalism', in Carmen Mangion's words below – to the diverse ways in which individuals thought and acted internationally, or reached beyond national borders to imagine or create international connections. This is not to say that international organizations and institutions play no role here: they have featured centrally in many histories of internationalism, and they do so in the chapters in this volume. They represent concrete and often contested sites of activity and debates about international cooperation. Many of them also left behind rich archives in which historians can find traces of internationalism in practice. International organizations such as the League of Nations, the Comintern, the International African Institute, the United Nations Relief and Rehabilitation Administration, the Food and Agriculture Organization, and the Disabled People's International, to name but a few, feature centrally in the following chapters. But the contributors use them above all to try to understand how they affected and were shaped by the people involved with their work – including individuals on the ground, in the field, in the local offices or refugee camps. In other words, all the authors in this volume seek to restore a sense of the lived experience of internationalism. None are writing about an organization as an end in itself, and all of them supplement institutional archives with a range of other primary sources. In this they are building on recent research that has set out to rethink the history of international organizations, challenging familiar chronologies and geographies of internationalism in the process.[19]

---

[19] See, for example, Madeleine Herren, ed., *Networking the International System: Global Histories of International Organizations* (Heidelberg: Springer, 2014), and Simon Jackson and Alanna O'Malley, eds, *The Institution of International Order: From the League of Nations to the United Nations*

Individuals, both those who worked with international organizations and those who were targeted as the recipients of their schemes, as well as other 'agents of internationalism', are at the heart of this volume. Uncovering their perspectives can reveal the divergent social and political ideas which underpinned international projects. Understanding internationalism as a lived experience involves paying particularly close attention to language and methods of communication as a linchpin of transnational and international contacts. The chapters show how the successes of international programmes depended on participants' ability to communicate across linguistic, political, cultural and economic borders, and how often organizations' failures rested in practice on failed communication attempts. The chapters also shed light on the widespread appeal of technocratic solutions to many social and political problems, and particularly on the roles played by technical experts and infrastructure in forging international connections and the political contexts in which they operated. As they show, assumptions about the universalism of scientific, technical or technocratic internationalism were shared by many Europeans at key moments in the twentieth century.

Overall, in this volume we want to foreground a 'bottom-up', actor-focused approach to the history of internationalism, by exploring the perspectives of local and national actors and thereby laying bare a complex set of agendas which underpinned international collaborations in practice. By bringing together commonly disconnected strands of European history and history from below, this volume seeks to promote a deeper understanding of internationalism in its many historical guises.

(ii) Europe and Europeans

Reacting against the old Eurocentrism (of both history and historiography), much of the recent scholarship on the history of internationalism has justifiably shifted attention to other parts of the globe. Many important new insights have emerged from research into the relationship between internationalism, imperialism and decolonization.[20] International organizations played an important role in the development of European imperial rule in the twentieth century. The European imperial powers, for example, attempted to use the League of Nations to protect and strengthen their empires, although in practice the Mandates Commission they created provided a platform for colonial nationalists or non-colonial states to challenge their rule.[21] Mark Mazower has argued that the UN, just like the League before it, was a product of empire and imperial thought.[22] The influence of imperial powers over international organizations was gradually undermined by the creation

(Abingdon: Routledge, 2018); Haakon A. Ikonomou and Karen Gram-Skjoldager, eds, *The League of Nations: Perspectives from the Present* (Aarhus: Aarhus University Press, 2019).

[20] In addition to the works cited below, see Jeronimo and Monteiro, eds, *Internationalism, Imperialism and the Formation of the Contemporary World: The Pasts of the Present* (Cham: Palgrave Macmillan, 2018).

[21] Susan Pedersen, *The Guardians: The League of Nations and the Crisis of Empire* (Oxford: Oxford University Press, 2015).

[22] Mark Mazower, *No Enchanted Palace: The End of Empire and the Ideological Origins of the United Nations* (Princeton: Princeton University Press, 2013).

of a new wave of independent states from the late 1940s. But the process was not a straightforward one. Jessica Pearson, for example, has recently shown how France fought a vigorous rearguard battle to prevent the UN and agencies such as the World Health Organization from threatening its colonial authority.[23] By the early 1960s, the UN had become a battleground between imperial states trying to protect and defend their influence, and post-colonial states seeking to overturn the inequalities of the colonial era.[24]

The UN General Assembly's adoption of proposals for a New International Economic Order in 1974 is increasingly held up by historians as evidence of the growing influence and assertiveness of post-colonial states on the international stage.[25] But in many ways it represented the culmination of important strands of anti-colonial internationalism and anti-colonial activity within international organizations which had been developing since the start of the twentieth century. Pan-Africanists worked throughout the twentieth century to develop a set of ideas and institutional structures which both borrowed from and critiqued the liberal internationalism of Western states and imperial powers.[26] Vibrant communities of anti-colonial activists emerged in cities like London and Paris, particularly during the interwar period, helping to develop many of the ideas which would go on to shape the process of post-war decolonization.[27] Black women internationalists played a particularly active role in these networks, but one which has until recently been often overlooked.[28] After the Second World War, anti-colonial nationalists explored new models of federalism and cooperation between post-colonial states, and fought to establish a new, more equitable international system.[29] In the context of the Cold War, many Afro-Asian states sought to carve out a 'third way' between the two superpowers, mirrored by an increasingly vibrant network of activists, intellectuals and other non-state actors building ties across the Global South.[30]

These and other works have helped to expand the geographical scope of the study of internationalism, with important consequences for our understanding of the dynamics of power. But it is noteworthy that this geographical expansion has been fundamentally uneven, with some dense areas of interest and others which

---

[23] Jessica Lynne Pearson, *The Colonial Politics of Global Health: France and the United Nations in Postwar Africa* (Cambridge, MA: Harvard University Press, 2018).

[24] Alanna O'Malley, *The Diplomacy of Decolonization: America, Britain and the United Nations during the Congo Crisis 1960-1964* (Manchester: Manchester University Press, 2018).

[25] Getachew, *Worldmaking After Empire: The Rise and Fall of Self-Determination* (Princeton, NJ: Princeton University Press, 2019), ch. 5. See also the special issue of *Humanity* on the NIEO, 6, no. 1 (2015).

[26] Hakim Adi, *Pan-Africanism: A History* (London: Bloomsbury, 2018).

[27] Mark Matera, *Black London: The Imperial Metropolis and Decolonization in the Twentieth Century* (Oakland: University of California Press, 2015); Michael Goebel, *Anti-Imperial Metropolis: Interwar Paris and the Seeds of Third World Nationalism* (Cambridge: Cambridge University Press, 2015).

[28] Imaobong D. Umoren, *Race Women Internationalists: Activist-Intellectuals and the Global Freedom Struggles* (Oakland: University of California Press, 2018); Keisha N. Blain and Tiffany M. Gill, eds, *To Turn the Whole World Over: Black Women and Internationalism* (Urbana: University of Illinois Press, 2019).

[29] Getachew, *Worldmaking*.

[30] Special issue on 'Other Bandungs: Afro-Asian Internationalisms in the Early Cold War', *Journal of World History* 30, nos. 1-2 (June 2019).

are completely left out. As European historians, we find that Europe, in particular, has been badly served by both old and newer studies. Although Britain, France and perhaps Germany often featured in the older literature as 'international players' or as venues of big international organizations or meetings, Europe overall was not explicitly examined. In the newer scholarship on internationalism and transnationalism, Europe and Europeans have often fallen out of view completely, as scholars have turned to research South-East Asia, Africa or Latin America. Where European actors or projects do feature, narratives still often continue to be dominated by Anglophone perspectives as the supposed 'yardsticks' according to which other developments are being judged. However, what has been lost in the process is an understanding of Europe's own diversity of ideas and change over time, as well as the knowledge that important debates about internationalism originated in non-Anglophone parts of the continent. We cannot tell the history of internationalism without thinking about the role of eastern European (including Russian and Soviet), southern European and northern European actors. Anglo-French models of liberal international cooperation, for example, looked very different from those of Soviet revolutionaries, Albanian technicians, Yugoslav refugees, Spanish or Dutch Catholics, Norwegian disability activists, or Czechoslovak doctors. As a number of the chapters in this volume show, Central, Eastern and Southern Europe served as laboratories for international projects before they were applied to other parts of the world. They also take seriously the roles played by the Soviet Union in enabling and hindering possibilities for international collaboration. Ultimately, we cannot understand twentieth-century internationalism as a global phenomenon without also rethinking its specifically European dimensions.

The volume seeks to recover a sense of the geographical specificity and the diversity of perspectives within Europe, and of the roles played by ideas, people and organizations originating in Europe in the broader history of internationalism. None of these European ideas and projects were developed in isolation from the rest of the world. Some contributions in this volume illustrate the extent to which nominally 'international' projects were actually European ones, governed by European perspectives and driven by European actors, or tested out within European peripheries. Others think about European involvement in broader global developments, tracing the ways in which European actors formed parts of international movements which incorporated or were dominated by other regions, or how non-European ideas and projects were developed in opposition to European models. Incorporating such a diverse range of perspectives is vital to taking Europe's role seriously, but also of recovering its global context and judging its relative significance at different points in time. The volume's focus on the varieties of internationalism developed by Europeans in the course of the twentieth century represents an important intervention in the historiography of internationalism, and one which helps to set the agenda for the Bloomsbury series on Histories of Internationalism, which it launches. The series will feature case studies from around the world, including but not limited to Europe – but, like the chapters in this volume, it will seek to foreground actors, agency and the distribution of power in the history and geography of internationalism.

Structure

The chapters in this volume are divided into four parts, each of which foregrounds a particular dimension of the history of internationalism. Part I addresses some of the questions that Martin Geyer and Johannes Paulmann would consider the 'mechanics' of internationalism: issues of language, communication and technical infrastructure which underpinned the practice of cooperation across borders, but which have often been overlooked by historians who have accepted the logistics of international cooperation as an invisible, static fact.[31]

Two chapters address the history of international languages. International auxiliary languages, of which Esperanto was the best known and most successful, exploded in popularity in the early twentieth century as people sought out new means to communicate across borders. Brigid O'Keeffe's chapter opens up an important new field of study by exploring the history of Esperanto and Esperantists in the Soviet Union after 1917. 'How', she asks, 'could the workers of the world unite without a common language in which to communicate?' For Esperantists, the answer was simple – an international language was necessary to overcome the barriers between working people across different countries, and would solve many of the practical difficulties faced by practitioners of socialist internationalism. But there were many practical and political difficulties standing in the way of the adoption of Esperanto as the socialist lingua franca, not least the widespread multilingualism and ingrained Eurocentrism of many international socialist elites, and it was Russian that eventually won out as the core language of socialist internationalism. Valeska Huber highlights the case of Basic English, a simplified version of the language popular both within and beyond Europe in the interwar period. A project firmly grounded in British imperialism, its designers and promoters sought to develop a language which could reach beyond a narrow internationalist elite to enjoy mass appeal. But their technocratic and often authoritarian approach prevented the kind of flexibility and adaptation which would have been needed to make the project a success.

If language represents the 'software' of international cooperation, the other two chapters in Part I turn their attention to its 'hardware' in the form of physical transportation and communication infrastructure. Heidi Tworek's and Elidor Mëhilli's chapters combine the two approaches. Tworek introduces us to the often fractious debates about telegraphic codes ('hidden Esperantos') which took place in and around the International Telegraph Union in the early 1920s. These debates revolved around technical questions of how to organize and administer codes that would function across borders. But they also reflected contested ideas about language, power, openness and accessibility. Codes often privileged Western Romance languages, institutionalizing linguistic hierarchies between Europe and the rest of the world, but also between Western and Central-Eastern Europe. Mëhilli turns to radio as an important medium of socialist internationalism in the Cold War. Through the little-known example of Albania's Radio Tirana, he shows how radio provided the technical means for a small rural state on Europe's periphery to speak to, imagine and in some

---

[31] Compare with Geyer and Paulmann, *The Mechanics of Internationalism*, op cit.

ways shape the socialist world. But as with telegraph codes, radio broadcasting was about much more than the technical diffusion of information across borders. Radio was crucial to socialist nation-building in post-war Albania, but it also mirrored the contours of Albanian foreign relations and socialist internationalism during the Cold War, with radio broadcasts reflecting Albania's conflict with Yugoslavia, it's alignment with Moscow, and it's later partnership with China following the Sino-Soviet split.

The chapters in Part II explore what happens when members of international organizations encounter actors in specific local contexts, questions which international historians have often struggled to address. Histories written solely from the archives and perspectives of international organizations, NGOs or international elites have often glossed over the complexities of cooperation on the ground, as international projects came into contact with very particular local circumstances. The chapters in this part focus on these complex interactions. Jo Laycock shows how international organizations and Soviet authorities worked together on refugee relief and resettlement in Soviet Armenia during the 1920s, exploring their cooperation, conflict and (mis) communication, and the ways in which the supposed language of technical expertise helped to bridge some personal and ideological divides. Kornelija Ajlec presents the complex story of Yugoslav refugees fleeing the Nazis in the Second World War and their reception by the Allies in Southern Italy, who sent them on to British-run refugee camps in Egypt. By focusing on personal relationships and interactions on the ground, Ajlec draws attention to the political, cultural and linguistic factors which refugees and relief workers navigated – questions on which the success or otherwise of large-scale international projects often depended. Sławomir Łotysz's chapter shows how local scientific experts in Czechoslovakia fundamentally shaped the way in which UNRRA's penicillin plants sent from the United States and Canada to central Europe actually operated, in ways that had not been foreseen. Finally, Carmen Mangion shifts the focus towards the work of British religious sisters in Peru from the 1970s. Missionary work was arguably one of the earliest forms of internationalism. Mangion shows how global changes within the Catholic Church and interactions with locals in the barrios of Peru helped the Sisters of Mercy develop a new model of international missionary work based on bottom-up initiatives, solidarity and social justice.

Part III focuses on 'activists' as an influential category of international actor, encompassing individuals campaigning for particular groups or causes on the international stage. Daniel Laqua uncovers a history of student activism that long predated the well-known one of 1968 and that created a myriad of organizations and institutions through which students attempted to shape their futures. As a result of their activities, League of Nations officials in the 1920s, Comintern activists in the 1930s and Cold Warriors in the 1950s all tried to tap into the potential of university students. Monika Baár's chapter focuses on the emergence of international disability self-advocacy institutions in the 1970s and 1980s, thereby challenging monolithic, top-down views of internationalism. She pays close attention to the roles of disabled people in setting up the disability rights movement, and the ways in which different models of international activity and activism came to be incorporated in it. Kristy Ironside's chapter, in turn, looks at a particular case of 'activism': the efforts by the American communist writer Howard Fast to obtain royalties for his publications from the Soviet government, and the significance of arguments about internationalism in his campaign. Soviet authorities supported international culture but were unwilling to acknowledge copyright that required foreign currency. Finally, David Brydan brings to life an alternative model of international cooperation as presented by Catholic activists in the decades after the Second World War. He shows how their agenda to, first of all, prevent the spread of anti-Catholic policies within international organizations and, second, to fight communism, were mobilized in their international networks and programmes. Brydan shows the extent to which this activism cannot solely be understood as driven by the Vatican, but in practice drew upon the bottom-up engagement and support of Catholics across the world.

Part IV directly addresses the relationship between Europe and the rest of the world. Jessica Pearson explores the relationship between the international realm and Europe's overseas empires. The post-war period witnessed the rapid expansion of global tourism and air travel, and Air France was at the forefront of efforts to promote a positive vision of France's overseas empire both at home and at overseas. Through an analysis of Air France's promotional literature, Pearson shows how international air travel was used to reimagine 'Greater France' during a period of increasing international opposition to colonialism at the UN and elsewhere. Vincent Lagendijk's chapter turns our attention away from Europe. It shows how the New Deal-era Tennessee Valley Authority (TVA) became a global blueprint for development after 1945, serving as a nexus for international cooperation through efforts to transpose its model to the Mekong Delta. As an example of a US-led international development project emerging in the wake of Europe's imperial retreat from South-East Asia, it illustrates Europe's increasingly marginal role in many internationalist projects during the second part of the twentieth century. But a closer look at the origins of the TVA shows how many non-European international projects had their origin in earlier European initiatives, and particularly how parts of Europe acted as a testing bed for international development initiatives which were later exported to the rest of the world.

Part I

Communication and infrastructure

1

Building a communist Tower of Babel

Esperanto and the language politics of internationalism in revolutionary Russia

Brigid O'Keeffe

In his memoir, Jack Murphy recalled his time as a delegate at the Second World Congress of the Communist International (Comintern), held in Moscow and Petrograd in 1920. Murphy emphasized a regret that in many ways came to define his experience of working towards the goals of proletarian internationalism in the early Soviet republic. Dispatched to revolutionary Russia as a representative of British socialism, Murphy time and again encountered the language barriers that stood in the way of his ability to fully participate in the Comintern's planning for what was then heralded by the Bolsheviks and their allies as the imminent 'worldwide October'. This formidable language barrier especially pained Murphy when, on the opening day of the Comintern's Second Congress, he sat helpless as his hero V. I. Lenin addressed the delegates. 'How I wished I had studied foreign languages,' Murphy sighed. 'Like many more I had to wait for the translation, for of course Lenin spoke in Russian.'[1]

Murphy shared this frustration with many of his fellow socialists who travelled to revolutionary Russia intent on participating in the Comintern and its networks of international proletarian revolution. At the Comintern, engaging in the practical work of global communism immediately brought to the fore the inherent dilemmas and challenges of language diversity in an internationalist enterprise. For many proletarian internationalists who flocked to the Comintern, miscommunication and utter linguistic unintelligibility dominated their lived experience of this powerful node of interwar socialist internationalism. This chapter revisits their struggles and the wider, ultimately global politics of language in revolutionary Russia. It examines, too, the efforts of a distinct constituency within revolutionary Russian society that advocated what they believed was the best solution to the problem of language diversity among the global proletariat. That proposed solution was the international auxiliary language Esperanto.

---

[1] J. T. Murphy, *New Horizons* (London: John Lane, 1941), 111.

Scholarship on the Russian Revolution long took for granted the Bolsheviks' global pretensions. Recently, the history of Soviet internationalism has enjoyed a scholarly regeneration, opening productive avenues for understanding the construction of a twentieth-century socialist world.[2] Yet few have asked how the dilemmas of language diversity and international communication impacted Soviet internationalism, if at all.[3] The case of Esperanto provides a useful lens through which to examine how the global politics of language figured in the Russian Revolution and ultimately helped shape the twentieth century's socialist world. Esperantists posed a question of enormous practical and theoretical significance in revolutionary Russia: How could the workers of the world unite without a common language in which to communicate?

Upon the creation of the Comintern in 1919, Soviet Esperantists attempted to seize the moment because, they reasoned, only an international auxiliary language made practical and ideological sense for a transnational organization plotting a worldwide October. The Bolsheviks opted instead, however, for more traditional language politics. The Comintern made do, more or less, with a small handful of working national languages and a growing army of translators and interpreters. Given the Bolsheviks' primary preoccupation with the West, and with Europe in particular, the early Comintern privileged German as well as Russian, French and English as the working languages of socialist internationalism.[4] As the prospects for imminent world revolution faded, especially after the failure of German October in 1923, the Russian Revolution changed course. The Bolsheviks' first priority would be building socialism in one country. Ultimately, it was the Russian language – not German, and not Esperanto either – that the Bolsheviks would promote as the lingua franca of a new socialist internationalism unquestionably under the Bolsheviks' lead.

---

[2] See, for example, Rachel Applebaum, *Empire of Friends: Soviet Power and Socialist Internationalism* (Ithaca: Cornell University Press, 2019); Katerina Clark, *Moscow the Fourth Rome: Stalinism, Cosmopolitanism, and the Evolution of Soviet Culture, 1931-1941* (Cambridge, MA: Harvard University Press, 2011); Lisa Kirschenbaum, *International Communism and the Spanish Civil War: Solidarity and Suspicion* (Cambridge: Cambridge University Press, 2015); Michael David-Fox, *Showcasing the Great Experiment: Cultural Diplomacy and Western Visitors to the Soviet Union* (New York: Oxford University Press, 2011); Eleonory Gilburd, *To See Paris and Die: The Soviet Lives of Western Culture* (Cambridge, MA: Harvard University Press, 2018); and Elidor Mehilli, *From Stalin to Mao: Albania in the Socialist World* (Ithaca: Cornell University Press, 2017).

[3] A notable exception is Gilburd's *To See Paris and Die*, which provides an elegant analysis of how, during the Cold War, the Soviet Union embraced 'the "language" of culture' as a universal language for communicating across national, linguistic and ideological borders (quote on 55). For rare and valuable discussions of the dilemmas of communicating in the multilingual contexts of socialist internationalism, see Kirschenbaum, *International Communism*, Chapter 3 and Elizabeth McGuire, *Red at Heart: How Chinese Communists Fell in Love with the Russian Revolution* (New York: Oxford University Press, 2017).

[4] On the West, and Europe in particular, as the primary focus of (early) Soviet internationalism, see especially Gilburd, *To See Paris and Die*; Clark, *Moscow the Fourth Rome*; and David-Fox, *Showcasing the Soviet Experiment*. The Bolsheviks' early internationalism was also oriented towards 'the East' – their blanket category for the oppressed colonial peoples of the Middle East, Asia, Africa and even the Americas. Yet the West, and Europe, took first priority. See Masha Kirasirova, 'The "East" as a Category of Bolshevik Ideology and Comintern Administration', *Kritika: Explorations in Russian and Eurasian History* 18, no. 1 (2017): 7–34.

The imperial Russian origins of Esperanto

In 1887, L. L. Zamenhof (1859–1917), a Jewish subject of the Russian empire, published the first Esperanto primer in Warsaw. Zamenhof insisted that his new international auxiliary language would collapse the linguistic divides separating the world's peoples. Native to none, equally belonging to all, Esperanto would make it possible for all of humanity to 'come together in one family'. Esperanto was poised to solve the nagging dilemmas of Babel because it was uncommonly easy to master. Zamenhof boasted, 'The entire grammar of my language can be learned perfectly in the course of one hour.'[5]

It was no accident that Zamenhof's Esperanto primer entered the world's marketplace of ideas in an era of rapid industrialization, revolutionary telecommunications and expanding markets. Globalization inspired a craving for an international language that could facilitate commerce, travel, diplomacy and the international exchange of ideas and expertise.[6] Esperanto emerged during an era in which men and women creatively confronted the internationality of their self-consciously modern age.[7] This was also an 'age of questions' in which men and women agonized over human problems they believed required urgent and definitive solutions.[8] Zamenhof's answer to the 'international language question' proved especially compelling among educated Europeans eager to share ideas, exchange goods, communicate expertise and forge friendships with far-flung comrades. By the turn of the twentieth century, Esperanto had attracted internationalists and the globally curious across the ideological spectrum.

Esperantism's ascendancy in the late nineteenth and early twentieth centuries has largely been seen as western and central European phenomenon with France at the centre of the growing movement. Esperanto's appeal in its birthplace – late imperial Russia – has been overlooked. Commentators long assumed that the autocratic and largely agrarian Russian empire was 'hardly a soil on which an artificial language could be expected to thrive'.[9] Yet Russian Esperantists incubated the movement in its most vulnerable days. They were the first subscribers to Esperantist periodicals and the first to energetically pursue correspondence with other Esperantists both at home and

---

[5] Dr Esperanto [Zamenhof], *Mezhdunarodnyi iazyk: Predislovie i polnyi uchebnik* (Warsaw, 1887), 3–4. On how Zamenhof's late imperial Russian milieu profoundly shaped Esperanto as a utopian internationalist project, see Brigid O'Keeffe, 'An International Language for an Empire of Humanity: L. L. Zamenhof and the Imperial Russian Origins of Esperanto', *East European Jewish Affairs* 49, no. 1 (2019): 1–19.
[6] Roberto Garvia, *Esperanto and Its Rivals: The Struggle for an International Language* (Philadelphia: University of Pennsylvania Press, 2015); Michael D. Gordin, *Scientific Babel: How Science Was Done Before and After Global English* (Chicago: University of Chicago Press, 2015).
[7] Glenda Sluga, *Internationalism in the Age of Nationalism* (Philadelphia: University of Pennsylvania Press, 2015).
[8] Holly Case, *The Age of Questions or, a First Attempt at an Aggregate History of the Eastern, Social, Woman, American, Jewish, Polish, Bullion, Tuberculosis, and Many Other Questions over the Nineteenth Century, and Beyond* (Princeton: Princeton University Press, 2018). For Zamenhof, the international language question was always fundamentally about the Jewish Question. See Esther Schor, *Bridge of Words: Esperanto and the Dream of a Universal Language* (New York: Metropolitan, 2016).
[9] Joseph Rhodes, 'Progress and Prospects of Esperanto', *The North American Review* 184, no. 168 (1 February 1907): 282.

abroad. Esperanto societies operated in St Petersburg, Moscow and many other cities of the Russian empire. In the years following Russia's 1905 Revolution, publication of Esperanto materials in Russia surged. By 1912 there was an 'Esperanto' bookstore located on Moscow's central avenue.[10]

In the tsarist fin de siècle, imperial Russia's Esperantists published an array of Russian-language pamphlets hailing Esperanto's social, economic, cultural and even spiritual value in an increasingly globalized world. S. P. Rantov argued that the inescapable fact of modern life was its 'gravitation toward internationalism'. Modern inventions drew the peoples of the world ever more frequently together in international networks and transactions. In a globally interconnected world, he argued, Esperanto was a practical utility, not utopian folly.[11] V. A. Kolosov predicted that Esperanto would provide the world markets with a 'powerful, revitalizing jolt' once it had liberated international commerce from Babel's constraints.[12] Lev Argutin foretold a more genial geopolitics once Esperanto became the lingua franca of international diplomacy.[13] On a more fundamental level, Esperanto made it possible to correspond with foreigners, to learn about the world from pen pals and to travel abroad with relative ease. Many of Russia's Esperantists also saw in Esperanto the makings of a 'wonderful future, a kingdom of mutual love among peoples who speak different tongues'.[14] They embraced the spiritual sustenance they found in their growing global community of Esperanto speakers.

On the eve of the First World War, imperial Russia's Esperantists were among those both best and least prepared for the shocking devastation, violence and revolutions wrought by the Great War. They had warned of the dangers of a fractured world in an age of galloping globalization and proselytized the world harmony they believed Esperanto could achieve. As the tsarist government bumbled its way through what quickly proved an intractable global war, Russia's Esperantists did their best to persevere. When the February Revolution of 1917 collapsed the monarchy, they joined their compatriots in imagining and pursuing a wide variety of futures for a regenerated Russia and a humanity reborn.

Revolutionary possibilities

The February Revolution greeted Russia's citizens with uncertainty and chaos, but also offered them an unprecedented opportunity to grab a bullhorn and advocate for their varied ideological visions within the rowdy revolutionary public sphere. Within this climate, new Esperantist organizations sprouted throughout Russia. Until the Bolsheviks seized power in October, the Esperantist movement in revolutionary Russia

---

[10] P. Stoian and V. Neshinskii, *Neobkhodimye svedeniia ob Esperanto* (St. Petersburg: K. P. Shrader, 1912).

[11] S. P. Rantov, *Mezhdunarodnyi iazyk i sovremennaia zhizn'* (Saratov: Tipografiia B. L. Rabinovicha, 1914), 5.

[12] V. A. Kolosov, *Mezhdunarodnyi iazyk Esperanto, ego vozniknovenie, sostav, stroi, znachenie i rasprostranenie* (Simbirsk: Tipografiia Gubernskogo Pravleniia, 1911), 1.

[13] Lev Agurtin, *Mezhdunarodnyi iazyk* (Saratov: Tipografiia B. L. Rabinovicha, 1914), 14.

[14] Kolosov, *Mezhdunarodnyi iazyk*, 8.

operated as an ideological big tent. What united Russia's Esperantists in these days was a shared commitment to Esperanto. Yet new organizations of 'youthful Esperantists' and 'socialist Esperantists' embraced an increasingly radical Esperantist politics.

In agitating for Esperanto's essential role in the revolution, these young Esperantists deployed the key words and slogans of the evolving revolutionary discourse. They spoke of liberty, equality and fraternity. They also framed their arguments for Esperanto within the broad moral claims of the revolution and larger discussions of democracy, class and socialism. In this embrace of an early revolutionary discourse whose vocabulary was ubiquitous but whose meanings were not yet fixed, the Esperantists were joined by millions of their compatriots who were learning the political language of Russia's revolution as it evolved.[15]

One relatively radical approach to pursuing a role for Esperanto in Russia's revolution between February and October 1917 was the *Manifesto of the Union of Socialist Esperantists*. 'We, socialist Esperantists', the *Manifesto* explained, 'are the representatives of a new political worldview today freshly born from the smoke and ashes of the world war.' In all its devastating violence, the war had revealed the 'absurdity' of relying on international proletarian revolution to take place in the absence of an international language to unite the global proletariat. In order to vanquish capitalism, the proletariat needed to destroy the binds of national-chauvinism and the barriers of linguistic diversity. An international auxiliary language was a prerequisite of international socialist revolution because, without it, workers would feel a stronger psychological bond with their co-nationals even of the enemy classes than they would with their foreign proletarian comrades.[16]

The *Manifesto of Socialist Esperantists* captures well the breathless hopefulness in Russia's early revolutionary days. Yet this open-ended revolutionary moment soon passed. In the wake of the Bolsheviks' October Revolution, Russia's Esperantists quickly realized the need to marry their Esperantist ideals to the Bolsheviks' Marxism-Leninism. The Bolsheviks' seizure of power and, in time, their successes in the civil war made even the conceit of political neutrality unviable. Esperantism's former status in tsarist times as a largely 'bourgeois' affair and, in the wake of the February Revolution, as an ideological big tent was no longer tenable. Esperantists needed to embrace Esperanto *as politics* – namely as revolutionary, communist politics. They needed to convince sceptics that Esperanto was an essential weapon of international proletarian revolution.

Boris Breslau's *The International Language and the Proletariat* (1918) represents this ideological transition in its attempt to synthesize prerevolutionary Esperantist talking points with socialist ideals. Breslau argued that the world's workers could never unite without a shared international language to enable their pursuit of socialism. Knowledge of other national languages did not solve this problem of linguistic diversity among the global proletariat, Breslau argued, because workers had always been denied the

---

[15] Orlando Figes and Boris Kolonitskii, *Interpreting the Russian Revolution: The Language and Symbols of 1917* (New Haven: Yale University Press, 1999).
[16] R. Tsyvinskii and T. Sikora, *Manifest soiuza sotsialistov-Esperanistov* (Vyborg: Estra, 1917) (quotes on 2).

expensive 'bourgeois' luxury of foreign language study. Esperanto, however, was easy and cheap for workers to learn. Esperanto was the language of the future – a future shaped by 'the international proletariat, united in one close family'.[17]

Breslau's pamphlet takes on still more significance when considered alongside another of Breslau's revolutionary-era texts. In September 1917, Breslau had applied to Moscow's Institute for Esperanto seeking formal certification of his Esperanto language skills. He included in his application a brief autobiography and an essay on why he had become a 'fervent adept of Esperanto'. Born into a Jewish family in 1891 in the Pale of Settlement, Breslau explained, he was taught from an early age to prize education. In 1909, he became an Esperantist, drawn more to the language's spiritual meaning – its vision of global harmony – than to its practical utilities. Esperanto gave his life a distinct 'moral satisfaction' and nourished his 'interest in global life, art, and culture'. It opened to him a wide world of comrades, of kinship that defied borders. 'Speaking with an Esperantist', Breslau testified, 'I forget that he is from a different nation, class, office, or rank; I speak with a fellow-thinker, with a confrère.'[18]

Taking these texts of Breslau's together – one written some six weeks before the Bolshevik seizure of power in 1917 and the other published in 1918 – offers a personalized glimpse into how one Esperantist was doing his best to adapt to the shifting political winds of Russia's revolution. In 1918, Breslau embraced a vision of Esperanto as a weapon of global proletarian revolution. Sometime in that same year, he joined the Bolshevik Party.[19]

A proletarian international language in search of a proletariat

Despite the patent chaos and dislocations Russia's civil war, Esperantists continued to organize Esperanto clubs, lectures and courses in cities throughout revolutionary Russia. As the ideological tenor of Esperantist rhetoric shifted, so too did the sociological profile of Russia's Esperantists. In late imperial Russia, the Esperantist movement had been led by a wealthy, educated elite that did not apologize for its distance from the 'masses'. In the revolutionary era, young Esperantists organized anew, welcoming into their ranks working-class recruits to help advance the cause of an international language that they argued was essential for global proletarian revolution.

Esperantist youth organizations in Moscow, Petrograd, and a variety of provincial towns sent appeals to the various emerging People's Commissariats volunteering their Esperanto skills for the crafting of Soviet propaganda for both domestic and foreign audiences.[20] The young 'communist Esperantists' intensely lobbied the People's Commissariat of Enlightenment (Narkompros), urging it to adopt Esperanto as a mandatory subject in Soviet schools. They argued that Esperanto would help the proletariat to unseat the 'caste of privileged intelligentsia' who had dominated

---

[17] B. Breslau, *Mezhdunarodnyi iazyk i proletariat* (Saratov: Tip. P. N. Sibrina, 1918), 6.
[18] 'Breslau, B. M.', http://historio.ru/breslaux.php (accessed 15 March 2018).
[19] Ibid.
[20] Rossiiskii gosudarstvennyi arkhiv sotsial'no-politicheskoi istorii (RGASPI) f. 495 o. 99 d. 65 l. 7.

prerevolutionary life. The children of the revolution need not study the foreign languages of capitalist nations as the bourgeoisie greedily did in the days of old. Instead, they needed to learn to speak, read and write in their native language first, and in the 'proletarian international language Esperanto' second.[21]

In early 1919, Narkompros organized an investigatory committee to explore 'the question of international language'.[22] Yet this Narkompros committee concluded its deliberations almost as quickly as it had begun them. While acknowledging that Esperanto was a viable international language, and the only one with a proven and global track record, Narkompros washed its hands of the matter of decreeing an international language for use in Soviet schools, let alone in the Bolsheviks' international relations.[23] The commission encouraged the Bolsheviks to take seriously the issue of 'the international language question', but ultimately concluded that the answer to that question would be decided as a result of practical 'agreements between governments representing individual nations'.[24]

Although disappointed by Narkompros's decision, the Esperantists saw a fresh opportunity to lobby on behalf of Esperanto when, just a few weeks later, the Bolsheviks announced the establishment of the new Third International in Moscow. After all, they asked, what could a Communist International achieve without a distinctly proletarian international language? The workers of the world needed Esperanto in order to unite.

A new international

'Comrades, I deeply regret that I speak neither German, which Comrade Zinoviev yesterday called the "language of international socialism", nor Russian, which will be the language of international communism tomorrow.' One can imagine the sigh with which Jacques Sadoul, a self-declared representative of French Communists, began his speech to the founding Comintern Congress, held in Moscow in early March 1919. Apologetically, he explained: 'I must address you in French, the only language in which I am reasonably fluent, a language that for now, at least, can unfortunately be referred to only as the language of a revolution of long ago.'[25]

The founding congress of the Comintern met in a small Kremlin conference hall decorated with red banners 'with "Long Live the Third International" inscribed upon them in many languages'.[26] Yet the matter of language diversity at the first Comintern Congress was not as simple as it appeared on those banners. The official language of the conference was German, although Russian was also permitted. This decision was

---

[21] 'Vozzvanie tsentral'nogo biuro vserossiiskogo soiuza iunykh Esperantistov', *Zhizn' i tvorchestvo russkoi molodezhi* no. 22 (1919), 4 reproduced at http://historio.ru/zanovyj.php (accessed 9 May 2015).
[22] Gosudarstevennyi arkhiv Rossiiskoi Federatsii (GARF) f. A-2307 o. 2 d. 438 ll. 1-27ob.
[23] GARF f. A-2306 o. 15 d. 425 l. 28.
[24] RGASPI f. 495 o. 99 d. 66 l. 21.
[25] John Riddell, ed., *Founding the Communist International: Proceedings and Documents of the First Congress, March 1919* (New York: Pathfinder, 1987), 99–100.
[26] Arthur Ransome, *Russia in 1919* (New York: B. W. Huebsch, 1919), 214.

in keeping with German's decades-long standing as the unofficial lingua franca of the international Marxist left. Yet the congress proceedings proved both a test of the delegates' language skills and, at times, a revolutionary incarnation of the Tower of Babel. The British journalist Arthur Ransome reported that 'speeches were made in all languages, though where possible German was used, because more of the foreigners knew German than knew French'. Betraying his own linguistic limits, Ransome added: 'This was unlucky for me.'[27]

Ransome and Sadoul were not the only 'unlucky' ones in attendance for the founding meeting of the Comintern. Multiple national languages – German, English, French, Ukrainian and Russian, most prominently – were spoken throughout the proceedings. The official transcripts of the congress proceedings reflected the various logistical problems of translation encountered by the delegates who participated in the founding of the Comintern. Translators on hand did their best to render reports made in French or English into German and Russian. Yet the pace of the events often meant that those who needed translated drafts of resolutions had to wait; they were left proverbially lost in translation.[28] On the afternoon of the fourth day of the congress, it was suddenly announced that the remainder of that day's business would need to be delayed until the next day. The problem? Lack of translation staff. 'Comrades', it was announced, 'we must cut the session short. No translation is available from Russian to German. We have no choice but to propose ending the session at this point.'[29]

The translator-interpreters who served at the Comintern's founding congress were recruited from its very audience: they were themselves participating delegates or else leading Bolsheviks in attendance for the meetings. There was nothing particularly exceptional in this arrangement. One of the delegates who tirelessly provided translation and interpretation services at the founding Comintern Congress, Anzhelika Balabanova, had made a name for herself in previous decades as a one-woman 'living incarnation of the International' – so nicknamed because of her devoted application of her linguistic skills to translating and interpreting at meetings of the international Left.[30]

Moreover, the Bolshevik leaders' multilingualism was something they themselves generally took for granted. Most of the leading Bolsheviks were fluent in at least one, if not multiple, European languages in addition to Russian. Some of them were known for their agile multilingualism. Aleksandra Kollontai, who provided essential translation services at the First Comintern Congress, had learnt English, French and German from her foreign-born governesses in her privileged aristocratic youth. Many of her fellow Old Bolsheviks honed their foreign language skills while living abroad in revolutionary exile from the tsarist regime in Zurich, Geneva, Paris, Berlin, Vienna,

---

[27] Ibid., 215.
[28] See, for example, Riddell, *Founding the Communist International*, 149.
[29] Ibid., 220.
[30] Angelica Balabanoff, *My Life as a Rebel* (New York: Greenwood Press, 1968 [1938]), 87. The Bolsheviks, in their effort to bury the Second International, were also replicating its modes of dealing with language diversity at its international conferences. The Second International adopted the practice of consecutive interpretation and French, German and English as its working languages. Prior to the First World War, some delegates argued in vain that the Second International should adopt an international auxiliary language. Kevin J. Callahan, *Demonstration Culture: European Socialism and the Second International, 1889-1914* (Leceister: Troubador, 2010), 11–15.

London and Rome. For Russian Marxists living in exile in the two decades prior to the Russian Revolution, their native Russian language was a devalued currency and rarely useful except when they were talking among themselves. Preparing for revolution meant foreign language study as much as theoretical debate or gunrunning. Some, like Stalin, were ultimately embarrassed not only by their lack of experience abroad but also by their lack of foreign language fluency.[31] While training for revolution, Stalin had attempted to engage in some self-study of English, German and French. While in tsarist prison, he reportedly studied Esperanto, telling a cellmate that it was 'the language of the future'.[32] Nothing much came of these endeavours. Stalin would never live down the shame of not mastering German, the prerevolutionary lingua franca of the European Left. His nemesis Trotsky, meanwhile, flaunted his agility in foreign languages. At the international congresses of the early Comintern, Trotsky often served as his own translator, awing the audience as he delivered his lengthy speeches in Russian, German and French – a task that at least once famously exceeded six hours.[33]

Thus, the Comintern relied on multilingual comrades to facilitate its work. Adopted lingua francas – of international socialism (German) and of the global communist future (Russian) – more or less transacted Comintern affairs. Comrades who had the ability to translate from German or Russian into French, Italian or English helped to bridge linguistic gaps. Despite the logistical problems of language diversity encountered at the first Comintern Congress, the Bolsheviks were confident in both the imminence of world revolution and their ability to make do with their revolutionary lingua francas. In a rousing speech delivered at the Congress's festive conclusion, Lenin waved in his hands a copy of the newspaper of the Italian Socialist Party – a newspaper whose Italian words he could not fluently read. Lenin pointed to the text, pronouncing the Italian words, '*Sovietisti russi*'. These were words, Lenin exclaimed, that, 'even though they are in Italian, can be understood all over the world'.[34] To thunderous applause, Lenin concluded, 'Now that the meaning of the word "soviet" is understood by everybody, the victory of the communist revolution is assured.'[35] The proletarians of the world could speak in their different national tongues and yet effectively express a shared communist meaning. When all else failed, there were always translators who could be put to work in the service of the global proletariat.

Traditional language politics at the new international

The founding of the Comintern in March 1919 came as welcome news to young Esperantists in revolutionary Russia. As one Esperantist pamphlet published in

---

[31] Sheila Fitzpatrick, *On Stalin's Team: The Years of Living Dangerously in Soviet Politics* (Princeton: Princeton University Press, 2015), 96–7.
[32] Ronald Grigor Suny, 'A Journeyman for Revolution: Stalin and the Labour Movement in Baku, June 1907-May 1908', *Soviet Studies* 23, no. 3 (1972): 393.
[33] Joseph Freeman, *An American Testament: A Narrative of Rebels and Romantics* (New York: Farrar and Rinehart, 1936), 629–30.
[34] Riddell, *Founding the Communist International*, 312.
[35] Ibid., 315.

1919 insisted, Esperanto *must become* the language of the Comintern. It was time, too, for a revolution in how people communicated internationally. Esperanto provided a means for the international proletariat to conquer the chauvinism of using a national language as their shared language of communication. 'Any literate worker or peasant could learn it, and in the shortest possible time.'[36] Without Esperanto, the pamphlet insisted, Marx's appeal to the workers of the world to unite was fated to 'remain an empty phrase'.[37]

While few at the Comintern cared to listen, energetic Esperantists campaigned vigorously throughout 1919 and 1920 for Esperanto's essential role in hastening worldwide proletarian revolution. Given its a-national quality as an international *auxiliary* language, they argued, Esperanto was inherently anti-imperialist and anti-chauvinist. Esperanto was also inherently 'proletarian' in a way that the national languages could never be. The revolution demanded an international language that would 'destroy the masses' dependency on translators and the handfuls of patented intellectuals who . . . could otherwise lay claim to leadership' of what was rightfully the *workers*' international revolution.[38] To conduct international relations in any of the existing national languages was to cave to 'imperialist traditional polyglottism' when what was demanded was 'proletarian revolutionary internationalism'.[39] To reject Esperanto or to ignore it was thus a counter-revolutionary act. The dilemma of international language, the Soviet Esperantists argued, presented a test case for the Bolsheviks' and the Comintern's revolutionary credentials. It was time for the Bolsheviks to serve as the vanguard on the international language front.

Yet when the Second Congress of the Comintern met at sessions held in both Petrograd and Moscow in the summer of 1920, traditional politics of language diversity prevailed. The Comintern welcomed 218 foreign delegates hailing from North and South America, Europe, the Middle East, Central and East Asia. To cope, the Comintern now resolved upon three working languages for its proceedings: German, Russian and French.[40] This expanded list of official languages adopted by the Second Congress did not solve the problem of language diversity as it impacted delegates' ability to fully participate in and understand the proceedings. Stenographic reports reveal that much of the discussion was conducted in German or French, but Russian, English, Turkish and other languages were spoken throughout the event. Translators did their best to keep up, yet the imperfect system left gaps of understanding. Moreover, the Comintern's system for consecutive interpretation slowed the pace of proceedings. After each report or speech, the delegates would break into special groups by native language, so that an interpreter could relay what had been said. Those who did not require translation could afford to break for conviviality or deal-making with comrades, or else sit and wait in boredom for sessions to resume. As a result, congress sessions typically extended well past midnight. The participants' nerves quickly began to fray.

---

[36] V. P. Artiushkin-Kormilitsyn, *Mezhdunarodnyi iazyk revoliutsionnogo proletariata Esperanto* (Petrograd: n.p., 1919), 7.
[37] Ibid., 14.
[38] RGASPI f. 495 o. 99 d. 66 l. 8ob.
[39] GARF f. A-2306 o. 2 d. 591 l. 20.
[40] John Riddell, ed. *Workers of the World and Oppressed Peoples, Unite! Proceedings and Documents of the Second Congress* (New York: Pathfinder Press, 1991), 1: 1–16.

The American communist John Reed was exasperated. In the first three sessions, Reed three times unsuccessfully put forward a motion to have English added to the Congress's working languages. 'The number of English-speaking delegates in this hall exceeds the number of those using French,' Reed complained. 'We have been promised an English translator, but we have not got him yet.'[41] Reed was not the only English-speaking delegate aggrieved by the Comintern's language politics. The American and British delegates ultimately staged a boycott, refusing to attend a whole day of sessions. According to one of the British delegates, the English speakers were fed up with having to hope for the occasional 'garbled translation' offered them by a sympathetic comrade.[42] Eventually, at the Congress's ninth session, the Comintern adopted English as a working language for its work. It was a belated concession to Anglophone delegates for whom so much of the proceedings had been incomprehensible. It did not solve all the Anglophone delegates' problems either. One tellingly complained, 'Radek's speech, which lasted two hours, was given to us in a twenty-minute translation.'[43]

Although debate over organizational and programmatic issues remained the Comintern Congress's priority, it was becoming increasingly clear that the Bolsheviks' improvised style of providing for translation and interpretation was in many ways untenable. Just as the Esperantists had anticipated, the routine work of international proletarian revolution entailed the practical challenges of linguistic diversity. Consecutive translation of speeches into the Comintern's working languages exhausted the delegates, draining their enthusiasm. Angel Pestana, a delegate from Spain, recalled: 'The sessions began to lose their appeal. The number of translations required made the discussions endless ... the whole thing was immensely time wasting.' Morale was 'becoming desperate', Pestana explained, as the necessary demands of consecutive interpretation proved a drag on the world revolution. Responding to the mood of the crowd and the ticking clock, interpreters began to take drastic measures. 'The translations were shortened more and more until there scarcely remained anything of what the speaker had actually said.'[44]

On the penultimate day of the Second Congress, Pestana proposed a different strategy for dealing with the linguistic confusion and time-wasting that prevailed at the Comintern congresses. Instead of resigning themselves to their linguistic woes, he argued, the Comintern should adopt Esperanto as the single working language of translation. 'I propose that in the future every speaker use whatever language they find easiest, and that translation take place into the auxiliary language Esperanto,' Pestana explained. 'This language is readily learned and quite appropriate to our needs. We can save much time and labor by using it for translation.'[45]

---

[41] Ibid., 182.
[42] Quoted in James W. Hulse, *The Forming of the Communist International* (Stanford: Stanford University Press, 1964), 195.
[43] Riddell, *Workers of the World*, 2: 622.
[44] Francisco J. Romero Salvadó, 'Report on the Action Taken by the Delegate Angel Pestaña at the Second Congress of the Third International Which Was Presented by Him to the Confederación Nacional del Trabajo', *Revolutionary Russia* 8, no. 1 (1995): 68–9.
[45] Riddell, *Workers of the World*, 2: 772–3.

In response to Pestana's suggestion, the Comintern summarily charged a new committee, the Advisory Commission for the Introduction of an International Auxiliary Language in the Third International. When Esperantists throughout revolutionary Russia received this news, many of them no doubt celebrated. Yet, they were soon disappointed. The 'communist Esperantists' who had appealed to the Comintern since its founding were not invited to participate. They interpreted this as a clear signal that 'the center' was 'indifferent' to the idea of an auxiliary international language.[46] Moreover, the Esperantists' scepticism about the Comintern Advisory Commission appeared more than justified once plans proceeded apace for the convocation of the Third Comintern Congress in June 1921. The question of an international language was not placed on the agenda. Most tellingly, the Comintern kept to its traditional and plainly Eurocentric language politics. German, French, Russian and English were the working languages of the Third Comintern Congress and translators and interpreters were hired to provide, to the best of their ability, their services to the foreign delegates during the formal proceedings.[47]

Seeing that it was to be international language politics as usual at the Third Comintern Congress, revolutionary Russia's self-declared communist Esperantists decided that they needed to forge a place for Esperanto in the Soviet Republic that did not depend on the disinterested officials at the Comintern or Narkompros. In spring 1921, they commenced plans to establish their own 'all-Russian' organization – one that would be 'independent from the government and the Party'.[48] They needed an organizational foothold from which they could direct their efforts to make Esperanto an indispensable weapon of international proletarian revolution. In time, they would be better prepared to coordinate efforts with the Comintern, Narkompros and other Soviet organizations. In early June 1921, they convened an All-Russian Congress of Esperantists in Petrograd and established a new Union of Soviet Esperantists – an organization whose 'essential task' was 'to support, by means of Esperanto, the Soviet Government and to help it in the matter of fulfilling its international agenda'.[49]

Yet the Esperantists remained on the far periphery of the party's attention and much further removed in the minds of Russian society in general. Esperantists in the early Soviet republic battled the same dilemmas that dogged the Bolsheviks: the overwhelming poverty of their devastated country; a population that was overwhelmingly illiterate in its own native tongue; and a sorely needed proletarian revolution abroad that never arrived, to name just a few.

Shifting horizons

The summer of 1921 was a decisive one for reframing the Bolshevik imaginary of international proletarian revolution. At its Third Congress, the Comintern

---

[46] RGASPI f. 495 o. 99 d. 67 l. 9.
[47] John Riddell, ed. and trans. *To the Masses: Proceedings of the Third Congress of the Communist International, 1921* (Leiden: Brill, 2015), 47.
[48] RGASPI f. 495 o. 99 d. 67 l. 15.
[49] GARF f. A-2306 o. 1 d. 622 l. 12.

acknowledged that the international proletarian revolution was developing at a slower tempo than anticipated and the timetable for global revolution was uncertain. The Bolsheviks in 1921 were openly changing course in terms of their revolutionary tactics at home and abroad. The adoption of the New Economic Policy in March had inaugurated the Bolsheviks' controversial tactical retreat at home. The theses adopted at the Third Comintern Congress signalled their new 'defensive' as regards world revolution. Soviet Russia was the embattled headquarters of world revolution and it was unlikely to be relieved of this singular leadership position in the near future. Therefore, 'it was the international Communist movement that henceforth would have to shape its actions to serve the interests of [Soviet] Russia.'[50]

It was also made clear to the Soviet Esperantists that the prospect of the Comintern adopting Esperanto was incredibly unlikely. In June 1921, the Advisory Commission for the Introduction of an International Auxiliary Language in the Third International issued a communiqué arguing that the idea of using an international auxiliary language for the Comintern's work was attractive in theory, but unrealistic in practice given the inordinate 'expenditure of energy' that would be required to persuade Comintern members to learn Esperanto.[51] A French delegate to the Comintern confirmed the Esperantists' worst fears when he confided in a letter to a comrade, 'That Commission has practically done nothing.' In 1922, the Advisory Commission was dissolved without fanfare, and the question of an international auxiliary language for the Comintern's work was discarded.[52] For the Bolsheviks, Esperanto was at best a 'utopian luxury' that they and the global proletariat simply could not afford.[53] The Comintern Executive Committee struck the question of an international auxiliary language from even the long list of its agenda.[54] At its Fourth Congress held in November 1922, the Comintern persisted with its imperfect system of relying on translators and interpreters and its delegates were again to make do with German, Russian, French and English as working languages.

This privileging and reliance on European national languages reflected the Bolsheviks' Eurocentrism but also increasingly strained their working relationship with the so-called 'Eastern' comrades whom they recruited from among the colonial peoples of Asia, the Middle East and Africa. For the increasing number of 'Eastern' comrades sojourning to Moscow, joining the work of the Comintern and attending its congresses, the Bolsheviks' traditional and unapologetically Eurocentric language politics was an especial burden. These comrades were known to complain about the 'difficult position' they were in linguistically – most especially for those who did not know a single European language.[55] Soviet Esperantists, too, dared to question the

[50] Branko Lazitch and Milorad M. Drachovitch, *Lenin and the Comintern* (Stanford: Hoover Institution Press, 1972), 529.
[51] RGASPI f. 495 o. 99 d. 67.
[52] 'Dezorganizatory', *Biulleten' TsK SESS* 2 (February 1923): 10–11 (quote on 11).
[53] On the Bolsheviks' intolerance of cultural projects they regarded as 'utopian luxuries', see Lynn Mally, *Culture of the Future: The Proletkult Movement in Revolutionary Russia* (Berkeley: University of California Press, 1990), especially Chapter 7.
[54] RGASPI f. 495 o. 99 d. 70 l. 23.
[55] Josephine Fowler, *Japanese and Chinese Immigrant Activists: Organizing in American and International Communist Movements, 1919-1933* (New Brunswick, NJ: Rutgers University Press,

Eurocentric chauvinism of the Comintern's language politics. In his treatise *International Language in the Service of the Proletariat*, I. Izgur criticized the Comintern's reliance on European languages and incredulously asked, 'Can it be that the revolutionization of the proletariat of Persia, Turkey, and India is less important than the revolutionization of the proletariat of Romania, Switzerland, and Norway?'[56] Yet such complaints were frequently sidelined – to be resolved at a more opportune time, presumably once more cadres of interpreters and translators could be recruited to the Comintern's mission.[57] There was also the growing expectation, soon to become more prominent in Bolshevik strategy towards training its 'Eastern' comrades, that knowledge of the Russian language should be a prerequisite of communist internationalism.

After the decisive failure of the German Revolution in 1923, the Comintern began its aggressive pursuit of 'Bolshevization' within its ranks and, between 1924 and 1926 the CPSU debated and ultimately adopted 'socialism in one country' as the party line. International proletarian revolution remained a long-term goal, but the Bolsheviks' first priority was building socialism within the Soviet Union and defending it from capitalist enemies. These tactical and ideological shifts within the Comintern and the CPSU as a whole were soon reflected in the Bolsheviks' approach to the global politics of language and the struggle for world revolution. At the Fifth Comintern Congress in July 1924 – the first held since Lenin's death and the defeat of the so-called German October – German, Russian, French and English remained the working languages. Yet, a major linguistic shift took place that mirrored both the geopolitical shift that had taken place since the last Comintern congress and the jockeying for authority within the Bolshevik leadership that had begun in the wake of Lenin's death. At the Fifth Comintern Congress, for the first time, the Russian language eclipsed German as the primary language used in the proceedings. Bolshevik leaders who had at previous congresses typically given their speeches in German now did so in Russian.[58]

This elevation of the Russian language at the Fifth Comintern Congress signalled a profound shift in who was expected to lead international communism given the revised timeline of world revolution. It was not German (let alone Esperanto!) that was to be the language of international proletarian revolution, but Russian. This shift in the language politics of global communism was expressed neatly in the mid-1920s by the rector of the Communist University for the Toilers of the East (KUTV), a Soviet training ground for international revolutionaries who were to follow Comintern orders in pursuing revolution in their home countries. 'It's impossible to study Leninism without knowledge of the Russian language,' he explained. 'It's just as necessary as the study of German was, in its time, for Russian Marxists.'[59] At KUTV and other Comintern schools for foreigners, students engaged in intensive Russian-language coursework in

---

2007), 68. See also McGuire, *Red at Heart*, 79–80.

[56] I. Izgur, *Mezhdunarodnyi iazyk na sluzhbe proletariat* (Moscow: Novaia epokha, 1925), 17.

[57] Even at the end of the 1920s, seemingly no one in the Comintern's Far East Bureau could claim competency in Japanese. Sandra Wilson, 'The Comintern and the Japanese Communist Party', in *International Communism and the Communist International, 1919-1943*, ed. Tim Rees and Andrew Thorpe (Manchester: Manchester University Press, 1998), 295.

[58] Warren Lerner, *Karl Radek: The Last Internationalist* (Stanford: Stanford University Press, 1970), 131.

[59] Quoted in McGuire, *Red at Heart*, 77.

the 1920s and 1930s.[60] Recast as the language of global communism, Russian was seen not only as an essential requirement for deep study of Marxist-Leninism but also as loyal preparation for meaningful participation in Soviet-led world revolution.[61]

Elevating Russian to the first among equals on the Comintern's list of working languages, however, did not solve its problems of language diversity. So long as the Comintern functioned, language diversity bedevilled its operations and exasperated its comrades. To alleviate these problems, the Comintern ultimately chose to adopt a technological innovation that soon revolutionized the way interpretation services were provided at its meetings. At the Sixth Comintern Congress convened in Moscow in July 1928, the meeting hall was for the first time equipped with the telephone technology that made simultaneous interpretation possible.[62] As described by one of the interpreters hired for the event, 'On each Comintern delegate's seat was an earphone with five buttons marked Russian, French, German, Chinese, English. As the speaker talked, the interpreters, in low voice, translated his words into microphones connected with the earphones.'[63] By the time of the Seventh (and last) Comintern Congress in 1935, translation services were at last provided for Arabic speakers.[64]

In Moscow, the undisputed headquarters of international proletarian revolution, Russian was the language of Bolshevism and so of the 'new' socialist internationalism. At the Comintern, Esperanto did not upend traditional international language politics. Instead, traditional language politics were retrofitted with electronic headsets and put to the service of the Soviets' revised timeline for an international proletarian revolution that they were intent on leading.

Communist Tower of Babel

The February Revolution burst the door into an alternative Russian future wide open, inviting Russians across the political and socio-economic spectrum to imagine new possibilities for their homeland and the world. For Russia's Esperantists, it presented an unparalleled opportunity to advocate for Esperanto as essential for resurrecting Russia and transforming the globe. After the October Revolution, Esperantists adapted and learnt to make the case for Esperanto on a decidedly Marxist basis. They insisted that Marxism begged for an essential correction – an acknowledgement that workers of the world could never unite without an international auxiliary language to enable their

---

[60] See, for example, Yueh Sheng, *Sun Yat-sen University in Moscow and the Chinese Revolution: A Personal Account* (Lawrence, KS: University of Kansas, 1971), Chapter 5. As McGuire notes in her *Red at Heart*, this coursework was intensive, demanding and controversial, but not always effective (pp. 71–3; 129–31).
[61] Brigitte Studer, *The Transnational World of the Cominternarians*, trans. Dafydd Rees Roberts (London: Palgrave Macmillan, 2015), 131.
[62] Sergei Chernov, 'At the Dawn of Simultaneous Interpreting in the USSR', in *New Insights in the History of Interpreting*, ed. Kayoko Takeda and Jesus Baigorri-Jalon (Amsterdam and Philadelphia: John Benjamins Publishing Company, 2016), 135–65.
[63] Markoosha Fischer, *My Lives in Russia* (New York: Harper & Brothers, 1944), 43–4.
[64] Alexander Vatlin and Stephen A. Smith, 'The Comintern', in *The Oxford Handbook of Communism* (Oxford: Oxford University Press, 2014), 200.

communication, collaboration and camaraderie. Only Esperanto could serve the global proletariat in the fashion their revolution demanded; it was incredibly easy to learn, they claimed, even for undereducated workers and peasants. Esperanto did not belong to any singular nation and therefore acquitted itself of the chauvinist imperialism of using a national language for international relations. It was a necessary and righteous weapon in the global struggle to defeat capitalism and refashion human beings under the banner of socialism.

After the establishment of the Comintern in March 1919, the Esperantists campaigned for Esperanto as the logical choice as a working language – if not *the* working language – of the Comintern. In making their case, the Esperantists had an undeniable point, or rather a few, in their favour. On a sheer practical level, the reliance on communist polyglots to serve as translators and interpreters at the Comintern gatherings impeded efficiency, disrupted work and exhausted attendees. It also bred feelings of resentment among those who were ill-served by the Comintern's mere handful of working national languages. Comrades hailing from outside of Europe were especially disadvantaged and burdened by the Comintern's approach to language. The Bolsheviks recognized the limits and problems imposed by the conditions of linguistic diversity among the Comintern's agents of proletarian internationalism. Yet they reconciled themselves to traditional, unabashedly Eurocentric methods of dealing, or attempting to deal, with the global politics of language.

Prior to the revolution, the Bolsheviks had not given much demonstrative thought to the dilemmas of language and practical communication in a world that they endeavoured to refashion entirely. Many of the Bolshevik leaders were themselves polyglots who handily relied on the multilingualism their elite educations or years in revolutionary exile afforded them. Once their revolution was underway, the overwhelming and myriad practical challenges of securing political power and constructing a brave new socialist world from the rubble of nearly a decade of war were enough to convince most Bolshevik leaders that the question of international language was a niche interest and hardly one of their most pressing practical concerns. Traditional international language politics appeared to the Bolsheviks to be more practical and efficient than a utopian scheme to teach the still largely illiterate world an international auxiliary language.

Esperanto's lacklustre fate in revolutionary Russia did not, however, keep early Soviet Esperantists from hitching their cause to that of international communism and from promising to support the Bolsheviks' foreign policy in particular. Throughout the 1920s and early 1930s, the Bolshevik leadership tolerated Esperanto as a niche movement that might still offer them some small practical uses in advancing their revolution at home and abroad. It was not until Stalin's Great Purges that the Soviet state would punish its citizens for their participation in a global Esperantist community built on transnational relationships forged through communication in Esperanto rather than in Russian, the language of Lenin and communist lingua franca.[65]

---

[65] Ulrich Lins, *Dangerous Language: Esperanto under Hitler and Stalin*, trans. Humphrey Tonkin (London: Palgrave Macmillan, 2016), 2: chapters 1–2.

2

Coded internationalism and telegraphic language[1]

Heidi Tworek

In 1928, a 'revolutionary' proposal was put on the agenda at an international conference. The proposal was just one sentence, 'brief in its wording and substance, but extremely large in its import,' as American expert William F. Friedman observed. Only an expert could possibly characterize a change to one sentence in the Convention of the International Telegraph Union (ITU) with such fervour. It was 'so marked in its departure from the paths taken by all preceding conferences' that Friedman wrote an eighty-page report for the American government on its ramifications for international communication.[2]

The sentence proposed that 'code words must be formed of a maximum of five letters, chosen at the will of the sender, without any condition'. To twenty-first-century readers, it is hard to comprehend how this sentence mattered at all. In 1928, however, it represented the culmination of decades of debate on telegraphic language and the possibility of communication over cables. From the start of optical telegraphy around 1800 up to the 1930s, telegraphic codes were a disputed part of international communication and international language. Debates about code and code language morphed into disagreements over which languages were translatable, who could afford to communicate across borders, which 'European' languages could be 'international', and who could arbiter the boundaries of language at all.

International exchange happened for many reasons. Historians generally gesture to the telegraph as one of the major technologies fuelling the growth in information travelling across borders from the mid-nineteenth century.[3] What most have forgotten is the importance of telegraphic language, and particularly codes. These codes are more than just a footnote in the history of forgotten languages of internationalism. They are important because they show how experts, governments and businesses created

---

[1] Many thanks to Kilu von Prince for her help with the linguistic aspect of this chapter. I am grateful to Jessica Reinisch and David Brydan for shepherding this chapter and volume to completion.

[2] William F. Friedman, *Report on the History of the Use of Codes and Code Language, the International Telegraph Regulations Pertaining Thereto, and the Bearing of This History on the Cortina Report* (Washington, DC: United States Government Printing Office, 1928), 1–2.

[3] On the historiography of telegraphy, see Heidi J. S. Tworek and Simone M. Müller, 'Editorial – Communicating Global Capitalism', *Journal of Global History* 10, no. 2 (July 2015): 203–11.

international standards, and how contested those standards remained throughout telegraphy's existence. Telegraphic codes show how one of the first international organizations – the ITU – brokered between parties which disputed the reasoning, finances or linguistics behind certain telegraphic codes. Codes show the growing hegemony of certain Western languages over others. They show how codes helped to create certainty or trust in information. Finally, they show how technical forms of internationalism often tried to create distinct categories in areas like language that resisted strict divisions.

Like other international agreements over communications, arrangements about code were technical agreements. In the history of international communications, international technical standards have generally succeeded, while agreements over content have been hard to create.[4] Codes combined both: any technical agreement over code necessarily constrained or changed content. Agreements over code were possible because technical experts could hash out solutions with the ITU. Yet there was never one single standard code. For nearly seventy years, experts at the ITU, government officials, cable companies and the telegraphing public fought over the best codes to achieve their aims. Underneath these technical debates lay broader debates about the cost of telegraphy, the role of business versus government in international communications, secrecy versus openness, accuracy versus error, 'authorized' versus 'unauthorized' international languages, man versus machine. At base lay assumptions about how language worked that drew upon Western, in particular Romance, languages to create codes that had to work for telegrams sent all around the world.

The history of telegraphic codes reminds us how language could be used to create hierarchies, not only between Europe and elsewhere but also within Europe itself. In some ways, this history is a familiar story of Eurocentric internationalism: experts and organizations insistently based international guidelines on European practices with a clear linguistic hierarchy between Europe and the non-European world. But telegraphic codes also propagated and created linguistic hierarchies within Europe itself. Using purportedly technical linguistic justifications, the ITU drew distinctions between Romance and Germanic languages (and countries), on the one hand, and Slavic languages such as Polish on the other. In the ITU at least, Dutch mattered more than Russian.

Yuliya Komska, Michelle Moyd and David Gramling have argued that 'linguistic obedience' – or an adherence to certain norms of language and 'civil discourse' – is a key part of sustaining political hierarchies. Part of contemporary linguistic obedience comes from the 'complex and ubiquitous privileges of monolingualism'.[5] Linguistic obedience in the past also relied upon privileging a certain subset of European languages. Though not quite monolingualism, it was a highly selective multilingualism sustained by seemingly technical requirements of telegraphic code. Technical debates

---

[4] Heidi J. S. Tworek and Simone Müller, 'Introduction: The Governance of International Communications: Business, Politics, and Standard-Setting in the Nineteenth and Twentieth Centuries', *Journal of Policy History* 27, no. 3 (2015): 405–15.

[5] Yuliya Komska, Michelle Moyd and David Gramling, *Linguistic Disobedience: Restoring Power to Civic Language* (Cham, Switzerland: Palgrave Macmillan, 2019), 18.

on telegraphic code made language another element in bolstering imperial European countries' dominance in internationalism.

To understand the significance of the sentence in 1928, we need to unpack multiple distinctions created in the first decades of international telegraphy and the ITU. Creation of hard-and-fast categories proved elusive but continual search for them is one way to understand technical expertise – the continual discovery that words escape categorial meanings and characterizations. Attempts to create dichotomies and exclusive categories are characteristics of technical standards, but language proved too slippery and too difficult. It could not be subjected to the clean divisions that technical experts demanded.

Code both freed and constrained. It freed up capacity and finances; it reduced fears of mistakes; it facilitated international exchange. But it constrained the types of reporting, the languages and the people with access to a fast form of communication. Alongside spoken languages, telegraphic codes were another vital, contested and long-neglected language of internationalism.

The creation and contestation of coded internationalism

Telegraphic infrastructure first and foremost enabled information to travel faster than goods and people. Particularly after the first successful transatlantic submarine cable was laid in 1866, telegraphy seemed to connect the world (or rather the white, Euro-American world). Within a few decades, cables spread from Europe to India, Latin America and Australia.[6] But for international telegraphy to work, there had to be a universal language to transmit telegrams, codes that cut across linguistic boundaries and could ensure that a message sent from London could reach India ungarbled, even though it had to travel through non-Anglophone territories like the Ottoman Empire.

Telegraphy also relied upon human operators who would receive the messages sent in Morse code and then either translate them into the telegrams for customers or send them on the next telegraph line to their destination. These operators were generally poorly paid and had to work at high speed to transmit as many telegrams per hour as possible. They often did not speak the language of the telegram being sent, though they were generally expected to speak or read one European language. Most Ottoman telegraph operators were required to know French, for instance.[7] This would have helped with transmitting messages in English from Britain to British colonial territories in Asia, but also opened up the potential for significant errors and misunderstandings.

---

[6] Simone M. Müller, *Wiring the World: The Social and Cultural Creation of Global Telegraph Networks* (New York: Columbia University Press, 2016); Simone M. Müller and Heidi J. S. Tworek, '"The Telegraph and the Bank": On the Interdependence of Global Communications and Capitalism, 1866–1914', *Journal of Global History* 10, no. 2 (July 2015): 259–83; Roland Wenzlhuemer, *Connecting the Nineteenth-Century World: The Telegraph and Globalization* (Cambridge, UK: Cambridge University Press, 2012).

[7] Yakup Bektas, 'The Sultan's Messenger: Cultural Constructions of Ottoman Telegraphy, 1847-1880', *Technology & Culture* 41, no. 4 (2000): 688.

Historians have long paid attention to how language travelled internationally, whether Latin in the early modern period or English in the twentieth century.[8] Historians of science have shown how English, French, and German became the main scientific *linguae francae* in the late nineteenth century and how English came to dominate over the twentieth century.[9] Meanwhile, historians of translation have explored how Japanese and Chinese translations of Western legal texts in the late nineteenth century created new words and concepts in a kind of legal internationalism.[10] Others have examined how control over language was key to colonialism and anti-colonialism.[11]

The late nineteenth and early twentieth centuries were also times of linguistic invention in the service of universalism and internationalism. Language has become an important part of international history too. Overview works on internationalism would be incomplete without including Ludwig Zamenhof's invention of Esperanto in the 1880s. Mark Mazower, for example, has portrayed Zamenhof's attempt to create a universal language as 'characteristic of late-nineteenth-century confidence in the potential of internationalism'.[12] Brigid O'Keeffe has emphasized how Zamenhof's upbringing as a Jewish man in imperial Russian territory shaped his vision of Esperanto.[13] Others created languages for the visually and orally impaired, such as Louis Braille and innovators in sign languages in the early and mid-nineteenth century; these developments also sparked heated debates in the deaf community about oral versus visual communication.[14] Meanwhile, histories of visuality have reminded us that language is not only spoken in words. Humanitarian photography, for example, conveyed a vernacular of Christian morality from the nineteenth century up to the present.[15]

There were also technical languages of internationalism, which remain surprisingly underexplored. If we take language broadly to mean communication between entities, then that language need not be spoken or visual. It could be a language of library catalogue systems, statistics or other measurements.[16] It could be a language of

---

[8] On the global spread of Latin, see Stuart McManus, 'The Global Lettered City: Humanism and Empire in Colonial Latin America and the Early Modern World' (Ph.D., Harvard University, 2016).

[9] Michael D. Gordin, *Scientific Babel: How Science Was Done Before and After Global English* (Chicago: The University of Chicago Press, 2015).

[10] Lydia He Liu, ed., *Tokens of Exchange: The Problem of Translation in Global Circulations* (Durham, NC: Duke University Press, 1999).

[11] Rachel Leow, *Taming Babel: Language in the Making of Malaysia* (Cambridge, UK: Cambridge University Press, 2016).

[12] Mark Mazower, *Governing the World: The History of an Idea, 1815 to the Present* (New York: Penguin Books, 2013), 112.

[13] Brigid O'Keeffe, 'An International Language for An Empire of Humanity: L. L. Zamenhof and the Imperial Russian Origins of Esperanto' (forthcoming).

[14] Gerald Shea, *The Language of Light: A History of Silent Voices* (New Haven: Yale University Press, 2017); John Tabak, *Significant Gestures: A History of American Sign Language* (Westport, CN: Praeger, 2006). On disputes about whether deaf people should focus on lip-reading or sign language, oral or visual communication, see Kim E. Nielsen, *The Radical Lives of Helen Keller* (New York: New York University Press, 2004).

[15] Davide Rodogno and Heide Fehrenbach, eds, *Humanitarian Photography: A History* (New York: Cambridge University Press, 2014).

[16] Daniel Speich Chassé, 'The Roots of the Millennium Development Goals: A Framework for Studying the History of Global Statistics', *Historical Social Research / Historische Sozialforschung* 41, no. 2 (2016): 218–37; Daniel Speich Chassé, *Die Erfindung des Bruttosozialprodukts. Globale*

engineering standards.¹⁷ It could also be a history of codes. Few have examined codes beyond histories of intelligence.¹⁸ Simone Müller has explored their use for telegraphic chess games, which 'became emblematic of a bourgeois experience of "instantaneous globality"' as well as 'ideologies of civilisation and Euro-American supremacy'.¹⁹ Thomas Mullaney has looked at the difficulties for Chinese telegraphy, which had to translate a character-based written language into Morse code. Mullaney notes that historians of Chinese telegraphy have focused on the financial, political and legal aspects of the technology, while generally eliding 'the unavoidable place of language in this history'.²⁰

Codes were a vital part of telegraphy from the start. They were useful for secrecy and economy. Secrecy was an obvious advantage for certain types of communication, like banking or intelligence. Economy was also critical for controlling costs, as telegrams were so expensive. Codes saved words and letters. This saved time and money because it was quicker to cable something short. One code, for example, used combinations of artificial words and suffixes to convey questions or sentences in one word. ACCESAFIZI meant 'What would you advise them to do?' ACCESA meant 'What do – advise – to do?' FI meant 'you' or 'yours', while 'ZI' meant 'they' or 'them'. A combination of the root artificial word with the two suffixes condensed a question with seven words into one word and meant that the telegram cost one-seventh of a plain-language message.²¹ But there needed to be standard codes, or at least widespread usage, for codes to work effectively across borders.

Disagreements over how to standardize code existed almost from the very start of telegraphy. The struggles over code started in the mid-nineteenth century and continued into the interwar period. They centred around discussions at the ITU (from 1932, the International Telecommunication Union). One of the first international organizations, created in 1865, the ITU helped to create a technical international language of code.²² Cable companies and governments brokered solutions, sometimes

---

Ungleichheit in der Wissensgeschichte der Ökonomie (Göttingen: Vandenhoeck & Ruprecht, 2013); Markus Krajewski, *Paper Machines: About Cards & Catalogs, 1548-1929* (Cambridge, MA: MIT Press, 2011), chap. 6; Theodore M. Porter, *Trust in Numbers: The Pursuit of Objectivity in Science and Public Life* (Princeton, NJ: Princeton University Press, 1995); Quinn Slobodian, 'How to See the World Economy: Statistics, Maps, and Schumpeter's Camera in the First Age of Globalization', *Journal of Global History* 10, no. 2 (2015): 307-32.

[17] Craig N. Murphy and Joanne Yates, *The International Organization for Standardization (ISO): Global Governance Through Voluntary Consensus* (London and New York: Routledge, 2009).

[18] The classic text is David Kahn, *The Code Breakers: The Comprehensive History of Secret Communication from Ancient Times to the Present* (New York: Scribner, 1996). Kahn deals with telegraphic code on pp. 837-50, though he states that he mainly relies on Friedman.

[19] Simone M. Müller, 'Chess by Cable: On the Interrelation of Technology and Sports in the Making of the Modern World', *Icon* 19 (2013): 114.

[20] Thomas Mullaney, 'Semiotic Sovereignty: The 1871 Chinese Telegraph Code in Historical Perspective', in *Science and Technology in Modern China, 1880s-1940s*, ed. Benjamin A. Ellman and Jing Tsu (Leiden: Brill, 2014), 154.

[21] Friedman, *Report on the History of the Use of Codes and Code Language*, 22.

[22] For overview histories of the ITU, see Léonard Laborie, *L'Europe mise en réseaux: la France et la coopération internationale dans les postes et les télécommunications (Aanées 1850-années 1950)* (Brussels: Peter Lang, 2011); Francis Lyall, *International Communications: The International Telecommunication Union and the Universal Postal Union* (Farnham, UK: Ashgate, 2011). For the latest history, see Gabriele Balbi and Andreas Fickers, eds, *History of the International Telecommunication*

privately, sometimes through the ITU, which enabled shorter and cheaper messages to travel around the world.

Code could enable internationalism, but also constrain it and privilege particular Western languages over others. No one telegraphic code dominated, just like no one universal language succeeded. The ITU would discover that its experts' continual attempts to create categories of language could not contain the myriad varieties of linguistic expression. In the end, the ITU opted in the interwar period to regulate only the length of codewords, but not content. The ITU enabled codes to be transferred around the world by creating the framework conditions for coded language, whether the length of words or their pronounceability. The system was flawed, but it also enabled international exchange.

The debates about coded internationalism were lengthy and convoluted. Since the foundation of the ITU in 1865, discussions about code were not 'scientific, nor built upon a logical foundation', according to one of the organization's 'oldest and most experienced members'.[23] Almost every ITU conference since its foundation had debated how to improve telegraphic code. By the mid-1920s, these debates reached a head. The ITU conference in Paris appointed a fifteen-delegate subcommittee to consider the issue in greater depth. After meeting for nearly a month in 1926 at Cortina d'Ampezzo in Italy, the committee finished what became known as the Cortina report. It contained two sets of recommendations: one from the majority of fourteen delegates and one from the British delegate. The Cortina report contained the 'revolutionary' proposal for five-letter codewords that Friedman found so important.

To understand why the proposal was controversial and why it took nearly six decades to get there, we need to delve into how technical debates sought to create stark categories where only fuzzy distinctions existed. Years of expertise were invested into finding solutions to problems that telegraph administrations themselves had created. In what would become a typical pattern, 'infractions of rules and regulations always led to attempts on the part of the nations constituting the Telegraph Union to correct conditions and prevent abuses by drawing up new regulations, only to find that the latter were no better than the ones they replaced'.[24] By the late 1920s/early 1930s, the solution would be creating parameters for the length of code words, but not attempting to universalize language like in earlier debates. By the interwar period, experts had realized that the only universal language was one of parameters.

The ITU had been founded in 1865 on the premised need for a universal language of technical standards. Switzerland brokered a compromise between two different systems within Europe that had threatened to forestall telegraphy functioning across borders. The Swiss role in the ITU's foundation enabled Switzerland to create an image of itself as a neutral nation, relatively shortly after its rather violent revolutions in 1848.[25] It also led to the foundation of the first major international organization

---

Union: Transnational Techno-Diplomacy from the Telegraph to the Internet (Berlin: De Gruyter, 2020).
[23] Friedman, *Report on the History of the Use of Codes and Code Language*, 2.
[24] Ibid., 11.
[25] Gabriele Balbi et al., *Network Neutrality: Switzerland's Role in the Genesis of the Telegraph Union, 1855-1875* (Bern: Peter Lang, 2014).

after the creation in the early nineteenth century of the Central Commission for the Navigation of the Rhine, which regulated river traffic.[26]

At the second ITU conference in 1868 in Vienna, talk turned to code language. The Portuguese delegation proposed creating a universal language for international telegraphy, but this was rejected. Delegates for decades afterwards would debate the framework to make telegrams translatable across borders. At stake was not just secrecy and economy, but the possibility of electric communication at all. That possibility depended, or at least delegates long thought, on making distinctions in a language that could enforce their regulations.

To see how deep the 'splitting' impulse went, let us explore the categories that experts tried to create and why they would sow the seeds of a problem that flowered well into the twentieth century. By the early 1930s, the solution was not ever lengthier regulations, but something far simpler. Unusually, experts simplified rather than complexified.

The first key distinction was geographic. Code had a geography from the very start. Europeans had used code for telegraphy long before North Americans because Europeans had used a form of telegraph before the electric telegraphy. The French had developed a system of semaphoric, or aerial, telegraphy around 1800. European countries had used codes for semaphoric telegraphy and transferred many of these codes into electric telegraphy. They also drew on naval signals.[27] The United States had not had aerial telegraphy, and thus codes really began with the spread of Morse's telegraph from the late 1840s. As the nineteenth century progressed, European states came to control telegraphy within their borders (the British nationalized telegraphy in 1870). Quarrelling continental European states settled their differences in 1865 to create the ITU. Meanwhile, the telegraph network was private in the United States.

Another overlaid distinction was between North America and elsewhere. The United States and Canada used a different version of Morse code (American Morse) than every other country, which used International Morse. The United States did not join the ITU because the ITU's regulations often assumed state jurisdiction over landline cables. Technically, the United States was thus not bound by ITU regulations, though its cable companies had to comply with some of them when sending international cables. Even non-members never quite escaped the ITU's reach.

Although it had been founded the year before the first successful transatlantic submarine cable was laid in 1866, the ITU did not just consider landline cables. It also dealt with the 'extra-European regime' of submarine cables. After 1866, a rash of cable-laying soon connected Europe to Australia, Asia, and the Americas.[28] Private multinational cable companies laid these cables; their representatives attended ITU

---

[26] On the CCNR, see Robert Mark Spaulding, 'The Central Commission for the Navigation of the Rhine and European Media, 1815-1848', in *Exorbitant Expectations: International Organizations and the Media in the Nineteenth and Twentieth Centuries*, ed. Jonas Brendebach, Martin Herzer, and Heidi J. S. Tworek (London and New York: Routledge, 2018), 17–37.

[27] Steven Bellovin, 'Compression, Correction, Confidentiality, and Comprehension: A Look at Telegraph Codes' (preliminary version, 2009), 3–4. http://www.cs.columbia.edu/~CS4HS/talks/codebooks.pdf

[28] Müller, *Wiring the World*.

conferences. Although they did not have the right to vote, representatives could participate in discussions and their preferences did influence decisions.

For discussions about code, the geographic divide between Europe and extra-European telegraphy was crucial. Code was most important for long distances where cable capacity was limited and prices very high. European correspondence had less need for code unless customers like banks wanted to communicate in secret. Most of the problems with code and violations of regulations, then, happened outside Europe. Yet the ITU's major members were European. In other words, one of the ITU's central problems lay mostly outside its jurisdiction to solve. Many code regulations would distinguish between Europe and outside Europe, entrenching geographic boundaries.

Beyond geographic distinctions, successive conferences sought to make linguistic distinctions. At the third ITU conference in 1872 in Rome, delegates defined the difference between plain language and code words. Code language meant that telegrams could only be deciphered with a key. Plain language was defined as conveying 'intelligible meaning in any one of the languages used in the territories of the contracting States, or in Latin'.[29] While this sounded initially like common sense, even basic distinctions like these soon became problematic. Most obviously, plain language implied that people who did not speak a language would be able to recognize messages as plain language. For example, a French person reading German would be able physically to read the letters but might not be able to judge the intelligibility of meaning. A French-speaking telegraph operator in the Ottoman Empire might not know if an English word actually existed or not.

Within code language, there were several subdistinctions on the level of words. Words in code languages could be real or artificial. Real words were dictionary words that conveyed a different meaning in the particular code. For instance, juniper could signify a meaning that had nothing to do with the tree. Artificial words were not dictionary words; they could be used for secrecy. Or they could be used to save money because the artificial word contained a phrase or designation that would otherwise have cost a great deal more to cable. The distinction between real and artificial words was sometimes also known as the difference between 'bona fide' words and not.

Initially, code language was charged at the same rate as plain language, though the code had to use dictionary words. Codes swiftly proliferated. Many different types of codes emerged around the world to convey different sorts of information. They became part of financial, religious, political and cultural life for anyone who could afford to send a telegram. Codes helped to transmit financial information or convey business information for sectors like oil, gas, shipping, banking or even fruit dealers.[30]

[29] Article 9, International Telegraph Convention, 1872 Rome. http://search.itu.int/history/HistoryDigitalCollectionDocLibrary/5.3.61.fr.200.pdf
[30] Business Code Co, *Oil and Gas Code, for Telegrams and Cables* (New York: Business Code Co, 1923); H. R. Meyer, *The International Mercantile Telegraph Code: For the Use of Bankers, Merchants, Manufacturers, Contractors, Brokers, Shipowners, &c. / Compiled by H.R. Meyer* (London: Hamilton, Adams & Co, 1880); Joseph H. Wilson, *The United States Telegraphic Cipher, Adapted to the Use of Dealers in Fruit and Produce, and Merchandise Brokers* (New York: CH Parsons, 1893), http://hdl.handle.net/2027/mdp.39015009793715. On codebooks, see Katherine Hayles, 'Technogenesis in Action: Telegraph Code Books and the Place of the Human', in *How We Think: Digital Media and Contemporary Technogenesis* (Chicago: University of Chicago Press, 2006).

Meteorological codes disseminated information about weather, including from places like Brazil.[31] There were chess telegraphic codes produced in London.[32] There were codes for tourists and travellers.[33] Some governments like New Zealand produced codes for their ministers, high commissioner and treasury.[34] Even some churches, like the National Council of the Churches of Christ in the United States, produced a 'missions code'.[35] Some codebooks explicitly noted in their title that their primary function was 'to cheapen telegraphy'.[36] This was done by compressing phrases into single or a few code words. Others stated that their telegraphic code was intended to 'insure privacy and secrecy in the transmission of telegrams'.[37]

Codes swiftly tested the boundaries of the ITU's regulations. The 1872 conference had set the maximum length of a word at seven syllables; code compilers found ways to create words that were extremely lengthy but with few syllables, such as CHINESISKSLUTNINGSDON, which had twenty-one letters but only six syllables.[38] At the 1875 conference in St. Petersburg, word length was fixed at a maximum of fifteen characters for inner-European telegrams and ten characters for outside Europe.

This did not, however, solve the problem that telegrams continued to mix code and plain language in telegrams. Telegraph operators often could not tell which words were code and which plain language.[39] Some codes used very unusual words as code words, which caused further confusion, particularly for operators who did not speak the language of the telegram they were transcribing. Operators 'are not and can not be expected to be highly skilled linguists'.[40] From the start, it was difficult to procure the 'right quality of operators', as one commentator put it in 1855.[41] Particularly in the mid-nineteenth century, physical conditions were often poor. A mirror galvanometer was used in some places to display Morse code. This was a simple device that displayed the electric currents of Morse code as flashes of light. Some operators went partially blind after staring at shifting light for a few years.[42] They often worked long hours and were

---

[31] Nuno Alves Duarte Silva, *Codigo mnemo-telegraphico com applicação á meteorologia* (Rio de Janeiro: Typ Leuzinger, 1910).
[32] Edwyn Anthony, *Chess Telegraphic Codes* (London: Waterlow and Sons Ltd., 1890).
[33] Thomas Walter Hartfield, *The Atlas Universal Travelers' and Tourists' Telegraphic Cipher Code* (New York: American Bank Note Company, 1896).
[34] James B. Heywood, *New Zealand Government Telegraph Code: For Use of Ministers, High Commissioner, and Treasury* (Wellington, NZ: Government Printer, 1911).
[35] National Council of the Churches of Christ in the United States of America, *The Missions Code* (New York: National Council of the Churches of Christ in the United States of America, 1930).
[36] Anglo-American Code and Cypher Co, *Anglo-American Telegraphic Code to Cheapen Telegraphy and to Furnish a Complete Cypher* (New York: Tyrrel, 1891), http://hdl.handle.net/2027/nyp.3343 3019285554.
[37] Frank Miller, *Telegraphic Code to Insure Privacy and Secrecy in the Transmission of Telegrams* (CM Cornwell, 1882), http://hdl.handle.net/2027/nyp.33433019287345. On American and polyglot code books, see Hayles, *How We Think*, 152–61.
[38] Friedman, *Report on the History of the Use of Codes and Code Language*, 14.
[39] This problem continued into the era of radiograms. For examples, see Bellovin, 'Compression, Correction, Confidentiality, and Comprehension', 10.
[40] Friedman, *Report on the History of the Use of Codes and Code Language*, 16.
[41] O'Shaughnessy, cited in D. K. Lahiri Choudhury, 'Of Codes and Coda: Meaning in Telegraph Messages, circa 1850-1920', *Historical Social Research / Historische Sozialforschung* 35, no. 1 (2010): 135.
[42] Friedman, *Report on the History of the Use of Codes and Code Language*, 19.

not particularly well paid. Oxbridge graduates were not becoming telegraph operators. But the ITU regulations expected linguistic competency on that level.

Unsurprisingly, errors abounded. Some were, perhaps, inevitable, given that telegraph operators transcribed Morse code at high speed. But many were exacerbated by the wild variety of codes, often using myriad unusual dictionary words in multiple languages. A 436-page book published in 1890 listed some 70,000 errors made in actual telegrams.[43] Codes made international telegraphic communication less reliable and far less seamless than we often imagine in retrospect.

There were three main types of error. First, orthographic, meaning that operators muddled like-sounding or like-written words such as 'jeering' for 'peering'. Second, there were telegraphic errors. An operator might mix up dots and dashes so the letter 's' (three dots) could be heard as 'u' (two dots, one dash). Third, phonetic errors were common, like writing 'serial' instead of 'cereal'. The third category presented the most errors. As one expert noted in 1880, this was 'to a great extent due to the defective codes'.[44]

Error-riddled international telegrams with real words led to the proliferation of artificial words, which were 'safer'. Artificial word codes at this point combined real words with artificial prefixes and suffixes. For example, DEXTER meant in one code 'order in force for three months' while DEXTERITY meant 'order in force for six months'. To express 'order in force for four months', a code might make up a word like DEXTERABLE.[45] Any sharp distinction between the real (dictionary word) and the artificial made increasingly little sense.

Artificial word codes grew exponentially, although technically only bona fide words were allowed. Artificial codes were created in several different ways: by combining syllables and condensing words, or root and terminal systems. Root and terminal systems combined code words to create thousands of potential phrases. For example, the root APARL could mean 'we order 1500 at 28 shillings', while terminal ANFRO meant '140 lb. jute sacks Duluth Imperial, net c. i. f. London'. Combining the two created APARLANFRO to mean 'we order 1500 140 lb. jute sacks Duluth International at 28 shillings, net c. i. f. London'. A different terminal might alter the meaning slightly, for example, APARLANERE changed the destination from London to Liverpool. Although bona fide words were supposed to be easier to handle (in the eyes of some experts), many telegraph operators found artificial words simpler, because most artificial words had a basic consonant-vowel (CV) syllable structure to ease pronunciation.[46] The rules dictated use of bona fide words; the practice used artificial words and came closer to achieving the spirit of the rules – error-free international communication.

For delegates to the ITU, the spread of artificial words was a problem. The solution, as so often, seemed to be to create new distinctions: between official and unofficial

---

[43] *Guide to the Correction of Errors in Code Telegrams* (London, 4th edn, 1890).
[44] *Washburne's Cable and Telegraph Manual and Error Detector* (New York, 1880), cited in Friedman, *Report*, 20.
[45] Friedman, *Report on the History of the Use of Codes and Code Language*, 23.
[46] Friedman, *Report on the History of the Use of Codes and Code Language*, 25. On the history of jute, see Tariq Omar Ali, *A Local History of Global Capital: Jute and Peasant Life in the Bengal Delta* (Princeton: Princeton University Press, 2018).

vocabulary. In 1890, Belgium proposed the idea of an 'official vocabulary' because it was 'indispensable to put an end to the abuses' of code language.[47] But the provision was only applied to Europe and was optional for extra-European telegraphy. Ironically, codes were mainly used outside Europe, making official vocabulary a time-consuming and somewhat pointless exercise. The International Bureau published an official vocabulary in 1894 of 256,740 words. Criticized for many reasons including bad word choices and typographic mistakes, it was most opposed by code compilers and firms because it seemed to restrict their ability to save money through codes.

Official vocabulary was even less effective, because the American position had evolved. A Western Union rulebook in 1893 had for the first time officially allowed artificial words if they were pronounceable groups of letters. Of course, the key question was, pronounceable by whom? Different languages have different phonotactics, meaning the rules about how to combine sounds into syllables and words. Something highly pronounceable in one language could seem highly unpronounceable to a speaker of another. As became clear from the ITU's debates, pronounceability was a constructed political category too.

In the United States too, artificial words swiftly became widespread domestically and American users began to attempt to use their looser system internationally. The ITU still tried in the late 1890s to compile larger books of official vocabulary from existing code books. By 1903, the official vocabulary had expanded from 256,740 words to nearly 1.2 million words.[48] The work was in vain. The British delegation at the ITU conference in London in 1903 argued that Chambers of Commerce and 'the telegraphing public' disliked the imposition. Plus the British delegation questioned the assumption that bona fide words were easier for non-native speakers than artificial words. On the contrary, the British claimed, a telegrapher might find an artificial word like DEMINABAM easier than English words like 'awkwardly'. Furthermore, the Americans would not contemplate joining the ITU if it outlawed artificial code words that had now become so widespread on continental North America.[49]

The British delegation's arguments were both technical and political. As disputes would continue, the British focused on the technical arguments. Andreas Fickers has described this dynamic as 'techno-political diplomacy' or 'the inscription of political and symbolic capital into debates over technical standards'.[50] Especially for the British and Americans, supposedly technical arguments about language were also about securing the increasing dominance of English language in codebooks.

The distinction between unofficial and official vocabulary was now abandoned because it had proven unpractical. Instead of abandoning classifications, however, delegates at the 1903 conference created another category: pronounceability. The

[47] *Documents de la conférence télégraphique international de Paris* (Berne: Rieder & Simmen, 1891), 164 http://search.itu.int/history/HistoryDigitalCollectionDocLibrary/4.22.51.fr.200.pdf
[48] 'De l'emploi du langage convenu dans la correspondence télégraphique', *Journal télégraphique*, no. 4 (April 1926): 64. Permanent URL: http://handle.itu.int/11.1004/020.3000/ITU011-1926-04-fr
[49] Ibid., 64–5. On how business interests affected ITU debates, see Simone M. Müller, 'Beyond the Means of 99 Percent of the Population: Business Interests, State Intervention, and Submarine Telegraphy', *Journal of Policy History* 27, no. 3 (July 2015): 439–64.
[50] Andreas Fickers, 'The Techno-Politics of Colour: Britain and the European Struggle for a Colour Television Standard', *Journal of British Cinema and Television* 7, no. 1 (2010): 96.

introduction of pronounceability had a 'hundredfold more profound and far-reaching effect than the official vocabulary, either dead or alive, could possibly have had', William Friedman observed in retrospect.[51] ITU delegates changed Article 8, paragraph 2, on code language to read: 'the words, whether real or artificial, must be formed of syllables capable of being pronounced according to the usage of one of the following languages: German, English, Spanish, French, Dutch, Italian, Portuguese, or Latin.' Code words were also not allowed to be longer than ten characters.

While seemingly innocuous, this change introduced several new distinctions that reframed and reinforced linguistic hierarchy. First, it introduced the idea of pronounceability versus non-pronounceability. Second, it introduced the distinction of a syllable. Third, it solidified the hierarchy of eight 'authorized' languages whose pronunciation mattered. Finally, it made illogical assumptions about the overlap between a written syllable and its oral pronounceability.

The debate obscured a fundamental fact about pronounceability: it is relational. In other words, a word can be easy to pronounce for speakers of some languages and not others. My surname is easy to pronounce for Polish speakers and hard for many who only speak English. Arguments about whether something is pronounceable depend upon who is doing the pronouncing. That relationship overlapped with political power. Certain languages were deemed more pronounceable because powerful delegations spoke them. Politics underlay pronounceability.

Initially, the Belgian delegation proposed that the ITU should only recognize euphonious syllables for artificial words, 'euphony' meaning that which can be pronounced. The Germans and French quickly argued that not all languages offered euphonious syllables. For the French, the Polish language was an obvious example. Polish had the tongue-twister 'Chrzaszcz brzmi w trzcinie' ('the maybug is boring into the reed'). These words had syllables that were 'assuredly not' euphonious and yet they were technically pronounceable for Poles. The German delegation thus suggested that pronounceability would only exist as a criterion for the eight 'authorized languages'.[52] All of these languages were Romance or Germanic, all of them languages of imperial powers, or Latin. Slavic languages were excluded from the realms of pronounceability, as were Slavic understandings of language, like consonant-only syllables. Only 'authorized languages' were deemed euphonious or, rather, as languages that fit the ITU delegations' constructed categories of pronounceable language broken into syllabic bites.

After the new regulations went into effect in July 1904, compilers produced masses of code books with artificial, pronounceable words. These code books used five-letter code words; two could be combined to make the maximum word length of ten characters. These five-letter code words reduced errors for several reasons. One was that all words had the same number of letters. That type of uniformity could work. Code books also started to employ the principle of the 'two-letter differential'. This meant that every code word would have at least two letters different from any other code word. Most telegraph operators made at most one mistake per word. One mistake

[51] Friedman, *Report on the History of the Use of Codes and Code Language*, 36.
[52] Ibid., 37.

would not spell another code word so the operator would know that they had made a mistake. The reasonably priced 'Bentley's Code' for general business matters appeared in 1906 and quickly spread quite widely, because it helped to cut costs massively. Soon reprinted in 1909, Bentley's promised 'nearly 1000 million combinations' that generated coded telegrams 'with a minimum saving of 50%'.[53] Five-letter code words were barely used in 1904; by 1910, they were the norm.

Predictably, though, the more content-focused categories of pronounceability and syllables soon broke down in practice. First, it turned out that a syllable could mean two things – either a single vocal sound or characters/letters representing that sound. Each of the eight languages approached this differently. In English particularly, syllables were far from pronounceable. If the French had objected to Polish for its consonant clusters, shouldn't the French have objected to English syllables like 'spry'? Plus combining syllables from real English words could create code words like AWKMNEPNEU. Each syllable was technically pronounceable according to the ITU article and yet, the aggregate word was unpronounceable.[54] The problem here was that some consonant clusters function within words (such as pneu) but may not function as independent syllables. The ITU guidelines confused syllables with independently pronounceable syllables. They also obscured the relationality of pronunciation itself.

To the ITU delegates working on assumptions about Western languages in 1903, pronounceability and syllables had seemed like simple categories. This was particularly true for delegates from Romance language countries, where every syllable has consonants and vowels. Every syllable in Romance languages is also pronounceable even when separated from the words in which it is used. These assumptions had undergirded the Belgian proposal, but English alone had proven them unworkable. English was just as tricky as Polish in many respects, but the ubiquity of English and its state sponsors meant that delegates still sought solutions to the problems it caused. It did not occur to them simply to expand the number of official languages to include Slavic and other tongues. English exceptionalism prevailed over practicality.

Disputes over pronounceability started to plague telegraph operators. They were asked to adjudicate pronounceability. One telegraph official noted that telegram senders would 'manage by means of facial contortions to pronounce words containing up to four or five consecutive consonants'.[55] This wasted precious time and caused great acrimony (and hopefully occasional laughter) at the telegraph office. 'Poor charging clerks at the telegraph counters' were being asked to solve questions so technically complex that they 'would tax the knowledge and experience of expert phoneticists, orthoepists, orthographers, and lexicographers'. Pronounceability, just like official or bona fide words, was a category 'built manifestly upon an illogical, unscientific basis from the beginning'.[56] It simply could not be measured as the officials and some technical experts had believed.

---

[53] E. L. Bentley, *Bentley's Complete Phrase Book* (New York: American Code Company, 1909), title page. https://archive.org/details/bentleyscomplete00bentuoft
[54] Friedman, *Report on the History of the Use of Codes and Code Language*, 47.
[55] Cited in Ibid., 51.
[56] Ibid., 48.

These breakdowns meant that the question of code language dominated the next ITU conference in 1908 in Lisbon. The categories of 1903 had made some aspects of international telegraphy even more problematic. 'The language euphonic had become the language cacophonic,' quipped a French delegate.[57] The Russian delegation pointed out that many of the regulations on code language were 'contradictory'. Trying to point out the problems facing Slavic languages, the Russian delegation complained that a telegram in Polish in plain language was allowed, but a telegram using Polish words was rejected if the telegram as a whole was not comprehensible, that is, if Polish words were used as code words.[58]

Delegates in 1908 skirted the issue. The only solution was to add the word 'current' to the idea that syllables had to be pronounceable (i.e. pronounceable according to 'current usage') and to outlaw diacritics for artificial words. English, the only orthography without diacritics, became by default the only language whose full alphabet could be rendered in code words. And it was obvious even at the conference that many syllables in common words were not always pronounceable. What if, for example, a code word used the first syllables of the words 'psychology' and 'phthisis'. Was a code word like PSYCHPHTHI pronounceable, as delegates at the time understood it?[59]

Ideas of authorized languages and pronounceable syllables had thus created new hidden hierarchies of language. Most obviously, only Romance and Germanic languages were included and only their problems considered. Languages like Polish were used as examples of why they did not deserve to be included as 'authorized'. Even more hidden were writing systems (orthographies) that did not use the Roman alphabet like Arabic or Chinese. Character-based languages like Chinese had proven the most challenging since the 1870s. Telegrams in Chinese used multiple different systems, including number-based ones, to translate characters into Morse code. They were often classed as code, simply because operators could not deduce their meaning. This made telegrams in Chinese often more expensive than they were supposed to be if they had been classified correctly as plain language. The Chinese search for what Thomas Mullaney has called 'semiotic sovereignty' was even more hidden from ITU's debates over coded internationalism than languages like Polish or Russian.[60] The dead language of Latin was considered more universal than any non-Western (and non-Western European) language.

By this point, American cable companies had run out of patience with endless ITU debates. Western Union and Postal Telegraph both changed their rules to allow pronounceable and unpronounceable groups of letters.[61] As English became increasingly dominant in telegraphy, American usage disregarded what companies saw as pointless distinctions. While the concept of the pronounceable syllable seemed self-evident to speakers of Romance languages, they made less sense for English speakers, and thus less sense for international telegraphic language that increasingly

[57] Ibid., 52.
[58] 'De l'emploi du langage convenu dans la correspondence télégraphique', *Journal télégraphique*, no. 12 (December 1911), 288. http://handle.itu.int/11.1004/020.3000/ITU011-1911-12-fr
[59] Friedman, *Report*, 54.
[60] Mullaney, 'Semiotic Sovereignty', in Ellman and Tsu, *Science and Technology in Modern China*.
[61] Friedman, *Report*, 71.

used English. The American move anticipated the ITU by more than two decades; it also precipitated the ITU's debates because American companies were so important for international telegraphic traffic.

The outbreak of the First World War postponed further discussion of pronounceability until the next major ITU conferences in the mid-1920s, when the Cortina report devoted dozens of pages to the intricate details of the issue. The imprecision of pronounceability had continued, and was not just a feature of English codewords.[62] Some actual telegrams handled by the Dutch telegraph administration in December 1925 had included examples like YLGMFPAHVY or IAMKHZVESK. Dutch words may include such consonant clusters within them, but that does not make them syllables linguistically. Thus, these consonant clusters were unpronounceable on their own, even though the individual syllables came from pronounceable words.[63] Once again, the examples came from a Germanic language with different principles than Romance languages.

The majority opinion from the Cortina report (fourteen out of fifteen delegates) recommended removing the category of pronounceability. This was not necessarily simply a recognition that hard-and-fast 'technical' divisions of language had failed. It also arose from a new division: between man and machine. In the nineteenth century, signallers and operators exercised 'hermeneutic power over the telegraph's language and transmission of information', at the same time as the telegraphic system erased the identity of humans behind the scenes.[64] This made the transition to machines unnoticeable to many outsiders. By the mid-1920s, automatic printing machines had become highly ubiquitous. These machines automatically printed out the Morse code sent over telegraph. While there had been versions of tickers for decades, particularly for financial information, the new automatic teletypers now increasingly eliminated the job of the telegraph operator, at least in North America.[65] Automatic printing was now used for 85 to 90 per cent of land telegraphy in Canada and the United States.[66] Pronounceability was irrelevant to a machine, the delegates to Cortina realized. Ironically, one inventor had received a patent in 1928 for a cryptographic machine that automatically generated pronounceable syllables.[67] But it would soon prove useless.

The prevalence of machines printing telegrams meant that pronounceability made little sense as an aid to accuracy. One study by the Cortina subcommittee actually found that it took as much time to transmit code as plain language, using some types of telegraph equipment. This 'occasioned considerable surprise among the members of the Cortina committee'.[68] It also made pronounceability an ever more irrelevant category. Machines did not fall prey to many of the so-called psychological errors made by human operators like transposition. Machine errors were more related to

---

[62] Irvin Stewart, 'The International Telegraph Conference of Brussels and the Problem of Code Language', *American Journal of International Law* 23, no. 2 (1929): 293.
[63] Friedman, *Report*, 57.
[64] Lahiri Choudhury, 'Of Codes and Coda: Meaning in Telegraph Messages, circa 1850-1920', 136.
[65] Alex Preda, *Framing Finance: The Boundaries of Markets and Modern Capitalism* (Chicago: University of Chicago Press, 2009).
[66] Friedman, *Report*, 62.
[67] Hayles, *How We Think*, 141–2.
[68] Friedman, *Report*, 63.

transmission. This was thus an important milestone in what Katherine Hayles has described as 'a steady movement away from a human-centric view of code toward a machine-centric view'.[69]

Now, delegates to the ITU were more focused on reducing errors. This took them away from the six decades of debate about language to a discussion about the length of code words, not their content. The German delegate to Cortina noted that it vastly decreased errors if words were transmitted in five-letter groups, rather than grouped into ten-letter code words.[70] After debate, this then was the recommendation by the Cortina group (or at least fourteen of the fifteen delegates) to the ITU.

At the 1928 ITU conference in Brussels, the Cortina report was the main subject of debate. The United States cared more than we might expect from a non-member. The US government had commissioned Friedman's detailed report. It also sent Friedman as part of a large American delegation with unofficial standing to the conference.[71] The concern made sense more because it could severely impact American cable companies and their international reach. It also fit into a pattern where the US government often represented communication companies' interests at international conferences, such as the Washington conference in 1927 on radio and determining the international division of spectrum.[72]

The Cortina report's attempt to dissolve categories did not succeed at first. The lone minority voice of the British delegation ensured that, at least in 1928, the simple Cortina sentence did not pass. Instead, a compromise proposal created two categories of code language. Category A was for telegrams with words of no more than ten letters, composed of either bona fide words from one of the eight authorized languages or artificial words. The artificial words had to include at least one vowel if they were five letters, two vowels if they were between six and eight letters, and three vowels if they had nine or ten letters. After the Romance language countries had abandoned their commitment to euphony, the British had retained it. The International Chamber of Commerce as well as the London-based Eastern & Associated Companies agreed with the British delegation that the ITU should retain pronounceability and the status quo.[73] The second category, Category B, followed Cortina and allowed telegrams to be formed of no more than five letters with no further restrictions.

As per usual, categories proved unworkable. Together with another mathematician, William Friedman calculated that there were only about 150,480 words in category A, while there were around 400,000 in category B.[74] At the 1932 ITU conference, experts

---

[69] Hayles, *How We Think*, 124.
[70] Friedman, *Report*, 71.
[71] Howard S. LeRoy, 'Wrestling with the International Telegraph Code', *American Bar Association Journal* 445 (1929): 445–7.
[72] James Schwoch, 'The American Radio Industry and International Communications Conferences, 1919–1927', *Historical Journal of Film, Radio and Television* 7, no. 3 (1987): 289–309.
[73] 'Report of the American Delegation to the International Telegraph Conference of Brussels, 10–22 September 1928, accompanied by a Translation of Documents of the Conference as Published by the International Office of the Telegraph Union and Other Related Documents' (Washington, DC: U.S. Government Printing Office, 1929), 73.
[74] William F. Friedman and Charles J. Mendelsohn, 'Note on Code Words', *American Mathematical Methods* 39, no. 7 (1932): 394–09.

finally ceased their tireless categorization. They agreed that pronounceability would no longer be required from 1934 and agreed upon a maximum length for words of five letters. What seemed like a simple bureaucratic change was the culmination of nearly seventy years of technical wrangling. These minutiae do not just tell us that telegraphic communication was not as simple as often portrayed. They also tell us something about the nature of international technical expertise. That sought to create 'simple' categories of language like 'real' and 'artificial' words to enable coded internationalism. In the end, though, no linguistic category was simple. The only workable solution was stepping back from regulating content at all.

Although coded language ceased to be a controversial issue, one of the people who had engaged most intensively in the debate would put those skills to use in another coded context. Author of the eighty-page report on Cortina and a technical expert sent by the United States to the 1928 ITU Brussels conference, William Friedman would later use his technical expertise on coding to great effect. Friedman would be critical for US intelligence during the Second World War and would crack PURPLE, the Japanese equivalent of the German ENIGMA machine.[75] Friedman also helped the CIA to fund Crypto AG, a Swiss-based company that produced encryption devices for governments around the world, which we now know had back doors for the CIA and West German intelligence services.[76] Sometimes known as the 'dean of American cryptography', Friedman's intensive engagement with coded internationalism is forgotten.

Conclusion

In December 1932, the ITU journal noted that the optimal code 'from a purely technical point of view' was simply composed of five letters with no further conditions attached.[77] There was no such thing as the 'purely technical'. Even the final agreement on these regulations was affected as much by the global economic downturn, which had killed the last resistance to Cortina, as anything else.

Telegraphic codes were an expression of technical internationalism, taken to new heights in the late 1920s. They are also a forgotten part of the history of trying to find universal language. Katherine Hayles has called telegraphic code a 'subsurface lingua franca' whose potential was more fully realized with computer code.[78] It makes more sense to see codes as hidden Esperantos. Like Esperanto, no code ever became universal.

---

[75] Other scholars who later linked mathematics and communication, like Claude Shannon, also worked on code-breaking during the Second World War. John Guillory, 'Genesis of the Media Concept', *Critical Inquiry* (2010): 351, footnote 48.

[76] Greg Miller, 'How the CIA Used Crypto AG Encryption Devices to Spy on Countries for Decades', *Washington Post* (11 February 2020), https://www.washingtonpost.com/graphics/2020/world/national-security/cia-crypto-encryption-machines-espionage/

[77] *Journal télégraphique*, 64, no. 12 (December 1932): 330. https://www.itu.int/bibar/ITUJournal/DocLibrary/ITU011-1932-12-fr.pdf

[78] Hayles, *How We Think*, 162.

But code compilers, cable companies and ITU delegates tried to find universalizing mechanisms to govern coded international language.

It was not just about codes, but also about the standardization of languages. Telegraphic codes had to be precise and standardized to function across borders. What officials soon found was that their categories for standardization could not be measured as universally as they initially believed. 'If "pronounceability" were a condition susceptible of physical measurement, if it were a thing that could be weighed, a thing or a condition to which definite, unvarying, standard constants or measures of precision could be applied, the weight of the argument would be greatly increased. But is such a thing possible?' William Friedman asked.[79] It was one thing devising standards for physical objects or statistics. It was another to do so for language, which morphed within and across borders as well as over time.

While Friedman and other ITU delegates mostly complained about feasibility, the ITU's deliberations on telegraphic language also concealed assumptions about hierarchies in the international system. Romance languages were often taken as a baseline to understand the possibilities of language itself. The idiosyncrasies of Germanic languages like English and Dutch were tolerated; the consonant-heavy nature of Slavic languages was not. These supposedly technical discussions about syllables or pronounceability concealed deeply held assumptions about which European languages were worth accommodating and which were not. Even more fundamental was the complete disregard for non-European or character-based languages like Chinese. The ITU's regulatory debates around codes thus reinforced linguistic, political and economic hierarchies within and outside Europe that had emerged in other international realms like science, trade and international law.

The history of coded internationalism reminds us that technical expertise often meant creating categories with strict, commensurable divisions that prove unworkable in the real world. Technical expertise rests in the belief that these divisions are possible. Theoretically, codes made international telegraphy seamless and simple. In reality, international exchange was messy, hierarchical and error-riddled. But it could still work, somehow.

---

[79] Friedman, *Report*, 56.

3

An international language for all

Basic English and the limits of a global communication experiment

Valeska Huber

In 1938, at the height of India's struggle for independence, Jawaharlal Nehru advocated the use of Basic English in India, a radically reduced language of 850 words which had been developed in the 1920s by the Cambridge academics Charles Kay Ogden and Ivor Armstrong Richards. For Nehru, Basic English carried the promise of being astonishingly easy to acquire by anyone as the 'whole vocabulary and grammar can be put down on one sheet of paper and an intelligent person can learn it in two or three weeks'. Nehru concluded that 'where we teach English as a foreign tongue, and we shall have to do this on an extensive scale, Basic English should be taught'.[1] Nehru's support came at a surprising moment, given that India was entering the final phases of its long resistance against the British colonizers. Yet, for Nehru, even after independence English would be an essential tool for the participation in global communication.

Nehru did not stand alone in his promotion of Basic English. Against the backdrop of the promises of new media, above all the radio, and of new theories of learning, an international language for all became a central topic in internationalist circles. Internationalists of many different shades were soon enlisted as supporters of the Basic English project. Among them were Sven Hedin, the Swedish explorer of Central Asia, Julian Huxley, a British biologist and later UNESCO general secretary, and the Japanese-Austrian founder of the Paneuropean Union Richard Nikolaus Coudenhove-Kalergi. The American philosopher John Dewey figured together with playwright George Bernard Shaw and the author and social critic H. G. Wells. Henry Jacob and Joseph A. Lauwerys of the New Education Fellowship equally argued that global communications, such as the radio and the aeroplane, now called for new languages to bring humankind closer together intellectually as well, with Basic English as their preferred choice for this endeavour.[2]

---

[1] Jawaharlal Nehru, 'The Question of Language', Congress Economic and Political Study No. 6, in Adolph Myers, *Basic and the Teaching of English in India* (Bombay: Times of India Press, 1938), 1.
[2] Henry Jacob, *On the Choice of a Common Language*, with a Preface by Joseph A. Lauwerys (London: Sir Isaac Pitman & Sons, 1946).

If, for these internationalists, communication and the related technologies were key to interwar and post-war internationalism and to the unfolding of global processes more generally, it is not surprising that they have resonated with historians of global history and internationalism alike. In contributions to these fields, connections based on new modes of mobility and communication are paramount. Yet in contrast to the supporters of Basic English, recent global histories often concentrate on the 'hardware' of communications technologies, reflected for instance in the growing literature on infrastructures such as steamships and telegraph lines.[3] Furthermore, they tend to focus on technological innovations themselves rather than emphasizing the varied uses and questions of access that came with them.[4] Even those interested in more intangible concerns such as the circulation of news and the emergence of global publics in sports, culture and politics often pay less attention to questions of (imagined) participation and widening audiences.[5] In order to come closer to an understanding of use, access and participation, be they planned, projected or realized, it is necessary to complement the histories of technologies and infrastructures of communication with research on the 'technologies of the intellect' such as languages and translations, access to reading material and forms of publicity.[6]

A similar neglect of the 'software' of communication and the possibilities to communicate in a mutually comprehensible way holds true for the more precisely defined settings of international conferences and associations.[7] Many histories of internationalism mention language and communication merely in passing.[8] Rarely do we ask which language the participants at such meetings used to inform themselves or to communicate with each other. Internationalist projects of course depended on communication, even if the official protocols and transcripts sometimes disguise questions of language acquisition, translation and misunderstandings. Most fundamentally, language provides the link between international organizations and individuals, both among experts and in regard to broader populations that increasingly formed the audience of internationalism. The correlations of language and internationalism have only recently started to become the subject of systematic

---

[3] See, for instance, Roland Wenzlhuemer, *Connecting the Nineteenth-Century World: The Telegraph and Globalization* (Cambridge: Cambridge University Press, 2012); Dirk van Laak, *Alles im Fluss: Die Lebensadern unserer Gesellschaft – Geschichte und Zukunft der Infrastruktur* (Frankfurt am Main: S. Fischer, 2018); Emily Rosenberg, ed., *A World Connecting: 1870-1945* (Cambridge, MA: The Belknap Press of Harvard University Press, 2012).

[4] For a critique of this focus on innovation, see David Edgerton, *The Shock of the Old: Technology and Global History Since 1900* (Oxford: Oxford University Press, 2007).

[5] Heidi Tworek, *News from Germany: The Competition to Control World Communications, 1900–1945* (Cambridge, MA: Harvard University Press, 2019); Barbara J. Keys, *Globalizing Sport: National Rivalry and International Community in the 1930s* (Cambridge, MA: Harvard University Press, 2013). Tobias Werron, *Der Weltsport und sein Publikum: Zur Autonomie und Entstehung des modernen Sports* (Weilerswist-Metternich: Weilerswist Velbrück Wissenschaft, 2010).

[6] For the expression 'technologies of the intellect', see Jack Goody, *The Domestication of the Savage Mind* (Cambridge: Cambridge University Press, 1977), 16; Walter Ong, *Orality and Literature: The Technologizing of the World* (Abingdon: Taylor & Francis, 1982), 172. There is of course a large literature criticizing Goody's take on literacy.

[7] For 'software' and 'hardware' of communication, see Marshall McLuhan, *Understanding Media: The Extensions of Man* (Abingdon: Routledge, 1964).

[8] See as just one example of a burgeoning field Glenda Sluga and Patricia Clavin, eds, *Internationalisms: A Twentieth-Century History* (Cambridge: Cambridge University Press, 2017).

inquiry going beyond individual case studies.⁹ In this newer research, the uses of media and technologies are placed on the same level with the physical infrastructures that facilitate them. Focusing on the propagation of simplified versions of English on a worldwide scale, this chapter develops a set of more precise arguments regarding the connection of language and internationalism. Following the case of Basic English, it sheds light on three areas that can further the study of European internationalism more generally.

First of all, the project of Basic English illustrates a specific British imperial version of Western or European liberal internationalism, highlighting the complicated relationship between Britain and Europe, but also turning the gaze towards the English-speaking big brother, the United States. The chapter traces some debates around international languages in the interwar period, showing how contemporaries argued for the need for linguistic simplification in a complex world. English, unlike its frequently cited competitor Esperanto, is often seen as strangely separate from internationalist endeavours and merely linked to the rise of US capitalism and entertainment in the period after the Second World War.¹⁰ Yet many British internationalists of the interwar period were in favour of expanding English as a means of international communication. Often, these internationalists, being involved in both colonial and international projects, showed how imperialism and internationalism coexisted quite comfortably in this period. Secondly, in relation to internationalist concerns with English, the chapter questions the elite focus of much of the literature on interwar internationalism. It highlights, instead, that some communication projects revolved around the tension between elite communication in expert circles and the necessity to reach out to new audiences. While much of the research on internationalism concentrates on those elites meeting at conferences and other internationalist events, it is high time to expand the frame of the study of internationalism beyond these circles. Basic English and its journey from European internationalist circles into the world might be a probe for methodologies that could help us alleviate this bias, if not overcome it completely. Thirdly, the example of Basic English illuminates a specific technocratic and scientific way of reaching and possibly transforming people's minds. If the expansion of English is often seen as a mere corollary to American commercial expansion, the proponents of Basic English were part of a more general belief in technocracy and planning which was visible in many other fields of governance during the same period.¹¹

---

⁹ See the conference Languages of Internationalism, held at Birkbeck College, London, 24–26 May 2017.

¹⁰ There is an extensive literature on the rise of global English. See, for instance, Robert McCrum, *Globish: How English Became the World's Language* (New York: W. W. Norton & Company, 2010); David Crystal, *English as a Global Language* (Cambridge: Cambridge University Press, 1997); Nicholas Ostler, *The Last Lingua Franca: English Until the Return of Babel* (London: Allen Lane, 2010); David Northrup, *How English Became the Global Language* (Basingstoke: Palgrave Macmillan, 2013); Jennifer Jenkins, Will Baker, and Martin Dewey, eds, *The Routledge Handbook of English as a Lingua Franca* (Abingdon: Routledge, 2017); Diana Lemberg, '"The Universal Language of the Future": Decolonization, Development, and the American Embrace of Global English 1945-1965', *Modern Intellectual History* 15, no. 2 (2018): 561–92.

¹¹ On planning ideologies more generally, see Valeska Huber, 'Global Histories of Social Planning', *Journal of Contemporary History* 52/1 (2017): 3–15. See also David Engerman, 'The Rise and Fall of Central Planning', in *The Cambridge History of the Second World War: Volume 3, Total War: Economy, Society and Culture*, ed. Adam Tooze and Michael Geyer (Cambridge: Cambridge

Despite the European focus (reflecting the overall aim of this volume), this chapter does not seek to paint a triumphalist story of English for all, quite the contrary. Scholars working on post-colonial English have long pointed at the hegemonic or even coercive features of English as well as showing how non-European actors have appropriated the language and made it their own.[12] It might not come as a surprise that the unifying vision of Basic English coupled with a technocratic approach of dissemination gave rise to the dystopic ideas of George Orwell's novel 1984, with its artificial language Newspeak famously modelled on Basic English. As the last part of this chapter shows, the Basic English pilot projects connect with British-American dreams of hegemony, leaving little space for divergent voices and criticisms. At the same time, once put into practice none of these pilot projects were successful in the long run and the technocratic approach to global language dissemination gave way to a more organic development of a plurality of World Englishes.[13]

Speaking like an expert: Competing international language projects in the interwar period

The question of a common second language 'for all' and the political claims attached to any such second language gained importance inside as well as outside international meetings and organizations in the 1920s. In the interwar world of empires, the predominantly European and American expert publics at internationalist conferences had to process and simplify ever more information.[14] At the same time, they made increasingly wide-reaching claims regarding the audiences and constituencies of such international information. 'World understanding', as it was propagated by the League of Nations and other institutions, thus carried a double meaning. In its most frequent (idealistic as well as ideological) use, it was about world peace through learning and knowing about others. Yet it was also about the appropriate language to be used, which would be understood by a maximum number but at the same time carry as little bias as possible.

To note that language provides one of the thresholds for access and participation in internationalist endeavours is stating the obvious. Already in the nineteenth century, when international diplomacy and conferences were frequently conducted in French, non-European participants were acutely aware of their disadvantage in partaking in debates in a language in which they did not feel comfortable.[15] After centuries of the

---

University Press, 2015), 575–98; Stefan Couperus, Liesbeth van de Grift, and Vincent Lagendijk, 'Experimental Spaces: A Decentred Approach to Planning in High Modernity. Introduction', *Journal of Modern European History* 13/4 (2015): 475–9.

[12] See Robert Phillipson, *Linguistic Imperialism* (Oxford: Oxford University Press, 1992); Edgar W. Schneider, *Postcolonial English: Varieties Around the World* (Cambridge: Cambridge University Press, 2007).

[13] Markku Filppula, Juhani Klemola and Devyani Sharma, eds, *The Oxford Handbook of World Englishes* (Oxford: Oxford University Press, 2017).

[14] On expertise, see, for instance, Patricia Clavin, *Securing the World Economy: The Reinvention of the League of Nations, 1920-1946* (Oxford: Oxford University Press, 2013), 347.

[15] See the case of the Persian delegate and reformer Mirza Malkom Khan at the 1866 International Sanitary Conference: Valeska Huber, 'The Unification of the Globe by Disease? The International

predominance of French as language of diplomacy, the use of both English and French as the official languages of the 1919 Treaty of Versailles granted the former equal status on the international stage for the first time.[16] At the international conferences that followed the First World War, English occupied an increasingly central role as a lingua franca, even if translations were still provided in many settings, thus sidelining other European languages, such as French and German.[17]

In the 1920s and 1930s, internationalists of different origins and orientations reflected on language as the concrete basis of the lofty idea of world understanding. If the world grew together through the new technological opportunities of travel and communications, the coexistence of 1,500 separate languages represented a larger obstacle than ever before: 'For an expansion of trade, for the organization of peace, and for the development of science a simple and reasoned international language may be at least as important as the gold question,' stated an article in *The Times* in 1935.[18] Beyond the idea of world understanding in more general terms, for these experts, the main issue was therefore how understanding could happen in the more practical realm of everyday communication.

Focusing on the competing languages of internationalism, the international auxiliary language movement, with the International Auxiliary Language Association (IALA) at its helm, was explicitly concerned with world understanding in the literal sense of language acquisition and learning. The IALA was founded in 1924 in New York by Alice Vanderbilt Morris, a vocal and prosperous proponent of Esperanto who devoted both her money and her time to further its cause.[19] Through campaigns and publications, the organization wanted to come closer to 'World Unity through World Understanding'.[20] Over the course of a series of conferences, participants initially focused on the establishment of scientific criteria on the basis of which the most suitable existing auxiliary language could be selected. Under the direction of the linguist Dr Alexander Gode between 1943 and 1953, the IALA ultimately took the decision to reject the existing auxiliary languages, including Esperanto, on the basis that their schematic nature made them unintuitive. Instead, they argued that it was not necessary to invent an entirely new language, but rather merely to take the vocabulary and grammatical structures which were common to multiple European languages and to simplify and standardize them in a project called Interlingua.[21]

Despite the ideas of Alexander Gode and others at the IALA, the use of an existing language for international communication had many advantages. In the context of vivid

Sanitary Conferences on Cholera 1851-1894', *Historical Journal* 49/2 (2006): 453–76, at 463.

[16] Margaret Macmillan, *Paris 1919: Six Months That Changed the World* (New York: Random House, 2003), 55–6.

[17] Ruth A. Roland, *Interpreters as Diplomats: A Diplomatic History of the Role of Interpreters in World Politics* (Ottawa: University of Ottawa Press, 1999), 134. Fernand de Varennes, 'Language Policy at the Supranational Level', in *The Cambridge Handbook of Language Policy*, ed. Bernard Spolsky (Cambridge: Cambridge University Press, 2012), 149–73.

[18] *The Times*, 11 June 1935.

[19] Julia S. Falk, *Women, Language and Linguistics: Three American Stories from the First Half of the Twentieth Century* (London: Routledge, 1999).

[20] League of Nations Archives, Geneva, BPC Cooperation intellectuelle/Paix et langages, Box 73: World Unity through World Understanding, Mexico/Rome: Mondi Lingua Academi, no year.

[21] Frank J. Esterhill, *Interlingua Institute: A History* (New York: Interlingua Institute, 2000).

debates surrounding the necessity of a world language for international understanding and a lasting peace after the First World War, many supported English as an alternative avenue to Esperanto and Interlingua, or other language projects such as Volapük, Ido, Novial and Parlamento – to mention just the best known of the international auxiliary languages mushrooming in the period.[22] Among the most vocal of them were philosopher, psychologist and linguist C. K. Ogden (1889–1957) and literary critic I. A. Richards (1893–1979). The two Cambridge academics had started to collaborate around 1910, and in 1923 published *The Meaning of Meaning*, a philosophical treatise on 'the influence of language upon thought', which resonated with the larger interest in language philosophy and the quest for unambiguous communication of the period.[23]

From the outset, Ogden and Richards' work transcended questions of language philosophy and spilled over into the more practical world of interwar internationalisms. Following from their philosophical investigations, they set themselves the aim to de-emotionalize language and to debabelize the world.[24] In the eyes of Ogden and Richards, English was much more suitable than Esperanto as it was already spoken by millions, even if it came with the problem of being tainted by imperialism as commentators readily acknowledged. Furthermore, according to Ogden, English was more suitable once an expansion beyond Europe was in the picture as most of the other internationalist languages often consisted of a clearly European agenda, reflected in the preference of a Romance vocabulary:

> Esperanto, in particular, is just one more European dialect constructed at a time when the problem of the East was only a small cloud on the horizon. If Orientals were to agree to promote some modification of Cantonese or Hakka, similar in many respects to Chinese and Japanese, as an international auxiliary language for Europe, its claims to 'neutrality' would hardly be taken seriously.[25]

Ogden's quote highlights how, in a British imperial setting, the global dominance of English was detached from its European origins and instead firmly placed within the context of a British-American liberal order as the dominant form of internationalism. It became a clear indicator of Britain's ambivalent role in Europe as well as its self-perception as a global power. For Ogden and Richards, the choice of English was justified by turning internationalism into a global project transcending the European

---

[22] Roberto Garvía, *Esperanto and Its Rivals: The Struggle for an International Language* (Philadelphia: University of Pennsylvania Press, 2015); Esther Schor, *Bridge of Words: Esperanto and the Dream of a Universal Language* (New York: Metropolitan Books, 2016); Brigid O'Keeffe, 'Building a Communist Tower of Babel: Esperanto and the Language Politics of Internationalism in Revolutionary Russia', in this volume.

[23] C. K. Ogden and I. A. Richards, *The Meaning of Meaning: A Study of the Influence of Language Upon Thought and of the Science of Symbolism* (London, K. Paul, Trench, Trubner and Co., 1923).

[24] C. K. Ogden, *Debabelization: With a Survey of Contemporary Opinion on the Problem of a Universal Language* (London: K. Paul, Trench, Trubner & Co., 1931); Christine Holden and David M. Levy, 'From Emotionalized Language to Basic English: The Career of C. K. Ogden and/as "Adelyne More"', *Historical Reflections* 27/1 (2001): 79–105; James McElvenny, *Language and Meaning in the Age of Modernism: C. K. Ogden and His Contemporaries* (Edinburg: Edinburgh University Press, 2017).

[25] C. K. Ogden, *Basic English Versus the Artificial Languages* (London: K. Paul, Trench, Trubner and Co., 1935), 8.

and elite bias that came with it in many settings. In order to overcome the limitations of artificial languages while at the same time keeping their advantages, a new 'neutral' and 'scientific' method of teaching English was needed that would, at least in theory, enable a standardized and planned expansion.

Learning English the simple way: Basic English and internationalism for all

Despite the constantly evoked language of humanity, humankind and world understanding, internationalism can often appear as an elite affair, limited both geographically and socially.[26] Board rooms and conference halls in Geneva, New York, London and Paris provide its principal locations. From the early twentieth century onwards, these were complemented by an exponentially growing number of international meetings held at a wider variety of places, albeit mainly in European and American urban centres. Even if some of these events, like the international expositions, turned into tourist hubs and drew in a wider public, most of them clearly targeted bounded groups of participants such as scientists or public administrators. While the world was constantly mentioned on these occasions, the world of many internationalists therefore remained rather small, despite the fact that all-embracing expressions appeared in many internationalist writings. To mention but one example, we can turn to H. G. Wells's conception of a world encyclopedia which he called 'the mental background of every intelligent man in the world', leaving open what the entry threshold into this category actually was.[27] Despite using a myriad of similar universalist expressions, thinkers of the international rarely addressed questions of access and its limits.

Consequently, regardless of the growing use of English in internationalist meetings and beyond, a lingua franca of any kind often targeted a clearly bounded functional public. Such a public might spread geographically from Geneva, New York or elsewhere after a meeting had drawn to a close and its participants had travelled back home. But at the same time, it stood on a very narrow social basis. This facet is shared by the debates around common languages of the interwar period and the longer history of lingua franca. Neither Latin nor French was ever spoken by all.[28] In fact, David Crystal argues that a global language is by no means about the numbers who actually speak it.[29] The point is echoed by Nicholas Ostler: 'Elitism is a weak point in the profile of

---

[26] While this elite bias was true for contemporary actors, it still characterizes much of the scholarship. See Mark Mazower, *Governing the World: The History of an Idea* (London: Allen Lane, 2012). Sluga and Clavin, *Internationalisms: A Twentieth-Century History* point to the need of including new voices in their introduction and in the last section of their volume.

[27] H. G. Wells, World Encyclopedia. Lecture delivered at the weekly evening meeting of the Royal Institution of Great Britain, 20 November 1936, *World Brain* (London: Methuen, 1938).

[28] Nicholas Ostler, *Ad Infinitum: A Biography of Latin* (London: Harper Press, 2007); Jürgen Leonhardt, *Latin: Story of a World Language*, trans. Kenneth Kronenberg (Cambridge, MA: Harvard University Press, 2013).

[29] Crystal, *English as a Global Language*, 7.

every global language. Every lingua franca is a partial language – in the sense that not everyone knows it. Global languages divide the societies that make use of them'.[30] This is also true of those link languages defined by trade and religion rather than culture and politics such as Arabic or Persian, despite the fact that inclusion and exclusion might follow different parameters.[31]

Even those who actively sought to expand beyond the European and American circles of internationalism often targeted an elite public. Take Florence Wilson, the former head librarian of the League of Nations library who in the late 1920s journeyed to the Middle East for the Carnegie Foundation in order to garner support for the foundation's project of fostering world peace and understanding through the creation of international relations clubs and international mind alcoves in libraries. The audiences she identified for these efforts consisted mainly of English-speaking students at the American universities in the Middle East, for instance in Cairo or Beirut.[32] Many internationalists used expressions relating to the whole world or all of humanity. Yet if internationalism was to be expanded at all, this seemed foremost a geographical rather than a social concern. When it came to broader populations beyond non-European elites, European and American liberal international experts preferred to speak about populations and how they could be managed rather than to address them directly.[33] Neither the more general community of internationalists nor those who worried about overpopulation and proposed more or less radical schemes to alleviate it reflected on how the global 'masses' were to be incorporated into communicative processes.

At the same time, these 'broader populations' of course occupied an increasingly central role in the political regimes taking shape after the First World War. For democratic and authoritarian political regimes alike, the question of who had a voice in political affairs (and how this voice could be shaped and modified) became of central importance. Language and literacy formed part and parcel of efficient state propaganda while also being intimately tied to questions of identity and subjectivity.[34] In Turkey or Russia, the standardization and simplification of a language for all citizens

---

[30] Ostler, *The Last Lingua Franca*, xvii.
[31] Nile Green, ed., *The Persianate World: The Frontiers of a Eurasian Lingua Franca* (Berkeley: University of California Press, 2019).
[32] See Valeska Huber, Tamson Pietsch and Katharina Rietzler, 'Women's International Thought and the New Professions, 1900-1940', *Modern Intellectual History* (2019). On Middle Eastern universities, see Valeska Huber, 'International Agendas and Local Manifestations: Universities in Cairo, Beirut and Jerusalem after World War I', *Prospects* 45/1 (2015): 77–93.
[33] As Alison Bashford and others have shown, in the 1920s and 1930s intellectuals were increasingly concerned with the problem of a growing world population. Alison Bashford, *Global Population: History, Geopolitics, and Life on Earth* (New York: Columbia University Press, 2014); Matthew Connelly, *Fatal Misconception: The Struggle to Control World Population* (Cambridge, MA: Harvard University Press, 2008); Heinrich Hartmann and Corinna Unger, eds, *A World of Populations: Transnational Perspectives on Demography in the Twentieth Century* (New York: Berghahn Books, 2014).
[34] Christopher A. Bayly, *Remaking the Modern World 1900-2015: Global Connections and Comparisons* (Hoboken: John Wiley & Sons, 2018), 194–214; Alexandra Gerstner, Barbara Könczöl and Janina Nentwig, eds, *Der neue Mensch: Utopien, Leitbilder und Reformkonzepte zwischen den Weltkriegen* (Frankfurt am Main: Peter Lang, 2006); Greg Eghigian, Andreas Killen and Christine Leuenberger, eds, *The Self as Project: Politics and the Human Sciences* (Chicago: University of Chicago Press, 2007).

accompanied the more wide-ranging restructuring of the society. For the modernizing governments of Atatürk's Turkey or the Soviet Union, the acquisition of the new language among their populations could not be fast enough. The simplification and standardization of languages was a more general phenomenon of the interwar period, often connected with the simplification of national languages and literacy campaigns and figuring under the term of linguistic planning or linguistic engineering.[35]

In this context of mass politics and with the desire to overcome the elite bias sketched earlier, some internationalist experts, such as Ogden and Richards, grew increasingly interested in expanding the publics of internationalism. Even if their most total visions remained utopian, it pays to look at their conceptions of the world population as a possible audience for top-down propaganda efforts and bottom-up attempts to create a world of learners. Coming back to language initiatives in the realm of internationalism, the conversion of new audiences to the internationalist project gained increasing importance. Language therefore had a double function for the international experts interested in the matter congregating at meetings of the IALA, and other similar organizations. One concern was about creating an international community of experts that could talk to each other and circulate complex findings. Another was about mediating their expertise to a wider public, which often went hand in hand with simplification. The translation of internationalist agendas to broader publics increasingly became a concern, pointing to a tension between a passive audience of propaganda and the dissemination of information as an enabling tool for political agency.[36]

Those, like Ogden and Richards, who were convinced that English was the most suitable language of internationalism therefore turned to the question how to spread it further. As in the case of the language projects connected to nationalist modernization, in the internationalist debates of the 1920s, simplification, efficiency and speed became the central keywords. Ogden's and Richard's answer to the dilemmas of increasing complexity and the restriction to elite publics was Basic English, which takes its name from the acronym of British American Scientific International Commercial. In the 1920s, they established the Orthological Institute in Cambridge where the scientific simplification of the English language was to be perfected and professionalized. The Basic English vocabulary consisted of just 850 words through which everything could be expressed. The carefully chosen selection of operators, necessary names, qualifiers and common things could, together with the summary of rules, fit on one single sheet.

---

[35] Richard Bauman and Charles Briggs, *Voices of Modernity: Language Ideologies and the Politics of Inequality* (Cambridge: Cambridge University Press, 2003); Geoffrey Lewis, *The Turkish Language Reform: A Catastrophic Success* (Oxford: Oxford University Press, 1999); Hale Yılmaz, 'Learning to Read (Again): The Social Experiences of Turkey's 1928 Alphabet Reform', *International Journal of Middle East Studies* 43/4 (2011): 677–97; Jeffrey Weng, 'What Is Mandarin? The Social Project of Language Standardization in Early Republican China', *Journal of Asian Studies* 77/3 (2018): 611–33; Laurence Brockliss and Nicoloa Sheldon, eds, *Mass Education and the Limits of State Building, c.1870-1930* (Basingstoke: Palgrave Macmillan, 2012).

[36] See, for instance, Harold D. Lasswell, Daniel Lerner and Hans Speier, eds, *Propaganda and Communication in World History* (3 vols, Honolulu: East West Center, 1979–80); Stephen Wertheim, 'Reading the International Mind: International Public Opinion in Early Twentieth Century Anglo-American Thought', in Daniel Bessner and Nicolas Guilhot, eds, *The Decisionist Imagination: Democracy, Sovereignty, and Social Science in the 20th Century* (New York: Berghahn Books, 2018), 27–63.

The artificial language followed very strict, if minimal, rules and represented the maximum reduction of language imaginable.

According to Ogden, the new language could be learned by everyone on the entire globe in no more than seven weeks while most people would be able to communicate after seven days: 'Basic English is an attempt to give to everyone a second, or international, language, which will take as little of the learner's time as possible.'[37] Basic was designed as an international auxiliary language for politicians, scientists and businessmen, but it also clearly reached beyond them to a truly global audience. In order to live up to this ambitious, if not megalomanic, plan, the Orthological Institute churned out material addressing a number of different groups. It constructed learning materials and courses, 'translated' literary works into Basic English and co-produced films such as the *March of Time* series. It also developed material to guide the novice of English, for example, *From Basic to Wider English*.[38]

Despite Ogden and Richards' self-fashioning as original inventors of a unique scheme, they would soon encounter competitors in their quest to simplify English and make it useable everywhere, such as *Streamline English* and *World English*. All these initiatives shared an emphasis on scientific planning and standardization in order to reach new strata of the world population and to counter diversification and fragmentation into various Englishes. But how to go about achieving this goal? The Canadian teacher Michael West proposed: 'We are to do scientifically what every successful language-learner already does empirically: he limits the field and becomes perfect within its limitations, and he defines when he cannot express directly. And we are to standardize this limitation so that all may be able to comprehend as well as to express.'[39] In his article he explained that the English language consisted of over 250,000 words, yet educated adults only used 10,000 to 20,000 of them. For a *World English*, the reduction to a 'Minimum Adequate Vocabulary', 'the smallest set of words adequate for all ordinary purposes', had to go much further.[40] Against the idea of organic development and the creative use of language, linguists proposed systematic reduction and simplification. It is of course no coincidence that these attempts took shape at the same time as the appeal of technocracy and planning as a model of managing social relations was at its highest. Many experts believed that every political and social problem could be solved scientifically. It might therefore not come as a surprise that this belief in science and planning prevalent in governance and social policy more generally was also applied to the field of language.

Some supporters of Basic English went even further in their own quest for a universal language. Otto Neurath, part of the Vienna circle around Rudolf Carnap, is a case in point. Just like C. K. Ogden, he came to thinking about language from a philosophical position.[41] As part of the Red Vienna movement, Neurath was

---

[37] Ogden, *Basic English versus the Artificial Languages*, 13.
[38] Catherine M. Nesbitt and William B. Mumford, *From Basic to Wider English* (London: Evans Bros, 1940–41).
[39] Michael West, 'English as a World Language', *American Speech* 9/3 (1934): 163–74, at 174.
[40] West, 'English as a World Language', 163.
[41] James McElvenny, 'International Language and the Everyday: Contact and Collaboration between C.K. Ogden, Rudolf Carnap and Otto Neurath', *British Journal for the History of Philosophy* 21/6 (2013): 1194–218.

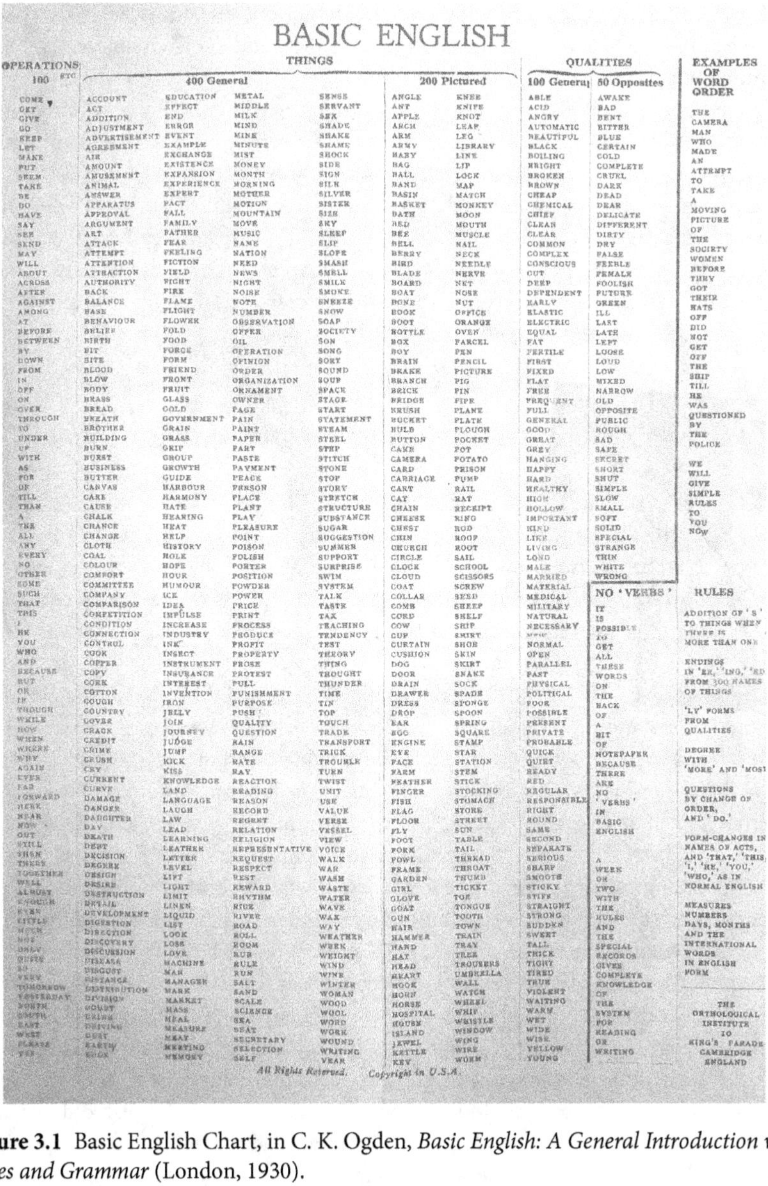

Figure 3.1 Basic English Chart, in C. K. Ogden, *Basic English: A General Introduction with Rules and Grammar* (London, 1930).

forced into exile in 1938, first to the Netherlands and then on to Oxford in 1940. Originally interested in transmitting information about social and economic facts to a broad audience through museum work, in 1925 he established the Gesellschafts- und Wirtschaftsmuseum in Vienna with the purpose of explaining to citizens from all backgrounds the basic workings of the economy and the welfare state. From this point of departure, he developed the International System of Typographic Picture Education, 'Isotype' for short, which would allow complex issues to be communicated to anyone in no time at all through the use of pictograms. In connection with Basic, it would be possible to supply information to the widest audience possible in an entirely unambiguous way.

If Isotype, just like Basic, ran into troubles in the implementation of their grandiose plans, both language experiments shared the belief in unambiguous communication in any cultural context which was accessible to all in the true sense of the word. What unites debates around Basic English and other simplified universal languages for all is the attempt to provide a communicative answer to the increasing complexity of the interwar period, marked by new states, new pressure groups and new political concerns, through the creation of a single linguistic tool easily available to everyone.

Talking back: Basic English in a world of many tongues

In H. G. Wells's science fiction novel *The Shape of Things to Come*, published in 1933, Basic English had become the official medium in air and sea control. It had left Spanish and French wide behind as an international language and 'by 2020 almost everyone was able to make use of Basic for talking and writing'. This quote expressed in Basic English highlights not only the highest hopes one could attach to the project but also its inherent problems. Perhaps not surprisingly, in conventional English the phrase reads slightly more elegantly: 'by 2020 there was hardly anyone in the world who could not talk and understand it.'[42] The phrase gives us a flavour what was lost in the translation process from 'Wider' to 'Basic' English. This stiltedness and unnatural sound was only one of the criticisms connected with Basic English as it became more widely applied.

From the 1930s to the 1950s, Basic English moved away from the specialist spheres of British liberal internationalists and linguists. As it left the drawing board of the Orthological Institute in Cambridge, it quickly ventured beyond its original conception in the context of peace building and international understanding. In the more turbulent decades following the 1920s, the project became embroiled in the global politics of English within the larger context of the declining British Empire. It is therefore worthwhile to follow the journeys of Basic English beyond the European internationalist circles where it originated. These journeys illustrate debates around language acquisition and language rights, but also the failures of an internationalist project and the resistance it could meet. Not surprisingly, Basic English did not unify the world of learners in the way Ogden and Richards had projected. Rather, the critical voices highlight the central tension of elite and mass education bringing out the very inequalities and hierarchies that Basic English originally wanted to overcome.

In the context of an expansion of colonial education, Basic English had a market. It appeared as a means to reverse the disappointing story of English teaching in the colonies: W. B. Mumford, lecturer at the Colonial Department of the London Institute of Education and a supporter of Basic English, argued that English instruction had so far not diminished misunderstandings, but had in fact provoked them and therefore needed to

---

[42] H. G. Wells, *The Shape of Things to Come* (London: Hutchinson, 1933).

be reformed.[43] I. A. Richards saw this rise of English teaching in the colonies as a chance to be seized. Yet it soon became evident that this meant the departure from the idea of a rational, de-emotionalized language and therefore cast Basic English's neutrality once again into doubt.

Already in 1939, I. A. Richards was writing with passion to the Editor of the Times: 'The way to preserve the splendor and dignity of English, as it spreads through the schools of the world, is to see that what is learned is well learned and thoroughly understood.'[44] He went on to lobby for Basic English in China and India, pleading for the importance of languages in social planning and social engineering. In this process he made very clear that his vision was not neutral but in fact carried the values of a specifically Western European civilization:

> I think we have a better way of teaching English, but while you're teaching beginning English, you might as well teach everything else. That is to say, a world position, what's needed for living, a philosophy of religion, how to find things out, and the whole works – mental and moral seed for the planet. In this way the two-thirds of the planet that doesn't know how to read and write would learn in learning how to read and write in English, the things that would help them in their answers to 'Where should man go?'[45]

Basic English was taken up with various success in India, China, Sri Lanka and other locations such as refugee camps after the Second World War.[46] The British Council experimented with it as a teaching tool and Voice of America and the BBC tested the use of Basic English on their listeners.[47] T. T. S. Hayley, publicity officer to the government officer of Assam, employed Basic English in wartime propaganda through loudspeaker cars. This use had its own problems, as he noted, because the language was not marked by passion or liveliness: 'The language is colourless and lacks conviction. Strong emotions are only expressed with difficulty and a sense of vividness is necessarily absent.' In order to be able to use it at all, he also had to introduce new words such as 'victory' and 'defeat'.[48] After the war, UNESCO used Basic English to teach workers in its groundnut scheme in Tanganyika.[49]

In these different testing grounds, Basic English could not fulfil the expectations of its founding fathers. For one, this was due to the rigidity of its rules. Once put into

---

[43] The National Archives, Kew (TNA), ED 52/2: Dr. W. B. Mumford, The Place of Word-Function and Word-Frequency Vocabularies in the Teaching of English in the Dependencies, originally published in the Year Book of Education 1940.
[44] I. A. Richards to the Editor of the *Times*, 3 June 1939.
[45] Quoted in Rodney Koeneke, *Empires of the Mind: I. A. Richards and Basic English in China, 1929-1979* (Stanford: Stanford University Press, 2004), 213, interview 1968.
[46] TNA, ED 52/14: Memorandum on the Spread of Basic English in China; ED 52/2 War Cabinet: Memoranda on Basic English.
[47] TNA, ED 52/2; ED 52/15; BW 1/35: Records of the British Council.
[48] TNA, CAB 21/886: TTS Hayley, Publicity Officer to the Government of Assam, Shillong to the Chairman, Basic English Committee, c/o The India Office, Whitehall, London, England, 21 September 1943.
[49] TNA, MAF 83/1853. On the spectacular failures of the groundnut scheme, see, for instance, Joseph Hodge, *Triumph of the Expert: Agrarian Doctrines of Development and the Legacies of British Colonialism* (Athens: Ohio University Press, 2007), 209–14.

practice, Basic English quickly became a matter of ridicule. The quotation by H. G. Wells or the complaint of Assam's colonial publicity officer during the Second World War already showed that the artificial language lacked elegance and flexibility. This was also illustrated in George Orwell's novel *1984*, where the language Newspeak, modelled on Basic English, became a major tool for the suppression of any free opinion.[50]

When it came to teaching Basic English to those unfamiliar with English itself, the inflexible tools of the artificial language did not make it appealing as it became more complicated to unlearn the rules when moving on to wider English than to start with a larger set of rules at the beginning. Also, the radical reduction of words did not prove advantageous, as it seemed more complicated to remember various uses of the same word than several words with more specific meanings.[51] In practical terms, flexibility was preferable to scientific rigour and learners benefited from a variety of experiences rather than simplicity. The fact that rules and rigidity made Basic English undesirable for teachers and learners alike shows that in this case the scientification of language was taken too far.

What is more, despite the purging of any superfluous words and the maximum reduction of vocabulary and rules, the language never achieved the neutrality it aimed for. The 'residual colonialism of language' that came with the expansion of English in the twentieth century has been analysed in various circumstances, and it did not spare Basic English.[52] Even if Nehru, as seen at the beginning of this chapter, saw no way of circumventing English if India was to find its position as a global power, Basic English could not deliver its promise of neutrality.

The clearest proof to the impossibility of a neutral language was provided by Churchill's support of Basic English during wartime in his promotion of an Anglo-American post-war order. During the Second World War, Churchill was a most vocal proponent of Basic English. In a talk at Harvard in 1943, he stated that '[t]he empires of the future are the empires of the mind'.[53] As a pilot project, Churchill ordered the 1944 Atlantic Charter in a Basic English version.[54] A world of Basic English would be an essential instrument to bring global populations in line and to bolster the connection between Roosevelt and Churchill, in line with Churchill's later expression of the three great circles referring to empire and commonwealth, English-speaking world and a united Europe, voiced at the Conservative party mass meeting in 1948. However, Churchill's wartime engagement for Basic English brought critics to the

---

[50] George Orwell, *Nineteen Eighty-Four* (London: Secker & Warburg, 1949). See also George Orwell, 'Politics and the English Language', *Horizon*, April 1946.
[51] See, for instance, TNA, CAB 21/886 Pte. Clive A. Bentley, Basic English as a Universal Language.
[52] Bayly, *Remaking the Modern World 1900-2015*, 274–8.
[53] Koeneke, *Empires of the Mind*; Qing S. Tong, 'The Bathos of a Universalism: I. A. Richards and His Basic English', in *Tokens of Exchange: The Problem of Translation in Global Circulations*, ed. Lydia H. Liu (Durham, NC: Duke University Press, 1999), 331–54.
[54] The Atlantic Charter, and the Prime Minister's Statement on Basic English of 9 March 1944; in their original form, and in Basic English, for purposes of Comparison, presented by the prime minister to Parliament by Command of His Majesty March 1944, House of Commons Parliamentary Papers Online, 1943–4 Cmd. 6511; republished in Jacob, *On the Choice of a Common Language*.

scene. 'What about winning the war?' Earl Winterton asked Churchill during a debate in parliament. 'This is in connexion with winning the peace,' Churchill countered.[55] The Canadian teacher James G. Endicott remarked that '[s]ome German PhD is sure to submit a thesis before too long on Basic English as an instrument of Power Politics in the New Geopolitic of Anglo-Saxon World Domination'.[56]

The post-war promotional campaigns of the Basic English Foundation furthermore show the problems of seeking and receiving attention in an age of global campaigning. The archives of the foundation contain many letters seeking to secure financial supporters or grant money, whether from organizations such as UNESCO or from private individuals. Yet the Basic English Foundation was losing out to its more powerful competitor, the British Council, and Churchill himself abandoned his support. This problem of competing successfully in a global market of potential English learners was due not only to limited resources but also to the problem of establishing Basic English as a successful brand. Non-European elites in colonial and post-colonial settings hoping for increased social mobility through access to English refused to be fobbed off with a basic form of English while its complex version was reserved to Europeans and Americans, and they grew increasingly vocal in voicing this concern. The replies to a questionnaire sent to officials in various colonies show that among colonial elites, Basic English was perceived as second-rate English which would cement difference in status rather than lowering entry barriers.[57] A textbook that had Oxford or Cambridge on the cover seemed much more appealing than a version of English called 'basic'.

At the same time, the problem that had driven C. K. Ogden and I. A. Richards in the first place had not disappeared. Linguistic fragmentation was still being heavily criticized. The German newspaper *Die Zeit* wrote in 1956 that the multiplicity of languages led to the 'loss of intellectual energy', which could rather be used for the welfare of all humanity, and opted for a constructed language with a minimal grammar.[58] In the 1954 issue of the main UNESCO journal, the number of languages spoken was assessed as 3,000, ranging from 450 million to a few hundred speakers only. The French literature professor Felix Walter despised this 'jigsaw pattern of the world's languages' and lamented:

> We can devise atom bombs to wipe out half of the world or jet planes to girdle it, but, so far as the tangle of languages is concerned, we are still in the era of the Tower of Babel.[59]

---

[55] *The Times*, 10 March 1944.
[56] TNA, CAB 21/886: James G. Endicott, English Department of West China Union University to Winston Churchill, 17 December 1943.
[57] See TNA, CAB 21/889: Basic English Attitude of Colonies. Questionnaire sent to officials in different British colonies.
[58] Erich Köhler, 'Ist die Grammatik an allem schuld?', *Die Zeit* 15/1956.
[59] Felix Walter, 'The Jigsaw Pattern of the World's Languages', *UNESCO Courier* 7/1 (1954): 5–7.

Conclusion

In 1963, the death of Basic English was officially announced.[60] The case of an international language experiment and its problems enables us to draw several conclusions that go beyond the specific examples explored in this chapter. Even if language planning often brought about unintended consequences, it highlights the variety of internationalist actors who wanted to have a say in the world order taking shape after the First and Second World Wars. An examination of the Orthological Institute and the Basic English Foundation that were supposed to carry the project of Basic English to fruition brings into the open the multifarious networks of internationalism, but also highlights the limits of campaigning.

Despite these limits, the case of Basic English shows how liberal internationalist, British imperialist and American capitalist global orders could come together and intersect. If Basic English as a global brand was not successful, the different audiences it sought and the different agendas of its creators and supporters highlight the existence of competing internationalisms and the role of individuals in promoting or undermining internationalist projects. Through actors such as C. K. Ogden, I. A. Richards and, more prominently, Winston Churchill, this example reveals the importance of colonial connections and the special position of Britain in Europe and in the history of interwar and mid-century internationalism.

The failed internationalist project of Basic English furthermore gives us insight into the connection of interwar internationalism to planning ideologies. In this way, it draws our attention to some central tensions of the mid-twentieth century, namely between simplification and complexity, and between planning and unstructured growth. The case of Basic English shows how the two visions of a highly structured international order and of a more chaotic capitalism unchained were not always opposed but could sometimes go hand in hand. Homogenization and hybridization, as well as simplification and complexity, come together in the intellectual world of the creators of Basic English and their followers.

This tension between complexity and simplification is captured in an ideal manner in debates around language and communication. The 'hegemony of Global English' coexisted with the vision of English as an ideal tool to participate in global debate.[61] Basic English and its competitors illustrate the role of language in twentieth-century national and international politics. The British promoters of Basic English demonstrate the attempt to maintain British hegemony through language politics. Yet the intense debates over languages, from Otto Neurath's pictograms and the quest for a neutral language, to the national language engineering in Russia

---

[60] TNA, CO 1045/1262: Death of 'Basic English', The Language of the Future, Carlino Sera Bologna, 17 August 1963.

[61] See, for instance, Zohreh R. Eslami, Katherine L. Wright, and Sunni Sonnenburg, 'Globalized English: Power, Ethics, and Ideology', in *Going Global: Transnational Perspectives on Globalization, Language, and Education*, ed. Leslie Seawright (Cambridge: Cambridge Scholars Publishing, 2014), 2–16; Nasia Anam, 'Bangladeshi Anglophone Literature: Rerouting the Hegemony of Global English', *Interventions* 20/3 (2018): 325–34.

and Turkey, highlight the importance of communication for the creation of political subjectivity more broadly.

In the long run, however, hybridity and diversity seemed both more desirable and more realistic than the quest for simplification and unambiguity driven forward by the supporters of Basic English and other proponents of planning. If Nehru's idea of the importance of English for the future of India did not seem entirely mistaken, Basic English as a method disseminated from Britain into the world was criticized from the outset. Even if English has appeared as the winner in the game over a global language, a strictly speaking 'international' English has failed.

4

Radio and revolution

Tirana via Bari, from Moscow to Beijing

Elidor Mëhilli

In a span of three decades, the main radio station of a small rural country became a global voice of communism. This chapter explains how this came to be. It recounts Radio Tirana's modest beginnings in the 1930s, shaped by fascist-era Italian involvement, the Soviet-style programming of the 1950s and the adoption of Chinese technical assistance in the 1960s. Such foreign contacts mirrored Albania's tumultuous political alliances in this era. This offers an opportunity to analyse how radio served as an instrument for making socialist subjects at home and how it became a weapon for waging ideological warfare abroad. After the liberation from Germany in 1944, radio served to mark a new socialist temporality. As relations with neighbouring Yugoslavia soured in the late 1940s, it turned into a tool for communicating with Moscow. Then, following the 1960s Sino-Soviet dispute, and as Tirana sided with Beijing, broadcasting took an anti-Soviet turn. Mao's China helped amplify Radio Tirana's signal, bringing it to remote parts of Albania's rugged terrain, as well as to aspiring revolutionaries around the world.

To capture broadcasting as both a local and a globalized practice is to bring into view how international engagement shapes processes of nationalization. Early on, the state's capacity to create a national audience was limited. As economic and political relations expanded abroad – and as they broke down – opportunities to deploy technology also changed. After the ruptures with Yugoslavia and the Soviet Union, addressed in the first half of the chapter, it became necessary to devise a register for speaking to a fragmented socialist world. Radio Tirana emerged as a site of competing forms of socialist internationalism, from early Soviet-influenced notions of cooperation to later forays (thanks to Chinese imports) across the Iron Curtain. The party state spoke exuberantly of having conquered land and air. A closer look at broadcasting shows that some Albanian peasants were in fact less connected to Tirana's voice than foreigners around the globe. This brings to mind contemporaneous developments with Soviet radio, as analysed in the fine accounts of historians Kristin Roth-Ey and Stephen Lovell.[1] A history of broadcasting illuminates the ambition, the insecurity

---

[1] Kristin Roth-Ey, *Moscow Prime Time: How the Soviet Union Built the Media Empire That Lost the Cultural Cold War* (Ithaca: Cornell University Press, 2011); Stephen Lovell, *Russia in the Microphone Age: A History of Soviet Radio, 1919-1970* (Oxford: Oxford University Press, 2015).

and the vanity of self-described world revolutionaries. But it can also show how the medium itself became a site for defining and redefining the contours of socialist internationalism.

The chapter's other aim is to introduce an overlooked example of Cold War-era broadcasting to a literature that has expanded unevenly. Within it, the study of Western broadcasting dominates, as illustrated by the centrality of the US-funded Radio Free Europe/Radio Liberty (RFE/RL).[2] There was too much cacophony in Cold War broadcasting to have a body of work so heavily tilted to Washington, Munich and London.[3] To look beyond the usual players is to move away from a prevailing fixation, to give an example, on Western radio's influence on Eastern Europeans.[4] Radio Tirana's history captures the multi-directionality of Cold War-era competition and the work that went into recasting the geography of socialism. Telling this story as polyphonic is important because not only the actors involved were aware of this fact, but they acted in response to it. Cold War-era broadcasting fuelled comparative urges from the beginning.

An analysis of broadcasting, finally, has something to say about the location and periodization of internationalism.[5] Internationalism does not appear here as the domain of grand intellectual projects in the anglophone world, let alone the exclusive realm of liberalism or legal thought.[6] Broadcasting reminds us that internationalism happened at different scales, and not always in public. It cropped up in places that might seem unexpected from the vantage point of national historiographies. It could

---

[2] An apt survey is offered in Marsha Siefert, 'Radio Diplomacy and the Cold War', *Journal of Communication* 53, no. 2 (June 2003): 365–73. More accounts have been published since then, including Richard H. Cummings, *Cold War Radio: The Dangerous History of American Broadcasting in Europe, 1950-1989* (Jefferson, NC: McFarland, 2009) and his *Radio Free Europe's 'Crusade for Freedom': Rallying Americans Behind Cold War Broadcasting, 1950–1960* (Jefferson, NC: McFarland, 2010); A. Ross Johnson, *Radio Free Europe and Radio Liberty: The CIA Years and Beyond* (Washington DC and Stanford: Woodrow Wilson Center Press and Stanford University Press, 2010); A. Ross Johnson and R. Eugene Parta, eds, *Cold War Broadcasting: Impact on the Soviet Union and Eastern Europe* (Budapest: CEU Press, 2010). Indicative of a broader scope in recent scholarship are entries in Alexander Badenoch, Andreas Fickers and Christian Henrich-Franke, eds, *Airy Curtains in the European Ether: Broadcasting and the Cold War* (Baden-Baden: Nomos, 2012) as well as in a special issue: 'Radio Wars: Broadcasting during the Cold War', *Cold War History* 13, no. 2 (2013): 145ff.

[3] The potent combination of empire, the English language and the BBC has also shaped the scholarly footprint. The last of Asa Briggs's monumental five-volume *The History of Broadcasting in the United Kingdom* (Oxford: Oxford University Press, 1995) placed the BBC's post-war challenges in the context of the Suez Crisis, the rise of new technologies and geopolitical competition. More recent examples include Alban Webb, *London Calling: Britain, the BBC World Service and the Cold War* (London: Bloomsbury, 2014) and Simon James Potter, *Broadcasting Empire: The BBC and the British World, 1922–1970* (Oxford: Oxford University Press, 2012).

[4] Former agency insiders have authored many of the volumes on Radio Free Europe/Radio Liberty. Measuring radio's impact on listeners was a top priority for administrators, so it is not surprising that the theme endures in the literature, too.

[5] On how radio's rise and fall is typically given a chronology, and the importance of the German examples, see Yuliya Komska, 'West Germany's Cold War Radio: A Crucible of the Transatlantic Century', *German Politics and Society*, 32, no. 1 (Spring 2014): 1–14.

[6] My thinking owes much to the agenda set out in Jessica Reinisch, 'Agents of Internationalism', *Contemporary European History* 25, no. 2 (May 2016): 195–205. An example that successfully expands the thematic frame for studying forms of internationalism is Glenda Sluga and Patricia Clavin, eds, *Internationalisms: A Twentieth-Century History* (Cambridge: Cambridge University Press, 2017).

also be sporadic. Radio histories highlight the importance of state structures, but they can also be opportunities to capture internationalism's unintended outcomes. One way to do this is to focus on the interaction of geopolitical conflict with technology. For this purpose, this chapter spotlights the Sino-Soviet conflict not as a diplomatic event, but as a longer process. Competition between Moscow and Beijing, the chapter's second half shows, encouraged a remapping of socialist internationalism. It emboldened a radio station along the Mediterranean to reimagine its reach, to take up more foreign languages and to pursue more ears in faraway places.

Inconvenient origin

Founded in 1941, Albania's Communist Party lacked organizational experience but turned to neighbouring Yugoslavia for guidance and support. The contacts with Belgrade continued past the Italian occupation of the country, the ensuing German occupation and the partisans' victory in late 1944. The incoming leaders quickly declared a historic victory, but they also found themselves inescapably bound to the Yugoslavs. This helps explain why the second half of the 1940s was marked by both boundless euphoria and a sense of subordination. The oft-repeated rallying cry was to fashion workers out of the masses of illiterate peasants. But the capacity was meagre and the needs great: building towns, feeding the populace, dealing with real and invented enemies of the state. The ruling clique, presided over by the charismatic and cunning Enver Hoxha, felt compelled to rely on the support and expertise of its Yugoslav partners. The building of socialism was understood as history driving a peasant society forward. Geopolitical uncertainty remained, however, and so did the sense of lagging behind other socialist states.

Nationalization brings to mind an economic process and the confiscation of mills, housing stock, hidden valuables and gold. Yet it was about more than property claims. Aware of social fragmentation from north to south, the new regime understood the need to develop a national voice. Doing so, however, meant relying on foreigners and their technologies. Take the example of Radio Tirana. It had begun regular broadcasting in 1938, thanks to a small Italian-supplied short-wave station.[7] Some years earlier, Radio Bari had also issued Albanian-language broadcasts, with Rome's blessing.[8] Italian cultural involvement deepened after the invasion in 1939.[9] Radio Tirana then issued news bulletins, music and comedy, but also – notable, given later developments

---

[7] Skifter Këlliçi, *Historia e radio-televizionit shqiptar: (1938-1990)* (Tiranë: TPE, 2003), 10.
[8] Franco Monteleone, *Storia della radio e della televisione in Italia: società, politica, strategie, programmi, 1922-1992* (Venezia: Marsilio, 1992), 99; Antonio Rossano, *1943: 'Qui radio Bari'* (Bari: Dedalo, 1993), 22. Once it came under allied control, Radio Bari continued to serve as a tool for spreading anti-fascist messages to resistance groups in Italy and abroad.
[9] King Zog, the country's ruler, issued frantic messages on the radio urging his subjects to put up a fight against the Italians. 'Few Albanians owned radios', one historian has explained, 'so few heard the appeal'. Bernd Fischer, *Albania at War, 1939-1945* (West Lafayette: Purdue University Press, 1999), 24.

– targeted programmes on health and agrarian affairs.¹⁰ Creating 'national radio citizenship', to put it in historian Heidi Tworek's terms, had been a shared imperative in the interwar period, from London to Berlin and across the Atlantic.¹¹ Such echoes were fainter in this corner of the Balkans. But Italian cultural officials (and, later, the Germans) understood the importance of direct communication in a largely illiterate country. The anti-fascist guerrilla leaders would come to appreciate the importance of the medium too.

For a regime bent on breaking with the past, the radio's pre-communist precedents were inconvenient. Gjergj Bubani, the agency's former director, was put on trial, accused of using the radio to collaborate with enemies. Some of his colleagues insisted that he had been a patriot. He was sentenced to prison anyway.¹² Along with the purges, it became imperative to establish a new birthdate for socialist radio. Official accounts would eventually settle on the moment of the country's liberation in November 1944. The party boss had delivered a radio speech at that time, and this marked radio's new beginning.¹³ Later oral histories with veterans served to buttress this chronology, emphasizing the strategic importance partisan fighters had placed on broadcasting.¹⁴ In fact, there was conspicuous continuity across 1944 – both material and biographical. Some of the Italian personnel were not allowed to leave, since their technical skills could not be readily replaced.¹⁵ The equipment, described by witnesses as 'war booty', remained in use well into the post-war period.¹⁶ According to one testimony, a recorder left by the Nazi armed forces served to produce socialist programming for years.¹⁷ To have broadcasting power was to be modern. The new regime sought to claim radio as *its own*. This, however, was possible precisely because broadcasting had already become associated with state power.

Post-war radio programming reflected two parallel goals: to emancipate listeners and to remind them of the dangers lurking outside national borders. As broadcasting

---

10 Alessandro Pes, 'Fascist Propaganda in Albania: Schools, Cinema and Radio', in *Images of Colonialism and Decolonization in the Italian Media*, ed. Paolo Bertella Farnetti and Cecilia Dau Novelli (Newcastle upon Tyne: UK Cambridge Scholars, 2017), 57–66. On radio's social function as a source of health information over time, see Xhelil Aliu, *Radioja që më përfshiu të tërin: Mbresa nga puna 40 vjeçare në Radio-Tirana* (Tiranë: Expo, 2015), 43, 185, and Agron Çobani, *Ju flet Tirana: histori, kujtime, personazhe nga RTSH* (Tiranë: Toena, 2010), 59–60.
11 Heidi J. S. Tworek, 'The Savior of the Nation? Regulating Radio in the Interwar Period', *The Journal of Policy History* 27, no. 3 (2015): 465–91, quote at 485. On the afterlife of Anglo-American wartime communications and the later US-led effort to deploy the concept of 'freedom of information' against the Soviet Union, see Jennifer Spohrer, 'Threat or Beacon? Recasting International Broadcasting in Europe after World War II', in *Airy Curtains in the European Ether*, 29–50.
12 'Kurrë nuk është vonë', documentary film, Radio Televizioni Shqiptar (Albania), 6 August 2018, based on the recollections of Viktori Xhaçka; Kliton Nesturi, *Gjergj Bubani, i harruari i përkohshëm* (Tiranë: Omsca-1, 2010).
13 Akademia e Shkencave e RPSSH, *Fjalor enciklopedik shqiptar* (Tiranë: Akademia e Shkencave e RPSSH, 1985), 902.
14 'Like the heart pumping blood through the body, our radio-station will spread our Party's word so that people will rise for freedom.' *Flasin heronj të Luftës Nacional-çlirimtare* (Tiranë: Botim i Drejtorisë Politike të Ushtrisë Popullore të R.P.SH, 1971), 318.
15 This included the chief of the Italian army orchestra, who reportedly stayed on to lead the radio orchestra. Këlliçi, *Historia e radio-televizionit shqiptar*, 20.
16 Bedri Mata and Sali Mensori cited in Aliu, *Radioja që më përfshiu të tërin*, 187–8.
17 Emil Plumbi referenced in Këlliçi, *Historia e radio-televizionit shqiptar*, 51.

hours expanded, so did the range of programmes.[18] The summer of 1946 featured a short morning session, followed by afternoon comedy and an evening programme ('rhythmic music', 'the worker's hour', Balkan music, current affairs, a 'special hour devoted to women', more dance music.)[19] Administrators also embraced the emancipatory value of opera (once weekly) in addition to local amateur musical bands, which were common.[20] Seeing radio as a nationalizing tool, administrators sought to familiarize listeners with the new government, its rules and its social vision. This explains the importance attached to segments on railroad construction or sessions like 'Getting to know our laws' and 'Health advice'. The idea was to combine the practical with the political. At the same time, the broadcasts echoed the regime's insecurity. Some of the comedy-hour jokes from October 1946, for example, took jabs at Greece's aims at the Paris Peace Conference, castigating Athens for claiming southern Albanian territory. Other quips touched on the thorny issues of Trieste and war reparations.[21] Entertainment was hardly divorced from international politics.

The effort to create a national radio audience faced obvious difficulties. First of all, the technology was rudimentary and the equipment shared across agencies. At one point in 1946, transmission equipment became so overused that some telegraphic and telephonic services had to be suspended. Administrators recommended a regular rest day for the equipment.[22] Local managers complained that they lacked spare parts, but options for imports were limited. Even more importantly, the number of receivers in the country was small, with most of the units confined to the main cities and households supplied with electricity.[23] In the meantime, authorities installed wired loudspeakers in public areas and workplaces. Workers might occasionally obtain receivers as prizes for participating in labour competitions. It took many years, however, for receivers

---

[18] In early 1945, the station added a half-hour midday session to its evening broadcasts. Ministria e Shtypit, Propagandës dhe Kulturës Popullore (Sekretariati) to Këshilli N. Çl. të prefekturës, n.d. (February 1945), Arkivi Qendror Shtetëror (Tirana, hereafter AQSH), Fondi (F.) 566, Viti (V.) 1945, Dosja (Dos.) 158, Fleta (Fl.) 1.

[19] Radio-Tirana, 'Programi i ditës së Djelë më 16 Qershor 1946', n.d., AQSH, F. 566, V. 1946, Dos. 40, Fl. 1.

[20] Përgjegjësi i Radio Tiranës, untitled memo dated 17 February 1945, forwarded 19 February 1945, and response by Drejtoria e Radio Propagandës, 'Mbi programin e Emisioneve', 23 February 1945, in AQSH, F. 566, V. 1945, Dos. 158, Fl. 3-6. My focus here is on Radio Tirana, but it was not the only station that merits study. For other examples, see Nicholas Tochka, *Audible States: Socialist Politics and Popular Music in Albania* (New York: Oxford University Press, 2016), 48–9.

[21] Undated comedy-hour transcripts from October 1946, AQSH, F. 566, V. 1946, Dos. 41, Fl. 1-4.

[22] Stacioni i Radios to Ministria e Punve Botore, 26 June 1946, and Ministria e Punve Botore to Kryeministria, 19 July 1946, both in AQSH, F. 499, V. 1946, Dos. 855, Fl. 1-1 verso, 3-3 verso. In another illustration of material continuity across 'the national liberation', some of the correspondence was typed on old letterhead bearing the insignia of 'The Kingdom of Albania' and the names of its ghost institutions.

[23] Reported numbers of receivers vary across sources, as reflected in the difficulties US intelligence analysts had in making sense of the figures. Estimates for the early 1950s were under 20,000. Cf. 'Foreign Radiobroadcasting Reception Potential in Albania' (Secret), 4 February 1954, CIA Records Search Tool (hereafter CREST), CIA-RDP79-01093A000400130001-0 and Economic Intelligence Report, 'Post and Telecommunications Services in Albania, 1950-58', August 1959, CREST, CIA-RDP79R01141A001500070002-5. One Albanian source cites a figure of 100,000 receivers for the mid-1960s. Këlliçi, *Historia e radio-televizionit shqiptar*, 121.

to become more common in households, thanks in part to Eastern bloc imports.[24] Party authorities vowed to spread the revolution from the lowlands to the mountains. Limited domestic radio coverage, however, was a constant reminder of the staunch urban–rural divide.[25]

Politically, the year 1948 was a turning point. As Stalin quarrelled with Yugoslavia's Josip Broz Tito, Albania's leadership found itself caught in the middle.[26] The Soviet party boss had initially supported Yugoslav tutelage over the less-developed neighbour. But when disagreements erupted that year, Hoxha saw an opportunity to escape the Yugoslav clutch, declaring loyalty to the Soviet party boss. For a number of years, local propagandists had glorified the 'brotherly' relations with Yugoslavia. Now they accused Belgrade and Tito of having plotted to colonize Albania by way of exploitative economic arrangements. In this telling, Stalin became the nation's saviour. For Hoxha and his collaborators, it became possible to bypass Yugoslav intermediaries and forge direct links with the Kremlin. As an added benefit, the political schism in 1948 came with scapegoats – accused domestic allies of the Yugoslavs – who could be blamed for planning failures and other abuses. As relations with Belgrade crumbled, a Yugoslav ship bringing a medium-wave radio station (purchased in France) is reported to have turned back without unloading the cargo.[27] But there was hope. As in other areas of economic life, authorities turned to Moscow for help.

The urgency of internationalization

Throughout the 1950s, Moscow stood as the promise of socialist advancement and technical aid. At the same time, the schism with Belgrade physically detached Albania from the Eastern bloc. Propagandists used newspapers, documentary film and radio to dramatize this notion of 'encirclement' by enemies (Greece, Italy and Yugoslavia). Such geopolitical reality, the party line went, coupled with Anglo-American security threats from the West, required constant vigilance and sacrifice. In retrospect, talk of living 'under siege' might appear overly dramatic, but this was more than a metaphor. After 1948, in fact, the CIA in coordination with British intelligence services saw Albania as an ideal experimental site for removing a communist regime from power – one of the earliest and most overlooked of such Cold War attempts, preceding the coups in Iran and Guatemala. The agencies developed a plan to infiltrate Albanian exiles with the aim of fomenting a mass revolt. They airdropped millions of Albanian-language

---

[24] A state store in the northern city of Shkodër was reported to stock Czech, Yugoslav and Soviet sets, but they were not cheap. 'Sources of Domestic and Foreign News/Purchase of Radios/Shortage of Spare Parts' (Confidential), 5 April 1954, CREST, CIA-RDP80-00809A000500440168-5.

[25] On the introduction of radio to rural life, framed by the experience of land collectivization, see Aliu, *Radioja që më përfshiu të tërin*, 9.

[26] For the implications of the Moscow-Belgrade rift, see Norman Naimark, *Stalin and the Fate of Europe: The Postwar Struggle for Sovereignty* (Cambridge, MA: The Belknap Press of Harvard University Press, 2019), 54–87.

[27] Këlliçi, *Historia e radio-televizionit shqiptar*, 60.

Figure 4.1 Peasants hear the clandestine radio blaring 'Death to Communism, Freedom to Albania' in the early 1950s. (Source: CIA, 'Schedule of BGFIEND-VALUBLE Leaflet Drops', Nazi War Crimes Disclosure Act collection).

leaflets and operated a clandestine radio station (Voice of Free Albania) beginning in September 1951, urging locals to resist communist rule.[28]

The experiment proved a disaster, as local security operatives ambushed the infiltrators and as Radio Tirana angrily blasted the Anglo-American meddling.[29] There was no regime change in 1950s Albania, after all. In fact, the episode served to feed the regime's paranoia. But the sense of outside pressure was concrete, and it was multidirectional. Hostile radio signals originated not only in the West (the BBC, The Voice of America, Rome and the Vatican) but also from the north and the south (Belgrade, Athens). 'Because of its unique location', noted a 1954 US intelligence report, 'virtually surrounded by the non-Soviet Bloc countries, Greece, and Yugoslavia, and with Italy only a short distance away across the Adriatic Sea, and because of the absence of extensive local jamming activities, Albania is quite vulnerable to the reception of

---

[28] At first, broadcasting consisted merely of slogans like 'Down with Communist tyranny!' See '"Free Albania" Committee's Radio Station', n.d., The National Archives of the United Kingdom (London), FO 371/95038; 'Clandestine Station 'Radio Free Albania', 3 December 1951, CREST, CIA-RDP80-00809A000500730246-5. For a fuller context, see Albert Lulushi, *Operation Valuable Fiend: The CIA's First Paramilitary Strike Against the Iron Curtain* (New York: Arcade, 2014).

[29] In the words of a former wartime British liaison in Albania, the operation merely served 'to make Hoxha's long-standing propaganda line about the hostility of the capitalist powers and their nefarious intentions from the wartime onwards appear more plausible, and to give Hoxha another pretext for tightening "revolutionary" controls'. Reginald Hibbert, *Albania's National Liberation Struggle: The Bitter Victory* (London and New York: Pinter Publishers, 1991), 235.

Western broadcasts.'[30] Another information report deemed Belgrade's broadcasts to be more effective propaganda, since the Yugoslavs knew enough about internal Albanian affairs to tailor their attacks. As much as the Americans liked to think they knew how to speak to communism's 'captives', nothing seemed to breed resentment like a broken intra-communist bond.[31]

Along with emphasizing the idea of encirclement, radio reminded listeners that they also had allies abroad, including the world's most powerful socialist state. 'Our freed people today have the opportunity to listen and benefit greatly from the Albanian-language broadcasts of Radio Moscow,' one newspaper article declared, urging listeners to write appreciative letters to the Soviet broadcaster. 'Every evening, the voice of Radio Moscow blasts on our streets and inside our homes relayed via Radio Tirana.'[32] Soviet technology also helped boost Tirana's capacity and reception. In 1952, Moscow supplied a higher power transmitting station, improving not only the domestic medium-wave reception but also the signal's reach abroad.[33] Soviet specialists provided technical advice about station locations, though locals also took into account the earlier advice provided by the Italians. Almost all telecommunications equipment had to be imported from the socialist world – in particular from the Soviet Union and Czechoslovakia. Training depended on foreign assistance, too. It took years to develop local curricula in industrial electronics, so promising students enrolled in technical programmes in other friendly states.

In the 1950s, then, Radio Tirana was a reflection of the yet-incomplete task of creating a national audience as well as the regime's ambition to internationalize its claims. As shipments of Soviet equipment arrived, the Italian-era material legacy was still evident, which meant that technological solutions and spare parts might still be needed in the West. At the same time, personnel changes at Radio-Difuzioni, the public broadcasting agency, reflected a greater opening to the socialist world. In addition to editors for Albanian folk music, there were now specialists tasked with Soviet music, as well as staff covering Eastern bloc affairs, and translators from Russian, Bulgarian, Romanian and Serbo-Croatian.[34] Radio Tirana's own foreign-language broadcasting expanded, including in Greek, English, Serbo-Croatian, French, Italian, the languages of the Eastern bloc and a special Albanian-language service for the diaspora. To internationalize broadcasting was not merely desirable; it became a party-backed ideological imperative, even as domestic reception continued to be poor and uneven.[35]

---

[30] 'Foreign Radiobroadcasting Reception Potential in Albania' (Secret), 4 February 1954, CIA-RDP79-01093A000400130001-0. Western daily broadcasts to Albania, however, continued to be shorter than those of Moscow and Belgrade. Richardson to Dunning (Strictly Confidential), 14 June 1961, Radio Free Europe/Radio Liberty Corporate Records, Box 1665, Hoover Institution Archives, Stanford, California. On the Vatican's broadcasts, see Settimio Stallone, *Ritorno a Tirana: la politica estera italiana e l'Albania fra fedeltà atlantica e 'ambizioni' adriatiche (1949-1950)* (Rome: Edizioni Nuova Cultura, 2011), 30.

[31] 'Radio Propaganda Beamed to Albania' (Secret), 11 March 1955, CREST, CIA-RDP80-00810A006100290013-2.

[32] F. Veizi, 'Radioja jonë ecën në shëmbullin e Radios Sovjetike', *Bashkimi*, 2 July 1950, 2.

[33] 'Radio në Shqipëri', n. d., AQSH, F. 509, V. 1952, Dos. 2, Fl. 41.

[34] Këshilli i Ministrave, approval of radio agency personnel, 21 March 1949, AQSH, F.490, V. 1949, Dos. 610, Fl. 12-16.

[35] 'International Aural Radiobroadcasting Services of the Soviet Orbit' (Appendix G), n.d. (most likely 1953), CREST, CIA-RDP92B01090R000300020043-6. An earlier report had observed that

What did a typical radio programme during this period look like? It might start with a morning gymnastics session, followed by Soviet music (duets, Russian polka, Azerbaijani folk) and the reading of the lead article of the party paper *Zëri i Popullit*. The midday session (after 1:00 PM) might feature Russian dances, short pieces by Albanian musicians directed by Soviet conductors, Chopin, Tchaikovsky, Ukrainian music, stories read by Soviet pioneers, lectures and comedy numbers. The Albanian-Soviet Friendship Society-sponsored programme ('Getting to know the Soviet Union') was typically scheduled once per week. The evening session, finally, which started at 5:30 PM and concluded at 11:00 PM, would consist of the Albanian-language edition of Radio Moscow, traditional Albanian folk dances, medical curiosities and some combination of Dvořák, Rachmaninoff, Prokofiev, waltzes, poetry and partisan songs.[36]

Petraq Kolevica, at the time a young aspiring architect, later recalled this flooding of the airwaves with Soviet sounds: 'The radio never stopped informing us about the Soviet Union and broadcasting Russian songs.' Referring to the traditional Russian and Albanian string instruments, he wrote that the balalaika 'overwhelmed the *çifteli*'. Kolevica studied architecture between 1952 and 1957, and Soviet planning examples had become formulas to follow in design, too. He would later write in his memoir that the Soviet ready-made blueprints seemed foreign to him. So did Russian music and literature. He was accustomed to Italian *canzonette* and found it difficult to connect to Feodor Chaliapin or the bass Mark Reizen. The fact that Kolevica became a celebrated translator of Russian poetry is, in retrospect, an apt illustration of how cultural reception works. The introduction to Soviet culture, the architect and translator later admitted, was 'a painful phenomenon, love mixed with hatred'.[37] Constant propaganda about Soviet culture was staggering, but it was possible to admire Soviet culture *despite* of it.

One might be tempted to read this Soviet cultural offensive as an external imposition. In reality, domestic broadcasters could not yet fill all the broadcasting hours with local recordings, let alone original productions. Therefore, Soviet and Eastern bloc material was also a pragmatic choice. Imported music from the East helped to fill hour-long gaps in airtime.[38] By mid-decade, the relative weight of locally produced reporting increased, and so did the ranks of technicians, speakers and editors. Special programmes now targeted youth, peasants and women. Broadcasts of local orchestras, choirs and amateur groups similarly expanded. Nevertheless, programmes about the Soviet Union and the Eastern bloc did not disappear.[39] In fact, in a sign of not limiting themselves to the

---

diction and grammar in Radio Tirana's foreign programmes were poor. 'Radio Broadcasting: Programmatic Characteristics and Techniques' (unevaluated), 30 March 1951, CREST, CIA-RDP80-00809A000500730212-2. Parts of this section stem from my book *From Stalin to Mao: Albania and the Socialist World* (Ithaca: Cornell University Press, 2017).

[36] Examples are drawn from early 1950s radio programmes published in the main newspapers *Zëri i Popullit* and *Bashkimi*.

[37] Petraq Kolevica, *Arkitektura dhe diktatura* (Tiranë: Logoreci, 2004), 40–1.

[38] Beginning in the late 1940s, the broadcasting agency devised bilateral agreements with its Eastern bloc counterparts. 'Drejtorisë së Radiopërhapjes së Shtetit', 2 June 1949, Arkivi i Ministrisë së Punëve të Jashtme (Tirana, hereafter AMPJ), V. 1949, Dos. 132, Fl. 29; Albanian Mission (Bucharest) to Tirana, 18 July 1951, AMPJ, V. 1951, Dos. 244, Fl. 19; 'Mbi materialin kultural që u dërgohet Radiodifuzioneve të Demokracive Popullore', 29 February 1952, AQSH, F. 509, V. 1952, Dos. 2, Fl. 6.

[39] The radio programme for Saturday, 13 December 1958, included Bulgarian composer Pancho Vladigerov, Soviet music, songs selected by employees of the airport and patients in the capital's

continental sphere of socialism, programming chiefs occasionally added Korean and Chinese music to the mix, while continuing to censor Western music.

In thinking about radio's educational role, culture officials favoured simple messages and short sentences. Radio announcers employed the technique of continuous repetition of certain key phrases. Conveyed ideas had to be simple, crafted in a way that listeners could mimic. But this was not exactly easy, since there was regional variation in the use of the Albanian language. According to a French-language 1955 RFE/RL Research Institute field report, Radio Tirana used a 'mélange' of the two prevailing local dialects with the intention of addressing as many inhabitants as possible.[40] It is difficult to assess the reception of such efforts. The programmes were not recorded – a common problem with radio histories in general but compounded, in this instance, by the dearth of first-person accounts. Moreover, official government reports could be prone to hyperbole. Radio had not yet become a mass activity around the country. In some workplaces, however, and especially newly built industrial settlements, it was becoming a vehicle for socialization.

The idea of radio as a tool for socializing urban party types is perhaps best illustrated by the fact that such socialization backfired against the authorities that promoted it in the first place. The year 1956 is a good example of this. In February, Soviet leader Nikita Khrushchev famously delivered his anti-Stalin 'secret speech' in Moscow. An uprising in Budapest followed later that year, crushed by Soviet troops in November. Scholars analysing the Hungarian events have typically underlined and debated the role of Radio Free Europe during the crisis.[41] A broader lens, however, reveals how the socialist states' own radio promotion had unintended outcomes. Dora Vargha, for example, has brilliantly captured the role of amateur broadcasting, RFE and the transportation of an iron lung (a machine used to treat polio patients) during the crisis.[42] In Tirana, months before the turmoil in Budapest, mid-level party members criticized the leadership at a party conference.[43] The ruling circle had sought to keep Khrushchev's speech secret. Word got out anyway. Among the first to discuss it were administrators who had *access*: employees of agencies with international ties like the newspapers, the news service, the 'foreign affairs' government sections and the radio agency. They felt emboldened by the news coming from Moscow.

These individuals, after all, had been socialized into Eastern bloc affairs.[44] They listened to (and could understand) foreign broadcasts. For them, emulating Soviet

---

hospital, along with current affairs items and medical advice on ulcers. *Zëri i Popullit*, 13 December 1958.

[40] 'Radio Tirana', 8 July 1955, HU OSA 300-1-2-59823, Records of Radio Free Europe/Radio Liberty Research Institute: General Records: Information Items, Open Society Archives (OSA) at Central European University, Budapest, Hungary.

[41] Cf. Charles Gati, *Failed Illusions: Moscow, Washington, Budapest, and the 1956 Hungarian Revolt* (Washington, DC and Stanford: Woodrow Wilson Center Press and Stanford University Press, 2006), 183–5; Johnson, *Radio Free Europe and Radio Liberty*, ch. 3.

[42] Dora Vargha, *Polio Across the Iron Curtain: Hungary's Cold War with an Epidemic* (Cambridge: Cambridge University Press, 2018), 61–5.

[43] Ana Lalaj, 'Konferenca e Partisë e Tiranës, një pranverë e dështuar e së majtës në Shqipëri (14-19 prill 1956)', *Studime historike*, nos. 1–2 (2009): 109–32.

[44] Socialization nurtured intra-elite comparisons, competition and discontent. As outlined in an RFE/RL Research Institute field report, Radio Tirana's section chiefs were paid less than their counterparts at the main newspaper. A main complaint levelled at the Tirana party conference

examples had become a routine. Except that now emulation meant publicly envisioning a set of reforms. One of these individuals was Vehip Demi, who spoke passionately on behalf of the radio agency's party organization. He criticized news censorship, pointing to instances when criticism of Stalin had been taken out of published translations. The press, he complained, had not adequately covered the Moscow party congress and the related articles in *Pravda*. When radio staff had opted not to censor recent critical Polish materials, superiors had reprimanded them. Faced with mounting criticism, Hoxha made an urgent appearance at the conference, where he attacked the critics. Socialized by Soviet news and radio, as had been expected, they now stood accused of having conspired with one another. Demi and others were expelled; some were imprisoned. Colleagues who had approved Demi's statements at the radio agency were transferred to other jobs. The punishments sent the unmistakable signal that defiance would not be tolerated. Albania's de-Stalinization campaign failed to launch.

The government had spent money and effort bringing the Russian language into schools, shipping promising youths abroad to obtain university diplomas, educating translators that could act as cultural intermediaries between national borders. Officials had demanded that the airwaves get inundated with the sounds of the bloc. The events of 1956 brought to surface the problem of socialist connectivity: its potential for contamination. Just like they could be invaded by capitalist signals, the country's airwaves were also susceptible to influences from the other 'people's democracies'. It was not a coincidence that after party members spoke against the cult of personality at the Tirana conference, the party boss framed such charges as nefarious 'theses' emanating from Western radio stations.[45] Later that year, the leadership was warned that youths were in danger of being corrupted by outside influences.[46] For a geopolitically insecure state, internationalization was an urgent task. The events of 1956, however, show that the notion of foreignness was not static. It changed over time to accommodate domestic needs and unexpected developments abroad. The socialist map of friends and enemies required constant revision.

Socialist internationalism remapped

After 1956, Hoxha and his lieutenants paid lip service to Soviet advice, but they avoided substantial reforms. There was no rehabilitation of political prisoners, for example, and no durable rapprochement with Yugoslavia. When Khrushchev visited Albania in the spring of 1959, the celebrations went on for days and the rhetoric was boastful. Bilateral talks behind closed doors, however, revealed a number of discrepancies. The Soviet party chief refused to discuss Yugoslavia and pressured his interlocutors to rethink their economic plans. It made no sense, he argued, to keep demanding more Soviet

---

concerned unequal distribution of material privileges within the party's echelons. "Radio Tirana", 8 July 1955, HU OSA 300-1-2-59823.
[45] Enver Hoxha, *Vepra*, vol. 13 (September 1955 to June 1956) (Tiranë: Naim Frashëri, 1973), 479.
[46] 'Informacion', n.d. (December 1956), AQSH, F. 14/AP, OU (Organet Udhëheqëse), V. 1957, Dos. 7, Fl. 4-5.

loans to fund heavy industries in the context of a small agrarian economy. Albania could instead become an agricultural supplier to the Eastern bloc. Such talk reflected the Soviet leader's vision for an international distribution of socialist labour. But it hardly took into account the profound sense of insecurity among his counterparts. For them, economic self-reliance could not be divorced from the fact of geopolitical 'encirclement'.[47]

As Sino-Soviet relations tumbled in the summer of the 1960, Hoxha saw yet another opportunity to escape the pressures of a more powerful state. The more Moscow demanded that the leadership in Tirana fall in line, the more sympathy the Albanian side voiced for the Chinese criticism of Khrushchev's policies. For their part, Chinese officials were pleased to find a tiny but vocal ally. Like Hoxha, Mao deemed that de-Stalinization had been a mistake. The notion of a 'peaceful coexistence' with capitalism seemed tantamount to a betrayal of Leninism. Moreover, the anti-Yugoslav (and anti-revisionist) rhetoric of the Chinese received a warm reception in Tirana, where the top party brass had been implicated in the anti-Yugoslav hysteria of the late 1940s. These converging interests brought the Albanian and Chinese parties closer. When the Soviets retaliated in 1961, withdrawing their advisers, Beijing agreed to supply aid, including much-needed wheat – greeted with a special announcement by Radio Tirana.[48]

Shifting from Moscow to Beijing raised its own problems. Year after year party functionaries had extolled the friendship with the Soviet Union. Radio Tirana had described at length Soviet achievements across numerous time zones. A generation of specialists owed their careers to their Soviet credentials and their Russian-language skills. The friendship was now dead, which raised the question of how a vulnerable regime could reposition itself in international affairs. Some observers doubted whether China could effectively provide the technical assistance that was so desperately needed. After all, China was itself a poor country. For others, the split encouraged speculation that the turn away from Moscow might signal a Yugoslav-style opening to the capitalist West. When Radio Tirana introduced some Western music in its programme, listeners wondered whether a broader political opening might be imminent. Taking note of the anti-Soviet turn in Tirana, Radio Free Europe administrators wondered whether it might make sense to restart Albanian-language broadcasting.[49] Within and across national borders, listeners tried to decode Radio Tirana for geopolitical clues.

Instead, the party leadership insisted that it would uphold Marxism-Leninism, no matter the economic predicament. It blamed Moscow for reneging on its internationalist duties, pointing to the fact that Soviet technology would have helped build a large radio antenna in the locality of Shijak. Because the Soviets had withdrawn their technical personnel, local technicians were forced to figure out how to install the antenna on their own. In official parlance, such acts became evidence of 'sabotage' and symptoms of an

---

[47] 'Protokoll', 25 May 1959, AQSH, F.14/AP, M-PK(b)BS, V. 1959, Dos. 24.
[48] CIA/SRS-14, 'The European Satellites and the Sino-Soviet Difference', 3 November 1960, CREST, CIA-RDP80-01445R000100190001-7.
[49] They were not overly enthusiastic about the prospects: 'The target is too small; the politics are too complicated', one memo put it. 'Should RFE Broadcast to Albania?', 8 March 1962, Hoover Institution Archives, RFE/RL Corporate Records, Box Nr. 1665.

international 'blockade'. The battle to expand the radio's signal *despite* the Soviet Union turned into a kind of symbolic crusade. The radio antenna became an achievement of local workers and engineers, who impressed their Chinese counterparts, as one author explained, with their iron resolve.[50] Traces of an earlier era remained; a recent hire at the radio in 1965 was advised he would hear Russian and Italian technical words at work.[51] Chinese technical presence, however, became conspicuous. As the official party line put it, the two regimes stood as defenders of Marxism-Leninism on opposite ends of a world retreating into revisionism. In reconfiguring a place for itself, Albania's establishment was confronted with the need to redraw this world map.

One way to think about this process is to imagine it as proceeding along three tracks, addressing the past, present and future of socialism. First, party functionaries did not reject the Soviet legacy wholesale but rather Moscow's political leadership. This allowed them to cast themselves as heirs to Stalinism and the true legacy of the Russian Revolution. Secondly, in terms of the immediate planning needs, they vowed to build socialism by adopting Chinese technology and expertise. To mark the twelfth anniversary of the People's Republic of China, Tirana dedicated a week to Chinese music.[52] In November 1961, Radio Beijing began transmitting Tirana's Albanian-language programme, which had been relayed by Sofia.[53] Within a few years, extensive cultural agreements between the countries followed.[54] Beyond the Soviet past and the Chinese present, finally, party higher-ups increasingly pushed to project the idea of a revolutionary future by establishing contacts with militant movements across Latin America, Africa and Asia. And there was hardly a more convenient vehicle for doing this than Radio Tirana.

A decade earlier, when the Soviet Union had supplied a broadcasting station, one observer had fretted to Western researchers that the Kremlin was about to make Radio Tirana the voice of Moscow to 'the Moslem peoples of the Middle East'. Soviet-inspired 'red propaganda', this source had explained, would 'attempt to convince devout Arabs from Morocco to the Persian Gulf that there is no basic conflict between the principles of Marxism-Leninism and the Mohammedan religion'.[55] The evaluators had appeared sceptical of the religious connection. In later years, however, Khrushchev did indeed speak about turning Albania into a socialist showcase for the decolonized world, and the importance of Arabic-language broadcasts kept coming up.[56] This kind of

[50] Murat Klosi, *Ndërtimet në pushtetin popullor* (Tiranë: Naim Frashëri, 1968), 132–4.
[51] Çobani, *Ju flet Tirana*, 12.
[52] GDR Embassy in Tirana to MfAA, 'Information. Die Würdigung des 12. Jahrestages der Gründung der Volksrepublik China in der Volksrepublik Albanien' (Confidential), 11 October 1961, Politisches Archiv des Auswärtigen Amts -Ministerium für Auswärtige Angelegenheiten (Berlin) C 274/75, 20–8.
[53] FBID Chief to Bureau Chiefs, 'Letter of Information' (Secret), 22 November 1961, CREST, CIA-RDP83-00586R000300210004-4.
[54] 'Plan për zbatimin e marrëveshjes së bashkëpunimit kulturor midis Republikës Popullore të Shqipërisë dhe Republikës Popullore të Kinës për vitet 1963-1964', n.d., AQSH, F. 511, V. 1963, Dos. 87.
[55] 'Radio Tirana to Be Focal Point of Soviet Propaganda to Arabs', 12 September 1952, HU OSA 300-1-2-25033, OSA.
[56] 'We proposed to Albania that a powerful radio station be built that could serve the aims of propaganda', Khrushchev later recalled. 'We wanted to use this radio station to promote our ideas,

thinking reflected Soviet anxieties about US-centred globalism much more than actual aspirations in Tirana at the time. Still, to the extent that such rhetoric translated into more Soviet loans and gear, the Albanian side went along. The irony is that after the Sino-Soviet schism, Albania's elites did in fact enthusiastically embrace Khrushchev's vision of becoming a socialist voice speaking to the decolonized world – this time, by chastising Moscow.

Seen from this perspective, the split with Moscow emerges not as a single diplomatic event but as a longer and wider process. It meant confronting the past, present and future of socialism in more places and in more languages than had been the case before. The 1960s map of hostile territories expanded in several directions beyond Rome, Belgrade and Athens. In both Western and Eastern Europe, for example, Radio Tirana could try to speak to sympathizers who had sided with China. But party directives also raised the possibility of using radio as a weapon against Moscow in Europe and around the world. This meant continued broadcasts in English, French, Arabic, Greek, Serbo-Croatian and Italian. Later, addressing the Third World meant developing programmes in Spanish, Portuguese and Indonesian. The urgency of foreign languages, in other words, was also a reflection of geopolitical imperatives. By the mid-1960s, radio had multiple targets beyond the capitalist West: the Albanian diaspora abroad; rival states within the socialist world; as well as revolutionaries outside of Europe. Sino-Soviet squabbles thus pushed radio propagandists to internationalize their voice.[57]

It also became necessary to develop an editorial voice. As the propaganda sector saw the problem, the new geopolitical reality of the 1960s required not simply more words in more foreign languages. Up until then, administrators had thought of translation as a technical obstacle: the mechanical act of rendering the same text into several languages. Such uniform communication, officials explained, would no longer work. The world was changing and what was needed was more effective 'counter-propaganda'. This meant creating country, or at least region-specific programmes. Seen over time, in other words, the turn from Moscow to Beijing signalled a need to globalize broadcasts but also to filter and tailor content for a wider range of foreigners. Such tasks required more translators and speakers of foreign languages – the foreign propaganda section more than doubled in 1967 – and also more information, and, above all, hard currency.[58]

A stronger radio signal was also necessary. Two new stations in the 1960s were the result of government agreements with China. Beijing supplied equipment, teams

---

our policies, and the policies of all the Communist parties.' This would have made Albania 'a vivid example for countries gaining their freedom from colonial oppression, thus demonstrating the advantages of the socialist system'. Sergei Khrushchev, ed., *Memoirs of Nikita Khrushchev*, vol. 3 (Pennsylvania State University, 2007), 517. On Soviet-encouraged broadcasting in Arabic: 'Relacion mbi vajtjen e delegacionit të radios shqiptare në Moskë', 17 December 1957, AMPJ, V. 1957, Dos. 56, Fl. 28; Albanian Embassy (Moscow) to Tirana (Top Secret), 12 March 1958, AMPJ, V. 1958, Dos. 63, Fl. 14.

[57] 'Mbi propagandën për jashtë të ATSH-s dhe Radio-s', addressed to Enver Hoxha, dated by hand 15 July 1961, and 'Vendim Nr. 222' (Secret), 15 July 1961, both in AQSH, F. 14/AP, OU, V. 1961, Dos. 55, Fl. 72-80; 'Vendim Nr. 38' (Secret), 10 February 1965, AQSH, F.14/AP, OU, V. 1965, Dos. 4, Fl. 139. By 1980, Radio Tirana issued broadcasts in nineteen languages.

[58] 'Relacion', 3 December 1965, AQSH, F. 490, V. 1965, Dos. 901, Fl. 32-33; 'Relacion', 6 March 1967, and 'Vendim Nr. 29', 20 March 1967, AQSH, F. 490, V. 1967, Dos. 53, Fl. 1-2, 5.

of technicians and training for Albanian engineers. Since the government sought to reach remote parts of the country, a group of local and Chinese specialists travelled around to test signal reception. Diplomats in Turkey and Egypt were asked to confirm the quality of sound in their respective locales. Officials were especially concerned with radio reception along borderland regions. This fact reminds us that borders with Yugoslavia and Greece required more than physical policing. As investigators noted, inhabitants in these regions often compared Radio Tirana's weaker signal with 'enemy' stations from across the border. To address this problem, the radio's chief proposed building mini-stations in cooperation with the army in order to drown the sounds of Corfu and Athens.[59]

This enduring obsession with the intersections of aerial and physical borders can be traced from 1950s Sakhalin to 1960s Tirana to late-socialist Bucharest.[60] It fuelled fantasies of control but also exposed the limits and frustrations of jamming technology. The challenge of dealing with enemy signals came up for discussion at the Politburo in Tirana. 'Ten foreign radio stations broadcast in the Albanian language,' a multi-department report explained in 1965, totalling eight hours per day. The report singled out not only the usual culprits (Voice of America, Belgrade) but also Moscow – once the source of inspiration now morphed into an antagonist. It also explained that London produced 'the most intelligent propaganda' (ironically, the BBC suspended its Albanian service two years later), whereas the Greek and Spanish services piled on the insults and the Vatican kept on issuing history lessons.[61]

Assessments of the power of broadcasting can seem heavy-handed in retrospect. Western administrators seem to have been, if anything, pessimistic about the value of broadcasting to a place for which they did not even have basic audience data.[62] Albanian chiefs fretted about powerful Western sounds, but Hoxha himself admitted at the Politburo that Radio Tirana could hardly drown them out. Listeners wanted to hear Western music. What to do about that? If Tirana did not broadcast it, listeners would tune in to foreign stations for the music and get a dose of propaganda along with it.[63] Still, a continued emphasis (and exaggeration) of foreign radio had its domestic uses.[64] To be attacked on the airwaves was to be relevant – worthy of sustained effort. This allowed local officials to ask for more resources from higher-ups. As the havoc of the Cultural Revolution had engulfed China, Beijing sought to relay Chinese broadcasts aimed at the Soviet Union and other 'revisionist' states via a station in Albania.[65]

[59] 'Mbi ndëgjimin e radios në vendin tonë', 6 May 1968, AQSH, F. 490, V. 1968, Dos. 559, Fl. 4-8.
[60] Lovell, *Russia in the Microphone Age*, 156; Dana Mustata, 'Geographies of Power: The Case of Foreign Broadcasting in Dictatorial Romania', in *Airy Curtains in the European Ether*, 156–7.
[61] 'Raport mbi propagandën e armikut, detyrat e kundërpropagandës dhe forcimin e propagandës në botën e jashtme', dated by hand 10 February 1965, AQSH, F.14/AP, OU, V. 1965, Dos. 4, Fl. 128-129.
[62] Hart to Ott, 11 January 1967, Hoover Institution Archives, RFE/RL Corporate Records, Box Nr. 1665.
[63] 'Proces-verbal', 10 February 1965, AQSH, F.14/AP, OU, V. 1965, Dos. 4, Fl. 175.
[64] On the political uses of Western broadcasting in the Soviet Union, see Roth-Ey, *Moscow Prime Time*, 133. On the Hungarian establishment's uses of Western broadcasting – and related myths that outlived the Cold War – see István Rév, 'Just Noise? Impact of Radio Free Europe in Hungary', in *Cold War Broadcasting*, 239–58.
[65] 'Informacion mbi ndërtimin e një stacioni të ri në Fllagë dhe të një qendre kontrolli nga pala kineze', 20 March 1968, AQSH, F. 509, V. 1968, Dos. 5, Fl. 1.

It was at this time that the Party of Labor launched a campaign to instil a revolutionary spirit in daily life (*revolucionarizimi i jetës*). Radio also reflected this ethos. Broadcasts featured more historical programmes designed to celebrate the country's past struggles – from the Ottoman Empire to the Second World War – in addition to reportages on the need to eradicate 'backward' social customs, 'bourgeois residues', and religious practices. Alongside with this, the regime vowed to bring electricity to remote villages by 1970. A centralized state could marshal resources to electrify villages, but precisely that state's obsession with industrial output – and the hefty amounts of energy required – also placed a burden on broadcasting. Industrialization required so much power that when the radio signal did finally reach certain areas of the country, it was reported to be feeble. Since the power grid and the telephonic and telegraphic lines had not been coordinated, listeners reported signal interferences. Some reported merely noise. In rural communities, radio receivers continued to be scarce. One report mentioned villages in which local administrators distributed the few receivers that had become available by picking names by luck of the draw. The hope was to avoid resentment among the inhabitants.[66]

The picture that emerges here does not conform to the idea of a prevailing East-West conflict. Instead, I have sketched out uneven campaigns waged on multiple fronts: to conquer rugged territory within the country, to spread the radio's signal in an increasing number of foreign languages abroad and, finally, to counter foreigners from both East and West. Analysing these processes as multidirectional allows us to see how they interacted over time. They were marked by unpredictability. Technological exchanges did not perfectly align with ideological affinities. Soviet technology, it turned out, could end up serving anti-Soviet goals. Some Western foreign stations slashed budgets and ceased Albanian-language programming, but other interferences might emerge, inviting a kind of remapping of the outside world. Placed in the context of broadcasting, the Sino-Soviet schism emerges as a drawn-out geographic, temporal and linguistic realignment. State-backed broadcasting hardly lacked ambition, but this is also a story of contingency. Because television developed relatively late in Albania (as in China), radio remained a key medium of information warfare for longer than was the case in Western Europe and the United States.

'Hört Radio Tirana!'

By the 1970s, Radio Tirana spoke to more peasants in the country but also far-flung revolutionaries around the globe. For the party apparatus, using radio as a link to the outside world made practical sense. It was an administrative way to pay foreign allies by hiring them as translators, editors and speakers.[67] A notable example was Kazimierz

[66] 'Mbi ndëgjimin e radios në vendin tonë', 6 May 1968, AQSH, F. 490, V. 1968, Dos. 559, Fl. 7.
[67] Back in 1961, Hoxha told his colleagues that foreign Marxist-Leninists supported Albania 'out of sentiments of internationalism' but they nevertheless would 'easily accept a donation'. 'Proces-verbal i mbledhjes së Sekretariatit të KQ të PPSH të dates 19 qershor 1961' (Secret), 19 June 1961, AQSH, F. 14/AP, OU, V. 1961, Dos. 54, Fl. 223-248. On Tirana's support for foreign factions, see Nicola Pedrazzi, *L'Italia che sognava Enver: partigiani, comunisti, marxisti-leninisti: gli amici italiani*

Mijal, the Polish Marxist-Leninist who aligned with Beijing after the Sino-Soviet split. He set up shop in Tirana in 1966 and used the radio service's Polish programme to beam his revolutionary messages back to his homeland.[68] Another was Nils Andersson, the founder of Switzerland's Marxist-Leninist outfit, who was banished from his country at the same time and re-emerged with a position at Radio Tirana.[69] José Catalán Deus, the Spanish activist detained in 1973, clandestinely travelled to Tirana after his release, working with the Spanish-language section.[70] Tirana's exhortations eventually appeared in the amateur publications of Scandinavian Marxist-Leninist groups.[71] They popped up among Marxist-Leninists in both Germanys. In the West, the Kommunistische Partei Deutschlands/Marxisten-Leninisten encouraged its sympathizers to listen to the voice 'of the only socialist country in Europe'. Since the group also agitated in East Germany, the transmissions of once-friendly Tirana surfaced as an intelligence topic for the Stasi.[72]

Tirana's militant voice – 'as if from a different dimension' – thus crisscrossed the Iron Curtain, transcribed by fringe groups and minuscule factions. State security operatives dutifully noted the on-air rants, thus creating a transnational archive for what otherwise might have been lost.[73] Some of the listeners were Western leftists amused by the spectacle of an angry voice from the Stalinist past. Others were pro-Chinese agitators of various levels of organization and seriousness, as captured in a recent fascinating dissertation by the historian David Spreen.[74] Tirana also gathered a following, as memoirs attest, among anti-dictatorship activists in unexpected places, from the Iberian Peninsula to South America. In Franco's Spain, a young man by the name of Antonio Nieto became politically active while listening to the broadcasts.[75] The Portuguese security police kept track of foreign radios, including references to

---

dell'Albania popolare (1943-1976) (Nardò: Besa, 2017) and Ylli Molla, *Guerilas made in Albania: historia e Arafatit, Kabilës, Lulës, Amazonas dhe luftëtarëve nga 11 shtete, që u përgatitën politikisht dhe ushtarakisht nga pedagogët shqiptarë* (Tiranë: Botart, 2016).

[68] Margaret K. Gnoinska, 'Promoting the 'China Way' of Communism in Poland and Beyond During the Sino-Soviet Split: The Case of Kazimierz Mijal', *Cold War History* 18, no. 3 (2018): 343–59; Gasztold Przemysław, 'Maoizm nad Wisłą? Działalność Komunistycznej Partii Polski Kazimierza Mijala', *Pamięć i Sprawiedliwość*, no. 32 (2018): 290–318.

[69] Nils Andersson, *Mémoire éclatée: de la décolonisation au déclin de l'occident* (Lausanne: Éditions d'En bas, 2016), esp. 350–8.

[70] José Catalán Deus, *Del FRAP a Podemos: Crónica de medio siglo: un viaje por la reciente historia española con Ricardo Acero y sus compañeros*, vol. 3 (Sarrión: Muñoz Moya Editores, 2016), 322–3.

[71] *Røde Fane*, published by the Norwegian Arbeidernes Kommunistparti, featured material from Radio Tirana. On the context: Hans Petter Sjøli, *Mao, min Mao: Historien om AKPs vekst og fall* (Oslo: Cappelen, 2005).

[72] Der Bundesbeauftragte für die Unterlagen des Staatssicherheitsdienstes der ehemaligen Deutschen Demokratischen Republik (BStU, Berlin), MfS HA XXII Nr. 425/2; 'Auskunftsbericht', forwarded October 1979, BStU MfS-BdL/Dok. Nr. 006260, Bl. 1-40.

[73] Ardian Vehbiu, *Sende që nxirrte deti* (Tiranë: Dudaj, 2013), 253.

[74] David Spreen, 'Dear Comrade Mugabe: Decolonization and Radical Protest in Divided Germany, 1960-1980' (PhD diss., University of Michigan, 2019). On Maoism's wide-spanning footprint in the 1960s, see Julia Lovell, *Maoism: A Global History* (New York: Knopf, 2019).

[75] Antonio Nieto interviewed by Luis Martín-Cabrera and Elize Mazadiego, 14 July 2010. Testimony of the Spanish Civil War and the Francoist Dictatorship, University of California, San Diego, https://library.ucsd.edu/dc/object/bb20831135 (accessed 1 January 2020).

Tirana in local clandestine papers.⁷⁶ Under the military dictatorship in Brazil (1964–85), Radio Tirana cultivated a following among guerilla fighters during the Guerrilha do Araguaia. It served as an intercontinental channel of communication for activists like Rosa da Fonsêca, Maria Liège Santos Rocha and others. In turn, Brazilian couples were stationed in Tirana to handle translations, as were Australians, New Zealanders, Spaniards and others.⁷⁷

This also was a form of lived internationalism. Capturing it invites work with not only official sources but also memoirs, oral history and unpublished accounts in different languages. Such an approach to internationalism is especially pertinent for addressing the recent history of authoritarian regimes where the past has been periodically purged in line with the state's needs. Just as it attracted listeners abroad, Albania's regime launched a domestic assault on 'foreign influences' in the early 1970s. This raises the question of how states can pursue some forms of international engagement even as they reject the prevailing international order, and how forms of technology can produce transnational attachments but also reinforce a sense of distance. We tell histories of internationalism that are about ideas and states. Radio is a reminder that internationalism was also about people and the stories they tell. One colourful account that informed this chapter was written by the radio veteran Agron Çobani. In the preface to his book, he explained that a question bothered him as he set out to write: Would anybody care to read about this story? I wrote this chapter also as an answer to this question.

Acknowledgements

Funding for archival research was generously provided by the Presidential Awards at Hunter College of the City University of New York and the PSC-CUNY Research Awards.

---

⁷⁶ Exhibit on foreign radio stations, clandestine publications and the PIDE/DGS, Museu do Aljube – Resistência e Liberdade, Lisbon, Portugal, visited on 1 June 2017; José Pacheco Pereira, *"O um dividiu-se em dois": origens e enquadramento internacional dos movimentos pró-chineses e albaneses nos países ocidentais e em Portugal* (Lisbon: Aletheia Editores, 2008), 41-64.

⁷⁷ Elio Gaspari, *A ditadura escancarada*, 2nd edn (Rio de Janeiro: Intrínseca, 2014); Érico Firmo, *Rosa da Fonsêca* (Fortaleza: Edições Demócrito Rocha, 2017); 'Detyrat që kryejnë shokët e huaj të radios dhe pagat e tyre', 20 August 1973, AQSH, F. 14/AP, STR, V. 1974, Dos. 546, Fl. 2-3.

Part II

Local encounters

5

Speaking the language of humanitarianism or 'Speaking Bolshevik'

Visions and vocabularies of relief in Soviet Armenia, 1920–8

Jo Laycock

Over the course of the First World War, the Ottoman/Russian borderlands became the site of a protracted refugee crisis. From 1914, violence on the Caucasus front uprooted populations on both sides of the imperial divide. By December, 20,000 refugees had arrived in Erivan.[1] With the advent of genocidal massacres and deportations in Ottoman territories in spring 1915, thousands more Armenians fled to the relative safety of the Russian imperial provinces of Transcaucasia (the South Caucasus).[2] In the years that followed, complex patterns of displacement continued, driven by revolution, imperial collapse and the formation of new states. By the time the Soviet Republic of Armenia was established in December 1920, at least a third of its population were refugees.[3] Beyond the new Soviet state, Ottoman Armenian refugees remained dispersed across the territories of the former Russian Empire and, in even greater numbers, across the Middle East and Eastern Mediterranean.[4]

The refugee crisis meant that the Caucasus front became a site of prolonged international concern, where relief agencies, states and international organizations interacted through efforts to provide relief to refugees and shape a future Armenia. In

---

[1] The spelling 'Erivan' rather than the current 'Yerevan' was used during this period. Central Historical Archive of Georgia, Saistorio Tsentraluri Arkivi f.519, op.1, d.47. Chancellery of the Viceroy to Caucasian Committee for Victims of War, 25 December 1914.
[2] For the wider history of the Genocide, see Ronald Grigor Suny, *'They Can Live in the Desert but Nowhere Else'*: *A History of the Armenian Genocide* (Oxford: Oxford University Press, 2015); Raymond Kévorkian, *The Armenian Genocide: A Complete History* (London: I.B. Tauris, 2011).
[3] At the end of 1921 there were around 300,000 refugees in Soviet Armenia. Hayastantsi Azgayin Arkhiv, National Archive of Armenia (HAA), f.114, op.2, d.89. l.19 Report prepared for Harold Buxton, December 1921.
[4] The AND provided the following estimate: Syria 150,000, Greece 120,000, Bulgaria 20,000, Cyprus 2,000, Palestine 1,200, Mesopotamia 8,000 and Europe 20,000. Archives of the League of Nations, Geneva, (ALON) Fonds Nansen, R1763 / 48 / 36375 / 25899 Situation of Armenian Refugees Dr. Nansen's Report, Geneva, 1 May 1924.

the beginning, the response to Armenian displacement was driven by local Armenian organizations and the diaspora within the Russian Empire.[5] International relief agencies, including the British Lord Mayor's Fund (LMF) for Armenian Refugees and American Near East Relief (NER), played a smaller but significant role.[6] From the 1917 revolution, imperial collapse and the establishment of short-lived independent Georgian, Armenian and Azerbaijani Republics disrupted and reshaped both local and international relief efforts. With the Armistice, new opportunities for international aid arose, and the American Relief Administration (ARA) provided food supplies and coordinated relief in the region.

By autumn 1920, Turkish nationalist forces threatened the borders of the independent Republic of Armenia. The majority of international actors left the region. Caught between 'the Bolshevik hammer and the Turkish anvil', the Armenian government resigned, and by December a Soviet *Revkom* government had assumed power.[7] While Sovietization brought stability and security, the scale of the refugee crisis hardly diminished. The new government therefore invited international relief agencies to return to the region. It also opened relations with diaspora philanthropic organizations. By the mid-1920s, international entanglement in Soviet Armenia had reached a peak as diaspora organizations, relief agencies and the League of Nations cooperated in the development of the 'Nansen' agricultural resettlement schemes.[8] By the end of the 1920s, this short-lived but intense period of international engagement in Soviet Armenia had come to an end.

This ostensibly unlikely case provides a vantage point from which to examine the nature and the limits of international cooperation during the interwar period. The response to the Armenian Genocide has already been identified by historians as a 'critical' moment in the history of humanitarianism during which new conceptions of international responsibility, new modes of cooperation, as well as new thinking about human rights and law emerged.[9] This scholarship has however had little to say about the role of the Soviet Union in these processes, despite the fact that it was a Soviet Republic which became home to perhaps the greatest concentration of displaced

---

[5] On displacement in the Russian Empire, see Peter Gatrell, 'War, Refugeedom, Revolution', *Cahiers Du Monde Russe* 58, no. 1 (18 October 2017): 123–46. On the Caucasus front, Asya Darbinyan, 'Humanitarian Crisis at the Ottoman-Russian Border: Assisting Armenian Refugees of War and Genocide 1914–1915', in *Aid to Armenia: Humanitarianism and Intervention from the 1890s to the Present*, ed. Jo Laycock and Francesca Piana (Manchester: Manchester University Press, 2020).

[6] The Lord Mayor's fund was founded in London in October 1915. See Jo Laycock, 'Saving the Remnant or Building Socialism? Transnational Humanitarian Relief in Early Soviet Armenia', *Moving the Social* 57 (2017): 77–96. Near East Relief was first known as the American Committee for Armenian and Syrian Relief and then the American Committee for Relief in the Near East (ACRNE). The name Near East Relief was used from 1919 and is used here throughout for clarity.

[7] This was the phrasing of Simon Vratsian, Dashnak prime minister of the Republic, quoted in Razmik Panossian, *The Armenians: From Kings and Priests to Merchants and Commissars* (London: Hurst, 2006), 245.

[8] So called because the League's first High Commissioner for Refugees, Fridtjof Nansen, became their chief advocate.

[9] See for example Keith David Watenpaugh, *Bread from Stones: The Middle East and the Making of Modern Humanitarianism* (Oakland: University of California Press, 2015) and Michelle Tusan, '"Crimes Against Humanity": Human Rights, the British Empire, and the Origins of the Response to the Armenian Genocide', *The American Historical Review* 1:119 (2014):47–77.

Armenians during the interwar years. By focusing on relief in Soviet Armenia, this chapter examines the relationship between the Soviet Union and the international organizations and systems of humanitarian cooperation that emerged in the aftermath of the First World War. By focusing on communications between the multiple actors engaged in the response to displacement in Armenia, it demonstrates how international projects were shaped 'on the ground' by specific local contexts and actors.

The chapter begins by considering the ways that different Soviet actors, diaspora organizations, relief agencies and international organizations framed their engagement with Armenian refugees, demonstrating how conceptions of responsibility were transformed in the aftermath of war and genocide. It goes on to demonstrate how communication between actors within and beyond Soviet Armenia functioned, exploring how competing interests were managed through a combination of formal agreements and personal relationships, and showing how misconceptions and misunderstandings could shape an international encounter on everyday basis. Finally, it considers the extent to which institutional, ideological or even personal differences could be bridged through a language of technical or scientific expertise.

Rhetorics of international responsibility

International interventions in Soviet Armenia in the 1920s had a long prehistory.[10] Even before the Genocide, well-developed vocabularies of international responsibility for Armenians existed. Interventions on behalf of the Armenians since the late nineteenth century had relied upon the image of Armenians as deserving, suffering Christians on the edge of a 'barbaric' East; a semi-civilized people who had the potential to be reclaimed and rehabilitated as part of Europe.[11] In the context of war and genocide, the notion of Armenia as an international concern still resonated, but a new language of international responsibility emerged. In Britain, the Genocide was framed as a war atrocity and Armenia's status as a victim *nation* was emphasized.[12] The American response to Armenian suffering had long been channelled through missionary networks in the Ottoman Empire. These missionary roots meant that the American relief agencies NER portrayed their response to the Armenian Genocide as a Christian duty, but the organization also frequently couched its support for Armenians in national terms.[13] This emphasis on Christianity, civilization and

---

[10] See, for example, Davide Rodogno, *Against Massacre: Humanitarian Interventions in the Ottoman Empire, 1815-1914* (Princeton: Princeton University Press, 2012); Donald Bloxham, *The Great Game of Genocide: Imperialism, Nationalism, and the Destruction of the Ottoman Armenians* (Oxford: Oxford University Press, 2005). Ann Marie Wilson, 'In the Name of God, Civilization, and Humanity: The United States and the Armenian Massacres of the 1890s', *Le Mouvement Social* 227, no. 2 (2009): 27.

[11] Jo Laycock, *Imagining Armenia: Orientalism, Ambiguity and Intervention, 1879-1925* (Manchester: Manchester University Press, 2009), chapters one and two.

[12] Ibid., 109–16.

[13] Keith Watenpaugh emphasizes NER's shift towards a modern 'secular' form of humanitarianism in the Middle East. *Bread from Stones*, esp. 17–19. In the case of their work in the Caucasus, at least this shift seems to have been less complete.

nationhood continued to shape international responses to Armenian displacement in the Caucasus after the war.

It was not only the perceptions of external actors that shaped the international response to the Genocide. In the Russian Empire, the consequences of the Armenian Genocide were bound up with debates over imperial expansion and Armenian self-determination.[14] The organizations Armenians established to respond to the suffering of their compatriots became the crucible for debates over national rights.[15] Should Armenian refugees be returned to live under Ottoman rule, or should their homes be incorporated into the Russian Empire? Or, should an independent Armenian nation be created? In a parallel process, claims to post-war Armenian nationhood were articulated among diaspora elites and in international diplomatic circles, in particular, by Boghos Nubar Pasha, leader of the Armenian National Delegation (AND) in Paris.[16]

The hopes for Armenian nationhood which had been expressed in all of these different quarters seemed to have been fulfilled when the independent Republic of Armenia was established in May 1918. Ottoman surrender later that year seemed to make an expanded vision of Armenian nationhood, incorporating former Ottoman territory, a possibility. Both the Independent Armenian Republic and the AND sent delegations to the Paris Peace Conference.[17] The language of Armenian nationhood resonated strongly on the international stage during this 'Wilsonian moment', yet ultimately went unfulfilled. By the end of 1920, independent Armenia had become a Soviet Republic. By 1923, the Treaty of Lausanne and establishment of the Turkish Republic had put paid to hopes for an Armenia encompassing former Ottoman territories.

The failure to create an independent Armenian nation state meant that conceptions of international responsibility were transformed and refocused on the resettlement of refugees. The League of Nations emerged as the main forum for international engagement, and from 1923 its High Commission for Refugees extended its responsibilities to Armenians. While safeguarding Europe from the perils of displacement was the greater concern of the High Commission, advocates of the Armenian cause nonetheless quickly began to coalesce around it, viewing it as a means to fulfil their own aims.[18] The AND lobbied hard for the extension of the Nansen passport to Armenian refugees. Their interventions soon entangled the League in developing plans for the mass resettlement of displaced Armenians in Soviet Armenia.

---

[14] Peter Holquist, 'The Politics and Practice of the Russian Occupation of Armenia, 1915 – February 1917', in *A Question of Genocide: Armenians and Turks at the end of the Ottoman Empire*, ed. Ronald Grigor Suny, Fatma Muge Gocek, and Norman M. Naimark (New York: Oxford University Press, 2011).

[15] Peter Gatrell, *A Whole Empire Walking: Refugees in Russia during World War I* (Bloomington, IN: Indiana University Press, 1999), Chapter 7, esp. 150–4.

[16] The AND functioned as a kind of representation for the diaspora or 'government in exile' during and after the Armenian Genocide.

[17] Erez Manela, *The Wilsonian Moment: Self-Determination and the International Origins of Anticolonial Nationalism* (Oxford: Oxford University Press, 2007).

[18] For an overview, Claudene Skran, *Refugees in Inter-War Europe: The Emergence of a Regime* (Oxford: Clarendon Press, 1995), 170–7.

Much of the Armenian diaspora, especially the Dashnak Party (the former leaders of the independent Republic), remained intensely hostile to Soviet rule.[19] However, by 1923 the liberal-leaning AND and the associated philanthropic organization the Armenian General Benevolent Union, the AGBU, had reconciled themselves to working with the Soviet state on the grounds that a Soviet Armenian nation was better than no Armenian nation at all.[20] From the Soviet perspective, the situation was equally complex. On the one hand, engaging with the Armenian issue had the potential to derail good relations with the Turkish Republic. On the other hand, engaging with Armenian displacement on an international scale offered an opportunity for the Soviet Union to speak the language of the diplomatic agendas of the interwar period. During the Lausanne negotiations, Chicherin, commissar for foreign affairs, presented a note indicating the intention to settle a considerable number of Armenian refugees in Soviet territory.[21] Although they had been 'arbitrarily' excluded from discussion of nearly all of the questions at the conference, this note stated that they could still contribute to their solution.

Relief in Soviet Armenia: Terms of engagement

Like the Armenian Republic that had gone before it, the Soviet Armenian state was entirely unequipped to respond to the crisis that it faced. Across the former Russian Empire, existing organizations providing refugee relief had been centralized by the new Soviet authorities as *Tsentroplenbezh* (the Central Collegium for Prisoners of War and Refugees, later *Tsentrevak,* The Central Evacuation Commission). By the time the Soviet Republic of Armenia was formed, the work of these organizations was largely focused on repatriation. In Armenia, however, the logistics of repatriation did not pose the main problem – the refugees had nowhere to go 'home' to.[22] Instead, the challenge lay in caring for 300,000 refugees and orphans in a country devastated by more than six years of conflict. In these circumstances, the *Revkom* took the practical step of turning to relief agencies like NER and the LMF, which had prior experience of aiding refugees in the region.

NER had left Armenia in the weeks leading up to the Soviet takeover but almost immediately afterwards the *Revkom* decreed that the 'continuation and development' of NER's work was 'very desirable', offering them guarantees against requisitions and pledging the support of military and civil authorities.[23] By the following year, NER had

---

[19] Panossian, *The Armenians*, 365–71.
[20] See, Raymond H. Kévorkian and Vahé Tachjian, *The Armenian General Benevolent Union: One Hundred Years of History* (Cairo, Egypt: s.n., 2006).
[21] HAA f.430, op.1, d.578, l.4. Copy of a note verbale from the delegation of Russian, Ukraine and Georgian to the presidents of the Lausanne Conference 27 January 1923.
[22] *Tsentroevak* were involved in the repatriation of Armenians from the North Caucasus and the interior of Soviet Russia to Armenia.
[23] HAA f.114, op.1, d.46, l.24 Invitation to NER to resume activities, Bekzadian, commissar for foreign affairs, Revkom Erivan 14 December 1920, l.17, also letter to Yarrow, director of the Caucasus Branch of NER from Delegation of Armenian SSR for negotiations with NER, 1921.

formally returned to Soviet Armenia.[24] This echoed developments in Soviet Russia, where, in the face of impending famine, international agencies had been invited into the country to provide food relief.[25] But international presence in Armenia would prove to be more protracted than in Russia. Over the next few years, NER's work, which initially focused on the care of around 30,000 orphans sheltered in the city of Leninakan (formerly Alexandropol, now Gyumri), expanded to encompass what might be more readily termed 'development' work, from medical and agricultural training to public health.[26] The LMF also resumed work on a smaller scale. By 1922, it included an orphanage for 150 children, a shelter for 68 homeless children and a feeding station in Yerevan for 470 children. They employed 150 refugee women for lace-making, knitting and sewing, provided work renovating gardens in Yerevan with the Commissariat for Agriculture, and provided food and seed for 1,615 people in Ashtarak. And they managed the resettlement of around 6,000 refugees in an 'agricultural colony' at Gamarloo (Ghamarlu, now Artashat), close to the Turkish border.[27]

Working in the Soviet world presented new challenges for NER and the LMF. On the surface at least, the languages of Christian duty and liberal imperialism through which they articulated their responsibility to Armenians were at odds with the vocabulary and vision of socialist transformation that underpinned Soviet rule. Stephen Kotkin has characterized Soviet society as one which had had learned to 'speak Bolshevik'. By the 1930s, he argues, a new official language of public expression was both unavoidable for engaging with the state and was internalized, and gave meaning to people's lives.[28] Critics have suggested that Kotkin's formulation may create an unwarranted impression of the fixed nature of Soviet ideology across time and space.[29] Nonetheless, recognition of the centrality of language for the Soviet project has continued, and the notion of 'speaking Bolshevik', or the alternative, broader, formulation 'speaking Soviet', has gained currency beyond Kotkin's original articulation.

In Armenia, a new language of Soviet transformation was developing. Jeremy Johnson has explained how the Council of People's Commissars sought to assign to

---

[24] The NER Executive Committee acknowledged the offer but stressed that NER as a 'purely humanitarian philanthropic association' must remain free from political associations. Rockefeller Archive Centre: NER Acc 2010:002 Box 1 Minutes of the Executive Committee, 25 February 1921.

[25] Nansen was involved in this work and had also been involved in prisoner of war exchanges with Russia. See, Bertrand M. Patenaude, *The Big Show in Bololand: The American Relief Expedition to Soviet Russia in the Famine of 1921* (Stanford, CA: Stanford University Press, 2002).

[26] NER's official account of their work in the Soviet Caucasus is provided in James Barton, *The Story of Near East Relief* (New York: The MacMillan Company, 1930).

[27] HAA f.114 op.2 d.35 Report on the work of the British Relief Mission for the Commissariat for Foreign Affairs, 18 May 1922, D. S. Northcote. The Norwegian missionary Bodil Biorn also cared for orphans. Her work remained somewhat separate and is documented. Inger Marie Okkenhaug, 'Refugees, Relief, and the Restoration of a Nation: Norwegian Mission in the Armenian Republic, 1922–1925', in *Protestant Mission and Local Encounters in the Nineteenth and Twentieth Centuries. Unto the Ends of the World*, ed. Hilde Nielssen, I. M. Okkenhaug, and Karina Hestad Skeie (Leiden: Brill, 2011), 207–32.

[28] Stephen Kotkin, *Magnetic Mountain: Stalinism as a Civilisation* (Berkeley: University of California Press, 1997), 224.

[29] Anna Krylova, 'Soviet Modernity: Stephen Kotkin and the Bolshevik Predicament', *Contemporary European History* 23, no. 2 (2014): 167–92.

'core Soviet ideas, organizations, and institutions', 'historical Armenian translations or words derived from Armenian roots'. As Johnson points out, despite these efforts, there was often a 'slippage' between ideal and reality, as well as great potential for mistranslation and misinterpretation.[30] International relief interventions thus took place during a period of flux, where the leaders of the new Soviet Armenian government were themselves learning how to 'speak Soviet'. As an anti-Soviet uprising in Armenia was quashed in March 1921 and war communism gave way to the New Economic Policy (NEP) in spring 1921, the meaning of being, or speaking Soviet in Armenia was shifting. This was accompanied by a recognition from the centre that Transcaucasia was 'different', that the building of socialism would have a different pace.[31] Given these circumstances, it is perhaps not surprising that international actors' grasp of the evolving Soviet system and its vocabulary of rule and transformation was shaky. That they frequently referred to the Soviet Republic of Armenia as the 'Erivan Republic', sometimes reflected a desire to avoid using the term 'Soviet', but it also often reflected their confusion regarding the geography of Soviet power and their doubts about its future.

The evolving and uncertain meanings of socialist transformation in Soviet Armenia gave international relief agencies room to manoeuvre, leaving spaces open for them to pursue their own agendas. Against a background of upheaval they sought to formally define the terms of their encounter with the new Soviet Armenian authorities. Even in the interim period before NER formally returned, Clarence Ussher, a missionary doctor who had stayed behind when NER officially left Armenia, appealed to the new commissar for foreign affairs for a 'written guarantee' of the 'inviolability of American property'. He modelled this request upon his previous experience in the Ottoman Empire.[32] The British relief agent Hubert Harcourt soon requested a 'mandate' like that which had been granted to NER in May of that year.[33] Communications between NER and the Commissariat a few months later over the Soviet seizure of a property, the 'Nercessabad Farm', suggest that a formal mandate did not necessarily prevent misunderstanding.[34]

From 1922, the government of the Transcaucasian Federation (TSFSR), of which Armenia had become part of in December 1922, sought to formalize their relationship with international agencies, creating a special representative for foreign aid organizations. For much of this period this representative was Nariman Ter-

---

[30] In the 1940s, many of these terms were 'internationalized' using Russian-derived words. Jeremy Johnson, 'Speaking Soviet in an Armenian Accent', in *Empire and Belonging in Eurasia*, ed. Lewis Siegelbaum and Krista Goff (Ithaca: Cornell University Press, 2019), 138.

[31] This was articulated in Lenin's 'Letter to the Caucasian Communists'. Lenin urged 'greater gentleness, caution, concessions in dealing with the petty bourgeoisie, the intelligentsia and especially the peasantry'. Quoted in Ronald Grigor Suny, *Looking Toward Ararat: Armenia in Modern History* (Bloomington: Indiana University Press, 1993), 140.

[32] HAA, f.114, op,1, d.22, l.10 Letter Ussher to Bekzadian, 17 December 1920.

[33] HAA f.114, op.2, d.104, 19 Letter from Harcourt to Commissariat for Foreign Affairs, 19 September 1921.

[34] HAA f.114, op.2, d.22, l. 208, Sutton (NER) to Commissar for Foreign Affairs, 1 July 1921.

Ghazarian.³⁵ The representative was based in Tbilisi with offices in the main areas where NER initially worked – Erivan, Baku, Alexandropol and Djalal-Oghli. From 1922, a series of formal agreements outlined the responsibilities of international actors and the limits of their work.³⁶ These were renewed and sometimes renegotiated on a yearly basis. The 1923 agreement between NER and the TSFSR included provisions that the organization would support 25,000 orphans, providing the necessary food and clothes, as well as schools, agricultural training and medical aid. The 1924 mandate included a supplementary 'labour agreement' dictating the terms of employment for local staff employed by NER.³⁷

Such agreements are indicative of a growing desire on the part of the government of the Transcaucasian Federation to ensure that the work of international agencies did not encroach on key elements of Soviet transformation. They suggest that as far as the Soviet Armenian and Transcaucasian governments were concerned, international relief workers were neither equal partners nor entirely trustworthy. From the start, they placed strict limits on the activities of international agencies and explicitly forbade then from undertaking political, commercial or religious propaganda. Foreign workers who violated this clause could be expelled.³⁸ From 1923 more provisions were made to monitor educational work. The programme of NER schools and orphanages was to correspond to that of state schools and teachers were to be confirmed in their position by the 'Commissariat of Public Instruction'. Such sensitivity over education had pre-Soviet precedents. In 1919, NER had taken responsibility for orphans in the independent Republic. The decision to hand over the care and education of Armenian children to an international organization, as Nora Nercessian documents, had even then prompted protests and tensions with the Ministry of Education.³⁹ Despite the 1923 provisions, education continued to be a concern for the Soviet authorities. As Nercessian explains, they sought to counter the influence of NER-style education by cultivating secret communist boys clubs, *patkoms,* in the orphanages.⁴⁰

Channels of communication

Despite these official agreements, communication and cooperation were not always straightforward for those working in Soviet territory. In part, this was a matter of language. Eastern Armenian was adopted as the official language of Armenia, and the

---

[35] . Contemporary History Archive of Georgia, sakartvelos uakhlesi ist'oriis tsent'raluri arkivi (suita), suita, f.617, op.1, d.113, ll. 2-3, Report on the work of the representative of zaksovnarkom for foreign aid organizations in Transcaucasia and the activities of the American Committee for Relief in the Near East and British Aid Mission for Children.

[36] These echoed the agreements negotiated with the American Relief Administration. See Patenaude, *The Big Show in Bololand,* 39–48.

[37] suita f.617, op.1, d.193, ll. 14-18, 1923 agreement (Russian); Rockefeller, NER Acc 2009:104, RG1 (FA406), Series 1 project files, Box 9, 1924 agreement (English).

[38] suita, f.617, op.1, d.193, ll. 14-18, 1923 agreement.

[39] Nora N. Nercessian, *The City of Orphans: Relief Workers, Commissars and the 'Builders of the New Armenia' Alexandropol/Leninakan 1919-1931* (Hollis, NH: Hollis Publishing, 2016), 19; 48–9.

[40] Ibid., 257.

policy of *Korenizatsiia* (indigenization) meant that Armenian language was actively promoted as part of the Soviet Armenian nation-building project.[41] Language and literacy were instruments, in the words of Suny, to 'integrate the Armenians into the new political order'.[42] From campaigns to eradicate illiteracy to the use of Armenian language in arts, culture and education, this part of the Soviet agenda chimed with the agenda of both international relief agencies and the diaspora to use language as a means of preserving or cultivating Armenian identity.[43] By 1926, NER had even produced their own Armenian-language textbook for use in their orphanages and schools in Soviet Armenia. This shared commitment to the Armenian language thus reflected something much more fundamental to the ability of international actors and the Soviet Union to cooperate in Armenia, a shared recognition of the importance of cultivating Armenians as a *nation*.

Nonetheless, no matter the extent to which ideals of international cooperation were united, language could be the cause of complexities in communication. On his visit to Armenia in 1926, the League's High Commissioner for Refugees, Nansen, relied on translators for communication with Soviet commissars and technical experts. He did not hesitate to judge that 'the Armenian language did not sound well in speech-making; it is strong perhaps, but rather staccato, especially when compared to Russian, which is more fluid'.[44] Russian was used frequently in official communications within the Soviet Union. When the LMF sought new staff in 1926, they noted that 'a knowledge of the Russian or Armenian languages would be invaluable but not essential'.[45] Many Soviet officials and diaspora representatives meanwhile communicated in French. The LMF and NER both meanwhile relied upon Armenian staff, who played a vital role as intermediaries, making everyday work and communication possible. However, crucial though they were, their voices and experiences are much less present in the archival records of these agencies that those of international personnel.[46]

---

[41] On Soviet nationalities policy, T. Martin, *The Affirmative Action Empire: Nations and Nationalism in the Soviet Union, 1923-1939* (Ithaca: Cornell University Press, 2001); Yuri Slezkine, 'The USSR as a Communal Apartment, or How a Socialist State Promoted Ethnic Particularism', *Slavic Review* 53, no. 2 (1994): 414–52. On Armenia, Maike Lehmann, 'Apricot Socialism: The National Past, the Soviet Project, and the Imagining of Community in Late Soviet Armenia', *Slavic Review* 74, no. 1 (April 2015): 9–31.

[42] Suny, *Looking Toward Ararat,* 144.

[43] Emma Cushman, a missionary employed by the League of Nations Commission for the Protection of Women and Children in the Near East, described how in the Constantinople 'neutral house' children rescued from Turkish or Kurdish homes they had been taken into during the Genocide 'once more learned the Armenian language and sang Armenian hymns'. Cushman, report to the secretary general of the League of Nations, 16 July 1922, India Office Library L/E/7/1230/1585. Quoted in Gatrell and Laycock, 'Armenia: The Nationalisation, Internationalisation and Representation of the Refugee Crisis', in *Homelands: War, Population and Statehood in Eastern Europe and Russia, 1918-1924*, ed. Nick Baron and Peter Gatrell (London: Anthem Press, 2004), 97.

[44] Fridtjof Nansen, *Armenia and the Near East* (New York: Da Capo Press, 1976), 168.

[45] STC EJ 5 Armenia Correspondence 1926–7, Buxton to Ruth Fry, 13 January 1926.

[46] In 1923, about 3,000 staff worked for NER in Soviet Armenia. The British Relief Mission employed at this point just one British staff member and seventy-seven Armenians. Local staff working for NER were the object of particular interest for the Transcaucasian authorities, who sought to incorporate them into trade unions. suita, f.617, op.1, d.113, ll.3-4 on the work of the representative of zaksovnarkom for foreign aid organizations in Transcaucasia

The language situation was complicated further by the Soviet orthographic reforms undertaken between 1922 and 1924, which helped crystallize the distinction between the two variants of Armenian, Western (spoken by the Armenians of the former Ottoman Empire) and Eastern (the official language of the Soviet Republic).[47] While Soviet educational and literacy programmes utilized the reformed version, NER for the most part seemed to continue to use the pre-reform Western variant. In subsequent decades, an intense language politics evolved around the use and authenticity of Western and Eastern Armenian.[48] However, the archives of diaspora and relief organizations do not suggest that during the early 1920s they were particularly preoccupied by this issue.

Beyond the difficulties of translation, international actors working in Soviet Armenia also had to negotiate an alien bureaucracy and structure of government. Official lines of responsibility and authority shifted considerably during the period.[49] From 1922, Armenia was not a constituent Republic of the Soviet Union in its own right, but rather as part of the TSFSR. In practice, this meant that while the LMF and NER had arrived with the intention of aiding Armenians, they also had to contend with Moscow, as well as the sometimes conflicting interests of Georgia and Azerbaijan. This is an important reminder that Soviet Union did not necessarily engage in international projects as a single, monolithic bloc, republics and regions could also, to some degree, pursue their own local agendas.

Even within the different parts of the Soviet system concerned with Armenian refugees, there was rich potential for confusion and misunderstanding. In November 1925, for example, the Commissariat for Foreign Affairs complained to Sahag Ter-Gabrielian (representative of the Transcaucasian Federation to the RSFSR) about negotiations rumoured to be taking place in Constantinople to organize the resettlement of Armenians from Turkey in Soviet territory. Who was directing this without their permission? they demanded.[50] As the range of organizations involved expanded, so did the possibilities for misunderstandings. In May 1924, for example, Major Johnson at the High Commission wrote to Nouradoughian of the AND, reporting that Nansen's representative in Moscow, John Gorvin, had been told by a representative of the Soviet government that there were misapprehensions in Moscow about the scheme. Johnson appeared understandably frustrated, expressing his desire for the AND and the High Commission to arrive at a 'common programme'.[51]

---

[47] These reforms modified both the alphabet and the spelling of Armenian. A second reform in the 1940s reversed some of the changes made by the first. See Mouradian, *l'Armenie*, 185–202 and Johnson, 'Speaking Soviet'.

[48] As Claire Mouradian suggests, language often has a 'sacred' character for Armenians, 'like the cross, it is often worn as a medallion, as an emblem of identity' Claire Mouradian, *l'Armenie: De Staline a Gorbatchev, histoire d'une republique sovietique* (Paris: Editions Ramsay, 1990), 191. Western Armenian is an endangered language. UNESCO *Atlas of Endangered Languages* (2010 http://www.unesco.org/languages-atlas/).

[49] . The November 1922 'mandate' NER was signed by the representative of the RSFSR, Moscow. HAA, f.114, op.1, d.283, ll. 7-11. D. The 1923 mandate, in contrast, was signed by the TSFSR, Tbilisi, suita, f.617, op.1, d.193, ll. 14-18.

[50] NAA, f.113, op. 3 d.127, l.16, Commissariat for Foreign Affairs to Ter-Gabrielian, 25 November 1925.

[51] HAA f.430, op.1, d.1256, l.43. Johnson to Nouradoughian, 14 May 1924.

Among international agencies, there was often confusion regarding where authority lay as well as a readiness to subvert the complexities of the Soviet system. When conflict arose over religious education among orphans in Armenia, Harold Buxton, leading light of the LMF, suggested from afar that they should 'appeal to Moscow if necessary, over the heads of the Caucasian government'.[52] Attempts to take advantage of international incomprehension of the Soviet Union's workings was also not uncommon. For example, when the AND sought the assistance of the Rockefeller Foundation for public health work in Soviet Armenia in 1926, they stated to the Foundation's Paris office that the Republic of Armenia was 'entirely autonomous', and they had authority to negotiate with the Foundation 'without the approval of the government in Leningrad'.[53]

Some diaspora organizations also sought to bypass official Soviet lines of communication. In September 1921, the Hayastani Ognut'yun Komite (Armenian Aid Committee, HOK) had been established to cultivate diasporan involvement with the Soviet 'homeland'.[54] The liberal-leaning AGBU and AND, however, chose to manage their relationship with Soviet Armenia on their terms, initially making contact in Moscow through their representative Papadjanian, rather than through HOK channels.[55] As Vahé Tachjian has demonstrated, despite an apparent consensus over the status of the Soviet Republic as home for Armenian refugees, reconciling Soviet and diasporan priorities would prove difficult, with the relationship defined as much by conflict over aims, methods and funds as a shared vision of the Armenian future.[56]

Positive personal experiences and relationships, in contrast, could sometimes overcome negative stereotypes of the 'Bolsheviks' and smooth the process of cooperation. Soon after the Soviet takeover, Clarence Ussher wrote to NER contacts that 'the Bolsheviks are very moderate and very different from what we were led to expect from the stories of Russia.... One cannot help feeling sympathy for them and a measure of praise in spite of any mistakes they make.'[57] A year later, Harold Buxton, who had got to know Soviet Armenia in his capacity as secretary of the LMF, wrote in a report for Nansen's famine relief committee that 'it is obvious that the Soviet officials are now doing their best – working as they do under enormous difficulties, such as would tax the abilities of the most experienced administrators of any country. The

---

[52] Save the Children Fund, EJ16 Correspondence, Notes and reports of Rev. H Buxton 1920–8, Letter, Harold Buxton to Magda Coe, 9 November 1924. Bodil Biorn was forced to end her work in Soviet Armenia because of its over-religious dimensions

[53] Rockefeller Foundation Records, projects RG 1.1 (FA386) Series 804 Near East Region, Subseries 804.A: Near East Region – Medical Sciences, Folder 3 Medical Education in Armenia, Palestine and other minor Near East Countries, Preliminary Report, 'Inter-Office Correspondence – From Dr. Pearce's Diary', 21 May 1926.

[54] On the foundation of HOK, Vahé Sahakyan, 'Between Host-Countries and Homeland: Institutions, Politics and Identities in the Post-Genocide Armenian Diaspora (1920s to 1980s)' (PhD diss., University of Michigan, 2015), 159–60.

[55] Papadjanian was a former member of both the Duma and the Armenian Republic's delegation to the Paris Peace Conference; he thus had the communication skills and connections to connect with all parties concerned.

[56] Vahé Tachjian, 'Humanitarian Diaspora: The AGBU in Soviet Armenia 1920-1930', in *Aid to Armenia: Humanitarianism and Intervention from the 1890s to the Present*, ed. Jo Laycock and Francesca Piana (Manchester: Manchester University Press, 2020).

[57] HAA f.114, op.1, d.22, l.7 letter Ussher to Randolph and Mosher, Erivan 26 December 1920.

Commissars are uniformly sincere and hard-working men who share the poverty and privations of the whole people.'[58]

This is not to suggest that relations between the Soviet authorities and international actors were without conflict. The diaries of NER overseas director Barclay Acheson, documenting a visit to Soviet Armenia in July 1927, are full of frustration with the Soviet authorities, who had arrested some of their local staff: 'Knowing as I do that our organisation is full of spies, I don't see why the government should want to quiz these employees. We have never had any secrets anyway.'[59] Acheson's criticism was not restricted to the Soviet authorities. He could be equally critical about his own Caucasus staff: 'Miss Chickering' was said to be 'too fat to be energetic ... unless she is prodded up, she will degenerate in her work'.[60] There was also frequently a gap between the professed ideals of relief agencies and their practices. Individuals would not necessarily follow the instructions of their organizations and sometimes took matters into their own hands. Clarence Ussher claimed that when NER left the Armenian Republic, 'he took it [their work] up without waiting for authorisation and everything is going full swing.'[61]

Bridging the gap? Languages of expertise

As the interactions described earlier demonstrate, among the circles of Soviet and international actors engaged in relief in Soviet Armenia personal and professional relationships could both facilitate cooperation and be a source of conflict. As local and long-distance relationships between the different parties evolved, each also undertook to gain a more in-depth formal knowledge of the situation, producing reports regarding their own work and that of their partners. Soviet officials commissioned multiple reports on the situation in Armenia, gathering information on numbers, location and condition of refugees.[62] They also closely monitored the work of international relief agents.[63] Such reports passed between different branches of government and the different layers of Soviet power, from the Republic, through to the Transcaucasian Federation and ultimately to Moscow.

The Soviet Armenian and Transcaucasian authorities also produced extensive figures and reports for international agencies in Soviet Armenia. In turn, these organizations sent 'fact-finding' missions of their own to the Soviet Republic. Rather

[58] Rockefeller Foundation Records, Projects RG 1.1. (FA386), Series 100 International, subseries 100 N: International – war relief, Folder 724, Turkish relief general correspondence, July to December 1916. Copy of Report submitted to Nansen on Famine Conditions in Transcaucasia, January 1922, Harold Buxton and Archag Safrastian.
[59] Rockefeller Archive Center, NER Acc: Box 135, Acheson Diary, part II of II, 16 July 1927 entry.
[60] Rockefeller Archive Center, NER Acc: Box 135, Acheson Diary, part II of II, 30 July 1927 entry. More fundamental differences in NER's leadership would emerge in years to come over the question of the organization's future direction.
[61] HAA f.114, op.1, d.22, l.7 letter Ussher to Randolph and Mosher, Erivan 26 December 1920.
[62] E.g. HAA, f. 113, op. 3, d. 81, ll. 12–17, Report on Refugee Question (undated, likely 1925).
[63] suita, f.617, op.1, d.113, ll. 8-16, 'on the work of the Transcaucasian department of the American Committee for Relief in the Near East'.

than gathering eyewitness information about the refugees, these tended to be driven by the agencies' own priorities. NER's leadership visited the country repeatedly, as documented in Acheson's diaries. As the organization contemplated its future role, they sent a number of experts in the field of education and philanthropy to Soviet Armenia to assess their own work. In 1924, their work in the Caucasus was surveyed in *Reconstruction in the Near East*. The authors confidently assessed that the time was ripe for NER to bring about change: 'The Republics of the Caucasus are longing for something to happen.... Traditionalism has gone to the slag dump. The time is right for a new and better day.'[64]

In 1922, Save the Children (who provided the majority of funds for the LMF) had sent their director of European Relief, Dr Armstrong Smith, on a tour examining the situation in Armenia. His findings were not only compiled in the official Save the Children report but also shared with potential donors in a series of articles, 'A Doctor's Rounds', in their monthly publication.[65] Nor did the diaspora take knowledge of their proposed homeland for granted. The Armenian delegation sent multiple, sometimes overlapping missions to Soviet Armenia. Their principal purpose was to assess the viability of the country as a home for orphans in their care or larger resettlement programmes. Garikian, who visited in 1923, investigated 'industry, economic conditions and laws'. He was, his report stated, in 'constant and direct' contact with the 'commissars, bureaucrats and technical experts'. He placed the AND in a position of authority over the refugees as the 'supreme tutor of these remnants of our race', and concluded that they should be repatriated to Soviet Armenia.[66]

The reports of investigatory visits reflect the belief of the leaderships of relief agencies and diaspora organizations that in order to 'know' Soviet Armenia they needed the perspective of 'experts', rather than Soviet reports, the first-hand experiences of relief workers or even the perspectives of refugees themselves. Such official reports tend to occupy more space in the archival record that accounts of the mundane and everyday work of 'ordinary' relief workers, both international and local Armenian staff. Nonetheless, the importance of the everyday work in shaping both relations between the different actors and practices of relief on the ground in Armenia should not be underestimated.

The 'investigation' of Soviet Armenia took a new form after the Asia-Minor population exchanges provided for in the Lausanne Treaty put the Armenian refugee population sheltering in Greece under increasing pressure. At this point, the League began to seriously investigate the possibility of mass resettlement on Soviet territory, establishing a series of committees of inquiry. Plans for the irrigation and resettlement of four areas were presented to the League by representatives of Soviet Armenia. It was envisaged that the irrigation and drainage necessary for these schemes would be paid for by a loan from one of the European powers; once refugees had been resettled, the surplus from their plots would be sufficient both to support them and pay off the loan.

---

[64] Paul Monroe, R. Reeder, James Vance et al., *Reconstruction in the Near East* (New York, 1924).
[65] *Record of Save the Children*, no. 19, 15 June 1922, 292.
[66] HAA, f.430, op.1, d.346 Report by Garikian mission (French). On other AND/AGBU investigatory missions, see Tachjian, 'Humanitarian Diaspora? The AGBU in Soviet Armenia 1920-30s'

The League scrutinized the plans drawing on the technical expertise of a number of engineers. Their technical reports and discussions dominated the planning and investigation of the scheme.⁶⁷ The presentation of this project as a scientific or technocratic exercise had the benefit of distancing the project from its political context and the ideological conflicts that this may have raised. It also perhaps reflects the way that certain characteristics of *modern* states were evident in both the Soviet world and 'the west'.⁶⁸ Given this context, the shared use of languages of rational planning and commitment to 'scientific' interventions intended to transform society and economy that were evident in the Nansen schemes was hardly surprising. In these discussions, Armenian landscape was abstracted from the contemporary context and 'primitive' – not as a result of the recent war but more generally devoid of history, echoing Timothy Mitchell's observations of how modern 'development' relies on the construction of an 'object of development' which is entirely natural and outside social and political relations.⁶⁹ The landscape was also portrayed as inert or passive. Only through rational planning and the application of technical expertise could what NER's Charles Vickery termed the 'latent natural resources of Armenia' be awakened.⁷⁰

The planning of the Nansen schemes relied on a language of quantification and measurement. This was not simply a matter of measuring the landscape and environment, but also the population. Both relief agencies and multiple arms of the Soviet government collected data about the refugee population, measuring them against a series of 'norms'. The language used to describe the movement of refugees was often transactional: 'We note that you have been successful in carrying out the scheme of substituting five NER children for our five rejected ones for despatch to Cyprus.'⁷¹ The approach taken in the Nansen schemes echoed this. They were based on the figure of a standard refugee who represented a norm on which calculations could be based. This refugee (and by default his family) could then be assigned a regular amount of land which would yield predictable crops for subsistence and surplus. The success of this scheme thus depended on assumption of predictability which erased individual preferences and historical contingencies.

A shared commitment to rational planning could not overcome the financial barriers to the Nansen schemes, and by 1926 it had become clear that they would not come to fruition. The League turned its attention to resettlement in the Middle East, while the Soviet Union continued to work with the diaspora, on a much smaller scale,

---

⁶⁷ An engineer was sent by the League to Soviet Armenia in 1924 to work with the Transcaucasian irrigation engineers. William Kinder (formerly chief engineer to the Egyptian government) was sent to Erivan to scrutinize and finalize the plans in 1925. His reports were then assessed by Sir Murdoch MacDonald as part of a special League committee set up to review Nansen's reports. LON Nansen Fonds, Commission files, ILO, Russian Refugees, C1424/320/Ra.400/0/1 Special Armenian Committee Under Auspices of League of Nations (Erivan).

⁶⁸ For example, David Hoffman, *Cultivating the Masses: Modern State Practices and Soviet Socialism* (Ithaca: Cornell University Press, 2011); Stephen Kotkin, 'Modern Times: The Soviet Union and the Interwar Conjuncture', *Kritika* 2, no.1 (2001): 111–64.

⁶⁹ Timothy Mitchell, *The Rule of Experts: Egypt: Techno-Politics, Modernity* (Berkeley: University of California Press, 2002), 210.

⁷⁰ HAA f.430 op.1, d. 1251, ll. 1-3, Vickery (NER) to Nouradoughian (AND), 15 September 1923.

⁷¹ STC EJ8 Armenia Correspondence I 1923-27 Letter International Migration Service in Athens, 1 December 1925.

until the early 1930s. The LMF's exit from Armenia also came in 1926, as a result of diminishing funds and need in the Soviet Republic. In 1930, Barclay Acheson and Ter-Ghazarian signed a formal agreement regarding the liquidation of NER's remaining work in the Caucasus.[72] Ter-Ghazarian wrote cordially to Acheson, expressing gratitude for the NER's work.[73] The relationship ultimately ended in conflict, as a number of local Armenians employed by NER were arrested. In a communication to staff in the Caucasus, NER leaders in New York attributed this to political changes in the USSR: 'The central authority at Moscow apparently decided to disavow many of their previous arrangements with the semi-independent Caucasus governments and to dominate more completely Caucasus affairs. This led to the removal of some of our closest friends in high positions.'[74] International agencies would not return to the region until the very end of the Soviet period, in the aftermath of the Armenian earthquake in 1988.

Conclusions

In early Soviet Armenia, international cooperation was a product of improvisation and negotiation, in which there was little explicit discussion of internationalist ideals. All parties sought to formally define the terms of their engagement, but on the ground in the Soviet Republic, relationships were frequently makeshift and improvised, reflecting the priorities, prejudices and practical experience of individuals as much as the professed ideals of states and non-state organizations. Interactions on the ground were shaped by the circumstances of hardship and upheaval which characterized early Soviet Armenia. Communications between multiple actors, in multiple languages and sometimes across long distances, were slow and unwieldy, leading to frequent misunderstandings but also opening up possibilities to subvert or bypass regulations or prevailing assumptions.

The nature of the archival record means that the picture of international cooperation in Soviet Armenia remains incomplete. The records of international relief agencies like NER are vast, incomplete and often inconsistent, skewed towards the exceptional and the official rather than the mundane or routine. Soviet archives meanwhile provide plentiful, detailed reports about conditions and interventions but reveal much less of the personal opinions, experiences and interactions of those engaging with the displaced 'on the ground'. Nonetheless, paying attention to this case offers the opportunity to draw attention to actors often marginalized in interwar histories of humanitarianism, not least the diaspora activists who variously acted as lobbyists, intermediaries and sometimes antagonists. These actors do not fit neatly into the established categories of 'Soviet' or 'western', which frequently shape histories of internationalism and its limits.

Examining the nature of relief in early Soviet Armenia highlights the need for a more nuanced understanding of the place of the Soviet Union in interwar international

---

[72] Rockefeller, NER Acc 2009:104, RG1 (FA406), Series 1 project files, Box 9, folder 'Russian Contracts'.
[73] Rockefeller, NER Acc 2009:104, RG1 (FA406), Series 1 project files, Box 9, folder 'Russian Contracts', letter Ter-Ghazarian – Acheson, 7 August 1930.
[74] Rockefeller, NER Acc Box 134, Inter-state communications, 10 March 1931.

networks and organizations. In this context at least, the Soviet Union was not simply the 'other' of an emerging liberal international order and emerging refugee regime. Soviet engagements with Armenian displacement were by no means homogenous. Soviet Armenian government and society may have been *learning* to 'speak Soviet' during the 1920s, but this was not the only mode of communication available. Not only was the meaning of 'soviet' in this peripheral region of the Soviet Union in a state of flux, but it was still possible to deploy different registers in different contexts, in order to achieve particular ends. It is tempting to understand projects for the relief and resettlement of refugees in the Soviet Republic of Armenia as bridging an ideological divide, but on the ground international cooperation between the Soviet Union, diaspora organizations, relief agencies and the League of Nations in Armenia was characterized by an uneven picture of consensus and conflict which did not always map clearly onto a Cold War-style divide. Ideological differences certainly helped shape the encounter between Soviet and international actors, but they were not the end of the story.

6

Yugoslav refugees and British relief workers in Italian and Egyptian refugee camps, 1944–6[1]

Kornelija Ajlec

With Italy capitulating in September of 1943, a wide liberated area formed in the previously occupied territory that is now known as the Croatian Adriatic coast, consisting mostly of Dalmatia. Before the end of the year, the power vacuum created by Italy's withdrawal was filled by the units of the German Reich, despite great resistance from the Yugoslav National Liberation Army (YNLA) – the Partisans, led by Josip Broz Tito. During the interim period, civilians fled before the new occupier. Assisted by the Partisans, they migrated to the islands in the Adriatic Sea. The last point in this route was the island of Vis, which is one of the most distant islands from the continental coast and the island most fortified by the Partisans at that time. Within a short period of time the 8,000 inhabitants of Vis were joined by twice as many refugees, who inevitably started exhausting the food supplies.[2] As a result, the Partisan leadership decided to establish contact for the first time with the Anglo-American Allies in the south of Italy. On 23 December 1943, the Allies informed the Partisans that they would accept up to 1,000 Yugoslav refugees per day, but only on the condition that they would be transferred from Italy to refugee camps set up in Egypt, and as soon as possible.[3]

This chapter looks at what happened next. These Yugoslav refugees became one of the few population groups in Central and Southern Europe who managed to escape the advancement of the Axis powers in Europe. They came under the auspices of the Allies, who provided them with accommodation, food and other supply. Their subsequent paths were not completely unique: like them, groups of Greek[4] and Polish

---

[1] The research for this chapter was made possible by the national project *Refugees – A Never-Ending Story* (J6-8249) and the national programme *Slovene History* (P6-0325). I am grateful to all my colleagues and the editors of this volume to have taken the time to read and give comments on the paper.

[2] Albert Klun, *Iz Afrike v narodnoosvobodilno vojsko Jugoslavije* (Ljubljana: Partizanska knjiga, 1976), 243.

[3] Veseljko Huljić, *Lokalni, općejugoslovenski i medjunarodni značaj otoka Visa u narodnooslobodilačkoj borbi* (PhD diss., Philosophical Faculty, University of Belgrade, Belgrade, 1968), 190.

[4] Greek refugees took shelter in Aleppo in present-day Syria, Souk El Gharb in present-day Lebanon and Nuseirat in Palestine immediately after the invasion of the German Army in 1941. They also represented the first group of refugees in Egypt, for which the refugee camp was set up. At first it was placed in Cairo on the Gezira Island; however, in 1942 it was moved to the Moses' Wells oasis

refugees[5] also fled to the Middle East. However, what *was* unique about the Yugoslav case was how their camps in Egypt were run and organized, consisting of a two-tiered administration: the principal one carried out by the Western Allies and the secondary one carried out by the refugees themselves. For historians, this created unique meeting points of very different groups of people who each had very different ideas about the international management of refugees, and about internationalism more generally. As a result, this is a telling case study that provides us with important glimpses of the 'lived experience' of internationalism in the Allied-run refugee camps in Egypt, where various different and at times directly contradictory perspectives on internationalism came into contact, with important and lasting results for both Allied soldiers and administrators on the one hand and Yugoslav refugees on the other.

Regardless of which groups of refugees in the Middle East are under review, it is clear that relations between them, the civilian humanitarian workers and the military remain largely unexplored. The story of the Yugoslav refugees, in particular, has mostly been studied as a local case study, disconnected from any broader context and only sporadically understood in the context of the national framework.[6] However, a closer investigation of the archives and memoirs reveals that this micro-universe of refugee camps gave rise to an unexpected and unusual, yet important, dynamic of transnational cooperation, which can only be understood in the context of ideas about internationalism and international cooperation more broadly. The policies dictated by Washington or London only shaped developments here indirectly. Instead, it was the relationships on the ground that truly and fully shaped the reality of what transnational cooperation looked like. By contrast, the official histories about the Egyptian camps were largely written from the top-to-bottom perspective, often omitting interpersonal relations as irrelevant or of lesser importance.[7]

These individual stories were defined by a strict hierarchy, which placed the Allied military at the top and the refugees at the bottom. Communication between them was initially difficult since both sides stereotyped *the other*. Stereotypical labelling and attributing different personality traits to others was then and is now a daily occurrence. Group identity is also always characterized by attitudes towards other groups or group identities, especially towards those whom we believe contradict our own habits,

---

on the Sinai Peninsula. More in: Gary Wiener, *Refugees Throughout History: Searching for Safety* (New York: Lucent Press, 2018).

[5] After liberation in 1942, the liberated Poles from Siberian Gulags arrived in Persia, where they were placed in either civilian or military camps. Via Palestine and Egypt, some of the civilians were transferred to British refugee camps in East Africa and to Australia, and some even to Mexico. The soldiers made up the core of the Anders Army, which fought against German forces in Italy alongside the Allies. More in Jadwiga Szelazek Morrison, *From Exile to Eden: A Family Journal* (San Francisco: Turning Stone Press, 2012).

[6] By national framework, I am referring to Yugoslav framework prior 1991 and Croat framework after 1991 and the disintegration of Yugoslavia and Yugoslav historiography.

[7] George Woodbridge published UNRRA's history in a three-volume work in 1950. It was mostly based on the compilation of histories written by the chiefs of individual UNRRA missions and offices upon its closure. It does not include mentions of work on the ground or personal histories of those involved. The histories which formed the basis of his work are archived at the United Nations archives in New York City, while Woodbridge archive is at the Columbia University. George Woodbridge, *UNRRA. The History of the United Nations Relief and Rehabilitation Administration*, Vol. 1-3 (New York:Columbia University Press, 1950).

traditions and interests.⁸ When unfamiliar with 'the other', stereotypes and prejudice are inevitable. This reality proved paramount in the Egyptian camps from the start.

Yugoslavia overall was not directly influenced by Great Britain, with the partial exception of some upper-class Yugoslavs. Moreover, Britain was not the primary immigration destination for Yugoslav nationals. Until the first half of the twentieth century, the territory of Yugoslavia was not in the British sphere of interest. Consequently, the attitude of Yugoslavia's population overall towards the British was ambivalent at best, the vague negative stereotyping revolving around the proverbial British reservedness. At the same time, in the eyes of British writers of travelogues and fiction the territory of Yugoslavia and the Balkan area signified the border with the exotic East.⁹ It was never fully incorporated into the Orient, even though large areas of Yugoslavia had been a part of the Ottoman Empire for almost five centuries. The majority of the population in the Christian areas preserved their religion, and, unlike the Middle East, the Yugoslav provinces were never subjected to Western colonialism.¹⁰ The area thus remained relatively unknown in the West, forming a distinct identity. Some British books presented a romanticized image of Yugoslavia in the 1920s and 1930s – think *Murder on the Orient Express*.¹¹ Quite a few staff members of the Allied humanitarian organizations during and after the Second World War were attracted by this image and wanted to work in Yugoslavia or with Yugoslavs.¹² In Egypt, the early work done in the Allied refugee camps produced the blueprint for all the procedures later implemented in refugee camps across Europe after the end of the war, giving this story an important motive to further investigate it.

This chapter focuses on the administrators' and refugees' individual stories and viewpoints, emphasizing their struggles to understand *the other* through often-strained relationships. The focus here is less on the official reports and histories, which at best offered only a hazy idea of the situation on the ground. By contrast, this chapter draws heavily on personal notes and memoirs, which give a much clearer view of a complicated 'internationalism in practice' or 'lived internationalism'. As such, this chapter provides an important corrective to a historiography so often focused on the top sections of international organizations and their structures.

---

⁸ Janek Musek, *Psihološki portret Slovencev* (Ljubljana: Znanstveno in publicistično središče, 1994), 7; Theresa Vescio and Kevin Weaver. *Prejudice and Stereotyping*. http://oxfordindex.oup.com/view/10.1093/obo/9780199828340-0097 (June 2019).

⁹ Before the Second World War broke out, Robert Seton Watson, Agatha Christie, Rebecca West, Lawrence Durrell and others wrote about the Balkans and Yugoslavia. Eugene Michail, *The British and the Balkans. Forming Images of Foreign Lands, 1900–1950* (London: Continuum, 2011).

¹⁰ Milica Bakić-Hayden, 'Nesting Orientalisms: The Case of Former Yugoslavia', *Slavic Review* 54, no. 4 (Winter 1995): 917–31.

¹¹ According to Todorova, it is for this reason that the West invented the term 'Balkanization', which negatively stereotyped this region and continues to do so to this day. The term incorporates many structures and terms into what the Westerners in the first half of the twentieth century considered conservative and barbaric. Maria Todorova, *Imagining the Balkans* (Oxford: Oxford University Press, 2009), 11.

¹² Anne Dacie, an UNRRA employee, wrote the following: 'But I hadn't wanted to go to Italy to help Italians. I'd volunteered in the war to go abroad as a relief worker and help the Slavs, and I was bitterly disappointed at being sent to Italy.' Anne Dacie, *Instead of the Brier (Concerning Yugoslavs)* (London: The Harvill Press, 1949), 12.

Italy

The ship 'Bakar' was one of the biggest ships in YNLA's navy. On 12 January 1944, it sailed from the island of Vis to the Italian town of Molfetta, with hundreds of refugees on board. Most of them were women and children, who were joined by some seniors and wounded male Partisans. They followed the more than 10,000 refugees who had been evacuated in the two weeks prior. One of the people sharing the restless voyage with the convoy was the fourteen-year-old Vjera Nižetić. Her arrival on the Italian coast marked the first time she ever came face to face with representatives of the Western Allies, in her case the British military police. They settled her in the local cement factory, which served as a temporary emergency shelter. On the following day, she was transferred to a military camp, where a fence and barbed wire separated Vjera and the rest of the refugees from the British soldiers. Immediately upon arrival the group was sent to the camp bathroom, where they were ordered to strip naked and take a cold shower, after which they were dusted with DDT powder for the sake of disinfection from typhus-carrying lice. Then, they were put into a line and taken to the camp canteen, where they were given a thick soup, tea and rusk bread. This was the first full meal after a long time for the heavily malnourished refugees.[13]

Despite the strict military rules, the Yugoslavs perceived the British soldiers as benevolent, but they also feared them somewhat. The fear can most likely be attributed to the years of living under violent occupation exercised by uniformed Italian soldiers and police. But the fear was also undermined by their perception of the Allies as a symbol of safe shelter.[14] The representatives of the British Army, however, were much less positive in their initial perception of the Yugoslavs in their care. In their reports, they labelled the first groups of refugees as badly organized, and regarded some of them as unintelligent. Most likely this had to do with the fact that the two groups had a lot of problems with trying to establish communication, since there was a significant language barrier between them – neither spoke the others' language. In light of the quick decision of the British to accept Yugoslav refugees, there was a lack of suitable translators. This had important effects: we know that communication is an essential component in resolving humanitarian crises.[15] Although there were some translators among the refugees – most of them sailors and intellectuals who had learnt some English – the British soon realized that the refugees overall only knew a small number of basic English phrases, deeming them

---

[13] Vjera Nižetić, *U pustinji El Shatta. O doživljenom i pročitanom* (Split: Naklada Bošković, 2007), 64–8.
[14] Kornelija Ajlec, *Interview with Marija Knez nee Perić*, 11 June 2009.
[15] Nowadays, humanitarian organizations are still facing the same communication problems. There is a noticeable lack of information, for instance which language is spoken by the affected group, how well the group understands the language used by representatives of humanitarian organizations and which methods would enable the fastest and most efficient dissemination of information. *Putting Language on the Map in the European Refugee Response. Research Report. Translators Without Borders* by Mixed Migration Platform, September 2017. https://translatorswithoutborders.org/wp-content/uploads/2017/04/Putting-language-on-the-map.pdf (June 2019).

unhelpful.¹⁶ The transmission of clear instructions and information was crucial for the smooth relocation and supply of refugees. As a result, problems in communication heavily impaired this information flow and resulted in frustration on both sides. On the British side, it was expressed through negative stereotypes about the 'uncivilized' Yugoslavs. Only after the British had transferred the function of refugee care from the military police to the Middle East Relief and Refugee Administration (MERRA) did the attitude towards the refugees start to change. Although MERRA was part of the British Army, it was separately specialized to accommodate refugees and take care of them. However, its procedures for organizing and managing refugee convoys and camps made little attempt to hide its military origin.[17] Even its staff consisted of military personnel.

Along with the refugees, the Partisans sent 208 members of the Yugoslav Communist Party (CPY) to Italy.[18] They were delegated to the Central Refugees Board (CRB), a special management body that had already been established by the CPY on the island of Vis. CRB's task was to make sure the Yugoslav refugee group remained unified. At the same time, it was tasked to establish various communist organizations within the refugee camps, and to include the refugees in its operations with the purpose of indoctrination and general control over all aspects of life in refuge. During the first few weeks after the refugees entered Italy, however, the CRB was unable to perform its tasks, since it failed to establish adequate control in the chaos of constant movements and within the greater authority of the British Army. Consequently, the refugees did not trust the CRB, and at first outright rejected it.[19]

The main camps for Yugoslav refugees in Italy were located in Santa Maria al Bagno, Santa Cesarea and Santa Maria di Leuca – all in the south of the Puglia region. Here, MERRA housed the refugees on the outskirts of the towns, each camp consisting of at least 2,000 people. MERRA's own sources suggest that the British tried to provide the best care possible, which was a difficult feat to accomplish, since at the same time they also needed to provide resources for the Allied troops fighting on the front located to the south of Rome.[20]

CRB did, however, manage to quickly establish authority in these so-called permanent camps. Not only did it form an unarmed camp police that made sure any conflict – local or otherwise – was avoided, but it also managed to establish increasingly effective communication with MERRA. On 17 January 1944, Major P. B. Webb, a member of MERRA, sent a note to his superiors in Cairo, in which he described the Yugoslavs with greater affection than the first British reports had. He argued that the refugees were patriots who had experienced a great deal of hardship in the years of

---

[16] The claims are written in the unedited report that talks about the fourth refugee convoy in Italy. It is evident from other documents that the fourth convoy reached Italy on 5 January 1944. UNA (United Nations Archives), S-1312-0000-0022. *Report on fourth party Partisan Refugees*, Undated, 1.

[17] Ben Shephard, *The Long Road Home: The Aftermath of the Second World War* (New York: Alfred A. Knopf, 2011), 66–7.

[18] *Narodnooslobodilačka borba u Dalmaciji: 1941-1945*. No. 10, doc. 26 (Split: Institut za historiju radničkog pokreta Dalmacije, 1986), 147.

[19] Klun, *Iz Afrike v narodnoosvobodilno vojsko Jugoslavije*, 240.

[20] TNA (The National Archives, Kew), WO 204/6662, *Purchase of Foodstuffs by Troops*, 8 January 1944.

living under occupation and as fighters against fascism, albeit supporting a different ideology:

> The refugees are communists on Russian lines. All wear the Soviet five-pointed red star on their hats or clothes. They refer to each other as 'comrade' but use military rank when introducing their officers. . . . They use a military salute, but the hand is clenched instead of the fingers being extended in the usual way.
>
> They are extremely patriotic and on moving from place to place they shout 'Long live Yugoslavia', 'Long live Tito', 'Long live Stalin'. . . . Many of the women have been in the mountains for two years with the army and the women soldiers, usually dressed in khaki battle dress, are genuine 'killers', most of them having a 'score' of Germans to their credit.[21]

Webb even compared their 'mentality' to that of the British:

> The morale of these people is absolutely terrific. Their mentality seems to resemble closely the British. The worse their condition the louder they sing, exactly like the 'Tommy', and they appear to think much as we do. They are extremely reasonable; they will make plenty of requests but will accept without question refusal to these requests. In addition many look quite like the British people.[22]

As it had already been decided with the first agreement between the Anglo-American Allies and the Partisans, the end point for the settlement of Yugoslav refugees was Egypt. There were various reasons why the Allies opted for relocation: the main reason was ensuring the safety of the refugees, since in early 1944 the victory of the Allies who were stopped at the Gustav Line was not yet guaranteed. Considering that only a few hundred kilometres to the north intense battles were taking place, the relocation of refugees to Egypt also meant freeing up important supply lines for the army, and freeing up accommodation capacities for the Allied troops and prisoners of war.[23]

The location for the settlements of the first Yugoslav convoys was determined by the British Army on 20 January 1944. It chose the abandoned military base El Shatt in the Sinai desert, previously lodging the Eighth British Army during the El Alamein crisis.[24] However, news of the relocation was followed by a tide of rumours about the high mortality rate in the desert and the unbearable living conditions.[25] Ivan Kreft, who headed the CRB in Italy for a while, wrote in his memoirs that the refugees simply could not understand why they were not allowed to stay in Italy.[26] Cita Lovrenčič-Bole, a nurse in Santa Maria di Leuca, wrote that news about the 'deadly desert' was spread by Partisan fighters on their way from Egypt to their homeland as part of the so-called

---

[21] UNA, S-1312-0000-0022, *Report on the General Situation regarding Yugoslav Partisan Refugees at present in Italy*, 17 January 1944, 2.
[22] Ibid., 5.
[23] UNA (United Nations Archies), S 1021-0028-06, *History of the Middle East Office*, 60.
[24] Ibid., 55.
[25] Klun, *Iz Afrike v narodnoosvobodilno vojsko Jugoslavije*, 247.
[26] Ivan Kreft, *Spomini* (Maribor: Založba Obzorja, 1969), 248.

Prekomorske brigade (Overseas Brigades).²⁷ Even more so, accusations circulated of the Allies purposefully torpedoing the ships carrying Partisan refugees in the open sea.²⁸ Allegedly, the rumours had been spread by the political opponents of the Partisans – the representatives and supporters of the Yugoslav royal government-in-exile.²⁹ However, it would be too simple to attribute these rumours only to anti-Partisan propaganda. In many instances, they were a sign of basic human distress. For many of the refugees, Italy had already presented a remote, faraway land. Egypt was therefore an even bigger leap into the unknown, sometimes only known as the location of Bible stories or as the land of the 'Turks'. The fear of the Turks was still very much alive in Dalmatia and other Catholic parts of Yugoslavia, whose population had not forgotten the great Turkish invasions from the Ottoman Empire. In order to limit the opposition, the British tried to appeal to CRB's representatives to explain to the refugees the basic geographical and political properties of Egypt and Arabic culture. It seems, however, that they failed to sufficiently inform the CRB's representatives themselves, since one of the CRB's reports stated that the refugees going to El Shatt would be 'settled in the vicinity of the Suez Canal, which is full of forests and fertile land – the best land over there'.³⁰ Nothing could be further from the truth. In reality, El Shatt was only a railway station in the middle of the desert at the southern mouth of the Suez Canal. A report from the United Nations Relief and Rehabilitation Administration (UNRRA) Middle East Office from 1947 describes it simply as: 'The camp is desert and will return to desert. There is no such place [as El Shatt]. It is but a latitude and a longitude.'³¹ Of course, the statements of CRB's representatives might have been propagandistic, in hopes the refugees would be less disinclined towards going to Egypt. On the other hand, perhaps this information was the result of absent communication as a result of language barriers. Namely, complete understanding is crucial in preventing the spreading of fake news and manipulations. When the latter spread, they can lead to unrest, tension and even open conflict, which is dangerous both for the refugees and the relief staff.³²

---

²⁷ The Overseas Brigades were made up of Yugoslavs, mostly Croats and Slovenes, from the territories annexed by the Kingdom of Italy after the First World War. As its citizens, they were conscripted into the Italian Army, which also fought in North Africa. After the Battle of El Alamein, the Allies captured and interned them at prisoner of war camps, where they successfully segregated themselves from the Italian soldiers. After their segregation, differences started to become apparent regarding their political convictions, which is why the British Army allowed the soldiers to choose for themselves which Yugoslav army they wanted to join: units of the Royal Yugoslav Army, a part of which was located in Egypt at the time, or the YNLA. A large majority opted for the YNLA, which had established its military mission in Cairo. The first task of its military representation was the transfer of Partisan soldiers to Italy, where four overseas brigades had been established and later joined the battles for the liberation of Yugoslavia. Klun, *Iz Afrike v narodnoosvobodilno vojsko Jugoslavije*.
²⁸ Kreft, *Spomini*, 242.
²⁹ Klun, *Iz Afrike v narodnoosvobodilno vojsko Jugoslavije* 247; Kreft, *Spomini*, 242; Cita Lovrenčič-Bole, *Prekomorke* (Ljubljana: Borec / Lipa, 1988), 171–4.
³⁰ Mateo Bratanić, *Hrvatski zbjegovi u Egiptu: 1943-1946* (PhD diss., Philosophical Faculty, University of Zadar, Zadar, 2009), 66.
³¹ UNA, S-1021-0028-06, *History of the Middle East Office*, 55.
³² UNA, S-1021-0028-09, Middle East Office – ME2. *History of the Middle East Office. The Health Division*, 410.

Later, after the first refugees had already been settled in the middle of the rocky desert across the canal from the city of Suez, worrying news continued to reach Italy in which the Egyptian camps were described as 'places of great suffering'.[33] Such news was the result of a great measles epidemic, which had claimed a significant number of casualties, especially among the children.[34] Despite this, the British kept insisting until the summer of 1944 that all refugees in Italy needed to be transferred to Egypt. Only after the number of convoys coming through the Adriatic dropped did the British agree in August 1944 to allow the almost 8,000 refugees to remain in Italy.[35] These were able to return to their homeland by 8 March 1945, after Dalmatia and large parts of Bosnia and Herzegovina and Serbia had already been liberated.[36] Their return took place incomparably sooner than the return of the last group of the almost 29,000 refugees stationed in Egypt, who came back a year later – on 24 March 1946.[37]

Egypt

Besides El Shatt, the Yugoslav refugees were also placed in El Khatatba camp between April and August 1944. This camp was also a former military base, but on the western side of the Nile Delta on the edge of the Sahara desert. However, due to the unfavourable climate, the camp was soon closed down. After that, the refugees were allocated to the camp Tolumbat, on the Mediterranean coast between Alexandria and Abu Qir, where mostly women, children and patients suffering from tuberculosis were sent. A little over 3,000 Partisan refugees were stationed there. Before the Allies allocated Tolumbat to them, members of the Royal Yugoslav Army in the Middle East were stationed there. They were relocated to the military camp at El Arish on the Mediterranean coast. Later, a civilian camp was created next to the military camp, where the Allies sent those Yugoslav refugees who did not identify as Communists. It was the only Yugoslav camp that never fell under the CRB's administration.[38]

Even before the first official convoy set sail from the Italian port of Taranto, CRB's representatives agreed with MERRA's Major Webb to establish a two-tier administration

---

[33] Lovrenčič-Bole, *Prekomorke*, 173.
[34] Of all the refugees, 12.3 per cent were infected with measles, mostly those between the ages of three and thirteen.
[35] Dušan Plenča, 'Jugoslavenski zbjeg u Italiji i Egiptu', in *Istorija radničkog pokreta. Zbornik radova.* No. 4, ed. Pero Morača (Beograd: Institut za izručavanje radničkog pokreta, 1967), 344.
[36] Kreft, *Spomini*, 249.
[37] DASt (State Archives Split), 512, *Dodatak izvješću komisije, otprema devetnajstog (zadnjeg) transporta.*
[38] Not much is known about the El Arish civilian camp, which is considered the smallest UNRRA camp in the Middle East. Fragments from UNRRA's documents reveal that UNRRA supplied this camp as part of the Greek refugee camp in Nuseirat, Palestine, about 50 kilometres in the East. It was also partially supplied by the command of the Royal Yugoslav Army in the Middle East; however, there is no detailed information about that either in UNRRA's documents or in the documents of the Yugoslav government-in-exile in the Archives of Yugoslavia in Belgrade. Here too, the refugees had their own camp committee, which was independent of the CRB, yet less influential than the CRB. More in: UNA, S-1021-0028-06, *History of the Middle East Office*, 21.

in the Yugoslav camps, which was unheard of in all the other camps in the Middle East. The CRB took care of internal administration, which granted it authority over the kitchens, the sanitary service, the work brigades, the camp's security service, schools and cultural life. Meanwhile, MERRA provided all the necessary resources and medical care to the camps.[39]

The first official refugee convoy came to Egypt on 2 February 1944, five days after setting sail from Taranto. They were transported by the British merchant ship SS *Empire Pride* and the Polish steamboat M/S *Batory*,[40] which were boarded by 4,220 refugees coming predominantly from Makarska Riviera and the Adriatic Islands of Brač, Korčula and Hvar.[41] The voyage was described by the fourteen-year-old Ivo Srhoj:

> Two persons awaited us on the deck of the ship: one of our men, and an Englishman. They were counting us, so they would know how many of us boarded. We did this one after another, with no pushing or shoving. We descended via the staircase and came to the lower part of the ship, leaving two decks overhead. The lower area looked like a grand hall of some enormous hotel.[42]

MERRA representative Vivien Leallin also joined the first convoys on their voyage. On 12 February 1944, she sent a letter to Major Webb, in which she wrote that the refugees were mostly enjoying the trips, and that they were much more comfortably accommodated on the ships than they were while waiting to embark in Taranto. The ship's captain, Captain Troops, took care of the refugees with a 'fatherly warmth', and the crew handed out bags of candy and a chocolate bar to each of the children.[43] But not all the convoys' voyages were as pleasant. Frequently, the refugees would travel by less-luxurious ships, where they were placed in practically all areas, except the mechanical room and the boiler room. According to the accounts of the refugees, on their way to Port Said the convoys were also accompanied by ally torpedo boats, submarines and military aircraft, which frequently caused anxiety and panic among the passengers traumatized by war.[44]

The arrival in Egypt was a shocking experience for most of the refugees. After disembarking in the lively Port Said, the convoys then travelled by train to El Shatt, the very first convoy arriving in the afternoon heat on 2 February 1944. While taking the first steps on the red-tinted sand, the MERRA representatives witnessed various reactions: many deeply religious women started praying, some started screaming that they would never come back from the desert alive, while others quietly took off

---

[39] UNA, S-1312-0000-0022, *Report on the General Situation regarding Yugoslav Partisan Refugees at present in Italy*, 17 January 1944, 2–3.
[40] UNA, S-1312-0000-0022, *Report on Yugoslav Refugees in Italy*, 31 January 1944, 3.
[41] HDA (State Archives of Croatia), 1220, box 4, *Poročilo COB v Egiptu sekretariatu C.O.U.S.A.O.*, 1 January 1945, 1–2.
[42] Ivo Srhoj, *Sjećanje na El Shatt* (Dubrovnik: Self-published, 2000), 41.
[43] UNA, S-1312-0000-0022, *Report of Vivien Leallin to Major Webb*, 12 February 1944.
[44] Danica Nola, *El Shatt* (Zagreb: Školske novine, 1988), 10; Srhoj, *Sjećanje na El Shatt*, 42.

their winter clothes and came to terms with their new home.[45] An unnamed MERRA representative described their situation:

> They are thousands of miles from home, in the middle of the most barren piece of land that man has ever seen, and they cannot understand why they were brought to that place.... One must keep in mind that they are very simple people, fishermen, seamen, and farmers, and great many of them have never been away from their native land before, and who, in many instances, have lost their senses as a result of Nazi brutality.[46]

At the train station, the refugees were boarded on military trucks and taken to Camp I in El Shatt, the first of the five camp units that were subsequently set up. While the refugees were boarding the trucks, the Ghibli wind started blowing, which set off the first of many sandstorms. Besides that, there was not a lot that awaited the refugees at first, since it took about four months for camp provisions to start running smoothly, when the refugees were also finally able to sew their own clothes and make their own improvised footwear. The report of an unnamed MERRA representative, who visited the El Shatt around two weeks after the arrival of the first refugees, when there were already more than 4,000 of them stationed there, describes the feelings of helplessness and impoverishment the refugees felt in their new, vastly different living area:

> The people have absolutely nothing but the clothes on their backs, and even that is a figure of speech. Many are wearing parts of uniforms from killed Italian soldiers, others the cast offs of British troops, and all are in dire need of shoes.[47]

All the Partisan refugees staying in Egyptian camps were settled in the EPIP-class[48] British military tents, which had been prepared by the Yugoslav soldiers from the nearby POW camp in El-Geneifa and by the Royal Engineers unit.[49] They would connect the backs of the tents, thus creating a single unit. Later, the ground was concreted so they would not have to walk on the desert sand. Between eighteen and twenty people who usually came from the same area were grouped in each of the tents, so that individual village communities from the homeland could be kept together. About sixty-four tents, which amounted to about 1,200 people, formed an individual camp district. Each camp unit consisted of five such districts. The tents of Camp I were about 500 metres away from the old British military base, the buildings of which served as an operative frame for all camp units. MERRA's high representatives and their guests would settle in the three smaller buildings, while the biggest of the buildings, the so-called NAAFI,[50]

---

[45] Nižetić, *U pustinji El Shatta*, 73.
[46] UNA, S-1312-0000-0022, *Report on an over-all picture of UNRRA camps in Egypt*, undated, 4.
[47] Ibid.
[48] English personnel Indian pattern.
[49] Klun, *Iz Afrike v narodnoosvobodilno vojsko Jugoslavije*, 250; Vladimir Dedijer, *Dnevnik 1943-1945* (Ljubljana: Slovenski knjižni zavod, 1951), 51; UNA, S-1021-0028-06, *History of the Middle East Office*, 56.
[50] Navy, Army and Airforce Institutes.

was allocated to the refugees. The CRB was able to set up its office in NAAFI, while its larger part was used by the El Shatt central hospital.[51]

When Camp I began to function to MERRA's satisfaction, MERRA sent seventy-seven representatives of British and South African military units to El Shatt, along with members of the Greek Red Cross, American civilian medical doctors, nurses of the British Red Cross and volunteers of the Friends Ambulance Unit and the American Mennonite Central Committee.[52] This was a motley crew of conscientious objectors or those with a long tradition of humanitarian work from across the British Empire and the United States, who were in the first months governed by Major John Lyell Langman. He kept his commanding post even after MERRA had joined the newly founded international civilian organization, UNRRA, which took care of refugees in the liberated areas of Europe up until 1947. Its first mission had begun in the Middle Eastern refugee camps in May 1944.

By this time the CRB had already earned its authority over the refugees as well as the respect of the representatives of MERRA (and later UNRRA). It functioned as the extension of the Partisan rule in Yugoslavia, which, by that time, had already organized its body of representatives and its own government.[53] Therefore, the CRB was the Partisan refugees' highest body of authority in Egypt. Throughout the time the Partisan refugees remained in Egypt, approximately 500 members of the CPY were involved in the CRB and the rest of the Party's suborganizations. The members located there worked 'underground',[54] although the Allies according to an OSS[55] report had known about their ideological preferences ever since the first refugees came to Egypt and which they dully reported to the camp's administration:

> Although political talks and discussion with foreign people are avoided and refused by the evacuees, their political stand can be noticed by their attitude in meeting foreigners. Before giving us any information they wanted to know if any connection existed between us and the Yugoslav Government-in-Exile in Cairo.[56]

With the already-agreed terms of cooperation, the CRB mostly got along with the Allies. Although the requests of the refugees were usually modest, the CRB was understanding when the camp leadership was unable to fulfil some of them. On the other hand, MERRA/UNRRA staff tried – even by refugees' own accounts – very hard to provide the refugees with the best possible living conditions in the desert. What most of them pointed out was the selflessness of the representatives of MERRA and

---

[51] UNA, S-1021-0028-06, *History of the Middle East Office*, 57.
[52] Ibid.
[53] A representative body was the Anti-Fascist Council for the National Liberation of Yugoslavia (AVNOJ), while the government was the National Committee for the Liberation of Yugoslavia (NKOJ).
[54] Edvin Pervanje and Jože A. Hočevar, *Četrta prekomorska brigada* (Ljubljana: Knjižnica NOV in POS25 – III, 1969), 64.
[55] Office of Strategic Services (OSS) was a wartime intelligence agency of the United States and a predecessor to the Central Intelligence Agency (CIA).
[56] TNA, WO 204/1349, *OSS Report: Conditions at Yugoslav Evacuees Camp at Suez*, 26 February 1944, 4.

UNRRA, who put their hearts into their work. UNRRA deputy director of El Shatt camps, Lee C. Poole, for example, wrote:

> I have never, since being with UNRRA, actually enjoyed my work as much or felt I was doing something worthwhile as I have felt since I have been in camps.... I am most sincerely concerned that a good job is to be done and I am only anxious to make some contribution – that is why I joined UNRRA in the first place.[57]

This, however, does not mean that the relations were free from tensions. The relationship between the Allied leadership and the refugees went through its most severe test during the first months after arriving to Egypt, when Major Langman was in charge. This was a serious dispute, the basis of which was primarily ideological. The CRB was defending its stance that each refugee in the Yugoslav group was a supporter of Tito's Partisans. This was exactly the reason why the CRB did not acknowledge any potential 'renegades' among the refugees. However, immediately after the first groups began to arrive, a number of individuals contacted Major Langman and claimed that they did not feel safe in the Partisan camps, as they were the supporters of the royal government-in-exile. Some were family members of one of the royal government ministers, the others next of kin of a victim of the Partisans. As such they requested to be transferred to the royalist camp at El Arish. Major Langman then immediately met with CRB's representatives, with whom he tried to find a solution for the situation at hand. In the meeting, the representatives of the CRB agreed that all refugees who felt any 'actual sympathies for the King', should be transferred. Major Langman complied. The transfer, however, was accompanied with protests of other refugees, who threw rocks at the 'renegades'. This led to Major Langman deciding to once again meet with CRB's representatives, who ended up making the whole situation even tenser. President of the CRB Ivo Markić stated that MERRA was interfering with matters outside its jurisdiction, and claimed that the matters at hand were in the CRB's jurisdiction. Mr Markić also proposed to Langman that MERRA should deal with other matters, threatening that, otherwise, the CRB would no longer take responsibility for the violations of peace and order within the camp. Langman understood the accusations and threats as confirmations of numerous accounts that the CRB wanted to prevent the refugees from having direct contact with MERRA's representatives. Langman stood by his stance that, as the commander of the camp, he was responsible for all the refugees' safety, which meant that he would continue to transfer anyone who feels threatened.[58]

Later, it turned out that many of the refugees who asked to be transferred to a different camp were former Yugoslav government officials who had been interned by the Italians in the Apennine Peninsula at the beginning of the war, which is why they were unaware of the political development of events in Yugoslavia. They knew nothing about Tito and the political views of the CPY. They only joined the group of refugees in the Italian camps after being released by the Allies from Italian prisons. But the one

---

[57] UNA, S-1312-0000-0012. *Letter of Lee C. Poole to Jack Hughes*, 30 December 1945.
[58] UNA, S-1312-0000-0022, *Report on the Political Situation at El Shatt Refugee Camp up to 23rd Feburary 1944*, 23 February 1944, 1–2.

discovery made by Major Langman that stood out most was that the group of refugees included also many of those who had been forcibly evacuated from Yugoslavia by the Partisans.[59] Only after being interrogated did the representatives of the CRB admit themselves that the Partisan authorities had also transported potential traitors besides the actual supporters of Tito during the evacuation:

> Their main fear seems to have been that some of these people might betray to the Germans, possibly under pressure, who among the local Partisans were the leaders and who had been responsible for various incidents that had taken place. They had therefore in the interests of their own security forcibly brought with them everyone whom they could not trust. Some of such people had previously been threatened with death and some had already had their husbands and brothers shot by the Partisans in Yugoslavia. They were therefore in fear for their lives as they expected the Partisans to do the same to them at any moment.[60]

The wider outlook on the situation shows that the relationship between the Allies and the refugee leadership was especially burdened by mutual distrust, which was based on ideological differences, as well as the CRB's policy that was directed towards legitimizing the CPY's rule. After the incident, the Partisan leadership in the homeland reacted and decided to set up a military mission in Cairo. By setting up the mission, they tried to avoid new conflicts with the Allies. But they also showed that they never fully trusted the leadership of the CRB:

> Most likely the refugee authorities were unable to find a footing under the new, rather complicated conditions, far from home. We have therefore decided to shortly send representatives of our military mission to Cairo. . . . The representative office will have to obtain our authorisations in order to represent our interests in relations with the Allies and to represent our refugees.[61]

Simultaneously, they let the CRB's leadership know that its actions were wrong:

> Our relations have to be dignified and tolerant, as is befitting. . . . Yet it seems that our comrades among the refugees failed to understand that and are causing themselves great damage by being rigid.[62]

A few years later, the commander of the military mission in Cairo, Mate Jakšić, said in an interview in the *Vjestnik* newspaper that there were among the refugees 'many wonderful people, but also some dogmatists who tried to carry out a narrow-minded and inflexible policy and were unaware that they had to cooperate with the Allies, as they were no longer backed by the Partisan Army'.[63]

[59] Ibid., 3.
[60] Ibid., 4.
[61] Plenča, 'Jugoslavenski zbjeg u Italiji i Egiptu', 367–8.
[62] Ibid.
[63] Mate Jakšić, 'Partizanski grad u pustinji', *Vjesnik*, 31 November 1976.

Despite warnings from the Partisan leadership in Yugoslavia, the many actions and pledges made by MERRA, UNRRA and their commanders were perceived by CRB with a high degree of suspicion. Still, the Partisan leadership in the homeland was steadfast in insisting that the British, MERRA and UNRRA were obligated to take care of the Yugoslav refugees in cooperation with CRB:

> All the help from the Allies, including the care for our refugees, should be regarded as a sort of loan, which we have been earning since the first day of the war. It is their moral duty and obligation before all humankind to provide us with at least minimum aid . . . due to our great contribution to the general Allied interests in the battle against Nazi-Fascism we must not view this aid as alms but as something we have earned fair and square.[64]

Major Langman thus remained the source of disputes. In the reports that were sent to Tito at YNLA's main headquarters, it can be read that Langman supposedly propagated resistance against the Partisan leadership and that he cultivated the 'psychosis of fear' among the refugees.[65] According to the Yugoslav accounts, Major Langman was removed from his post at the insistence of the CRB on 8 August 1944, after managing the camps for eight months. Upon his removal, the relationship with UNRRA's officials improved, while attitudes towards Major Langman continued to be negative. In the later Yugoslavian historiography, he was accused of anti-communism and harmful attitude towards the refugees. Allegedly, Langman harmed CRB's functioning on a regular basis and allowed anti-Partisan propaganda to spread among the refugees.[66] Even more so, he was accused to have placed the El Shatt Camp II 8 kilometres east from Camp I, just so that he would break the refugee group's unity. In their accusations, the Partisan leadership refused to acknowledge the fact that the location where Camp II was placed included all the infrastructure needed for its functioning – a water tower, and buildings made of brick for the ambulance unit and for the offices of camp leaders. The buildings served the new groups in the same way as the buildings in Camp I did. The Partisans also accused Major Langman of having set restrictions on movement in the vicinity of the camp, as well as in Egypt in general, even though the restrictions had been set by the Egyptian government in its first negotiations with the British military. These negotiations were the very basis for the British to even be able to offer refuge to the Yugoslav refugees.[67] The attribution of this blame to Major Langman was perhaps the result of the many frustrations experienced by the CRB for being unable to assert its authority over all the refugees, particularly those with anti-Partisan views and a feeling that they were equal allies whose people should not be limited in their movements unless designated by the CRB.

Except for the official notices and one single report, Langman has not left behind any documented sources that would depict his attitude to the refugees. It is, however,

---

[64] Plenča, 'Jugoslavenski zbjeg u Italiji i Egiptu', 367–8.
[65] HDA, 1220, box 4, *Poročilo COB* . . . , 7.
[66] Ibid., 10.
[67] Kornelija Ajlec, 'Egipatska vlada i rješavanje izbjegličke problematike tjekom drugog svjetskog rata', *Časopis za suvremenu povijest* 46, no. 2 (2014): 295–318.

interesting to read the report written by Leon Dennen, a special correspondent of the Newspaper Enterprise Association,[68] which was published in 1945. The report clearly shows Major Langman's fondness of the Partisan refugees, whom he described with the following words:

> When Marshal Tito, due to German pressure, was forced to evacuate Dalmatia, he was particularly interested in saving the children so as to be able to bring them up in democratic spirit. After all, they are the future citizens of Yugoslavia. The women went with the children.[69]

Major Langman was much more unrelenting when it came to the supporters of the royal government-in-exile. He responded to Dennen's question about the reasons why so many young, lazy men could be found in the camp, when they could very well be fighting in their homeland by saying that

> they are unreliable elements, Chetniks,70 who have to be watched. Marshal Tito had the choice of dealing drastically with them or evacuating them. He chose a humanitarian solution[70].[71]

When Dennen asked him about the reasons why these men wore hats with red five-point stars on them, despite their views being anti-Partisan, Major Langman said that 'they [were] hypocrites'.[72] It is unclear as to why Major Langman's attitude towards those supporting the government-in-exile was so harsh in this account. It seems to lack the sensitivity that was prevalent in the previously mentioned report on segregation. At the same time, it could very well be that the Partisan reports exaggerated his negative stance towards them. Whichever way, with his actions Major Langman successfully established order within the camps.

Outlook and conclusions

After the hostilities in Yugoslavia and Europe ended, the refugees began their journey home. The repatriation was long, lasting more than a year, with the last convoy returning to Yugoslavia in March 1946. However, El Shatt did not 'return to a desert' immediately. It became a concentration camp for unrepatriable refugees of various nationalities, including the Yugoslavs from El Arish. They remained there until

---

[68] 'Leon Dennen', Obituary: The New York Times, 4 December 1974. https://www.nytimes.com/1974/12/04/archives/leon-dennen.html (accessed October 2018)
[69] Leon Dennen, 'Trouble Zone – Brewing of World War III?' in Balkan Reader. First-Hand Reports by Western Correspondents and Diplomats for over a Century, ed. Andrew Simon (Safety Harbor: Simon Publications, 2000), 243.
[70] 'Chetniks' is the name of the representatives of the royal army in Yugoslavia, which was led by Draža Mihailović. In the context of refugee camps in Italy and Egypt, the name is used to denote all persons with anti-Partisan views.
[71] Ibid.
[72] Ibid.

its closure in 1948, outliving UNRRA by a year,[73] when the International Refugee Organization (IRO) transferred them to Italy, where they remained until finally being resettled into the countries willing to accept them.[74]

The refugees longed for their homeland, attempting to recreate it by maintaining their culture and traditions. In most cases, they formed miniature communities similar to those at home with common features, such as family and neighbours, gardens in front of the tents and as much song, dance and sports as they could manage. However, they still longed for their typical Dinaric limestone from which their homes had been built, and a green landscape.[75] On the contrary, it is impossible to find references about homesickness in the British sources. The reasons for this are most likely multilayered: for example, it seems that the Allied authorities censored most of the personal letters by the relief workers. At the same time, extensive personal memoirs by relief workers in the camps had never been published. John Corsellis, who served as a relief worker from MERRA's inception until the closure of UNRRA, thought that the lack of homesickness was a result of the bureaucracy of the British colonial system:

> The highly privileged public schools – and I went to one of the most privileged public schools, the Westminster Public School right in the centre of London ... were pretty consciously providing people to run the empire and business, and elite.... We were sent off to prep school early on ... cutting the umbilical cord, not being homesick later on.[76]

The memoirs of refugees supporting the Partisans also highlight a reason for wanting to return home as soon as possible: their desire to be involved in the establishment of a new political system. It is therefore not surprising that early traces of the Cold War can be found at the level of the camps' administration. This aspect of the postwar international relations was reflected in the accusations against Major Langman, as well as in the claims that the lengthy repatriation of refugees was nothing more than an Allied retaliation for one of the earliest flashpoints of the Cold War, namely the territorial dispute between Italy and Yugoslavia over Trieste.[77]

Although the camps' two-tier administration generally received praise by both refugees and the British, there was a struggle for control being fought between the two lines. In reality, MERRA, and later UNRRA, had the highest level of authority, but the CRB, being the extension of the CPY, attempted to take over when it came to dealing

---

[73] UNRRA concluded all of its operations on 1 June 1947.
[74] Jacques Vernant, *The Refugee in the Post-War World* (London: George Allen & Unwin Ltd, 1953), 409–10.
[75] For example, Nižetić, *U pustinji El Shatta*, 129.
[76] Kornelija Ajlec, *Interview with John Corsellis*. Cambridge, 22 March 2014.
[77] Plenča, 'Jugoslavenski zbjeg u Italiji i Egiptu', 474. The Yugoslav-Italian dispute has been extensively researched in Italy (Diego de Castro, Raul Pupo and Giampaolo Valdevit) and Yugoslavia, particularly in Slovenia (Nevenka Troha, Janko Jeri, Jože Pirjavec, Dušan Nečak and Samo Kristen). For more on the Yugoslav-Italian dispute in English, see, for example, Christian Jennings, *Flashpoint Trieste: The First Battle of the Cold War* (Oxford: Bloomsbury, 2017); Glenda Sluga, *The Problem of Trieste and the Italo-Yugoslav Border. Difference, Identity, and Sovereignty in Twentieth-Century Europe* (Albany: State University of New York Press, 2001).

with the refugees. This was the CPY's way to try to legitimize its existence among the almost 30,000 strong group of refugees. It wished to do all this with the purpose of forming a strong supporting element that would help it take power in Yugoslavia after the end of the war.

In the three years of living and working together in the refugee camps, all groups largely succeeded to overcome the stereotypical notions of *the other*. This led to cooperation, the outcome of which was a significant improvement in the procedures and protocols in refugee care severely lacking in planning and experience of MERRA and UNRRA. The protocols established here became the basis for a much broader international relief and rehabilitation efforts in the newly liberated Europe. This was achieved by building on the certainty of each involved group that they were contributing to a common goal: a joint victory in the Second World War and the spirit of the 'United Nations' alliance. However, this triumph of international cooperation in this particular micro-space was overshadowed by another international occurrence: the ideological rift splitting formerly Allied populations in two ideologically opposing blocks. Britain and Yugoslavia were no longer on the same side. The legacy of this dominated the subsequent official narratives of the Egyptian refugee camps, reducing this interesting piece in the mosaic of the Second World War to a mere footnote.

In fact, Yugoslav collective memory of the camps and especially of the conduct of the British officers was very positive in the first years after the war. However, at the height of the Cold War these memories became heavily burdened by the growing Cold War tensions between Yugoslavia and the West. The Yugoslav literature written a decade or two after the repatriation of the refugees was influenced by the political reality of the time. It depicts the relationships in the camps in the framework of the stereotypical notion of the colonial master and his servant. As such, it also contains false information:

> El Shatt was not in Sinai . . . El Shatt was a refugee camp on the Egyptian side. One could see the refugee burial ground where thousands of Yugoslav people, women and children from Dalmatia were buried. The Allies were unable to feed them, they were starving. The English feel no shame because of this. They had their tea and their chocolate. . . . And their political bills that were paid for by the ordinary people.[78]

Such incidents indicate either complete ignorance of the events or a desire to discredit the Allies. In reality, not a single death from malnourishment is recorded in either MERRA/UNRRA's documents or in the available Yugoslav sources. People, however, did sadly die, in many cases due to contagious diseases.[79] However, in the Yugoslav cemetery in El Shatt, 571 burials are recorded instead of 'thousands'.[80] The Yugoslav attitudes towards the British in the CRB's documents were much more objective compared to later literary works such as quoted earlier. However, the British and

---

[78] Vladimir Kavčič, *Živalski krog* (Trst: Založništvo tržaškega tiska, 1982), 11.
[79] UNA, S-1021-0027-0005, *Origin of the Balkan Mission*, 135.
[80] Neven Bogdanić, *El Shatt naš nezaboravljeni. 50 obljetnica Hrvatskog zbjega na Sinaju 1944–1946* (Split: Crkva u svijetu, 1996), 49–63.

UNRRA sources present the largest amount of detail about these relationships. It is there and not in CRB's documents that we can find, for example, the farewell letter of the CRB's last president Andro Štambuk, who had spent all his time in refuge as a priest in Camp I, and Secretary Mate Barbić. The two wrote the letter when the last, nineteenth, convoy of refugees was leaving for Yugoslavia.

> In this moment of departure we would like to mention to you that we, the Yugoslav Refugees, are taking with us to our homes an unforgettable memory of a kind and friendly people which we will always cherish.[81]

The refugee experience had lasting influence on each person that took part in this story. Cita Lovrenčič-Bole became known for her work in family planning and reducing the mortality rate of women during childbirth in Yugoslavia.[82] After returning to Yugoslavia, Ivan Kreft became a professional diplomat.[83] With the third repatriation convoy on 5 May 1945, Vjera Nižetić also returned to her homeland.[84] Later in life, she became employed at a company that exported raw materials for cement. Among other things, she was in charge of the weekly export of marl to the cement factory in Molfetta – to the same cement factory where she had first encountered British soldiers as a fourteen-year-old refugee.[85]

Ivo Srhoj arrived in his homeland about two weeks earlier than Vjera with the second convoy. In his memoirs he wrote about feeling torn when returning home:

> When we sailed into the Adriatic Sea, we passed our ship sailing to Italy. . . . Both ships sounded their sirens for a long time, greeting each other, which meant that we would soon be arriving home. We sailed to Split and boarded the Sitinica steamship. I was simultaneously thinking about El Shatt and my birthplace; it was an internal struggle. I was happy to be returning home, but also troubled by having to leave. The struggle between the two is indescribable.[86]

Both Vjera Nižetić and Ivo Srhoj wrote their memoirs after retirement.

The fate of the Allied soldiers is harder to establish. Some of the nurses working at El Shatt later wrote a few journal articles.[87] The accounts of John Corsellis were among the first to be published[88]; however, he left his biggest mark in a book about Yugoslav

---

[81] UNA, S-1312-0000-0012, *The Letter of Andre Štambuk and Mate Barbić to brigadier Waddington*, 19 March 1946.
[82] Janez Kramarič and Irena Rožman, 'Cita Lovrenčič Bole', in *Pozabljena polovica: portreti žensk 19. in 20. stoletja na Slovenskem*, ed. Alenka Šelih et al. (Ljubljana: SAZU, 2007), 550–3.
[83] Enciklopedija Slovenije, vol. 5 (Ljubljana: DZS, 1991), 415.
[84] Nižetić, *U pustinji El Shatta*, 131.
[85] Ibid., 65.
[86] Srhoj, *Sječanje na El Shatt*, 152–3.
[87] Margaret G. Arnstein, 'Nursing in UNRRA Middle East Refugee Camps', *The American Journal of Nursing* 45, no. 5 (1945): 378–81; Ruth S. Faust, 'Trained at Yugoslav Refugee Camp', *The American Journal of Nursing* 45, no. 7 (1945): 549–52; Henry R. O'Brien, 'Other Nurses', *The American Journal of Nursing* 47, no. 10 (1947): 676–9.
[88] John Corsellis, 'Yugoslav Refugees in Camps in Egypt and Austria, 1944–47', *Refugee Participation Network*, vol. 17 (Oxford: Oxford University – Refugee Studies Center, 1994): https://www.fmr

refugee camps in Austria after the war.[89] After his departure from El Shatt, activities of Major Langman are mostly unclear. He did remain in the Middle East throughout the war, where he was promoted to a higher military rank. According to accounts, he did not discuss his activities during this time later in life; moreover, no personal correspondence has been preserved from the time he spent at El Shatt.[90]

As this chapter has demonstrated, for several years during the Second World War and its aftermath, El Shatt, located at the junction of Asian and African continents and strongly influenced by Europe, was a place where the Western and Eastern European worlds came into contact. Although at times it might have seemed it was the most remote place on Earth, it was closely connected to several different political and social worlds. Across the boundaries of the camps, external forces intruded and disrupted the lives of all who inhabited them. The camp seemed to have been some kind of a 'world in motion' not immune to prejudice based on national stereotypes, the inability to communicate, clashes surrounding ideological priorities in the early stages of the Cold War, as well as unlikely friendships, goodwill and kindness. Here, individual histories became interwoven, building new relationships and alliances. In turn, the consequences of these relationships and mutual (mis)understandings influenced global diplomacy's efforts for quick post-war reconstruction and the establishment of a new system of international relief. The history of the Allied-run refugee camps in Egypt, so often in the shadow of better-known and better-researched post-war refugee camps in Europe, is therefore a compelling example of transcending cultural and ideological boundaries, of 'lived internationalism', and, as such, an important addition to the history of internationalism.

---

eview.org/sites/fmr/files/HTMLcontent/rpn173.htm (June 2019).
[89] John Corsellis and Marcus Ferrar, *Slovenia 1945* (London: IB Tauris, 2005).
[90] Camilla Gibson, *John Langman* (e-mail), 3 February 2018.

7

Local and global

Religious institutes, Catholic internationalism and the Peru mission

Carmen M. Mangion

Women's religious institutes operating as religio-cultural networks were important contributors to the Catholic International. Individual religious congregations of sisters, often centralized with a female General Council directing its actions, expanded their remit internationally for the sake of evangelization and mission. Even enclosed, contemplative orders of nuns, managed autonomously, crossed national borders in founding new communities to expand their order's mission of prayer. Both modes of religious life were influenced by their international connections and transnational encounters and had a long history of internationalism, but the meaning and understandings of their internationalism shifted from the 1940s, but particularly in the 1970s and 1980s.[1]

This chapter explores these shifts in 'doing' internationalism through the lived experiences of the Sisters of Mercy, who contributed to the Leeds diocesan mission to Peru.[2] Missionary praxis diverged from the top-down structures of nineteenth-century internationalism to stress bottom-up solidarity and collaboration with both the peoples of Peru and other international groups. Their activities integrated global thinking revealing both a local mission done globally, as part of an extensive Catholic International and 'bearing witness' to Catholic communities in England, and a global mission done locally with Sisters of Mercy living in the *barriadas* and collaborating with Peruvians. As part of the Catholic International, female Catholic religious institutions such as the Sisters of Mercy were influenced in the 1970s and 1980s by discourses of social justice and liberation theology. From the 1970s, some British religious institutes left their institutional work running large schools and hospitals to move into new ministries. New ministries were both local and global, as women religious united by their emphasis on the marginalized worked locally utilizing the

---

[1] For my article on shifts in women religious 'being' internationalists, see Carmen M. Mangion, 'A New Internationalism: Endeavouring to "Build from This Diversity, Unity"', 1940-1990', *Journal of Contemporary History* 55:3 (2020), 579-601

[2] The Leeds Diocese, formed in 1878, is located in West Riding, Yorkshire, England.

global ideals of social justice. They were part of a larger movement of women religious (sisters and nuns) questioning socio-economic structures, gender relations and the dynamics of power and authority from within the convent and in the wider world.[3] Many, in considering systemic change, repositioned their work from solely the spiritual and corporal works of mercy to adding in the politics of mercy using the language of social justice. Motivated by faith and initially without an explicitly feminist or political agenda, women religious as internationalists negotiated how their internationalism was defined, lived and experienced.

The first section of this chapter examines how understanding the Catholic International adds to the broader scholarship on internationalism, exploring the religious and secular developments that motivated the shifts in Catholic internationalism. The case study that follows in the second section analyses Catholic internationalism in the foreign mission field interrogating how the Sisters of Mercy operated as internationalists working in the barrios of Peru.[4] Missionary work was one of the earliest forms of internationalism and intrinsic to the Catholic International, but the Peru mission offered a different way of 'doing' internationalism. They shared (with Peruvians) their technical expertise, personal labour and access to funding to create networks both in Peru and in England. Such quotidian practices linked to global ideas remind us how the paradigm of internationalism was enacted and lived locally by internationalists on the ground. This chapter argues that missionary work was in flux in the last half of the twentieth century. The Peru mission as both a local mission 'done globally' and a global mission 'done locally' was a response to global religious and secular developments that in emphasizing social justice strayed from the top-down imperatives of nineteenth-century internationalism to underscore solidarity and collaboration with both the peoples of Peru and other international missionary groups.

Employing a combined methodological approach using archived documentary sources and oral testimonies allows for a more nuanced analysis. The repositories accessed, diocesan and congregation archives, include circular letters and correspondence that give a sense of the day-to-day activities and lived experiences.[5] Oral narratives offered more emotive and subjective meanings and a view from

---

[3] See for example, Amy L. Koehlinger, *The New Nuns: Racial Justice and Religious Reform in the 1960s* (Cambridge, MA: Harvard University Press, 2007) and Susan Fitzpatrick-Behrens, 'Knowledge Is Not Enough: Creating a Culture of Social Justice, Dignity, and Human Rights in Guatemala: Maryknoll Sisters and the Monte María "Girls"', *US Catholic Historian* 24 (2006): 111–28.

[4] The Sisters of Mercy are an international congregation founded by Catherine McAuley in Dublin in 1831. They expanded rapidly in the nineteenth century, following the Irish diaspora to English-speaking nations and operating as autonomous communities until the twentieth century when communities began amalgamating. At the time of the Peru mission, the majority of Mercy communities in Britain operated within three larger bodies: the Federation of the Sisters of Mercy in Great Britain (formed 1969), the Union of Sisters of Mercy in Great Britain (formed 1976) and the Institute of Our Lady of Mercy (formed 1983). *Trees of Mercy: Sisters of Mercy of Great Britain from 1839* (Essex: Sisters of Mercy, 1993), 8–9.

[5] I am grateful to the Institute of Our Lady of Mercy, the Union of Sisters of Mercy in Great Britain and the Diocese of Leeds for allowing me access to their archives. Special thanks go to archivists Vida Milovanovic, Jenny Smith and Robert Finnigan and the individual sisters who agreed to be interviewed. The editors of this volume offered generous feedback that challenged me to broaden the post-war European context. Their suggestions have made this a stronger chapter. Any errors are my own. Research trips were financially supported by Birkbeck, University of London.

'ordinary' sisters whose lived experiences would be less likely to make their way into archives. All this, of course, gives oral sources their value, but also leaves them open to questions of reliability, authenticity, subjectivity, marginality and representativeness (and the same can be said of documentary sources). There is a distinctive subjectivity in these oral sources. The three sisters interviewed spent between fourteen and twenty-eight years in Peru. They contrast their lives before and after their experiences in Peru suggesting the intensity of the Peru mission, and this time as a radical marker of their lived knowledge of social justice. The Peru mission offers a prism with which to piece together the twentieth-century shifts in Catholic understandings of internationalism, particularly as it operated in the missions. However, this chapter is distinctively one sided in that sources of how the mission was received by Peruvians of the barrio in their own voices do not exist in the archives and are mediated in the testimonies. The transnational exchanges between different groups of missionaries are examined here, but the reception of the Catholic International is a gaping hole in the larger historiography of internationalism.

The Catholic International

Interactions between nations form the core of the usual definitions of internationalism as international relations, diplomacy and global economics. Internationalism, though, has a broader constituency, one that encompasses social, cultural and religious movements.[6] This expanding scope has spawned a large, growing body of literature where transnationalism and internationalism are often intertwined.[7] Internationalism has often been interpreted as a liberal and secular project.[8] Scholars of global civil society have persistently ignored religion, often because it did not fit their preconceptions of a global public sphere.[9] This belies the significance of religious internationalism to the reframing of both religious and internationalist identities on a world stage. Vincent Viaene argued that the 'threat of secularization focused identities and disciplined structures; multiplying the mobilizing force of organized religion'.[10] The Catholic Church's concerted efforts to strengthen religious identities and to reassert its authority was demonstrated by stronger church hierarchies, increased weight on doctrinal matters and a rigorous devotional culture. The Catholic International of the nineteenth

---

[6] For example, Martin H. Geyer and Johannes Paulmann, eds, *The Mechanics of Internationalism: Culture, Society, and Politics from the 1840s to the First World War* (Oxford: Oxford University Press, 2001), 1.

[7] Thomas Faist, 'Towards Transnational Studies: World Theories, Transnationalisation and Changing Institutions', *Journal of Ethnic and Migration Studies* 36 (2010): 1667; Patricia Clavin, 'Defining Transnationalism', *Contemporary European History* 14 (2005): 421–39.

[8] Reinisch has noted that 'non-liberal' forms of internationalism remain peripheral to the mainstream historiography. Jessica Reinisch, 'Introduction: Agents of Internationalism', *Contemporary European History* 25 (2016): 197.

[9] Abigail Green and Vincent Viaene, eds, *Religious Internationals in the Modern World: Globalization and Faith Communities since 1750* (Basingstoke: Palgrave Macmillan, 2012), 2.

[10] Vincent Viaene, 'International History, Religious History, Catholic History: Perspectives for Cross-Fertilization (1830-1914)', *European History Quarterly* 38 (2008): 579.

century was strengthened by the 'internationalisation of the Catholic masses' and the resulting modernization of the church.[11]

Women have only recently been integrated into the internationalist historiography. A growing number of studies engage with women's organizations whose feminist internationalist agenda includes work on the 'woman question' as well as political and humanitarian debates of liberal internationalisms.[12] The role of religion is rarely acknowledged in this literature. Religious women (and women religious) with and without a feminist agenda were internationalists. As my work has shown, women were an intrinsic, though often unacknowledged, component of the Catholic International.[13] Case studies such as this expand our knowledge of internationalism by acknowledging the perhaps unfashionable missionary enterprise as a form of 'doing' internationalism and by featuring small, female-led religious groups whose feminist and political agenda was muted in the 1970s and 1980s and whose members did not belong to a liberal elite.[14]

The work of Catholic religious institutes fits neatly into both the broader understanding of internationalism and the narrower Catholic International. From the nineteenth century, the transnational engines of the Catholic International were the armies of male and female religious that traversed the globe to recruit and form 'good' Catholics via the building of a Catholic infrastructure of schools and hospitals.[15] Religious institutes became 'international' as a result of their expansionist strategies. Unlike many of the organizations discussed in histories of internationalism, they were not national organizations that came together under an international umbrella with internationalist aims.[16] Instead, their internationalism was a by-product of their growth, not a purposeful coming together.

Catholic internationalism transformed in the last half of the twentieth century. Emblematic of this change was the Second Vatican Council (1962–5), a global event attended by over 2,000 cardinals and theologians from all over the world. As an event, and in its message of 'renewal', its aim was for the Catholic Church to maintain its relevance in a modernizing world.[17] Women religious were urged to re-examine female religious life and to relocate it from the narrow confines of a Catholic world to a more prominent place in civil society.[18] Three papal documents were particularly

---

[11] Vincent Viaene, ed., *The Papacy and the New World Order (1878-1903)* (Leuven: Leuven University Press, 2005), 10.
[12] For 'liberal' scholarship on internationalism, see Leila J. Rupp, *Worlds of Women: The Making of an International Women's Movement* (Princeton, NJ: Princeton University Press, 1997).
[13] Mangion, 'A New Internationalism'.
[14] For examples of the elite membership to some international organizations, see Rupp, *Worlds of Women*, 80–1.
[15] R. Scott Appleby, 'From State to Civil Society and Back Again: The Catholic Church as Transnational Actor, 1965-2005', in *Religious Internationals in the Modern World,* ed. Abigail Green and Vincent Viaene (Houndmills: Palgrave Macmillan, 2012), 330–2.
[16] Rupp, *Worlds of Women*; Christine von Oertzen, *Science, Gender, and Internationalism: Women's Academic Networks, 1917-1955* (Houndsmill: Palgrave Macmillan, 2014).
[17] The Second Vatican Council had an influential prehistory including the *nouvelle théologie* of the 1930s. Jay P. Corrin, *Catholic Progressives in England After Vatican II* (South Bend, IN: University of Notre Dame Press, 2013), 70–4. For research on Catholic internationalism before the Second Vatican Council, read David Brydan's and Daniel Laqua's chapters in this volume.
[18] Cardinal Leon Joseph Suenens, *The Nun in the World: New Dimensions in the Modern Apostolate* (London: Burns & Oates, 1962), 36, 64, 112–13.

meaningful. *Gaudium et Spes* (the Pastoral Constitution on the Church and the Modern World, 1965) suggested a two-way relationship between the church and the modern world which linked to a global vision and, for some, a radical egalitarianism.[19] *Lumen Gentium*, the Dogmatic Constitution on the Church (1964), redefined church, not as the hierarchy and clergy or as leaders and followers but as the 'People of God'.[20] Female religious interpreted this as an impetus to remove barriers between themselves and those who they ministered to, especially as they found themselves identified, not with a higher calling, but as laity. *Perfectae Caritatis*, the Adaptation and Renewal of Religious Life (1965), called for the renewal of religious life. Renewal included, among many things, ministerial renewal.

Apart from the Second Vatican Council, two other developments were fundamental to a shifting world view. The first development which straddled the religious and the secular worlds was the emergence of liberation theology.[21] The Second Conference of Latin American Bishops (CELAM) held in Medellín, Colombia, in 1968, and the later one in Puebla, Mexico, in 1979, articulated a particular response to poverty and oppression through the 'preferential option for the poor'. Liberation language became significant to the development of Catholic missions from the 1960s.[22] One tangible response, which will be discussed later in the chapter, was basic ecclesial communities (base communities), often created by the poor and marginalized, as a church *of* the poor rather than a church *for* the poor.[23]

And the second development was the secular world. Church teachings appeared congruent with some of the ideologies that informed the 1960s social movements. The 1960s were not exclusively about personal freedoms or challenging authorities and conventions; social movements of the long 1960s also engaged and acted on questions of social and economic justice for those living with socially constructed inequities.[24] Influenced by these developments, religious ministries relocated some works away from emphasizing charity to addressing social problems such as inadequate housing for single women, unliveable wages, limited job opportunities, occupationally compromised health and rationalized educational opportunities. Individual sisters and nuns also engaged with global movements such as ecological campaigns, anti-war movements and civil rights.

---

[19] John W. O'Malley, SJ 'Vatican II: Did Anything Happen?', *Theological Studies* 67 (2006): 12.

[20] *Lumen Gentium*, §33. The English text of papal documents can be found here: http://www.papalencyclicals.net/ (accessed 11 October 2019).

[21] Liberation theology was a radical movement that emerged from Latin America as a reaction to the poverty and oppression of the poor. Its most well-known theologian was Gustavo Gutiérrez. It has had a chequered history, embraced by many in the 1970s, but concerns of Marxism caused it to fall into disfavour. Timothy Gorringe, 'Liberation Theology', in *The Palgrave Dictionary of Transnational History* ed. Akira Iriye and Pierre-Yves Saunier (Houndsmill: Palgrave Macmillan, 2009), 659–60.

[22] For example, see Barbra Mann Wall, *Into Africa: A Transnational History of Catholic Medical Missions and Social Change* (New Brunswick NJ: Rutgers University Press, 2015), 84–90.

[23] Ellen M. Leonard, 'Ecclesial Religious Communities Old and New', *The Way Supplement* (2001): 123.

[24] Arthur Marwick, 'The Cultural Revolution of the Long Sixties: Voices of Reaction, Protest, and Permeation', *The International History Review* 27 (2005): 791.

The existing scholarship on women religious highlights a major shift in the ministries of sisters and nuns, charting the movement from traditional 'works of mercy' to social justice ministries.[25] My own work suggests a slow transition with a select few individuals leading the way in experimenting in social justice ministries. Demographic factors also undergirded shifts in ministry; the inability to fully staff because of declining numbers many of the large, institutional enterprises female religious managed led to their closure or transfer to outside bodies. New, often smaller, sometimes individual, endeavours reflected a broadening of ministries and the influence of the prominent discourse of social justice and secular social movements. There was both continuity and change from the mid-1970s and 1980s, as religious communities attempted to both maintain current ministries and accommodate the desires of sisters and nuns who requested permission to experiment with new ministries. Much of the social justice work done by religious institutes was initially ad hoc; by the late 1980s and 1990s, after a few decades of experimentation, many religious institutes developed more strategic ministerial visions. The determination to stand with the poor and marginalized was intrinsic to experimental ministries that would be political, without being overtly activist or protest-oriented.[26]

The Peru mission

Renewed Catholic internationalism, initiated by lay Catholics, clergy and female and male religious reflected the interconnectedness between Catholics and the social movements of a post-war Catholic and secular world. The case study in this chapter examines Catholic internationalism in the foreign mission field interrogating how the Sisters of Mercy in England sought the 'reform of society and politics by way of transnational cooperation'.[27] In doing this, it highlights first the ways in which Catholic foreign missions operated in the twentieth century, reworking nineteenth-century models of mission linked with salvation to embrace a post-war emphasis on social justice. This case study shows how concerns for social justice were lived locally in Peru, and globally through the new thinking on foreign missions which was often based on the principles of liberation theology. Second, the Sisters of Mercy operated a corporate mission interacting within a Catholic International connected with their international Mercy family and with other Catholic religious institutes, male and female, operating

---

[25] Jo Ann Kay McNamara, *Sisters in Arms: Catholic Nuns Through Two Millennia* (London: Harvard University Press, 1996), 639–41; Amy L. Koehlinger, *The New Nuns: Racial Justice and Religious Reform in the 1960s* (Cambridge, MA: Harvard University Press, 2007); Mary Beth Fraser Connolly, *Women of Faith: The Chicago Sisters of Mercy and the Evolution of a Religious Community* (New York: Fordham University Press, 2014).

[26] Carmen M. Mangion, *Catholic Nuns and Sisters in a Secular Age, Britain 1945-1990* (Manchester: Manchester University Press, 2020), Chapter 7.

[27] This chapter uses Paul Wende's definition of internationalism as a means to 'create international identities, *and* to reform society and politics by way of transnational co-operation, and the process of internationalizing cultural, political, and economic practices'. Paul Wende, 'Foreword', in *The Mechanics of Internationalism*, ed. Martin H. Geyer and Johannes Paulmann, (Oxford: Oxford University Press, 2001), v.

in Peru. This dynamic of connections has broader implications for how we can try to make sense of internationalism as lived experience.

The Catholic Church has always self-identified as a missionary church engaged in the salvation of souls through charitable work often educating the poor or healing the sick.[28] It rarely questioned poverty, assuming its inevitability and valorizing its participants. Pope Pius XII's encyclical letter *Evangelii praecones* (On the Promotion of Catholic Missions, 1951) introduced a different way forward for Catholic foreign missions. In criticizing both communism and capitalism and highlighting social justice, it proposed that charity was not enough: social and economic reform was necessary.[29] Pius XII's encyclical to Catholic bishops, *Fidei Donum* (On the Present Condition of the Catholic Missions, 1957) called for a 'keener interest in the missionary apostolate among your priests' and for bishops to make priests available for missionary activities.[30] Pope Paul VI also encouraged the Catholic missionary enterprise. Encyclical *Populorum Progressio* (On the Development of Peoples, 1967) highlighted the injustice of poverty and promoted development (with certain caveats). Apostolic exhortation *Evangelii Nuntiandi* (On Evangelisation of the Modern World, 1975) connected proclaiming and witnessing the Gospel with social justice. The Latin American episcopal conferences, particularly the ones in Medellín (1968) and Puebla (1979), added another dimension to missiology which identified with the 'church of the poor', linking together the poverty caused by injustice. Latin American bishops insisted that evangelization would not occur without transformation of the structures of Latin American society. They encouraged conscientization, the development of a critical consciousness through a process of reflection and action.[31] These documents and meetings encouraged a rethinking of missions from the nineteenth-century focus on salvation and a universalism that insisted on uniformity to a European way of being Catholic to an openness to rethink missionary praxis influenced by Latin American missiology.

'Doing' internationalism

In 1961, Bishop of Leeds, George Dwyer (1908–85) responded to the *Fidei Donum* appeal by sending diocesan priests to work with the Missionary Society of St

---

[28] Patrick Pasture, 'Dechristianization and the Changing Religious Landscape in Europe and North America since 1950: Comparative, Transatlantic and Global Perspectives', in *The Sixties and Beyond: Dechristianization in North America and Western Europe, 1945-2000*, ed. Nancy Christie and Michael Gauvreau (Toronto: University of Toronto Press, 2013), 371.

[29] Joe Holland, *Modern Catholic Social Teaching: The Popes Confront the Industrial Age, 1740-1958* (New York: Paulist Press, 2003), 282–3.

[30] *Fidei Donum* §4.

[31] Timothy McCarthy, *The Catholic Tradition: Before and After Vatican II, 1878-1993* (Chicago, IL: Loyola University Press, 1994), 253–9. The Latin American bishops were not all convinced of the effectiveness of economic development; nor were they all in agreement with a 'preferential option for the poor' or conscientization. Brazilian philosopher and educator Paulo Freire has utilized the concept of 'conscientization', a term grounded in Marxist critical theory and linked to social change, which considers that a critical consciousness can (in theory) be transformed into organized class solidarity.

Columban in Peru.[32] One of these priests, Gerald Hanlon, wrote requesting sisters to work with him in Tahuantinsuyo, a locale on the fringes of Lima, Peru.[33] In 1969, the Sisters of Mercy agreed to send a multi-community team of four sisters to the *barriada* of 30,000 in Tupac Amaru.[34] In 1984, another group of Sisters of Mercy founded a second mission at Villa Sol, also on the outskirts of Lima. Both groups began their ministries as they did in their founder Catherine McAuley's time by visiting the poor and sick, keeping in mind her admonition regarding visitations: 'act with great tenderness . . . relieve distress . . . promote the cleanliness, ease and comfort of the sick person . . . since we are always better disposed to receive advice and instruction from those who show compassion for us.'[35] In continuity with how ministries had operated throughout their history, evangelization was still a core feature of the missionary enterprise.[36] The Sisters of Mercy nursed the sick and in teaching the Catholic catechism educated children and adults. It was difficult, absorbing work complicated by a language barrier that often took years to overcome.[37] Sisters spoke of their initial inept language skills with embarrassment, highlighting their own frustration and the patience and good humour of local inhabitants. Some sisters came and went quickly, finding themselves unsuited for missionary work or succumbing to illness. Others were transformed by this new ministry, committing themselves to sometimes decades of service in Peru.

The Sisters of Mercy's missionary work was reflective of both the old and new ways of being missionaries. It was undergirded by their faith and methods of evangelization that promoted European ideas of orthodox Catholicism linked to the Universal Church. The church of their youth would have understood universalism as uniformity; the missionary endeavour informed and performed through a European lens focused on the salvation of the 'other'. Embedded in this universalism were hierarchies of ethnicity, class and gender and the superiority of a European Catholicism. These understandings can be read in one sister's report in the early years of the mission: 'The general opinion is that our people [the Peruvians] were baptized but never evangelized. To awaken them spiritually means first of all the eradication of superstition.'[38] These thoughts reflected the nineteenth-century views of the role of foreign missionaries to replace 'superstition' with European Catholic practices. However, the influence of social justice, later buttressed by liberation theology, led to other understandings and practice of ministry. In Peru, the Sisters of Mercy from England avoided the institutional emphasis

---

[32] The Missionary Society of St Columban evolved from the Maynooth Mission to China founded in 1918. In 1951, Columban fathers were missioned to Lima, where they were assigned a parish in the north side of the city.
[33] Gerald Hanlon, 'Letter from Lima', *The Far East*, December 1969, 4–6.
[34] Archives of the Institute of Our Lady of Mercy, Bermondsey (henceforth IOLM): IOLM/PERU/3/1, Peru Mission (flyer published by the Leeds Diocese); Archives of the Union of Sisters of Mercy in Great Britain (henceforth RSM Union): MISS/1, 'Papers re. Peru mission, 1980s–2000s, Villa Sol, Lima, Peru'.
[35] IOLM/PERU/3/1: 'Mercy Response to the Cry of the Poor', p. 19.
[36] RSM Union: MISS/1. 'Papers re. Peru mission, 1980s–2000s, Villa Sol, Lima, Peru'.
[37] Sisters were sent to the language school run by the St James Society in Lima upon their arrival where they studied for four months; they indicated that it took years to obtain linguistic proficiency.
[38] Sister M. Mildred McNamara, 'Our Sisters Write from Peru', *Leeds Diocesan Gazette*, August 1971.

that had been characteristic of nineteenth-century Catholic foreign missions.[39] Rather than build large educational or healthcare institutions that they expected to control and manage in perpetuity, they worked from within the community, encouraging the development of base communities that emboldened a Catholicism that was critically conscious and would become 'Peruvian' rather than 'European'.[40] The Sisters of Mercy did not control directly the knowledge they dispensed; they instructed catechists, barrio residents, who in turn taught Catholic doctrine and catechism and prepared their co-religionists for the sacraments of communion and confirmation. Barrio catechists became the primary agents of evangelization in their communities. They were connected to their local parish, involved in community activities including weekly formation meetings and prayer and youth groups who prepared the liturgy.[41]

Many initiatives were women-centred. They included organizing kitchens (*comedores*) throughout the barrio where local women cooked and provided meals at a nominal charge to the 70 per cent of the barrio inhabitants who were unemployed or underemployed. Tupac Amaru women created income-generating native crafts that were later sold by Mercy communities throughout England. This income gave women independent access to funds to help run their home and educate their children. One sister wrote describing her daily work:

> We help the sick; we help in the *comedores* or communal kitchens; we help with crafts; in fact we try to help the women move out of the isolation of their homes, often little more than a shack, so that they can learn to organise, share their concerns & find the support of friendship. For the women it is the food, medicines or money earned, that matter most. That is what makes the difference between life & death for them & their families. But we hope they see us as people who represent the God of life, interested in helping them & their families to live.[42]

Written in the 1980s, this excerpt demonstrates the Sisters of Mercy embrace of traditional 'caring' work of the corporal works of mercy. Yet the language suggests an approach that differs from the nineteenth century: sisters were 'work[ing] with the Senoras' rather than managing. Barrio women were expected to take the lead in these enterprises and to 'learn to organise'. The traditional work of the Sisters of Mercy, visiting the sick, was soon managed by members of a local women's group.

---

[39] Not all foreign missions chose this route. Many, including the Sisters of Mercy from Cork, Ireland opened institutions such as schools. See Phyl Clancy, *A Journey of Mercy: From Birth to Rebirth* (Congregation of the Sisters of Mercy, 1994), 153–61. Evelyn Bolster, *Mercy in Cork 1837-1987: A Sesquicentennial Commemoration* (Cork, Tower Books, 1987), 59–63. I am grateful to archivist Marianne Cosgrave of the Mercy Congregational Archives in Dublin for pointing me to these materials.

[40] Basic ecclesial communities grew rapidly in Latin America in the 1950s and 1960s. They were small non-hierarchical church communities. Some were connected to a local Catholic parish; others were stridently anti-institutional. They developed also in Italy, France and Spain, where Catholics unhappy with church hierarchy found a space to discuss and question church teachings and actively develop social justice and political initiatives not all of which would have been congruent with church teaching.

[41] IOLM/PERU/1/3, Circular Letter from Sister M. Mildred McNamara to Sisters dated 1985.

[42] Ibid.

Another group organized the *comedors*. One sister recorded their progress: 'Having already acquired the cooking utensils they must now provide a secure roof to safeguard this equipment.' The priority of the barrio women was the practical work of survival: 'food, medicines or money earned'. But it seems important too that these women 'share their concerns & find the support of friendship',[43] suggesting consciousness-raising (or perhaps the conscientization of the Puebla CELAM conference) of the larger social structures that were complicit in the poverty that oppressed them. Their aims were to encourage barrio residents 'to be actively involved in every effort being made to improve their lot – spiritually, physically and materially'.[44]

Clinics and special schools were initiated by the Sisters of Mercy, but they were intended to be run and managed by local constituents. The Sisters in Tupac Amaru in 1969 immediately opened up a clinic in their residence with (at least initially) one sister-nurse as the sole medical practitioner. By 1984, this had grown into a stand-alone brick structure, a Posta Medica that was managed by local administrators and medical personnel.[45] Sisters initially provided their technical expertise sharing standards of hygiene and biomedical practices, and creating employment opportunities; one sister wrote of 'getting some of our girls into the local hospital to be trained'.[46] Letters home to sisters in England share their lived experience of internationalism, recounting 'teaching the mothers the basics of nutrition and hygiene, with special concern for expectant mothers and new-born babies. The mothers are very anxious to cooperate, and Sister is training them, so that they in turn can help others'.[47] Another sister teamed with English priests and the Columban sisters to open a centre for children impaired with mental or physical ailments which also operated as an advice and advocacy centre. One sister explained how staff members became advocates for local people: 'So this centre became quite a centre, you know, where people gravitated towards, and we were able to help them go to the hospital if they needed callipers on their legs, or whatever it might have been.'[48] The teachers in the centre were Peruvian, and as teaching qualifications changed, they were funded by the mission to attend courses or obtain university training in order to meet national requirements. This enabling of expertise respected the quality of local training. The sharing of expertise, whether it be biomedical, pedagogical or organizational, was a feature of these smaller, community-run groups. This emphasis on self-help was also constituent in the ministries of religious institutes who chose to establish schools and hospitals where medical and educational infrastructures were non-existent. Influenced by social justice and liberation theology, these institutional ways of doing internationalism also shared technical expertise, often intending that institutions would transfer to local control.[49]

[43] Ibid.
[44] IOLM/PERU/3/1: 'Mercy Response to the Cry of the Poor', p. 4.
[45] IOLM/PERU/3/1: 'Mercy Response to the Cry of the Poor', Letter from Mother Imelda Keena to Sisters re: February to March 1985, pp. 51–2.
[46] McNamara, 'Our Sisters Write from Peru', August 1971.
[47] RSM Union: Miss/1: 'Peru 1978', Letter from Sister Mary Fitzsimons to Sisters undated.
[48] Interview RSM 011. The stories I heard were intensely personal and sometimes emotive, and some participants wished to remain anonymous so all the oral narratives have been anonymized for consistency.
[49] Wall, *Into Africa*, 152–3.

Sisters did not shy away from politicization of poverty. As agents of internationalism, they arranged for speakers to discuss with barrio residents 'more fully their position in a fast declining economy, as well as the various ways in which they may try to overcome exploitation'.[50] They organized Human Rights Groups and the 'building, furnishing & organising [of] a workshop for the Craft Group which will also provide an overnight refuge for battered women to be named "Casa de Misericordia"'.[51] They promoted native culture by organizing Peruvian Folk Groups that were 'essential', according to one sister, 'because many of the children born in the barrio have lost their "roots", be it religious/musical/dance, etc.'.[52] Barrio women were encouraged to organize, facilitate groups and raise funds, ultimately taking responsibility of their own communities and organizing in collaborative, non-hierarchical ways. The Sisters of Mercy acknowledged the political ramifications of what they did. One sister admitted: 'In such a complex scene, it is not easy to steer a middle course, in giving witness to Christian values of social justice and human rights, with sufficient sensitivity not to provide an excuse to someone in a power-position to retaliate against the very people our Sisters are trying to serve.'[53] One historian of Peru has called these forms of community organizing 'fraught with social and political implications'.[54] In a position paper dated 1987, the Sisters of Mercy reported on 'signs of life'. These included barrio residents organizing to put in basic services of water, sewerage and electricity. Disappointments could be intuited in this paper also, including the struggles to maintain democratic processes within the barrio structures. The position paper acknowledged that their aims, to create an active, Catholic populace with networks, confidence, skills and knowledge to address their own oppression, was far from complete.

Collaborations

Collaboration with other religious communities was also a new feature of the twentieth-century Catholic International. In the nineteenth century, successful missions to foreign lands would have been staffed by religious sisters from one religious institute. Declining numbers entering religious life limited the pool of missioners so cooperation between members of different religious congregations became more commonplace. One Sister of Mercy, alongside members from the Missionary Sisters of St Columban (Columban sisters) and Sisters of Mary Reparatrix, implemented religious programmes in ten centres for the physically impaired creating teaching materials for teachers and

---

[50] IOLM/PERU/3/1, 'Mercy Response to the Cry of the Poor', Letter from Mother Imelda Keena to Sisters re: February to March 1985, p. 54.
[51] IOLM/PERU/1/3, Circular Letter from Sister M. Mildred McNamara to Sisters dated 1985.
[52] IOLM/PERU/3/1, 'Mercy Response to the Cry of the Poor', Letter from Mother Imelda Keena to Sisters re: February to March 1985.
[53] IOLM/PERU/3/1: 'Mercy Response to the Cry of the Poor', Report on visit to Lima, 19 March–11 April 1987 by Mother Imelda Keena, p. 68.
[54] Jeffrey L. Klaiber, 'Prophets and Populists: Liberation Theology, 1968-1988', *The Americas* 46 (1989): 7.

parents.⁵⁵ They shared pedagogical expertise as they travelled throughout Peru giving one-day courses to local staff on preparatory programmes for first communion and confirmation, and tutoring Peruvian catechists.⁵⁶ Relationships between religious were more than simply collegiate.⁵⁷ One sister remarked: 'And you became very, the missionaries together, you became very close, you were like one family. You never thought of them as different orders. Yeah, worked with the Franciscans were lovely as well, and the priests were lovely, you know.'⁵⁸

The Columbans were central to coordinating the Leeds Peru Mission; they provided the intellectual, spiritual and physical hub of these Peruvian endeavours. They arrived in Peru in 1951, and by the end of the century, they, alongside priests, religious sisters and Catholic laity, were managing twelve parishes. They were vital to this experimenting though this was not without tensions.⁵⁹ Mission praxis emanating from liberation theology was political, and some were insistent the Columbans should stick to their pastoral role. Others, like Tiago G. Cloin, Redemptorist and Bishop of Barra in Bahia, Brazil speaking to the Columbans at a week-long study week, urged a more radical thinking:

> I would like to add only one thing about sending missionaries to Latin America. The missionary needs many qualities, but one is absolutely essential – a great feeling for social justice.⁶⁰

One sister acknowledged the significance of the Columbans to the mission: it was 'to them that all other priests and Sisters there converge for organization of mission projects, for organization of finances for collection of their mail, for advice, for the proverbial cuppa, and above all for the experience of real caring friendship'.⁶¹ Other occasions for collegiality and mutual support included the monthly meal shared by the Mercy sisters of Villa Maria and Villa Sol with nearby sisters of other religious institutes.⁶²

Sisters of Mercy, like other congregations, continued to imbibe spiritual and political sustenance through their association with the Columbans who organized regular retreats and meetings. One sister recalled at one of these meetings the influence of the foremost liberation theologian of their generation, Gustavo Gutiérriez: 'I remember hearing him, yeah. And some of the foreign priests would too, yeah. And every day there was different topics.'⁶³ Liberation theology became controversial

---

55 RSM Union: Miss/1: 'Peru 1978', Letter from Sister Joan Healy to Sisters dated September 1981.
56 RSM Union: Miss/1: 'Peru 1978', Letter from Sister Joan Healy to Mother Augustine Cahill dated August 1982.
57 Mangion, *Catholic Nuns and Sisters in a Secular Age*, Chapter 5.
58 Interview RSM 012.
59 Michael Fitzgerald, 'Changing Course', *The Far East*, November 1969, 4–6; Angelyn Dries, *Be Centered in Christ and Not in Self: The Missionary Society of Saint Columban: The North American Story (1918–2018)* (Bloomington, IN: Xlibris Corporation, 2017), 202–5.
60 Tiago G. Cloin, 'Latin America – Brazil', in *The Church Is Mission*, ed. Enda Mc Donagh (London: Geoffrey Chapman, 1969), 170.
61 RSM Union: Miss/1: Peru 1978, Letter from Sister Margaret Mary to Sisters dated March 1985.
62 Interview RSM 011.
63 Interview RSM 012. Peña in pointing out that 'protest language in liberation theology echoed that of an already mobilized popular sector' acknowledges already existing 'poor people's movements'.

in Catholic circles. Some were concerned it enabled the spread of Marxism, while others believed it strengthened the democratization process and 'awaken[s] the poor to the dangers of any form of political manipulation, whether from the right or the left'.[64] The mission to Peru, while adhering to some of the nineteenth-century ideals about 'care' for the poor, incorporated new thinking on liberation theology and its language of the margins politicized the missionary aims of the Sisters of Mercy. This terminology was used frequently in the recollections of individual sisters. One sister recalled:

> liberation theology was beginning to come in and the call of the Church as well, yeah, was saying to reach out to the poor. And we seemed to have everything, really. And it was, for me, I know you can't solve everything, but we can share.[65]

In acknowledging the 'we' in England who had 'everything', this sister was moved to 'share' though acknowledging the limitations of any permanent solution to the inequities of life for the poor in Peru. Sharing faith and evangelization was intrinsic to the Peru mission, but by harnessing the discourse of social justice the Sisters of Mercy were engaged with a political intent that was more than simply 'care'. They took the opportunity to respond to the 'preferential option for the poor' by redistributing resources and personnel to the mission field where support was needed. What underpinned these practical ministries was the desire to be 'present' to the poor; and to urge barrio residents to develop structures and skills they would use in their own journey of much hoped-for liberation.

The mission to Peru brought together sisters from several communities in England and also introduced them to other groups of Sisters of Mercy missioned to Peru from Ireland, the United States, Canada, Australia and New Zealand.[66] These autonomous groups became more interconnected from the late 1970s. North American groups of Mercies in Latin American united under the umbrella 'Mercy Union General of the United States'.[67] The Sisters of Mercy then expanded this grouping internationally, deciding it would be fruitful to connect as one body in Latin America though links to home countries remained in place. They were united in a Mercy identity that became stronger as they became 'more conscious of being part of Mercy – on all levels: local, Latin America, International'.[68] They held regular conferences, nationally, regionally and internationally. The Latin American and Caribbean conference of 1989 had as one of its aims to 'grow towards greater unity'. Together they drew up the 'Common

---

 Milagros Peña, 'Liberation Theology in Peru: An Analysis of the Role of Intellectuals in Social Movements', *Journal for the Scientific Study of Religion* 33 (1994): 43.

[64] Jeffrey L. Klaiber, 'Prophets and Populists: Liberation Theology, 1968-1988', *The Americas* 46 (1989): 14. Liberation theology also has a place in black and feminist movements.

[65] Interview RSM 012.

[66] Mary Beth Fraser Connolly briefly discusses the Chicago Sisters of Mercy Sicuani mission to Peru, which established schools and healthcare facilities. Connolly, *Women of Faith*, 162–3. For more on the United States missions, see Angelyn Dries, *The Missionary Movement in American Catholic History* (Maryknoll: Orbis Books, 1998), 179–246.

[67] RSM Union: MISS/1, 'Policy Regarding the Peru Mission', p. 5.

[68] RSM Union: MISS/1, 'Common Criteria for Formation Programs in L.A. [Latin America]'.

Criteria for Formation Programs in L.A. [Latin America]'. Many were also wedded to an understanding of mission which incorporated social justice language such as the desire to 'insert oneself among the poor (house, work, Heart)', 'allow the poor to evangelize us' and 'accompany the people in their struggles to defend life (justice initiative, co-ops, workshops, etc.)'.[69]

The educational remit of the Sisters of Mercy extended beyond the *barriada*. As agents of internationalism, their letters home were shared and discussed in Mercy communities. There were continued efforts to maintain links between the Sisters of Mercy in Peru and in England at a time of tumultuous change in religious life.[70] Regular visitors included congregation leaders and sometimes ordinary sisters. Mother General Augustine Cahill and Mother Imelda Keena of Doncaster spent eight weeks in 1980 with Mercy sisters in Tupac Amaru promoting community renewal. Upon her return, Keena was anxious to share her experiences, indicating: 'This is an opportunity for us to show our solidarity with our sisters working in the Third World, as well as giving us the chance of coming together for a few hours to renew our friendships and deepen our relationships.'[71]

In 'bearing witness', Sisters of Mercy also conveyed eyewitness accounts of political and economic injustices and structural inequities faced by barrio occupants to a larger English audience. 'Bearing witness', according to theorist Fuyuki Kurasawa, encompasses a 'web of cosmopolitan testimonial practices structured around five dialectically related tasks and perils': voice against silence; interpretation against incomprehension, empathy against indifference, remembrance against forgetting and prevention against repetition.[72] Media coverage of Peru in the Catholic parish, diocesan and national press included vivid accounts of Lima's poverty by the Bishop of Leeds, George Dwyer, alongside fundraising efforts of parish Justice and Peace groups, Friends of Peru and a folk-singing girl-group from Notre Dame High School.[73] Epistolary exchanges in the 1970s and 1980s were important means of communication in the early days of the transnational 'era of the witness' when media coverage was less instantaneous and relentless.[74] Bearing witness did not 'cure' or eliminate injustice, but it was, as Kurasawa highlighted, an 'act of resistance' that potentially enabled participation, empathy and knowledge to cross national borders.[75] 'Bearing witness' had a remarkable similarity to one of the 1979 Puebla commitments: to give public witness for the church's solidarity with the poor. Sisters of Mercy shared and criticized

---

[69] RSM Union: MISS/1, 'Common Criteria for Formation Programs in L.A. [Latin America]'.
[70] Mangion, *Catholic Nuns and Sisters in a Secular Age*, Chapter 1.
[71] RSM Union: Miss/1, Letter from Sister Mary Malachy Slavin to Sisters dated 7 February 1980.
[72] Fuyuki Kurasawa, 'A Message in a Bottle: Bearing Witness as a Mode of Transnational Practice', *Theory, Culture & Society* 26 (2009): 92.
[73] 'Parish Visit in Peru', *Catholic Herald*, 21 August 1964, 4; 'Mr Kieron Moore', *Catholic Herald*, 3 August 1977, 3; 'People and Places', *Catholic Herald*, 17 March 1978, 7; 'People and Places', *Catholic Herald*, 19 March 1978, 9; 'Christopher Howse Reports on the Differences in a Working Childhood', *Catholic Herald*, 29 February 1980, 2.
[74] Annette Wieviorka, *The Era of the Witness*, trans. Jared Stark (London: Cornell University Press, 1998/2006), 96.
[75] Kurasawa, 'A Message in a Bottle', 106.

the injustices lived daily by barrio occupants and expressed solidarity with the poor while conscientizing Catholics in England.

Concluding thoughts

The Sisters of Mercy in their missions to Peru sought to empower those marginalized by poverty by creating local institutions and processes that would be managed and supported by barrio residents, but were integrated into international missionary networks that were part of the Catholic International. They supplied resources in the form of technical expertise, personal labour, access to funding and knowledge of information, creating networks both in Peru and in England. This form of religious internationalism was born from a desire of Mercy sisters from England, and elsewhere, to engage with the assumed spiritual and known material needs of Peruvians. As Catholic missionaries, they shared an understanding of marginalization, seen through the lens of social justice and liberation theology. Scholars Emily Baughan and Juliano Fiori have stressed this form of humanitarian action, the empowerment of local actors, could be 'part of a politics of transnational solidarity':

> This is not a solidarity based on shared experience or characteristics, nor is it one that privileges the role of the outsider as an 'impartial spectator'. Instead, it is a solidarity between different agents with distinctive roles in pursuit of a common goal: a more just politics that challenges marginalisation, oppression, and subordination in their various forms.[76]

The mission of the Sisters of Mercy reflected a shift in the strategies of tackling of injustices through an interdependent relationship where giving and receiving was experienced by all parties.

Women religious were guided by a Catholic ethos that provided the religious motivation to engage with liberal, modern ideas of social justice. Historian Jaclyn Granick, in her examination of three faith-based organizations, called this 'sacralized humanitarianism' and argued that religious humanitarians drew on their faith 'for motivation, for justification, for empathy and combined it with the liberal ideas of the times. . . . They interpreted the world in light of their particular beliefs and adapted their organizations to navigate the balance of an ever-changing world and religious tradition.'[77] Social justice and liberation theology with its 'preferential option for the poor' allied with the idealism and activism of the long 1960s, informed the Sisters of Mercy mission in Peru. The sacred was personal, as well as political. The women I

---

[76] Emily Baughan and Juliano Fiori, 'Save the Children, the Humanitarian Project, and the Politics of Solidarity: Reviving Dorothy Buxton's Vision', *Disasters* 39 (2015): 129–45.

[77] Jaclyn Granick, 'Sacralized Humanitarianism: A Comparison of Three Faith-Based Private Associations', 2011, http://www.swiss-quakers.ch/ge/library/e-documents/7971-Granick2011.pdf (accessed 26 February 2016). Granick cites the work of Lisa Moses Leff on sacralized work. Lisa Moses Leff, *Sacred Bonds of Solidarity: The Rise of Jewish Internationalism in Nineteenth-Century France* (Stanford, CA: Stanford University Press, 2006), 169.

interviewed were guided throughout their ministerial work by their relationship with God; many found the new connections and relationships with the 'people of God' transformational, and this shaped and politicized their internationalism. Their decision to move outside of traditional convent ministries was not lightly taken, it was informed by a discourse of social justice that emanated from pontifical letters and encyclicals and their interpretation of the needs of the world. For women religious, these shifts in the 1970s and 1980s were 'radical' responses at a time of transition. Admittedly, such radicalness does not translate well in a secular world that identifies 'radical' with 'radical politics'. Ethnographer Marla F. Frederick suggested from her study of black women and faith that 'women's refashioning of their world may not always coincide with traditional interpretations of radical politics; nevertheless the communities they create and the life changes they inspire speak to the agentive possibilities of their faith.'[78] It is this agentive possibility that is salient to the radical nature of the early adopters of experimental religious ministries. For many women, the working for social justice was inherently political as it critiqued the inequities faced by the marginalized.

In the creation of internationalist identities and the 'doing' of internationalism from the bottom-up, female Catholic missionaries crossed boundaries in order to strengthen religious identities but also to reform and support societies through solidarity and collaboration. As part of a larger Catholic International, religious institutes were rethinking their internationalism in response to the spirit of *aggiornamento* of the Second Vatican Council, the development of liberation theology and the influential secular social movements of the long 1960s. Missionary work as a form of internationalism did not occur in a vacuum; it was aligned to the larger social movements of the post-war Catholic and secular world. Women religious were guided by global thinking and influenced by social justice rhetoric. Motivated by faith without an explicitly feminist or political agenda, women religious as internationalists negotiated how their internationalism was defined, lived and experienced. They were significant historical actors within the Catholic International. The Peru mission responded to global religious and secular imperatives; it diverged from the top-down structures of nineteenth-century internationalism to stress solidarity and collaboration with both the peoples of Peru and other international groups. These were collaborative ventures, Sisters of Mercy from England worked alongside other Sisters of Mercy, clergy, female and male religious and laypeople. New praxis in the foreign missions integrated global thinking revealing both a local mission done globally, as part of an extensive Catholic International and 'bearing witness' to Catholic communities in England, and a global mission done locally with religious sisters living and collaborating with the inhabitants of the *barriadas* of Peru. Internationalism, as this case study demonstrates, is more than a secular, liberal product of modernity.

---

[78] Marla F. Frederick, *Between Sundays: Black Women and Everyday Struggles of Faith* (London: University of California Press, 2003), 12.

8

Knowledge as aid

Locals experts, international health organizations and building the first Czechoslovak penicillin factory, 1944–9

Sławomir Łotysz

We tend to assume that international aid programmes, whether for ad hoc relief or long-term rehabilitation, are top-down initiatives formulated by politicians, with the scientists, engineers, doctors and relief workers only stepping in afterwards to actually provide the aid. This is the message conveyed by the media, which usually presents such programmes as being the result of political negotiations. But although the politicians have their place, the signing of agreements is, in fact, the last stage of what often begins as a bottom-up initiative triggered by local needs and devised by visionary locals, who understand both the problem and how it needs to be solved.

The history of the United Nations Relief and Rehabilitation Administration (UNRRA)'s penicillin plant programme is a good example of what skilled and eager local experts can do in formulating relief schemes. This programme was unique in the sense that apart from its humanitarian aspect, it was in fact a complex industrial rehabilitation project involving the changing hands of a highly advanced technology of potential military importance. The complex political situation on the brink of the Cold War did not make planning and carrying out the programme any easier.

This chapter aims to explain the Czechoslovaks' role in raising the question of Eastern Europe's independence from Western penicillin supplies, and their part in the formulation of this special rehabilitation programme's principles. In the broader context, this analysis will add to a better understanding of how international aid programmes relate to local settings, namely how they make use of existing expertise and how they contribute to local learning.[1]

[1] This research was funded by the National Science Centre, Poland, under grant number 2014/13/B/HS3/04951. Draft versions of this chapter were presented at the Seventh International Conference of the European Society for the History of Science in Prague in 2016, and at the Twenty-Fifth International Congress of the History of Science and Technology in Rio de Janeiro the following year. Some of the findings included in this chapter have been covered in a paper published in Chinese in the *Journal of the Social History of Medicine and Health*(Yīliáo shèhuì sh☒ yánjiū) in

Aid programmes designed arbitrarily by international aid and rehabilitation organizations, although invaluable to those in need, can in the long term be harmful to local initiatives and resourcefulness. As Philip Berke and Timothy Beatley observed in the case of post-hurricane aid programmes in the Caribbean, most top-down government actions were 'essentially authoritarian', while top-down NGO programmes 'tended to be paternalistic'.[2]

UNRRA relied heavily on the mutual cooperation of the population being assisted, which suggests that its approach was much more innovative than many of the international aid programmes of the time, and even of today. This 'local component' was embedded in how the administration actually worked: the supply division in Washington was empowered to arrange procurements and shipments only at the request of the UNRRA mission operating in each country. The mission, in turn, responded to specific needs articulated by local authorities, whether they were responsible for health, welfare, agriculture, transportation or industry. However, when the UN assumed many of UNRRA's duties after it was disbanded in 1947, it broke with this tradition of drawing on local expertise in defining its programmes, with most of its aid programmes being subsequently built on a 'top-down' approach. This change was unfavourable, as in general 'top-down' schemes are liable to specific deviations that render the assistance provided less effective and not as well targeted, and thus less effective overall than they could be. As D. John Shaw argues, it was only after disappointing results from these initiatives that the 'bottom-up' attitude was again adopted by the UN agencies.[3]

The lessons learned from UNRRA's practices have also been forgotten by the WHO, the immediate successor of UNRRA's health programmes. Even by the 1970s, the US-based Institute of Medicine emphasized in a report the importance of including the 'community mobilization component' in planning the WHO's programmes to improve sanitary and medical conditions in developing countries.[4] As for the reasons why most of these aid schemes followed the top-down approach, the report pointed out that 'relatively few program planners and administrators understood the requirements of effective use' of this factor. While summarizing the background of early post-war rehabilitation programmes, the report stressed that the planners considered the 'traditional societies' they were helping to be 'relatively closed systems – conservative homogenous and static, with individual behaviour being non-innovative and non-experimental'. Adopting such anthropological theories, originally coined to define low-income groups but now used to pigeonhole entire countries, could have in fact been an exemplification of the quasi-colonial attitude of the benefactors to their beneficiaries.

2017. This author wishes to thank the discussants at both meetings for their valuable comments, as well as the editors and reviewers of the above-mentioned journals. Last but not least, thanks go to the editors of this volume for their guidance and patient assistance.

[2] Philip R. Berke and Timothy Beatley, *After the Hurricane: Linking Recovery to Sustainable Development in the Caribbean* (Baltimore: Johns Hopkins University Press, 1997), 180.

[3] D. John Shaw, *The UN World Food Programme and the Development of Food Aid* (New York: Palgrave, 2001), 142.

[4] Institute of Medicine (US). Committee on International Health, *Strengthening U.S. Programs to Improve Health in Developing Countries* (Washington: National Academy of Sciences, 1978), 38–9.

Neglecting local conditions and renouncing vernacular participation in health-oriented programmes can indeed be considered colonial in its origin. During the anti-hookworm campaign in British Ceylon, launched in 1916, the personnel of the Rockefeller Foundation did not ask for the cooperation of the indigenous population as long as they were operating under the umbrella of the colonial authorities. But when the campaign expanded to other countries in the region, where colonial control did not exist, as Randall Packard has noted, the Foundation's International Health Board was forced to develop new communication strategies to overcome resistance to the painful treatment, and adapt it to existing conditions.[5]

Whether top-down or bottom-up, 'health interventions are more successful' than other aid programmes, according to William Easterly. Or at least, they might look that way, because their 'outcomes are specifically defined and easily observable – you can keep track of deaths from disease', he argues.[6] Still, UNRRA's penicillin plant programme does not easily fit into that category. It was part of the health activities of the administration, but embraced operations more typical of development plans, such as industrial investment and transfer of know-how. The latter was particularly vulnerable to failure, as it assumed that local specialists, who, for several years under Nazi occupation remained disconnected from the international circulation of knowledge, were capable of comprehending the latest advances in mycology, bacteriology, biochemistry and chemical engineering that had occurred mainly in the United States until then.

Although risky, this approach carried the promise of embedding the transferred know-how deeper and more efficiently in the local context. Nowadays, this is particularly visible in industrial development programmes, planned and managed like typical business ventures, yet financed by international institutions. According to Richard Ouma-Onyango, who analysed how the rehabilitation of Kenya's sugar industry was carried out in the 1980s, aid comes in packages that preclude local experts and stunt local learning.[7] While they do include the much-needed technology and know-how, they leave no room for existing local expertise and do not contribute to its advancement. In this sense, these programmes can create technological bubbles.

Within the quite extensive historiography on UNRRA activities, only very few works have even looked at its largest single rehabilitation project – the penicillin plant programme – let alone used it as a focal point.[8] Works on penicillin's general history do much better in this respect. Robert Bud gives a general overview of the uneasy implementation of the programme, although he does not explore its origins in depth.[9] Not enough justice has been done in detailing the Czechs' role as initiators of the

---

[5] Randall M. Packard, *A History of Global Health: Interventions into the Lives of Other Peoples* (Baltimore: Johns Hopkins University Press, 2016), 34.

[6] William Easterly, *The White Man's Burden: Why the West's Efforts to Aid the Rest Have Done so Much Ill and so Little Good* (Oxford: Oxford University Press, 2006), 158.

[7] Richard Ouma-Onyango, *Information Resources and Technology Transfer Management in Developing Countries* (London: Routledge, 1997), 95.

[8] With the exception of my recent book, which centres on it. See *Fabryka z darów. Penicylina za żelazną kurtyną 1945-1954* (Warsaw: Aspra-JR, 2020).

[9] Robert Bud, *Penicillin: Triumph and Tragedy* (Oxford: Oxford University Press, 2007), 84–6.

UNRRA programme and their contribution to its finalization.[10] While the story of the Czechoslovak plant is largely overlooked, the national historiographies in Italy, Poland and Yugoslavia cover their own parts more or less thoroughly.[11]

Using previously unpublished sources, this chapter sheds new light on how the programme was conceived, negotiated and then painstakingly carried out. It traces interventions by key figures, both world-famous and those less recognized internationally, but still important in national historiographies, as well as some who have been entirely forgotten, such as the engineers and UNRRA officers.

A 'miracle drug' in a morbid world

Late in 1946, the Czechoslovak minister of health Dr Adolf Procházka thanked Fiorello La Guardia, director general of the UNRRA, for making penicillin available to his fellow compatriots. 'We all well remember that penicillin was sent to this country with the UNRRA medical supplies for the first time a few weeks after the liberation,' Procházka said, adding that at present it was 'impossible to imagine' therapy without it.[12]

Procházka echoed the conclusions of their ministerial Penicillin Commission, who had reviewed the results of the first year of treatment of patients with this first antibiotic. But his enthusiasm was justifiable for yet another reason. By late 1946, all signs pointed to a complete penicillin factory – long since promised to Czechoslovakia by UNRRA and the result of even longer negotiations – finally reaching the country and being ready for swift assembly. This would bring great changes to the lives of the Czechs and Slovaks, who would be able to enjoy secure and stable supplies of the 'miracle drug' from the day after the factory was completed. Additionally, the plant was a golden opportunity for the Czechoslovak scientists to catch up with the British and Americans, who were currently leading the research on antibiotics.

Spirits must have been high on both sides, since Petr I. Alexeev, the head of the UNRRA Mission in Prague, expressed hope that the penicillin plant would be a

---

[10] See, among others, Karel Smolek and František Slanec, *Deset let československých antibiotik* (Prague: Státní zdravotnické nakladatelství, 1959); Bohumil Sikyta, 'Moderní vývoj biotechnologií. Příspěvek českých zemí', in *Vývoj biotechnologie a průmyslové chemie. Seria: Práce z dějin techniky a přírodních věd*, Vol. 12, ed. Jaroslav Folta (Prague: Národní technické muzeum, 2006), 3–61;Karel Sommer, *UNRRA a Československo* (Opava: Slezský ústav AV ČR, 1993).

[11] For Italian case, see Mauro Capocci, '"A Chain Is Gonna Come". Building a Penicillin Production Plant in Post-war Italy', *Dynamis* 31, no. 2 (2011): 343–62; 'Cold Drugs. Circulation, Production and Intelligence of Antibiotics in Post-WWII Years', *Medicina nei Secoli* 26, no. 2 (2014): 1–22; Daniele Cozzoli, 'Penicillin and the European Response to Post-war American Hegemony: The Case of Leo-Penicillin', *History and Technology: An International Journal* 30, no. 1–2 (2014): 83–103; Daniele Cozzoli and Mauro Capocci, 'Making Biomedicine in TwentiethCentury Italy: Domenico Marotta (1886–1974) and the Italian Higher Institute of Health', *The British Journal for the History of Science* 44, no. 4 (2011): 549–74. For the history of the Polish factory, see my papers: 'A "Lasting Memorial" to the UNRRA? Implementation of the Penicillin Plant Programme in Poland, 1946–1949', *ICON: Journal of the International Committee for the History of Technology* 20, no. 2 (2014): 70–91, and for Yugoslavian one, see Petar Bosnić, *Istorija jugoslovenskog penicilina 1945-1995* (Belgrade: P.B. Bosnić, 1995).

[12] United Nation Archives, New York, USA (hereafter UNA), S-1320-0000-0004, P. Alexeev to F. La Guardia, 3 December 1946.

'lasting memorial' to the administration, which was established in 1943 to bring assistance to countries ravaged by the war.[13] The main slogan behind the formation of the organization was 'Helping people to help themselves', and so providing them with a pharmaceutical factory instead of just sending periodic supplies of ready-to-use medicine was very much in line with UNRRA policy.[14]

The penicillin plant programme also included Poland, two Soviet Republics (Belarus and Ukraine) and Italy. The latter took the place of Yugoslavia, which was initially on the list but eventually withdrew.[15] At that time, the Belarusian and Ukrainian Republics were in fact superficial political entities, fully dependent on Moscow. Poland and Czechoslovakia had been liberated by the Red Army, which soon turned into an occupant itself, guaranteeing that the entire region would remain in the Soviet zone of influence. As for Italy, because of the strong position of their communist party, the country's future could not be foreseen with absolute certainty.

While tensions between the United States and the Soviet Union increased, the prospects of a new confrontation between former allies also loomed on the horizon. Even until 1948, certain Western policymakers were deluding themselves that pro-democratic tendencies in the 'curtain countries' could be sustained, thanks to the humanitarian relief offered to their populations.[16] This explains why the Soviets were so eager to accuse UNRRA of being a political tool in the hands of 'imperialists', and why the Western governments and societies became gradually more reluctant to continue this support, as in turn they were only receiving more hostility.

Although the unfavourable political climate might have endangered finalization of the programme, it was more likely to fall apart for another reason. Namely, that it was essentially a very ambitious grassroots initiative, aimed at establishing a new, highly sophisticated branch of industry in countries without a sufficient industrial environment or substantial scientific backing. It involved a transfer of knowledge and know-how in such varied disciplines as fermentation, analytical chemistry, microbiology, chemical engineering and mechanical technology. The antibiotics industry was still in its infancy then, and transplanting such incompletely developed technology carried the risk that without local personnel capable of overseeing the process, within a couple of years the entire investment would become a technological fossil.

---

[13] UNA, S-1339-0000-0010, P. Alexeev to L. Rooks, cable no. 2111, undated.

[14] United Nations Information Office, *Helping the People to Help Themselves: The Story of the United Nations Relief and Rehabilitation Administration* (New York: United Nations Information Office, 1943), 13.

[15] The reasons for their withdrawal, as well as its consequences, is covered in: Sławomir Łotysz, 'A Bargain or a 'Mousetrap'? Reused Penicillin Plant and the Yugoslavians Quest for a Healthier Life in the Early Post-war Era (1946-1950)', in *The Persistence of Technology. Histories of Repair, Reuse and Disposal*, ed. Stefan Krebs and Heike Weber (Bielefeld: Transcript, 2020), 7–25.

[16] Provision of this relief was not free of political motivation. For example, when Poland suffered from a dramatic shortage of grain in the summer of 1947, the US authorities contemplated sending supplies from other directions, assuming that it would be 'undesirable' for America to let the Poles become dependent on Soviet grain. Library and Archives Canada, RG 25, box 3892, 9255-B-40, F. Linville to G. Craig, 18 July 1947.

The wonder of organized science

The story of penicillin in the context of early post-war international aid is significant. It was not merely an important medicine that should not be denied to needy people for humanitarian reasons, but a tool for exercising political power, and even a potential tool of war. Penicillin made its great debut on the battlefields of Northern Africa and Italy in 1943, and was quickly adopted in therapeutic practices by military surgeons on all frontlines where Anglo-Saxon forces fought. The allies quickly grasped the military importance of the new drug. Marshal Bernard Montgomery, reporting on his advances in the North-West European theatre between mid-1944 and mid-1945, said: 'The healing of war wounds has been revolutionised by the use of penicillin. Many men, who in the last war would have been permanent invalids, were fit and ready to go back to the line within a month of being wounded.'[17]

The same view was presented by Vannevar Bush (1945), an American inventor, engineer and professor at the Massachusetts Institute of Technology, who headed the US Office of Scientific Research and Development during the war. Although in his report to President Herbert Hoover in July 1945 Bush acknowledged the science-based technologies as a warrant of America's health and prosperity in the post-war era, he also referred to their military importance. He called penicillin 'a most effective weapon ... in accelerating healing of wounds and burns'.[18] For Bush, penicillin – next to radar – was the greatest scientific achievement of that era. 'Science and the great practical genius of this Nation made this achievement possible,' he wrote in his report.[19] This was true in the sense that American research institutions were generously supported by their government. They worked in close partnership with private industry, and had succeeded in developing what had been crude, theoretical concepts flown out of Great Britain busy with war, into mature and fully operable technologies.

British research on penicillin was initiated in late 1939 at the University of Oxford by Ernst Chain, Howard Florey and Norman Heatley, who picked up the slack from Alexander Fleming, whose original discovery of the curative properties of penicillin mould in 1928 had remained merely a scientific curiosity. In 1941, Florey and Heatley flew to America with their notes, and the spores of *Penicillium* fungi. By mid-1943, the allied nations gained access to what was then called (with only very little exaggeration) 'a wonder drug'. Bud defines penicillin as a biological product of 'organized science', as its manufacture required integration of a variety of scientific and engineering disciplines on a previously unprecedented scale.[20]

It goes without saying that all reports on the chemistry of penicillin, its production methods and medical applications were made secret during the war. And with the Cold War tensions that dominated relations between the former allies, the ban was not so readily lifted. Holding the knowledge of the new drug, the editors of the fundamental

---

[17] Bernard Montgomery, *Operations in North-West Europe from 6th June 1944 to 5th May 1945*, 'Supplement to the London Gazette' no. 37711 (3 September 1946): 4452.
[18] Vannevar Bush, *Science, the Endless Frontier: A Report to the President on a Program for Postwar Scientific Research, July 1945* (Washington, DC: United States Government Printing Office, 1945), 46.
[19] Ibid., 5.
[20] Bud, *Penicillin: Triumph and Tragedy*, 23.

work 'The chemistry of penicillin', published in early 1949, explained this reluctance with reference to 'the extreme importance of penicillin as a military weapon'.[21] Although they were referring to the reasons behind the policy of secrecy that had been lifted by the end of 1945, communist propaganda exploited this phrase to accuse the United States of still limiting access to this knowledge as late as 1949.[22]

From mercy flights to factories

With production levels rising in the United States, Canada and Great Britain, more penicillin was gradually released to civilian patients, even before the end of the war. Subsequently, it became available in other Western nations that could afford to buy the drug on the free market, or that had managed to launch their own production. The Russians had some of their own making too, but their basic method of obtaining penicillin, which they had developed independently by 1944, did not offer much prospect of improving either the quality or availability of the drug. Other nations, too poor or too devastated by the war, depended entirely on the mercy of those who enjoyed an abundance of the new drug.

Penicillin has always been at the top of UNRRA's delivery lists to all recipient countries, just as Procházka said it was. But the Red Cross and other charitable organizations also had a hand in providing vials of the drug. The United Polish Relief Fund, for example, used to send the drug by planes. After one of their so-called mercy flights crashed in November 1945, it became clear that the health policy of multimillion-population nations could not be based on such expensive, unreliable and risky air bridges.[23] Further, in spite of all the sacrifices made along the way, there was still not enough penicillin for everyone. As a commodity that was still technically scarce, penicillin often found itself being stolen, smuggled and forged throughout continental Europe, both in the liberated countries and in occupied Germany – press reports from the time are full of such stories. Although in its early form this first antibiotic had to be kept in cold storage, it was really hot stuff on the black market.

There was only one way forward: let all nations have their own supplies of what would appear to be the basis of therapeutic practice for many years to come. Building factories, training local personnel and providing them with all the necessary know-how seemed to be the only logical, sustainable solution. It also seemed actually doable, since all of the minds behind developing the method of making penicillin – from Fleming to Chain, Heatley and Florey – had refused to patent the process, for the good of humankind.

[21] Hans T. Clarke, ed., *The Chemistry of Penicillin* (Princeton: Princeton University Press, 1949), VII.
[22] This was voiced at (among other places) the World Health Assembly in July 1949 by a Polish delegate, Irena Domańska. See 'Seventh Plenary Meeting, Second World Health Assembly, Rome, 13 June to 2 July 1949', *Official Records of the World Health Organization*, no. 21 (December 1949): 105.
[23] Five Canadian airmen were killed in the crash. See Hugh A. Halliday, 'Penicillin for Poland: A Tale of Two Plaques: Air Force, Part 48', *Legion Magazine*, 19 December 2011, https://legionmagazine.co m/en/2011/12/penicillin-for-poland-a-tale-of-two-plaques-air-force-part-48/ (accessed 30 April 2020).

Conceiving the inconceivable

The idea that the Czechs and Slovaks would need penicillin once the war was over came into being in 1944, when the country was still in the grip of the Nazis. The officials of the Czechoslovak government-in-exile in England initiated talks in London and Washington, investigating whether UNRRA would be willing to include a penicillin production equipment into its medical rehabilitation programme for the country. Since such a venture would have required some outlay from themselves, the Czechs had some concerns about its profitability, as the antibiotics industry was a new and rapidly evolving trade and there were rumours about the swift arrival of synthetic penicillin, suggesting that a price drop was coming. However, since new factories employing the biological process of making penicillin were being built all over the free world, it looked like everyone was taking the same risk.[24] Eventually, after encountering numerous difficulties the negotiations came to a halt. As the Czechs later summarized the outcome of their efforts, 'certain circles in London and Washington were not in favour' of their request.[25]

After liberation, negotiations were resumed by the new Prague government. Their medical delegate in Washington was Professor Josef Brumlik, a world-renowned cardiologist.[26] In the summer of 1945, Brumlik began inquiring as to whether UNRRA would be more willing to come up with the desired assistance. The Czechoslovaks envisioned a plant of forty billion units capacity, to be operated by a special joint-venture company closely supervised by the Ministry of Health and formed by the country's three largest pharmaceutical producers: B. Fragner, Interpharma and the Spolek pro chemickou a hutní výrobu (Association for Chemical and Metallurgical Production).[27]

The typical procedure in UNRRA's rehabilitation projects was that such requests were first made by their own regional missions. So, in late July 1945, after the Czechoslovaks touched base with UNRRA officials in Washington – or at least, after they thought they had – Vojtech Schlesinger of the Ministry of Health officially asked Petr I. Alexeev to initiate procurement of a complete penicillin plant for Czechoslovakia, adding that to his understanding the administration was 'willing in principal [sic] to supply such a factory'.[28]

The Czechoslovaks did not ask for the machines alone. They knew that they were useless without the knowledge to operate them, so Prague also requested training for two of their experts, either in the United States or in Canada, so that they could begin production at the plant as soon as it was complete. For this training, they had two particular people in mind – a bacteriologist, Dr Ivan Malek, from the Bacteriological

---

[24] Narodni archiv, Prague, the Czech Republic (hereafter NAP), MZd, M 1460/1945, Vladislav Kruta, Informace pro pana ministra, 13 November 1945.
[25] Ibid.
[26] Stanley B. Winters, 'Obituary. Joseph V. Brumlík (1897-1979)', *East Central Europe* 6, no. 1 (1979): 127–9.
[27] In 1945, they were still private enterprises, only being nationalized the following year.
[28] UNA, S-1327-0000-0010, V. Schlesinger to P. Alexeev, 31 July 1945.

and Serological Institute at Charles University, and Milos Harold, a chemical engineer from the B. Fragner company. As Prohazka noted, the two men

> have been working on the isolation of penicillin for some years, and have succeeded in finding the right method themselves, at a time when they were completely cut off during the Nazi occupation. They already know the flask method and some methods of isolation of the drug, and would certainly gain the necessary knowledge of the more modern procedures in the shortest possible time.[29]

The minister here referred to the now-famous story of Mykoin BF 510, the so-called Czech penicillin, developed in secrecy during the German occupation at the B. Fragner pharmaceutical plant in Dolní Měcholupy, East of Prague.[30] At first, the Czechs were not sure whether the active agent they had obtained was the same substance they had read about in a copy of *Schweizerische Medizinische Vochenschrift*, as being produced in Great Britain and the United States from *Penicillium notatum*. They simply did not have access to British or American drugs to test its chemical structure, or at least its curative properties. Only after the war was it confirmed that both substances, Penicillin and Mykoin BF 510, were identical.[31]

What happened next could have been considered an effect of multiple misunderstandings, communication problems or even proof that those 'certain circles' in Washington were still not in favour of Czechoslovakia's request: it appears that for the next two months, no official call ever reached UNRRA headquarters. While it isn't clear who should be blamed for this, it seems that it was not the Prague mission. Throughout August it repeatedly asked Washington 'whether UNRRA's [offer to build a] penicillin factory in Czechoslovakia [is] firm'.[32] Schlesinger had, in the meantime, been informed by the Czechoslovak embassy in the United States that UNRRA, although having taken some steps towards procuring the equipment, could not carry on until an official request arrived from the Prague mission. On the 24th of September, Schlesinger again asked Alexeev to 'kindly look to the matter', and pass it on to Washington if he found that 'the factory is really necessary in Czechoslovakia'.[33]

In early October, UNRRA finally responded, although it was not the answer the Czechs had been waiting for. Herbert Lehman, UNRRA director general, informed the Prague mission that 'consideration will be given' if the Czechoslovak government proposed (through the mission, of course) upgrading Prague's State Health Institute with a small-scale penicillin plant.[34] Lehman assured them that all divisions at his command – those responsible for health, medical supplies and industrial rehabilitation – were ready to procure the equipment and deliver it to Czechoslovakia.

---

[29] UNA, S-1327-0000-0010, A. Procházka to P. Alexeev, 17 November 1945.
[30] The history of these achievements is covered by, among others, Smolek and Slanec, *Deset let československých antibiotik*, 25–6; Sikyta, 'Moderní vývoj biotechnologií', 20–1; Bud, *Penicillin*, 77–8.
[31] Petr Fragner, 'Padesát let od přípravy prvního českého penicilínu', *Mykologické Listy* no. 50 (1993): 17.
[32] UNA, S-1339-0000-0010, UNRRA Prague Mission to UNRRA Washington, 6 August 1945.
[33] UNA, S-1339-0000-0010, V. Schlesinger to P. Alexeev, 24 September 1945.
[34] UNA, S-1339-0000-0010, H. Lehman to UNRRA Prague Mission, 3 October 1945.

As for the suggested inclusion of the plant into the structure of the State Health Institute, the rationale was quite logical. Since most of the products previously manufactured at the Institute's laboratory, namely biological preparations, had lost their usefulness with the growing availability of sulfonamides and antibiotics, the new production profile would have been a sort of compensation. It was also argued that since penicillin production is a very complicated process requiring special, expert knowledge, the plant should be incorporated as an independent unit within the Institute, in terms of administrative, financial and scientific matters.

From trainees to teachers

The programme was officially announced in mid-January 1946. There was, however, one fly in the ointment – the Czechoslovaks had initially asked for a penicillin plant with a monthly capacity of forty billion Oxford units, while the one offered by UNRRA was four times smaller. This was twice as much as they needed at that time, but still not enough to realize their bold plan: in asking for a larger plant, they hoped to establish 'a sort of a centre for the production and distribution of penicillin in Central Europe'.[35]

Besides, Czechoslovakia was not the only beneficiary, as the Poles, Byelorussians, Ukrainians and Italians (after the Yugoslavians withdrew from the programme) were also promised factories. In Prague, it was well understood that UNRRA would not favour one country over another by building up its export capacity, while paying no or little attention to others in need. UNRRA had curbed the Czechoslovaks' ambitions (and of all others, potentially) by imposing additional conditions. These included forbidding the factory from being run on a fully commercial basis. Instead, those small, pilot-like plants had to be included into their recipient countries' state health institutions and operated on a non-profit principle.

But beggars can't be choosers, and the Czechoslovaks agreed to these conditions. What was perhaps the most agonizing in their case, however, was that the whole penicillin plant programme, sometimes referred to as a 'lasting memorial' to UNRRA,[36] was the unanticipated result of their own actions. As early as 1944, the Czechs had understood both the significance of antibiotics and the fact that their country's need for penicillin could not be solely dependent on supplies from relief organizations, and had initiated talks in Britain and America to secure for the soon-to-be-liberated Czechoslovakia the delivery of a complete plant and know-how in penicillin making. After long and discouraging negotiations, the arrangement they arrived at was then extended to other nations, wrecking Prague's hopes for taking the favourable position as leader in antibiotic production in Central Europe.

Even before the first batches of equipment began to reach Czechoslovakia (not without problems, by the way), in April 1946 Malek and Harold took off for Toronto, Canada. They disembarked at Connaught Laboratories, part of the University of Toronto, where they were familiarized with a factory that had been chosen by UNRRA

[35] NAP, MZd, M 1460/1945, Vladislav Kruta, Informace pro pana ministra, 13 November 1945.
[36] UNA, S-1339-0000-0010, P. Alexeev to L. Rooks, cable no. 2111, undated.

as the standard model for the programme. While there, together with the trainees from the other countries included in the scheme, they studied the production process under the guidelines of the plant's actual designer, Dr Norman L. Macpherson, who also ran it. Besides the Czechs, there were two Poles, two Italians and two representatives of Soviet Belarus and Ukraine. All those attending were being sponsored by UNRRA on the condition that, upon their return to their home countries, they would be working for their respective state entities for two years. This rule clearly indicated that for the Americans and Canadians carrying humanitarian assistance did not mean, by definition, forgetting their own stakes. The European trainees were not allowed to make use of newly acquired knowledge in private companies under the assumption that the latter could have been more competitive than state owned institutions thus threatening the benefactor's mercantile interests.

Obviously, acquiring knowledge transmitted by the Canadians required from the trainees ample knowledge of microbiology and biochemistry, as well as their industrial applications. Considering their previous experience, Malek and Harold seemed to be well prepared for the training, but it was not so apparent in the case of others. As a CIA informant reported later, from among the UNRRA fellows, 'the Czechs were the brightest and got the most out of it', while 'the Italians were only fair', and the Poles – 'completely incompetent'.[37] The report blasted as worst both Soviet trainees, 'one of whom [...] couldn't speak English and could not grasp the theory at all'. As a result, 'the Soviet group did not learn a great deal because of the low caliber of their men', being – as the informant was convinced – 'political appointees'. However, to some extent he exculpated the East European fellows, who, for the previous six years have been disconnected from the mainstream research on antibiotics, and were not aware of new developments in antibiotics achieved during wartime.

In August, Malek and Harold were joined by Zdenek Kabatek, chief designer at Association for Chemical and Metallurgical Production. Kabatek was allowed to visit the Toronto factory for ten days only, during which time he busied himself studying the Canadian blueprints and devising a floor plan for their own plant that would meet Czechoslovak standards. He also copied the plans to give them to his Polish, Soviet and Italian counterparts.

The UNRRA programme did not only include the provision of equipment and training. The recipient countries were also promised the *Penicillium* spores and raw materials needed for six months of production, with their only job being to furnish a suitable factory building to house the production lines. This could be either a new building or an existing one, adapted to purpose. For Poland and Czechoslovakia, this simple task caused a lot of problems and led to significant delays in implementation of the programme. In both cases, it was the ambitions of some of the institutions involved – and sometimes their incompetency – that caused the trouble.

Initially, the Czechoslovaks planned to adapt a pharmaceutical plant in Rybitvi, near Pardubice (now the *Výzkumný Ústav Organických Syntéz a.s* – the Research Institute of

---

[37] Central Intelligence Agency Archive, CIA-RDP80-00926A003700020008-3, Details on Penicillin Plants Shipped to Europe by UNRRA, 29 June 1951, p. 2.

Organic Synthesis),[38] but in late March 1946 the governmental commission established to coordinate the enterprise approved a different location – an old varnish factory on the banks of Vltava river in Roztoky, near Prague. This location was problematic for many reasons, one being the risk of flooding. Nevertheless, the adaptation works continued, but at a very slow pace. Throughout all of 1947 and 1948, the national press repeatedly complained about the delays at the construction site. The headlines foresaw 'the mortality rate rising by 1,500'[39] a month in Prague alone and 'millions of dollars needlessly spent abroad'[40] if the construction continued to be delayed. The press called for more effort to be made, so that Czechoslovakia, having its own experts and a suitable industrial backing, would not be 'surpassed by other European nations only because there are not enough construction workers in Roztoky'.[41]

Although this competitive spirit was visible in the press of the era, as well as in official documents, the Czechoslovak experts were actually very much engaged in helping the other countries struggling with setting up their factories. The most significant example of this engagement was a conference held in Prague in June 1947. This was the initiative of John Bowring, chief of Supply and Distribution at the UNRRA mission in Prague, who was very well acquainted with the problems the Czechs were facing. Prague also wanted to invite Macpherson, as he was planning to visit Europe about that time anyway. Eventually though, UNRRA asked F. William Hendershott of the Canadian branch of Merck & Co. to come to Prague. Although the conference invitation went out to all of the countries involved, only the Polish experts came, and an American engineer from the UNRRA mission in Minsk, representing Belarus – simply because there was no Belarusian expert available.

Assessing the outcome of the conference is somewhat problematic. The previously mentioned CIA informant, most probably Hendershott himself, was very sceptical about the results of the meeting and the chances to launch production soon. According to him, the most advanced Czechs 'were in trouble and even the assistance' he could give them 'did not help a great deal. Although they were the smartest of all, they could not truly grasp the principle of the process'.[42] However, apparently the Czechs managed to make a good use of the Hendershott's visit. He explained and corrected some ambiguities in the blueprints spotted by Kabatek, and the UNRRA representatives promised to speed up delivery of the missing equipment. A detailed report from the meeting was sent out to all countries in the programme, even those who had not attended.[43] In this sense, for some time following the meeting, Czechoslovakia became a centre of research on penicillin for other countries in Central Europe, just as the Czechs had initially dreamed. The engineers from Poland particularly flocked to the

---

[38] Dagmar Broncová, *Historie farmacie v Českých zemích* (Prague: MILPO, 2003), 127.
[39] 'Kdy budeme vyrábět penicillin? Nepospíšíme-li si, zvýší se úmrtnost o 1500 osob', *Obrana Lidu*, 10 January 1948.
[40] 'Přes dva roky se táhne stavba továrny na penicilin. Miliony v dolarech zbytečně odplývají do ciziny', *Rude Právo*, 3 February 1948.
[41] 'ČSR střediskem evropské výroby penicilinu', *Národní Osvobozeni*, 28 June 1947.
[42] CIA-RDP80-00926A003700020008-3, Details on Penicillin Plants Shipped to Europe by UNRRA, 29 June 1951, p. 2.
[43] UNA, S-1339-0000-0010, Report on the penicillin conference held at the Ministry of Health in Prague on 16 June to 19 June 1947.

construction site in Roztoky to seek advice from the Czech experts on how to solve the problems they were encountering in their own plants.

However, shortly after the conference, on 30 June 1947, UNRRA was dissolved and all of its health programmes and duties were handed over to the Interim Commission of the World Health Organization. The transfer process revealed how little was known of what actually happened to the assistance and relief that the administration provided. The expression, used in the handover report, that UNRRA 'believed that they [the penicillin plants] were furnished to six countries' is both staggering and frightful, and begs the question of where responsibility in the provision of aid ends.[44] It was estimated that completion of the programme would have required further deliveries of missing machinery, as well as additional training of local specialists. The handover report also suggested 'bringing production methods up to date',[45] which was very much the same conclusion formulated by Dr Ernst B. Chain after his visit to Czechoslovakia in April 1948.

Chain in Czechoslovakia

From mid-February 1948, the Czechoslovaks sought the expertise of Ernst Chain, a Nobel laureate from 1945, which he had won jointly with Alexander Fleming and Howard Florey 'for the discovery of penicillin and its curative effect in various infectious diseases', or rather, speaking of his contribution – for developing an improved method of its production. After learning of Chain's method, Malek, Harold and other members of the ministerial commission urged Minister Procházka to invite Chain to Czechoslovakia, in the hope that he could advise them on possible ways out of the deadlock. Procházka sent the invitation just before resigning his post on 21 February 1948. He was an activist for the moderate Czechoslovak People's Party (*Československá Strana Lidová*, ČSL), and one of the twelve ministers of the coalition cabinet who stepped down to protest against the communist takeover attempt. A few days later, the communists and their puppets formed a new cabinet anyway, and this was the final act of the so-called February coup d'état. The new minister of health was Josef Plojhar – a 'fallen priest' and member of both the Roman Catholic clergy and the ČSL, who ostensibly favoured the communists.

After the coup, the official rhetoric on the lethargic progress of the penicillin factory changed dramatically. To a large extent, this was prompted by Plojhar himself and very much in line with the thinking of the new regime, which was ruthlessly squaring up to the democratic opposition. In May, at the government meeting, Plojhar emphasized that before the February change of power the progress at the construction site had been unsatisfactory, and that in some cases the activities of certain authorities in regard of this undertaking 'were directly bordering on sabotage'.[46]

---

[44] 'Stimulation of the Production of Penicillin', *Official Records of the World Health Organization*, no. 12 (1948): 11.
[45] Ibid.
[46] NAP, ÚPV-B 1402/68, karton 1081, Schůze vlády dne 18 května 1948.

What was a classic example of sabotage, according to Prime Minister Klement Gottwald, was the decision to locate the investment in Roztoky instead of Rybitví. The Ministry of Industry had proposed the latter because of a plant specializing in organic synthesis located there, but the Ministry of Health argued that 'the Americans would not supply the equipment' if the factory was located anywhere else than in Roztoky. 'If, then, the Ministry of Health had not insisted on setting up the factories in Roztoky, we would have been manufacturing our own penicillin for a long time now,' as Prime Minister Gottwald put it then. Today it is believed that the decision was not a mere minister's whim, but an effect of lobbying by Association for Chemical and Metallurgical Production, who owned the site. Roztoky was flooded in 1940, and four years later the plant was devastated by fire.[47] Thereafter, the company tried to get rid of the ill-fated building, finally selling it for a good price to the government.

But the new regime was not looking for enemies just from among their own ranks. As the source of all the trouble, Plojhar had pointed out UNRRA's unwillingness to pay the high patent fees for the newer devices employed in the improved method. He added that the equipment was 'actually already outdated by the time it was received from UNRRA, and is all the more so today'. Criticizing your predecessor's efforts is always easy, but the new minister apparently put the same amount of hope in Chain as Procházka had, perhaps even more so as the biochemist had, in Plojhar's opinion, a 'friendly and politically positive attitude toward Czechoslovakia'.[48]

Eventually, when Chain visited Prague in April 1948, he did so as a guest of the communist regime. As he recalled later, he saw no reason to cancel the trip because the purpose of his visit was not political, but concerned health issues. During his first visit to Roztoky (there were two more visits), Chain studied 'in detail the UNRRA-donated penicillin equipment, which had not yet been assembled'. It was clear to him 'that much of it was obsolete, in particular the extraction part'.[49] Here he was particularly referring to the Sharpless centrifuges, which had indeed seen widespread use in the pharmaceutical industry two years before, but which had been largely replaced by Podbielniak counter-current extractors since then. In the recommendations Chain sent to Prague shortly after completing his journey, he suggested replacing 'the extraction outfit supplied by UNRRA' with Podbielniak machines. He also added that after seeing Herbert R.Kaiser of Podbielniak Inc. it appeared to him 'that the supply of machines for Czechoslovakia would not meet with any difficulty'.[50]

Besides this, Chain recommended using special sterilizers and to make sure that the fermentation tanks were more resistant to corrosion. He also proposed modifying the final step of drying the penicillin salts. The method which the UNRRA penicillin plants based their process on was lyophilic drying of the penicillin solution. Chain offered to provide the Czechoslovaks with a method based on n-butanol extraction that he had developed himself, together with Flora J. Philpot, and patented in Great Britain. It was far from free though – he was willing to grant the license to Czechoslovakia for 5,000

---

[47] Jaroslav Huk, 'Prof. Miloš Herold', *Odraz*, no. 7–8 (2009): 6.
[48] NAP, ÚPV-B 1402/68, karton 1081, Schůze vlády dne 18 května 1948.
[49] Wellcome Library Archive, London, UK (hereafter WLA), PP-EBC-E.232, no title, p. 3.
[50] WLA, PP-EBC-C.4, E. Chain to B. Schober, 26 April 1948.

British pounds plus royalties of 3 to 5 percent of the total sales.[51] The method assumed the use of Podbielniak extractors, and it was believed that two machines would have enough capacity to handle the entire output of the Roztoky plant. The Czechoslovak medical authorities were very much in favour of Chain's offer, as it was a sound promise that the crystalline penicillin, more efficient and stable than its amorphous form, would be available to Czechoslovakian patients soon.

The deal, however, was not signed. Soon after the offer was made, the Czechoslovaks discovered that Chain's understanding of the Podbielniak machines' accessibility was wrong – which also came as something of a surprise to himself. As he noted a few years later, 'the situation was not nearly as simple as it appeared' because Podbielniak, Inc. was refused an export license to sell its machines to the Soviet zone on the grounds of 'security considerations'.[52] As Chain himself put it, 'some people in the State Department thought that these machines could be used for concentration of bacterial toxins', which 'of course, was nonsense', because – as he further explained – being proteins, bacterial toxins are insoluble in organic solvents and as such cannot be processed in Podbielniak extractors.[53]

Within a couple of months, the initial hopes in Chain's ability to help have vanished. The bitterness was so intense that at the meeting of the inter-ministerial committee to investigate the Roztoky case in October 1948, engineer Jan Kazimour, representing the chancellery of the prime minister, even accused Chain of spying by suggesting that he had come 'behind the iron curtain to check whether the works in Roztoky are well-sabotaged, and to make sure that no penicillin is being produced there yet'.[54] He proposed seeking advice in the USSR instead. In so far as the political correctness of such a call stands, it did not make much sense because the Soviet Union had no such technology itself. Consequently, Czechoslovakia, backed by Poland and Yugoslavia, then turned to international bodies to exert pressure on the United States to lift the ban.

Helpless helpers

In mid-November 1948, the three countries used the forum of the Conference of War Devastated European Countries in Geneva to broadcast their problems with obtainingexport licenses from the United States for the Podbielniak extractors.[55] Following this, in mid-January 1949, the WHO invited Czechoslovakia, Poland, Yugoslavia, Belarus and Ukraine to send their experts to a so-called Penicillin Plant Conference, to be held in Geneva the following month.[56]

[51] NAP, ÚPV-B 1402/68, karton 1081, Schůze vlády dne 18 května 1948.
[52] M. L. Hoffman, 'U.N. Health Body Seeks U.S. Penicillin Aid for Soviet Bloc, Which Charges Embargo', *New York Times*, 3 March 1949, 4.
[53] WLA, PP-EBC-E.232, no title, p. 6.
[54] NAP, ÚPV-B 1402/68, karton 1081, Zapis o 5. poradě meziminiaterské komise, pověřené vyšetřením případu penicillinové továrny v Roztokách n/Vlt., 18 October 1948, p. 6.
[55] 'Availability of Medical Supplies for Europe', *World Health Organization, Executive Board, Third Session*, EB3/20, Add. 2, 28 February 1949, p. 1.
[56] 'Annex, A letter sent to: Byelorussia, Czechoslovakia, Poland, Ukraine, Yugoslavia on 20 January 1949', *World Health Organization, Executive Board, Third Session*, EB3/20, Add. 1, 28 February 1949, p. 6.

The discussion at the meeting revealed that although none of the plants in question were operational, most of the equipment had already been installed.[57] Considering that construction of the plants was at such an advanced stage, and how much of the equipment was now either useless or still missing, the conference came up with two different solutions. The first, deemed relatively easy, was to launch the Czechoslovak and Polish plants using the old-fashioned production of amorphous penicillin with the Sharpless super-centrifuges already provided by UNRRA. In this case, only a few missing pieces of machinery would have to be sent in. The second scenario assumed adoption of Chain's method of making crystalline penicillin, which was considered 'not only a more economic proposition, but also a simpler process'.[58] The Poles and Czechs were free to follow this path despite it meaning redesigning the plants and actually obtaining the Podbielniak extractors, and this was something no one knew how to achieve in the current political situation.

The question of the export licenses was brought up again at the third session of the WHO executive board on 21 February 1949. At this meeting, Czechoslovakia, Poland and Yugoslavia accused the United States of suppressing their national anti-STD agendas by directly linking this question with their halting the deal on the Podbielniak extractors. Czechoslovakia and Poland were particularly determined to use the whole issue as a propaganda weapon, working on the theory that 'the United States will have a hard time convincing the world that shutting off supplies of medicine is an essential security measure'.[59] Both countries asked the WHO to obtain the missing equipment on their behalf, and declared their intention to withdrew from its ranks if the organization failed to do so. Through its Medical Supply Division, the thus-blackmailed General Secretariat of the WHO made a deal for six Podbielniak extractors – two each for Czechoslovakia, Poland and Yugoslavia.[60] Nonetheless, some of the WHO's experts were sceptical about how such support could be effective, and, indeed, the US Department of State turned down these demands too.[61]

The inability of the WHO to solve the escalating dispute over finalization of the UNRRA plan only fuelled the otherwise critical attitude of the Soviet bloc towards the organization. On 12 February 1949, Nicolai A. Vinogradov, the Soviet deputy minister of public health, announced that his country was leaving the WHO because its recent activities 'did not correspond to those tasks which were set [. . .] at the inaugural conference'.[62] During the year and a half that followed, practically all of the WHO's communist members withdrew from its ranks, from both Soviet Republics – Belarus

[57] 'UNRRA Penicillin Plants', *World Health Organization, Executive Board, Third Session*, EB3/20, Add. 1, 28 February 1949, p. 3.
[58] Ibid.
[59] Hoffman, 'U.N. Health Body'. One example of such a policy was a speech by the Polish minister of Labour, who criticized the embargo at a meeting of the International Labour Organization in Geneva in June 1949. See 'Min. Stańczyk o polityce dyskryminacji gospodarczej USA', *Życie Częstochowy*, 19 June 1949.
[60] Archiwum Ministerstwa Spraw Zagranicznych, Warszawa, Poland (hereafter AMSZ), 24/162/13, Sprawozdanie z III Sesji Rady Wykonawczej Światowej Organizacji Zdrowia, pp. 3–4.
[61] M. L. Hoffman, 'Penicillin Appeal Pushed in Geneva', *New York Times*, 10 March 1949, 8.
[62] *Official Records of the World Health Organization*, no. 17 (1949): 52.

and Ukraine – who left in February, to Poland bringing up the rear on 15 August 1950.[63] In this way, all the recipients of the UNRRA-donated penicillin plants went off on their own. The exceptions were Yugoslavia, which was quite independent in making its foreign policy after the Stalin-Tito split of 1948, and of course Italy. Leaving Belarus and Ukraine aside, this was a particularly mercenary move by the Czechoslovaks and Poles, because they both left the WHO only after their factories were completed (while the Czechs waited half a year, it took nearly thirteen months for the Poles to take that step). Both plants produced amorphous penicillin until the early 1950s, when their efforts to master the technology of making the drug in its purer, crystalline form finally succeeded – largely thanks to Chain, who eventually helped the Czechoslovaks first, who in turn helped the Poles.

Conclusions

The UNRRA penicillin plant programme originated in the prudence of Czechoslovak experts who foresaw the necessity of enhancing and strengthening the nation's ability to solve its own health problems. Under UNRRA's strategy, these experts were entrusted with partial responsibility for implementation of a programme that included adoption of a cutting-edge technology. In this respect, the penicillin plant programme was quite a bold endeavour, but eventually, these assumptions were proved largely correct, partially because within the UNRRA framework, the Czechs were able to employ the expertise they had won independently through work on antibiotics during the wartime. As a result, the penicillin plant programme, unlike many industrial rehabilitation projects nowadays that exclude existing expertise, did not create a technological bubble. On the contrary, the programme established a new supranational centre of expertise in antibiotic research and production. The Czechs then helped the Soviets and Poles to modernize their own antibiotic industries. It could be argued then that the key to this success lay in UNRRA's approach, which assumed an openness to local initiatives, and in its persistence in firmly grounding the teaching of self-help in the local context.

As it appears, the dual nature of the penicillin plant programme – partly health, partly industrial – caused substantial difficulties in the initial stages of its management in the recipient countries. At first, all the arrangements were carried out through the respective ministries of health of Czechoslovakia, Poland and Yugoslavia. Only later was handling of the investment transferred to their ministries of industry, which were deemed capable of completing the quite sophisticated industrial set-ups. Because the success of the health component of the programme was dependent on the practical, developmental part, final evaluation of the entire undertaking remained ambiguous for a long time, and this fuelled the propaganda machines of the communist regimes in these countries. The main line of argument was that by deliberately postponing delivery of technical equipment, the United States was torpedoing the national health improvement initiatives undertaken in these countries, particularly the campaigns to eradicate sexually transmitted diseases.

---

[63] *Dziennik Ustaw RP*, no. 41/1950, poz. 373.

When the representatives of the forty-four nations that met in Atlantic City in November 1943 decided to form an organization to coordinate post-war relief and reconstruction efforts, their main message was helping people in the soon-to-be-liberated countries so that they could help themselves. In spite of tremendous difficulties, and not without major setbacks, UNRRA largely fulfilled this task. In the case of its penicillin plant programme, however, this slogan should have been expanded with 'let them help you to help themselves'.

Part III

Internationalism as activism

9

Student activists and international cooperation in a changing world, 1919–60

Daniel Laqua

Mentions of student activism inevitably conjure up images of 1968 – a year in which protests on university campuses across the world were often framed in internationalist terms.[1] This chapter, by contrast, draws attention to earlier varieties of student internationalism: it focuses on a period that predated both the growing appeal of New Left currents and a substantial expansion in access to higher education. Many student organizations that operated internationally before the 1960s engaged in knowledge exchange and cooperation with international institutions to further the interests of their constituency. Revolving around associational work and expert collaboration, their brand of internationalism resembled other varieties that are being explored in this volume.

Prior to the 1960s, university students were but a small subsection of their age cohort. Notwithstanding national variations, the participation rate in interwar Europe barely surpassed 2 per cent.[2] By the late 1950s, this share had increased – but not in a way that drastically changed the overall picture.[3] In Japan, student numbers were proportionally higher than in Europe: 4 per cent in 1940 and 7.5 per cent in 1952.[4] The United States were an outlier, with around 8 per cent of young people attending college or university by 1940 as well as substantial expansion resulting from the G. I. Bill of

---

[1] For studies that emphasize the internationalism of student protests in and around 1968, see Robert Gildea, James Mark and Anette Warrring, eds, *Europe's 1968: Voices of Revolt* (Oxford: Oxford University Press, 2013); Martin Klimke and Joachim Scharloth, eds, *1968 in Europe: A History of Protest and Activism, 1956-1977* (Basingstoke: Palgrave, 2008); Vania Markarrian, *Uruguay, 1968: Student Activism from Global Counterculture to Molotov Cocktails*, trans. Laura Pérez Carrara (Oakland, CA: University of California Press, 2017); Martin Klimke, *The Other Alliance: Student Protest in West Germany and the United States in the Global Sixties* (Princeton, NJ: Princeton University Press, 2010).

[2] Fritz Ringer, 'Admission', in *Universities in the Nineteenth and Early Twentieth Centuries (1800-1945)*, vol. 3 of *A History of the University in Europe*, ed. Walter Rüegg (Cambridge: Cambridge University Press, 2004), 254–7.

[3] Vincent Carpentier, 'Expansion and Differentiation in Higher Education: The Historical Trajectories of the UK, the USA and France', *Centre for Global Higher Education Working Paper Series*, no. 3 (April 2018): 16.

[4] T. J. Pempel, 'The Politics of Enrollment Expansion in Japanese Universities', *The Journal of Asian Studies* 33, no. 1 (1973): 68.

1944.[5] In many other parts of the world, higher education remained even more of a minority experience than it was in Europe. The dynamics of empire were one major factor that shaped patterns of exclusion as well as scholarly mobility.[6] Limited college or university provision in regions under colonial control subsequently informed debates about colonialism and international development.[7]

As a select band of people, university students were subject to major expectations regarding their potential contributions to society. In this respect, perceptions of students as future leaders intersected with broader ideas about youth. In his study of post-1945 France, Richard Ivan Jobs has noted that 'young people as a group became the object of countless debates and innumerable government policies as they represented the hope of a future unburdened by the devastation of the recent past'.[8] Visions of youth as a force for the 'rejuvenation' of society can also be applied to the specific constituency of university students and to the international activities that they engaged in. League of Nations officials during the 1920s, communist leaders during the 1930s as well as Cold Warriors from both power blocs during the 1940s and 1950s supported student organizations or sought to influence their work. Such forms of engagement anticipated that university youth might play an important role in the future.

University students were not a cohesive group. There were significant national differences with regard to their social profile, even though the low number of working-class students was a widely shared feature across different education systems.[9] Women's participation in higher education tended to vary, too. Even within individual countries, the growth in the number of women students from the 1920s to the 1950s was by no means a linear process.[10] Political persuasions and religious beliefs added further complexity to the make-up of the student body. With regard to the religious dimension, it is worth bearing in mind that the higher education landscape comprised not only secular institutions but also colleges and universities that were run by churches or religious communities.

International student organizations mirrored the heterogeneity of the constituency that they catered for. Some organizations claimed to represent students irrespective of their backgrounds, while others addressed particular religious, ethnic or political groups. Meanwhile, the question of women's access to higher education underpinned the work of the International Federation of University Women.[11] Yet, despite the

[5] Paul Windolf, 'Cycles of Expansion in Higher Education 1870–1985: An International Comparison', *Higher Education* 23 (1992): 4 and 11.
[6] Tamson Pietsch, *Empire of Scholars: Universities, Networks and the British Academic World, 1850–1939* (Manchester: Manchester University Press, 2013).
[7] On issues and debates surrounding university development in West Africa, see Timothy Livsey, *Nigeria's University Age: Reframing Decolonisation and Development* (London: Palgrave, 2017).
[8] Richard Ivan Jobs, *Riding the New Wave: Youth and the Rejuvenation of France After the Second World War* (Stanford, CA: Stanford University Press, 2007), 7.
[9] Fritz Ringer has discussed the 'social origins of university students' before the Second World War in Ringer, 'Admission', 257–66. For developments from 1945 to 1970, see A. H. Halsey, 'Admission', in *Universities since 1945*, vol. 4 of *A History of the University in Europe*, ed. Walter Rüegg (Cambridge: Cambridge University Press, 2011), 223–6.
[10] See, for example, Gail Kelly and Sheila Slaughter, 'Women and Higher Education: Trends and Perspectives', in *Women's Higher Education in Comparative Perspective*, ed. idem (Dordrecht: Kluwer, 1991), 3–13. On the uneven development in Britain, France and the United States, see Carpentier, 'Expansion and Differentiation', 18.
[11] Marie-Elise Hunyadi, 'Promouvoir l'accès des femmes aux études et aux titres universitaires: un défi transnational? L'engagement de la Fédération internationale des femmes diplômées des Universités

diversity of actors on the international scene, student internationalism constituted a concrete and distinct phenomenon, as student leaders from different backgrounds, persuasions and associations interacted with one another in manifold ways.

In tackling the work of international student organizations, this chapter examines how student leaders positioned themselves within a changing global order, either consciously or implicitly. In particular, it discusses threads that connected the interwar period to the early Cold War – a chronological approach that has also informed other recent studies on internationalism.[12] Notwithstanding its thematic approach, the chapter highlights wider trends for the period between 1919 and 1960, notably the growing role of political pronouncements and non-European actors within the work of international student organizations.

A fresh look at student organizations contributes to the literature on internationalism in three major ways. First, it illustrates how war and conflict produced new collaborative patterns, as reflected in widening spheres of action for student organizations. Second, student internationalism covered a broad ideological spectrum and thus allows us to consider 'non-liberal variations of internationalism and transnationalism', which have only recently begun to attract greater scholarly attention.[13] Third, it shows that the history of European internationalism cannot be separated from extra-European internationalisms. Students from European colonies were present within imperial metropoles and engaged in international action. Moreover, student organizations often acted globally – be it because of missionary agendas or because the dynamics of decolonization forced organizations to extend their scope of action. In all of these respects, a phenomenon that at first appears to be relatively confined – namely the work of organizations that catered for small groups of young people – illustrates the spread and diversity of internationalism.

War as a spur for internationalist action

International student organizations had existed before 1914, yet the Great War and its aftermath transformed the work of such bodies. The conflict's impact was felt clearly within the World's Student Christian Federation (WSCF), which had been founded in Sweden in 1895 and thus was the oldest international student organization. In 1931, its secretary Suzanne de Dietrich articulated a sense of generational rupture. As she

(1919 – 1970)' (PhD thesis, Université de Génève and Université de Paris, 2019). See also Christine von Oertzen, *Strategie Verständigung: Zur transnationalen Vernetzung von Akademikerinnen 1917–1955* (Göttingen: Wallstein, 2012).

[12] See, for example, Talbot Imlay, *The Practice of Socialist Internationalism: European Socialists and International Politics, 1914–1960* (Oxford: Oxford University Press, 2018); Simon Jackson and Alanna O'Malley, eds, *The Institution of International Order: From the League of Nations to the United Nations* (Abingdon: Routledge, 2018).

[13] Jessica Reinisch, 'Introduction: Agents of Internationalism', *Contemporary European History* 25, no. 2 (2016): 197. Recently, an influential volume has sought to consider a 'broader spectrum of intellectual thought and action', encompassing 'ideological transactions that took place across the boundaries of the socialist and liberal strands of internationalism' and the use of internationalism by 'even . . . [its] most avowed enemies': Glenda Sluga and Patricia Clavin, 'Rethinking the History of Internationalism', in *Internationalisms: A Twentieth-Century History*, eds. idem (Cambridge: Cambridge University Press, 2017), 4.

suggested, the war had led to 'a displacement of interest from the spiritual to the social' and a 'passionate revolt against the "institutions of the past"', including 'Churches, missionary societies, any type of thought which might be labelled "conservative" or "conventional"'.[14] Research on the WSCF has noted that the organization did itself undergo significant changes in the 1920s, moving 'from an overt evangelical focus to a more inclusive and interfaith perspective'.[15]

More generally, the war experience created new contexts for student activism. Young people who entered higher education in the years following the Armistice had observed the consequences of military conflict; in many cases, they had undertaken military service themselves.[16] They were confronted with the war's manifold legacies – from political instability and social crisis to cultural transformations. In light of their experiences and as members of a new generation, students could cast themselves as uniquely equipped for overcoming past antagonisms and shaping the new international order. Such claims resonated with contemporary notions about 'Peace through Youth' – the motto of a large-scale Franco-German youth gathering in 1926.[17] This is not to say that such slogans can be taken at face value: wartime enmities proved just as pervasive among students as they did elsewhere.[18] Nonetheless, many student organizations affirmed their commitment to reconciliation and cooperation. The WSCF's first post-war meeting – held in St Beatenberg, Switzerland, in 1920 – featured delegates from former enemy countries.[19] WSCF member Ruth Rouse later noted a 'passionate determination to build international relationships on a new basis', as reflected in the decision to include an 'international objective' in the organization's agenda.[20]

After the Great War, a host of new student organizations joined the WSCF on the international scene, exemplifying the internationalist momentum of the era. WSCF officials noted the emergence of other 'student societies of an international character' and proposed 'to consider in a friendly spirit any openings for cooperation'.[21] Importantly, the post-war rebirth of internationalism produced new structures that allowed activists to promote their aims. Recent research has highlighted the role of

---

[14] Suzanne de Dietrich, 'A Tentative History of the Federation Message', *The Student World* 24, no. 2 (1931): 112–3.

[15] Johanna M. Selles, *The World Student Christian Federation, 1895–1925: Motives, Methods, and Influential Women* (Eugene, OR: Pickwick, 2011), 253.

[16] The war's impact on British university life, including the role of ex-service students therein, is the focus of a research project whose initial findings are presented in Georgina Brewis, Sarah Hellawell and Daniel Laqua, 'Rebuilding the Universities after the Great War: Ex-Service Students, Scholarships and the Reconstruction of University Life', *History: The Journal of the Historical Association* 105, no. 364 (February 2020): 82–106.

[17] Géraoid Barry, *The Disarmament of Hatred: Marc Sangnier, French Catholicism and the Legacy of the First World War, 1914–45* (Basingstoke: Palgrave, 2012), 128.

[18] I have explored this dimension in Daniel Laqua, 'Activism in the "Students' League of Nations": International Student Politics and the Confédération Internationale des Étudiants, 1919–1939', *The English Historical Review* 132, no. 556 (June 2017): 605–37, esp. 613–14.

[19] Yale University Divinity School, World Student Christian Federation Archives (RG 46 Series IX), A912 - General Committee Reports (hereafter MS WSCF): *Who's Who: Meeting of the World's Student Christian Federation, St. Beatenberg, July 30 – August 7, 1920*, 6–7.

[20] Ruth Rouse, *The World's Student Christian Federation: A History of the First Thirty Years* (London: SCM, 1948), 264–5.

[21] MS WSCF: *Minutes of the Meeting of the General Committee of the World's Student Christian Federation, High Leigh, England, August 7 to August 20, 1924*, 24.

the League of Nations as a focal point for many efforts.²² Among students, a range of local and national groups promoted awareness of the League and its work. From 1924, they were organized transnationally through the International University Federation for the League of Nations. Meanwhile, another body – the International Confederation of Students (*Confédération Internationale des Étudiants*) – bundled the efforts of national unions of students and worked with League officials, for instance launching an International Student Identity Card in 1926–7.²³

War-induced humanitarian emergencies stimulated new internationalist endeavours. There are various connections between recent scholarly interest in internationalism on the one side and humanitarianism on the other, including the attempt to problematize both phenomena rather than viewing them as inherently progressive or benign.²⁴ Humanitarian ventures can be approached through the conceptual lens of internationalism because they used patterns of international cooperation that were common to many internationalist ventures. If one bears this aspect in mind, it underlines the extent to which the interwar period was an internationalist era. The literature on humanitarianism treats the Great War as a transformative moment that produced an expanded, diversified and increasingly organized humanitarian landscape.²⁵ Recently, Tomás Irish has shown how aid efforts aimed at universities could combine a humanitarian impetus with ideas about the 'moral reconstruction' of a devastated continent.²⁶

The creation of European Student Relief in 1920 was one manifestation of this wider development. Georgina Brewis has appraised the former as 'a substantial contribution to the broader postwar aid movement', while Benjamin Hartley suggests that it 'may be considered the first international ecumenical relief agency'.²⁷ The aid effort had been initiated by WSCF members after encountering poverty and devastation in Central Europe. Ruth Rouse, a key figure in these endeavours, stated that as WSCF Travelling Secretary, she had witnessed much misery, but none on the scale she observed in

---

²² Andrew Arsan, Su-Lin Lewis and Anne-Isabelle Richard, 'The Roots of Global Civil Society and the Interwar Moment', *Journal of Global History* 7, no. 2 (July 2012): 157–65; Daniel Gorman, *The Emergence of International Society in the 1920s* (Cambridge: Cambridge University Press, 2012); Thomas Davies, *NGOs: A New History of Transnational Civil Society* (London: Hurst, 2014), 77–122. See also the plethora of examples in Daniel Gorman, *International Cooperation in the Early Twentieth Century* (London: Bloomsbury, 2017).
²³ Laqua, 'Activism in the "Students League of Nations"', 625–6, 628 and 637.
²⁴ See, for example, Emily Baughan's comment that 'humanitarian histories were ... part of a pushback against more celebratory narratives of internationalism and integration', in Matthew Hilton, Emily Baughan, Eleanor Davey, Bronwen Everill, Kevin O'Sullivan and Tehila Sasson, 'History and Humanitarianism: A Conversation', *Past & Present* 241, no. 1 (2018): e11.
²⁵ Bruno Cabanes, *The Great War and the Origins of Humanitarianism, 1918–1924* (Cambridge: Cambridge University Press, 2014); Peter Gatrell, 'General Editor's Introduction' to the 'Discussion: Humanitarianism', in *1914–1918 online: International Encyclopaedia of the First World War*, https://encyclopedia.1914-1918-online.net/article/discussion_humanitarianism (last accessed 22 July 2019).
²⁶ Tomás Irish, 'The "Moral Basis" of Reconstruction? Humanitarianism, Intellectual Relief and the League of Nations, 1918–1925', *Modern Intellectual History*, 17, no. 3 (2020): 769–800.
²⁷ Georgina Brewis, *A Social History of Student Volunteering: Britain and Beyond, 1880–1980* (Basingstoke: Palgrave, 2014), 54; Benjamin Hartley, 'Saving Students: European Student Relief in the Aftermath of World War I', *International Bulletin of Mission Research* 42, no. 4 (2018): 296.

Austria: 'Vienna was a wreck slowly but inevitably sinking.'[28] Her account demonstrated how religious beliefs and humanitarian concern could fuse with hopes for the post-war order. As she put it, 'The key to the salvation of the nations lay so obviously in the universities, the nurseries of future leadership.'[29]

European Student Relief attained a significant scale. By 1926, it reported to have 'raised over £480,000 and distributed them amongst their needy fellow students in Europe'.[30] Early on, it moved beyond Central Europe, for instance organizing aid for Russian students. As the immediate post-war situation gave way to new concerns, activists extensively debated the way forward for student-centred relief efforts.[31] In 1925, they renamed their organization 'International Student Service', and one year later adopted an institutional arrangement that provided greater independence from the WSCF. International Student Service continued to lead a range of aid efforts, for instance supporting refugee students in the 1930s. Norman Bentwich – a British academic who had worked for the High Commissioner of Refugees Coming from Germany in 1933-5 – later noted that it had been 'the agency chosen by common consent to deal with the refugee students from the Continent of Europe', and acknowledged its role in offering guidance, college placements and scholarships.[32]

In Ruth Rouse's view, involvement in relief efforts did not only benefit the recipients of aid: to those who participated in relief ventures, it offered 'a vast international education' and 'an experience of the richness of international fellowship'.[33] Early reports stressed this personal dimension. In 1920-1, submissions from WSCF branches in China, India and Japan suggested 'that nothing has helped their students so much during the past year to understand the Federation as the real sacrifices some of them have made for the E.S.R. [European Student Relief]'.[34] In China, students provided 'gifts for the relief of Vienna students' alongside help for famine sufferers at home. The Indian section proclaimed that the 'ready and generous response of students in money and sympathy has gone a long way to further their interest in the federation', while the report from Japan predicted that 'this spirit of doing for other students will increase their sympathy and friendliness towards all foreigners'.

If involvement in humanitarian ventures was an education in internationalism, its impact could also be observed in the trajectory of student leaders. The career of Mary McGeachy (1901-91) provides an illustrative example. As an undergraduate in Toronto,

---

[28] Ruth Rouse, *Rebuilding Europe: The Student Chapter in Post-War Reconstruction* (London: Student Christian Movement, 1925), 16.

[29] Ibid., 7.

[30] Swarthmore College Peace Collection, Subject File 'Youth/Students: Organizations A-N' (hereafter MS Swarthmore): leaflet 'International Student Service of the World's Student Christian Federation' (November 1926), 2.

[31] See, for example, *Minutes of the Meeting of the General Committee . . . , High Leigh*, 6-8. See also M. S. Swarthmore, *Fifth Annual Conference of International Student Service of the World's Student Christian Federation. Karlovci – Yugoslavia. July 24th– August 2nd 1926* (Geneva: WSCF, 1926), 19-24.

[32] Norman Bentwich, *The Rescue and Achievement of Refugee Scholars: The Story of Displaced Scholars and Scientists 1933-1952* (The Hague: Martinus Nijhoff, 1953), 24.

[33] Rouse, *Rebuilding Europe*, 53.

[34] WSCF, *Christ and the Student World: A Review of the World's Student Christian Federation, 1920-21* (London: Student Christian Federation, 1922), 27.

McGeachy joined the Student Christian Movement, which WSCF and European Student Relief formed part of. McGeachy later acknowledged that her university experience was formative in 'inspiring her to be a social activist'.[35] After graduating, she maintained close ties to student organizations, and in 1927 she attended a conference of International Student Service in Switzerland. Shortly afterwards, she was named editor for the organization's paper, *Vox Studentium*.[36] Later on, McGeachy worked for the British government and the League of Nations. In 1944, she became a leading official in the newly created United Nations Relief and Rehabilitation Administration – a body that also worked with World Student Relief, which had emerged from International Student Service.[37] If, as Mary Kinnear has put it, international cooperation was 'the organizing theme of her life', then student internationalism is key to understanding McGeachy's subsequent commitments.[38]

The Second World War both perpetuated and transformed the international structures and efforts that had characterized the interwar years. In the humanitarian realm, it led International Student Service to join forces not only with its long-standing institutional partner, the WSCF, but also with the Catholic student organization Pax Romana in setting up a War Emergency Relief Committee.[39] Furthermore, in 1947, the Student Commission of the World Federation of United Nations Associations established a post-war successor to the University Federation for the League of Nations. Finally, if a language of reconciliation featured prominently in some strands of interwar internationalism, the same goes for the post-1945 years. For instance, at its first post-war meeting, the WSCF 'rejoiced in the renewal of official contact with the Movement in Germany and the presence ... of its representatives' while also applauding the 'renewed activity of Protestant student groups in Austria and ... contacts made by Federation staff'. Even at this early stage, officials expressed a desire to support students from such countries 'to enter more deeply into the life of the Federation'.[40] These examples suggest that, in the face of war, genocide and destruction, some activists sought to strengthen their efforts for dialogue and cooperation. From a different angle, Richard Ivan Jobs has highlighted the emphasis on Franco-German youth links, with travel initiatives in the 1940s and 1950s being cast as 'journeys of reconciliation'.[41]

---

[35] Mary Kinnear, *Woman of the World: Mary McGeachy and International Cooperation* (Toronto: University of Toronto Press, 2004), 30.
[36] Ibid., 44.
[37] This relationship also included the secondment of World Student Relief personnel to UNRRA missions: World Student Relief, *Out of the Ruins: Fifth Report on Student Relief Activities April 1945 – March 1946* (Geneva: WSF, 1946), 27–8.
[38] Kinnear, *Woman of the World*, 7.
[39] Bentwich, *The Rescue and Achievement of Refugee Scholars*, 24. See also the reference to Pax Romana's participation in this venture 'on terms of equality with other student representatives' in 'Pax Romana Summary' (1947), in *American Students Organize: Founding the National Student Association after World War II. An Anthology and Sourcebook*, ed. Eugene Schwarz (Westport, CT: Prager, 2006), 747.
[40] MS WSCF: *Minutes of the Meeting of the General Committee of the World's Student Christian Federation, Chateau de Bossey, Céligny, Switzerland, August 9th to 20th 1945* (Geneva: Geneva, 1946), 24 and 28.
[41] Richard Ivan Jobs, *Backpack Ambassadors: How Youth Travel Integrated Europe* (Chicago: University of Chicago Press, 2017), 59–96.

Challenges to 'apolitical' conceptions of student internationalism

Like many humanitarian ventures, European Student Relief and International Student Service adopted a discourse of neutrality and impartiality. When International Student Service received its new legal status in 1926, its 'guiding principles and policy' pledged that it would operate 'on an impartial service basis' and 'irrespective of creed, race or nationality'.[42] Yet it was not only in the realm of humanitarianism that various student organizations claimed to be 'apolitical'. During the 1920s and 1930s, the International Confederation of Students insisted on refraining from political pronouncements. Its agenda, which focused on service provision, echoed the ways in which national unions of students, including those in France and the UK, interpreted their remit.[43] Such rhetoric evidently requires critical interrogation. For instance, the complex relationship between humanitarianism and politics is widely acknowledged.[44] And if claims about the apolitical nature of student internationalism were always tenuous at best, they rang particularly hollow in times of ideological polarization.

The political dimensions of student internationalism became evident in the 1930s, when communists gained ground within university circles in several countries.[45] In line with its Popular Front strategy, the Communist International and its youth wing increasingly sought to 'to forge links with the main body of "progressive" youth'.[46] University students offer a striking perspective on the phenomenon of communist internationalism, because student activism was less overtly shaped by social milieus or identities and, as such, the boundaries between the non-communist and communist worlds remained porous.[47] In December 1934, the creation of the World Student Association (*Rassemblement Mondial des Étudiants*, RME) highlighted the growing

---

[42] MS WSCF: *Minutes of the Meeting of the General Committee of the World's Student Christian Federation: Nybox Strand, Denmark, August 11th to 24th, 1926*, 12.

[43] On France, see Alain Monchablon and Robi Morder, 'Apolitisme, autonomie et indépendance dans le mouvement étudiant', in *Cent ans de mouvements étudiants*, ed. Jean-Philippe Legois, Alain Monchablon and Robi Morder (Paris: Éditions Syllepses, 2007), 195–204. With regard to 1960s Britain, a growing challenge to 'apolitical' conceptions of student union work is discussed in Caroline Hoefferle, *British Student Activism in the Long Sixties* (New York: Routledge, 2013), 67–9.

[44] Michael Barnett and Thomas G. Weiss, 'Humanitarianism: A Brief History of the Present', in *Humanitarianism in Question: Politics, Power, Ethics* (Ithaca, NY: Cornell University Press, 2008), 1–48. Maria Framke has used the term 'political humanitarianism' for 'a form of humanitarianism in which political motivations are particularly overt': Maria Framke, '"We Must Send a Gift Worthy of India and the Congress!" War and Political Humanitarianism in Late Colonial South', *Modern Asian Studies* 51, no. 6 (2017): 1970.

[45] Jacques Varin, 'Les étudiants communistes, des origines à la veille de Mai 1968', *Matériaux pour l'histoire de notre temps* 74 (2004): 37–49; Susan Whitney, *Mobilizing Youth: Communists and Catholics in Interwar France* (Durham, NC: Duke University Press, 2009), 161 and 163; Robert Cohen, *When the Old Left Was Young: Student Radicals and America's First Mass Student Movement, 1929–1941* (New York: Oxford University Press, 1993); Brewis, *A Social History of Student Volunteering*, 90–1.

[46] Kevin Morgan, *Against Fascism and War: Ruptures and Continuities in British Communist Politics, 1935–41* (Manchester: Manchester University Press, 1989), 39.

[47] The recent interest in the history of communist internationalism is exemplified by Kasper Braskén, *The International Workers' Relief, Communism, and Transnational Solidarity: Willi Münzenberg in Weimar Germany* (Basingstoke: Palgrave, 2015); Brigitte Studer, *The Transnational World of the*

communist engagement with student internationalism. Its original name included the by-line 'against War and Fascism' and thus resonated with the terminology of the Amsterdam-Pleyel movement and communist-dominated ventures such as the Women's World Committee against War and Fascism.[48]

Its overtly political character prevented the RME from developing formal relations with the League of Nations. In November 1936, its request to join the League's liaison committee for student representatives was declined because it seemed clear that the RME operated 'largely on the terrain of active politics'. The committee reiterated that, in representing student organizations with diverse constituencies, it had 'to abstain from all active politics' and could 'not depart from its traditional neutrality'.[49] Nonetheless, the RME cannot be treated in separation from other strands of student internationalism. For example, its members played a prominent part at the World Youth Congresses of 1936 and 1938, held, respectively, in Geneva and at Vassar College in Poughkeepsie, New York. The first of these events – with over 700 participants – originated in an initiative of the University Federation for the League of Nations. As such, it revealed how a communist body could even target initiatives that had originally been associated with liberal internationalism. Joël Kotek has highlighted the growing role of communist activists in international student ventures and noted the 'extraordinary network woven by the League of Young Communists' in the 1930s.[50]

Student internationalism was subject to conflicting impulses in its stance on military conflict – a tension that was implicit in the phrase 'against war and fascism': while pacifism enjoyed growing currency among some young people,[51] particular conflicts triggered militant solidarity. Both the Spanish Civil War and Japanese aggression in China resulted in the mobilization of young people.[52] In such instances, student solidarity created fresh alliances. For example, a meeting held at Bedford College, London, in 1936 featured not only Chinese students and members of International Student Service but also speakers from communist groups.[53] In 1938, an RME-led delegation travelled to Asia, 'to discuss how the world students can give practical aid to China'.[54]

Cominternians (Basingtoke: Palgrave, 2015); Patryk Babiracki and Austin Jersild, eds, *Socialist Internationalism in the Cold War: Exploring the Second World* (Charm: Palgrave, 2016).

[48] Jasmine Calver, 'The *Comité mondial des femmes contre la guerre et le fascisme*: Anti-Fascist, Feminist, and Communist Activism in the 1930s' (PhD thesis, Northumbria University, 2019).

[49] 'Neuvième reunion des Délégués internationals d'étudiants', *La Coopération intellectuelle*, no. 71 (December 1936), 12.

[50] Joël Kotek, *Students and the Cold War*, trans. Ralph Blumenau (Basingstoke: Palgrave, 1996): 16.

[51] Jean-François Sirinelli, *Génération intellectuelle: Khâgneux et Normaliens dans l'entre-deux-guerres* (Paris: Fayard, 1988), 134–6 notes the prominent role of pacifist views at the École Normale Supérieure in 1930s Paris. See also Brewis, *A Social History of Student Volunteering*, 111–16.

[52] For the British case, see Brewis, *A Social History of Student Volunteering*, 122–32. Tom Buchanan has discussed the wider resonance of these causes among the British left in *Britain and the Spanish Civil War* (Cambridge: Cambridge University Press, 1997) and *East Wind: China and the British Left, 1925–1976* (Oxford: Oxford University Press, 2012), 48–80.

[53] 'Internationale Solidarität: Internationale Studentenkonferenz für die Unterstützung des Kampfes der chinesischen Studenten', *Internationale Rundschau*, no. 14 (26 March 1936): 571–2.

[54] 'Round-Table Confab for I.S.D.', *China Forum*, 18 June 1938. See also 'Une délégation internationale d'étudiants est partie pour la Chine', *Revue Mensuelle*, no. 2 (15 May to 15 June 1938).

Communist investment in the wider project of student internationalism meant that the emerging Cold War tensions of the late 1940s also played out within student organizations. After the Second World War, the newly established International Union of Students (IUS) resumed earlier efforts to federate national unions of students. Maintaining a secretariat in Prague from 1946 onwards, the organization soon came under Soviet domination. In 1948, a Soviet memorandum acknowledged the division 'into two camps, one of which, led by the Soviets, was trying to politicize the Union, while the other insisted on a purely cultural outlook'.[55]

Despite growing misgivings, national unions from non-communist countries attended the early IUS meetings. International politics, however, caused major ruptures, as evidenced by the contrasting responses to the Stockholm Appeal of 1950. The latter had been launched by the communist-dominated World Peace Council and 'split the peace movement along cold war frontiers'.[56] The appeal reflected communists' adoption of the language of 'peace' and sustained portrayals of the Soviet Union as a peace-loving country.[57] Conflict surrounding the Stockholm Appeal and related issues characterized the IUS's Prague congress in 1950. British student leader Stanley Jenkins criticized that the self-proclaimed 'Defenders of Peace' were 'not against war in any part of the world, provided that it is a war fought for communist aims'.[58] Meanwhile, an American delegate argued that 'banning the atom bomb would not guarantee peace'.[59] Although such statements met with jeers from the majority of the congress audience, the position of non-communist delegates meant that the congress ultimately acknowledged 'that certain groups of students expressed their struggle against the use of nuclear arms through other texts than the Stockholm Appeal'.[60] The subsequent history of student internationalism highlights the impossibility of maintaining unified structures. Nonetheless, the existence of a communist strand connects the student internationalism of the interwar years to the Cold War period.

Beyond internationalisms on the left

When student internationalism took on overtly political features, it did not necessarily have to tilt towards the left. Recent work on the history of internationalism has insisted on its diversity, far beyond the varieties that bore liberal, socialist or communist inflections. In this respect, it is worth noting internationalism's close relationship

---

[55] Juliane Fürst, *Stalin's Last Generation: Soviet Post-War Youth and the Emergence of Mature Socialism* (Oxford: Oxford University Press, 2001), 90.
[56] Günter Wenicke, 'The Communist Led World Peace Council and the Western Peace Movements: The Fetters of Bipolarity and Some Attempts to Break Them in the Fifties and Early Sixties', *Peace and Change* 23, no. 3 (1998): 269.
[57] However, Günter Wernicke has argued that we should not treat specific kinds of 'peace commitment' as any less 'genuine' just because of their connection to 'a political world view': ibid., 267.
[58] *Report from Prague: An Account of the Second World Congress of the International Union of Students (August 1950)* (London: Student Labour Federation, 1950), 11.
[59] 'Students Hear Warning', *New York Times*, 20 August 1950.
[60] Didier Fischer, 'L'Unef et l'Union internationale des étudiants (1945–1965)', *Matériaux pour l'histoire de notre temps*, no. 86 (2007): 89.

with ideas of nationhood. As Glenda Sluga has argued, we should not regard internationalism as nationalism's 'other' but rather comprehend the two phenomena as intrinsically connected.[61] Nationalism featured prominently within some strands of internationalism – and internationalism provided a potential staging ground for national agendas.

European Student Relief was a case in point. As a vehicle for humanitarian aid, it may appear as an expression of cosmopolitan convictions. Yet the memoirs of Willem Vissert t'Hooft – subsequently a key figure in the ecumenical movement – point to the presence of strong national passions within the organization. In 1922, a motion to define 'world peace and fraternity' as key objectives for the organization triggered a 'long and testy debate'.[62] As Vissert t'Hooft noted, 'the severity of the rejection stemmed from the suspicion that European Student Relief might be a bait to harness European students for a specific American peace ideology'. Some delegates even construed the proposal 'as an attack on their national sentiment'. While a compromise formula subsequently spoke of 'international understanding' and 'international responsibility', the episode showed how national anxieties even reared their head in a humanitarian organization dominated by Christian activists.

The 1923 congress of European Student Relief further highlighted this aspect. At this event, the German delegation denounced the occupation of the Ruhr while Hungarian participants defended their government's anti-Semitic *numerus clausus*.[63] Moreover, Jewish students were forced to form a separate delegation as they had been excluded from several national delegations. Ruth Rouse argued that European Student Relief ultimately improved 'international and interracial relationships' in Hungary, helping Hungarian student leaders to see beyond the irredentist designs vis-à-vis Czechoslovakia and Romania and to question their anti-Semitism.[64] The overarching picture, however, remains ambivalent. In 1929, International Student Service acknowledged the discrimination that Jewish students experienced in different Central and Eastern European countries. Yet, rather than campaigning through public pronouncements, the organization chose to address the issue by organizing a conference featuring 'students of every shade of opinion, from Anti-Semite to Zionist'.[65]

The case of German student politics further illustrates internationalism's ambivalences. Throughout the Weimar years, the *Deutsche Studentenschaft* defined itself in pan-German terms, with a mission that extended beyond the borders of the German state. Early on in the 1920s, the association embraced *völkisch* policies; by 1931, it was dominated by National Socialist students.[66] Despite never joining the

---

[61] Glenda Sluga, *Internationalism in the Age of Nationalism* (Philadelphia, PA: University of Pennsylvania Press, 2013).
[62] Willem A. Visser't Hooft, *Die Welt war meine Gemeinde: Autobiographie* (Munich: R. Piper & Co, 1972), 21.
[63] Ibid., 23.
[64] Rouse, *Rebuilding Europe*, 124.
[65] M. S. Swarthmore, *Annual Report on International Student Service 1929–1930* (Geneva: ISS, 1930),
[66] I have discussed the *Deutsche Studentschaft*'s conflicts with the International Confederation of Students in Laqua, 'Activism in the "Students' League of Nations"', 613–15. See also the observations in Lieve Gevers and Louis Vos, 'Student Movements', in *Universities in the Nineteenth and Early Twentieth Centuries*, ed. Rüegg, 345–57.

International Confederation of Students, the *Studentenschaft* attended its congresses, provoking heated debates on several occasions. Even in the 1930s, it continued to participate in the International University Games. As late as 1937, the International Confederation discussed ways of bringing the *Studentenschaft* on board by creating the new membership category of 'Sporting Collaborators'.[67] Similarly, although German students withdrew from International Student Service in 1934, a 'German Circle for International Cooperation in Student Service' maintained links with it. International Student Service cooperated with the German Circle in hosting two Anglo-German conferences, held in Oxford (1937) and Dresden (1938), discussing issues such as 'the colonial question, the possibility of an economic settlement, disarmament, and the general conditions for the construction of a lasting European peace'.[68] These interactions are striking because, in the same period, International Student Service was busy organizing aid efforts for Jewish victims of Nazism. Such examples highlight the involvement of fascists within the internationalist field, despite their hostility to notions of dialogue and diversity.[69]

From a different ideological angle, Catholic student internationalism further demonstrates the highly variegated nature of internationalism. As expressions of lay action, Catholic student organizations covered a broad spectrum of social and political persuasions; even at the national level, political tensions existed among Catholic student groups.[70] Only recently has the interwar history of Catholic internationalism received detailed attention.[71] Catholic students began to organize themselves internationally after the First World War through the foundation of Pax Romana in 1921. The latter formed part of the wider associational landscape of interwar internationalism, maintaining relations with the League of Nations as well as other student organizations.

After the Second World War, Pax Romana was put on a new organizational footing, comprised of two major strands: the International Movement of Catholic Students and the International Movement of Catholic Intellectuals – the latter being informed by views that an 'international association of Catholic academics' might play 'an important role in the ideological struggle against communism'.[72] Anti-communism was indeed an important factor for Pax Romana. Accordingly, when Catholic students from America participated in the 1946 IUS congress, they were 'jarringly out of sync with the spirit

---

[67] 'Les relations entre la C.I.E. et la Deutsche Studentenschaft', *Bulletin officiel d'Information de la Confédération Internationale des Étudiants* 10, no. 1 (January–February 1937): 6–7.
[68] Swarthmore College Peace Collection, CDGB 'Switzerland – Collective Box': *International Student Service: Annual Report 1936–1937* (Geneva: ISS, 1937)
[69] Herren, 'Fascist Internationalism', in *Internationalisms*, eds. Sluga and Clavin, 191–212; Benjamin Martin, *The Nazi-Fascist New Order for European Culture* (Cambridge, MA: Harvard University Press, 2016).
[70] David Colon, 'Face aux églises, un siècle d'organisations des étudiants chrétiens', in *Cent ans de mouvements étudiants*, ed. Legois et al., 219–25.
[71] Giuliana Chamedes, *A Twentieth-Century Crusade: The Vatican's Battle to Remake Christian Europe* (Cambridge, MA: Harvard University Press, 2019); Cormac Shine, 'Papal Diplomacy by Proxy? Catholic Internationalism at the League of Nations' International Committee on Intellectual Cooperation, 1922–1939', *Journal of Ecclesiastical History* 69, no. 4 (2018): 785–805.
[72] Bernhard Salzmann, *Europa als Thema katholischer Eliten: Das katholische Europa-Netzwerk der Schweiz von 1945 bis Mitte der 1950er Jahre* (Fribourg: Academic Press Fribourg, 2006), 78.

of the conference'.[73] With regard to post-war Quebec, Nicole Neatby has described Pax Romana members as 'traditionalists among student leaders', stating that 'international cooperation between Catholic university students' was meant 'to check pernicious communist influences'.[74] Anti-communism could produce alliances with authoritarian regimes: in June 1946, Pax Romana held its first post-war congress in Francoist Spain. Giuliana Chamedes has suggested that on the one hand the event was 'a lavish display of old-style papal internationalism', taking place in Salamanca as a renowned seat of Catholic learning. On the other hand, the conference was also a forum 'to celebrate Spain as a bastion of anticommunist resistance'.[75] Shortly afterwards, Joaquín Ruiz Giménez – the Spanish organizer of the conference who had served as Pax Romana president since 1940 – travelled to Britain and North America, 'to speak with Catholic leaders and lobby on behalf of the regime'.[76]

This is not to say that Catholic student internationalism was exclusively anti-communist, conservative or right-wing. In 1946, the International Young Catholic Students (*Jeunesse Étudiante Catholique Internationale*, JECI) emerged as another international actor alongside Pax Romana.[77] This organization had its roots in social Catholicism which, while seeking to counter communist agitation, engaged with questions of social justice.[78] Some of its members embraced leftist ideas. Gérard de Bernis – president of the National Union of French Students in 1950 – had originally been a member of *Jeunesse Étudiante Catholique* and promoted ongoing contacts with the IUS upon his election in 1950.[79] He subsequently joined the French Communist Party and became a well-known Marxist economist. Moreover, by the early 1960s, 'JECI was in tune with progressive currents in the Catholic church', as Gerd-Rainer Horn has noted.[80] Such examples not only demonstrate the broad political spectrum covered by Catholic organizations but signify a wider feature of internationalism: the presence of a plurality of worldviews.

Cold War internationals

Sandrine Kott has argued that 'the Cold War solidified the position and operation of the two rival universalisms and their internationalism' while also facilitating 'the circulation of knowledge'.[81] The history of student internationalism illustrates both aspects. Cold War rivalry certainly manifested itself within the world of student

---

[73] Paget, *Patriotic Betrayal*, 35.
[74] Nicole Neatby, 'Student Leaders at the University of Montreal from 1950 to 1958: Beyond the "Carabin Persona"', *Journal of Canadian Studies* 29, no. 3 (1994): 26–44.
[75] Chamedes, *A Twentieth-Century Crusade*, 267–8.
[76] Stanley Payne, *The Franco Regime, 1936–1975* (Madison, WI: University of Wisconsin Press, 1987), 356.
[77] Louis Vos, 'Student Movements and Political Activism', in *Universities since 1945*, ed. Rüegg, 278–88
[78] The related case of the *Jeunesse Ouvrière* Catholique is discussed in Whitney, *Mobilizing Youth*.
[79] Fischer, 'L'Unef et l'Union internationale des étudiants', 89.
[80] Gerd-Rainer Horn, *The Spirit of Vatican II: Western European Progressive Catholicism in the Long Sixties* (Oxford: Oxford University Press, 2015), 209.
[81] Sandrine Kott, 'Cold War Internationalism', in *Internationalisms*, eds. Sluga and Clavin, 351.

organizations. In 1950, student leaders from non-communist countries launched the International Student Conference (ISC) to counter the Soviet domination of the IUS. To Philip Altbach, the history of these two bodies 'is, in microcosm, a history of the Cold War', while Louis Vos has described them as 'pawns on the chessboard' of a global ideological conflict.[82]

The ISC's credibility suffered a terminal blow in 1967 when *Rampards*, a counter-cultural magazine, revealed that the organization and its American member, the National Student Association, had largely depended on covert CIA funding.[83] Karen Paget has stressed the impact of American involvement from the very start of the organization.[84] Joël Kotek has argued that American funds were provided in secret partly because the climate of McCarthyism made it impossible to offer direct support to organizations that 'generally defended liberal and progressive causes'.[85] At the same time, he notes that the ISC, too, had an interest in obscuring the true source of its resources: as its leaders criticized the Soviet Union's role within the IUS, the organization's 'credibility would have been totally destroyed if it had admitted receiving 90 per cent of its funds from the State Department, let alone from the CIA'.[86] This interpretation echoes the arguments of some of the protagonists. For instance, Norman Uphoff, an elected official of the National Student Association, presented the situation in the following terms:

> Apart from the fact that open funding would have defeated its purpose – no student international would have operated with acknowledged funding from official sources in East or West – it was probably not possible. If the U.S. Congress balked at the political 'waywardness' of foreign governments receiving American aid, how much more difficult would it have been to appropriate money for an organization that would condemn U.S. allies such as Paraguay, Portugal, Spain and South Korea, and even the U.S. itself, as when it invaded the Dominican Republic.[87]

Such claims require further probing. In its early years, the ISC remained politically cautious, casting itself as less politicized than its Cold War rival. In other words, CIA funding was provided in secret even at a time when the organization was reluctant to make political pronouncements. That said, from the mid-1950s, the ISC indeed adopted a more overtly political stance which, as Uphoff's remarks indicate, extended

---

[82] Phillip Altbach, 'Introduction', in *The Student Internationals*, ed. idem and Norman Uphoff (Metuchen, NJ: The Scarecrow Press, 1973), 4.

[83] 'Ramparts Says C.I.A. Received Student Report' and 'Foundations Linked to C.I.A. Are Found to Subsidize 4 Other Youth Organizations', *New York Times*, 16 February 1967.

[84] Karen Paget, 'From Stockholm to Leiden: The CIA's Role in the Formation of the International Student Conference', in *The Cultural Cold War in Western Europe, 1945–1960*, ed. Hans Krabbendam and Giles Scott-Smith (Abingdon: Frank Cass, 2003), 134–67. See also Paget, *Patriotic Betrayal*, 65–49 on CIA involvement in student internationalism in the run-up to the ISC's creation.

[85] Joël Kotek, 'Youth Organizations as a Battlefield in the Cold War', in *The Cultural Cold War in Western Europe*, ed. Krabbendam and Scott-Smith, 182.

[86] Ibid., 208.

[87] Norman Uphoff, 'The Viability of Student Internationals: Reflections on Their Structure, Financing and Relevance', in *The Student Internationals*, ed. Altbach and Uphoff, 142. On Uphoff, see Paget, *Patriotic Betrayal*, 293–4.

to a critique of particular issues in the West. Karen Paget, whose work generally emphasizes the CIA's involvement in the ISC, suggests that by the 1960s American control over the organization seemed to be less certain and that the organization's annual gatherings 'were becoming a headache' for American officials.[88] The ISC's willingness to adopt politically inconvenient positions can be interpreted in two different ways. One is that in a Cold War context, the ISC sought to appeal to progressive youths. Some of the literature on the cultural Cold War suggests that the support for critical voices could reinforce notions of pluralism and thus offer a contrast to the Soviet bloc and its suppression of freedom of expression.[89] An alternative interpretation of the ISC's engagement with politics would go beyond the prism of Cold War politics and highlight students' agency.[90]

In 1957, an article in the ISC's magazine elaborated on the shift in the organization's position. Its author acknowledged that its initial stance was based on the premise 'that a national Union of Students is, by definition, an organisation of students of varying political orientation and ideology' and that 'its officers are not chosen to represent a political point of view, but to carry out practical services of benefit to all students who make up the organisation'.[91] Moreover, members of the ISC had argued that '[i]f the United Nations could not resolve the great issues of world politics by discussion and debate . . . the students could hardly be expected to do so'. The author suggested that a rethink had been triggered by events in Hungary, South Africa and Algeria. Indeed, students were protagonists in the Hungarian Uprising, the struggle against apartheid and the quest for Algerian independence. In other words, external events had made it clear 'that no sharp distinction could be drawn between student problems and political questions which concerned the student community'.[92]

By this point, the ISC had resolved its approach to political questions by establishing a Research and Information Commission, which was conceived as an 'independent fact-finding commission' that would document instances in which students faced political repression.[93] Alongside tackling human rights violations in the Eastern bloc, its reports addressed injustices in countries allied to the West, for instance the US-backed dictatorships of Venezuela, Paraguay and Cuba. Likewise, the ISC's magazine also dedicated space to human rights issues, for instance highlighting the repressive policies of the Batista regime in Cuba and the situation of African Americans in the segregated South.[94]

---

[88] Ibid., 256 and 197.
[89] See, for example, Frances Conor Saunders, *Who Paid the Piper? The CIA and the Cultural Cold War* (London: Granta, 1999). However, it has been noted that left-wing activists could also use such funding for their own purposes: Hugh Wilford, *The CIA, the British Left and the Cold War: Calling the Tune?* (London: Frank Cass, 2003).
[90] In this context, it is worth bearing in mind the argument that 'we must not rely solely on the projections of adult policy makers': Mischa Honeck and Gabriel Rosenberg, 'Transnational Generations: Organizing Youth in the Cold War', *Diplomatic History* 38, no. 2 (2014): 237
[91] Paul E. Sigmund, 'Research and Information Commission', *The Student* 1, no. 7 (June 1957): 14.
[92] Ibid.
[93] *RIC Yearbook 1955-1956: Reports on Higher Education in South Africa, Venezuela, Paraguay and East Germany* (Leiden: ISC, 1956), 2.
[94] 'Student Tragedy in Cuba', *The Student* 2, no. 1 (August 1957): 14; 'Racial Integration in United States Education', *The Student* 2, no. 4 (January 1958): 12–14.

This is not to say that there was a clear consensus on such matters. At a time when the Research and Information Commission was already up and running, the ISC's magazine still debated the question, 'Should National Unions Be "Political"?'.[95] The impossibility to ignore the political dimensions of students' experiences was brought to the fore two pages later in the same magazine issue, as the publication featured a series of photos from student protests.[96]

While not denying the role of Cold War dynamics, the nuances in the ISC's position illustrate why we must not treat student internationalism of the 1940s and 1950s in purely dichotomous terms. In themselves, national unions of students in Western Europe had no homogenous stance vis-à-vis Cold War tensions, as communists and radical socialists were involved in such bodies. For this reason, national engagement with the IUS was by no means consistent. In the UK, the National Union of Students had been a driving force behind creating the ISC as a rival to the IUS. At the same time, the presence of a significant cohort of communist student activists meant that disaffiliation from the IUS proved contentious. As a compromise, the National Union of Students withdrew its full membership and instead became an 'autonomous associate member' in 1950.[97] In 1961, the organization reiterated its desire 'to consolidate and extend friendly student relations between Britain and the U.S.S.R.'.[98] A similar degree of ambivalence applies to the French case. The National Union of French Students withdrew from the IUS in 1948, but renewed its relations on 'technical' questions in 1953.[99] Didier Fischer has suggested that there were parallels between Charles De Gaulle's foreign policy and French involvement in international student politics, namely the ambition to carve a distinct route amid the rivalry of great power blocs.[100] From a different angle, Jodi Burkett has observed a desire among British student leaders to act as mediators between activists from the two power blocs.[101]

The globalization of student internationalism

Internationalism could serve power-political agendas, and, as some of the examples in this chapter have illustrated, they could be appropriated by actors with exclusionary agendas. Internationalist practice – both within student organizations and elsewhere – was often construed within existing imperial hierarchies.[102] Johanna Selles has noted

---

[95] 'Should National Unions Be "Political"? A "Student" Forum on Vital Student Questions', *The Student* 2, no. 2 (October 1957): 8–9.
[96] 'Political Protests: Student Demonstrations in Different Countries', *The Student* 2, no. 7 (October 1957): 11–12.
[97] Kotek, *Students and the Cold War*, 177–81.
[98] Jodi Burkett, 'The National Union of Students and Transnational Solidarity, 1958–1968', *European Review of History* 21, no. 4 (2014): 546.
[99] Fischer, 'L'Unef et l'Union internationale des étudiants', 88 and 92.
[100] Ibid., 93.
[101] Burkett, 'The National Union of Students and Transnational Solidarity', 546.
[102] See, for example, Miguel Bandeira Jerónimo and José Pedro Monteiro, 'Pasts to Be Unveiled: The Interconnections between the International and the Imperial', in *Internationalism, Imperialism and the Formation of the Contemporary World*, ed. idem (Cham: Palgrave, 2018), 1–29. See also

that '[t]he goals of the WSCF were packaged in North American and British methods of organization and leadership'.[103] As Georgina Brewis has suggested, 'ideas of empire as a place for charitable aid and voluntary service fed into the British self-image as benevolent rulers'.[104] Moreover, universities themselves had manifold connections to the politics and practice of empire. However, student internationalism could also be deployed to challenge exclusion or external domination.

The WSCF offers some examples in this respect. Johanna Selles has argued that it 'gradually developed an appreciation of the diversity of its federated member groups and became less focused on conversion to Western Christianity'.[105] Indeed, in 1931, Suzanne de Dietrich suggested that '[t]he "prestige" of the West is gone for ever; tribute may be paid to Western science but no longer to Western civilization'.[106] Evidently, WSCF's work had been driven by missionary impulses and as such was entwined with imperial expansion. Yet the relationship between missionary activity and empire was never clear-cut, as the agendas of religious groups and secular authorities sometimes clashed with one another.[107] Some WSCF leaders argued that anti-colonial voices had to be taken seriously because any attempt to silence them would undermine both the international and the spiritual ambitions of their organization. By the 1930s, the WSCF discussed anti-colonial campaigns in its publications and at its conferences, for instance acknowledging Indonesia's 'thirst for national independence' in the context of the WSCF's Eastern Conference in Java (1933).[108]

The WSCF's engagement with anti-colonial matters needs to be seen in the context of the rise of anti-colonial student activism during the 1920s and 1930s. Recent work has shown how imperial metropoles such as Paris, London and Amsterdam became centres for anti-colonial movements in which university students from within the French, British and Dutch empires played a major role.[109] While such activism often unfolded at local or national levels, it interacted with internationalist ideas. For instance, African students in interwar Britain were involved in Pan-Africanism, which formed an international movement in its own right.[110] In this context, Hakim Adi has

---

Bandeira Jerónimo's chapter 'A League of Empires: Imperial Political Imagination and Interwar Internationalisms' in ibid., 87–126.

[103] Selles, *The World's Student Christian Federation*, 11.
[104] Brewis, *A Century of Student Volunteering*, 35.
[105] Selles, *The World Student Christian Federation*, 110.
[106] Dietrich, 'A Tentative History of the Federation Message', 113.
[107] Andrew Porter, *Religion versus Empire: British Protest Missionaries and Overseas Expansion, 1700–1914* (Manchester: Manchester University Press, 2004); Michael G. Thompson, *For God and Globe: Christian Internationalism in the United States between the Great War and the Cold War* (Ithaca, NY: Cornell University Press, 2015), 27–46.
[108] W. A. Visser't Hooft, 'National "Awakening" and the Thirst for National Independence', reprinted in *Memoirs and Diaries: The World Student Christian Federation (1895–1990)*, ed. Elisabeth Adler (Geneva: WSCF, 1994).
[109] Michael Goebel, *Anti-Imperial Metropolis: Interwar Paris and the Seeds of Third World Nationalism* (Cambridge: Cambridge University Press, 2015); Marc Matera, *Black London: The Imperial Metropolis and Decolonization in the Twentieth Century* (Berkeley: University of California Press, 2014); Klaas Stutje, *Campaigning in Europe for a Free Indonesia: Indonesian Nationalists and the Worldwide Anticolonial Movement, 1917–1931* (Copenhagen: NIAS, 2019).
[110] Hakim Adi, *West Africans in Britain: 1900–1960: Nationalism, Pan-Africanism and Communism* (London: Lawrence and Wishart, 1998). For a critique of the term 'black internationalism', see Hakim Adi, *Pan-Africanism: A History* (London: Bloomsbury, 2018), 4–5.

also highlighted the links between Pan-African activists and the world of communist internationalism.[111]

By the 1930s, communist internationalism, student activism and anti-imperialism intersected in several ways. The communist-backed RME repeatedly denounced colonial rule and imperial domination. As part of the RME mission to China in 1938, the organization's secretary James Klugmann visited several Indian cities, holding meetings with student leaders but also with Jawaharlal Nehru.[112] Furthermore, the RME's 1939 congress in Paris featured presentations of Indian and Vietnamese speakers who discussed independence movements and proclaimed their debt to the French Revolution. Meanwhile, a student association from Burma reported on the 'Burmese National Movement and the Struggle for Democracy'.[113]

Such ties went beyond sporadic congresses as communist engagement with anti-imperial and anti-colonial student activism continued in the post-war years. In challenging Western countries, the IUS provided a forum for anti-colonial voices. By 1948, the IUS and another communist-dominated body, the World Federation of Democratic Youth, supported an event that tackled national liberation movements in South-East Asia. As Philip Altbach noted, '[t]he conference took a strong anti-colonialist line and on several occasions criticized the IUS for its reliance on the moderate policies of its non-Communist Western members'.[114] Two years later, the IUS congress in Prague included a large contingent of non-Western delegates, who were celebrated for their participation.[115]

In some ways, Cold War dynamics effected a broadening of internationalist action: in its competition with the IUS, the newly founded ISC targeted students from decolonizing nations or recently independent states. In 1956, Western members of the ISC travelled to the Asian–African Students Conference in Bandung – a meeting that, in Karen Paget's words, 'decisively shifted the Cold War student battleground'.[116] The event evidently followed on from the previous year's Asian–African Conference, whose pivotal role in Third World politics is widely acknowledged; one newspaper account described the student event as the 'junior edition of the celebrated conference of last year'.[117] Paget suggests that the ISC involvement did not necessarily denote sympathy for anti-colonial struggles but was owed to fears that student movements

---

[111] Hakim Adi, *Pan-Africanism and Communism: The Communist International, Africa and the Diaspora, 1919–1939* (Trenton, NJ: Africa World Press, 2013).

[112] Geoff Andrews, *The Shadow Man: At the Heart of the Cambridge Spy Circle* (London: I.B. Tauris, 2015), 92.

[113] International Institute of Social History, Amsterdam, Rassemblement Mondial des Étudiants Collection, folder 15: documents 'The Influence of the French Revolution on the National Movement of Indonesia: Report by the Perhimpuan Indonesia', 'The French Revolution and the Indian National Movement: A Report by N. Chakravartty and C. Devanesan, Federation of Indian Students' Societies in Europe' and 'The Burmese National Movement and the Development of Democracy in Burma. Resume of the Report by the All-Burma Student Union' (all 1939).

[114] Altbach, 'Introduction', 27.

[115] See, for example, *Report from Prague*, 6.

[116] Paget, *Patriotic Betrayal*, 156.

[117] 'Bandung Juniors', *Manchester Guardian*, 7 June 1956. On the significance of the Asian–African Conference, see Vijay Prashad, *The Darker Nations: A People's History of the Third World* (New York: The New Press, 2008); Christopher J. Lee, ed., *Making a World after Empire: The Bandung Moment and Its Political Afterlives* (Athens, OH: Ohio University Press, 2010); Jürgen Dinkel, *The Non-*

in Asia and Africa might take a communist turn. As she argues, American members of the National Student Associations were partly seeking to 'sabotage its aims'.[118] Yet in itself, the need for ISC members to engage with this initiative indicates how the joint factors of Cold War and decolonization reshaped student internationalism.

Such shifting perspectives manifested themselves in the ISC's publications. For example, one of the Indian delegates stayed in Indonesia beyond the Bandung conference and subsequently reported on student life in Indonesia, praising the 'unique ... role of the students of Indonesia in their people's struggle for independence'.[119] This is but one example of the commitment to represent a more diverse constituency. The ISC's magazine covered issues such as 'Colonialism and the University in Africa' as well as discussing the first Pan-African students' conference.[120] In the magazine's debate forum on national student unions and politics, Dafalla El Hag Yousif, former president of the Sudan University Students' Union, argued that politics could not be ignored by students who experienced colonialism's 'adverse effects on culture, politics and economy'.[121] A related point about politics as a response to external factors was advanced by a Willie Abraham, a Ghanaian contributor. Abraham argued that in the late 1940s, when leaders of Ghana's independence movement were imprisoned, students had been active campaigners, whereas '[a]fter that the battle against political imperialism was more or less won', students had become more apathetic.[122]

As previously mentioned, student leaders cited the events in Algeria as a key factor for the politicization of the ISC. The Algerian question posed particular challenges for the National Union of French Students, whose stance on colonial matters underwent significant changes in the course of the 1950s. In 1953, its delegates had left the ISC conference at Istanbul in protest because a Senegalese organization had been admitted at a time when the French colonies in West Africa had not yet acquired independent statehood. Back then, the French leaders criticized the ISC for 'having engaged a bit too much on the political terrain and notably on that of anti-colonialism, while trying to impose its views upon the national unions'.[123] By the end of the 1950s, its position had changed. Alain Mounchablon has suggested that the Algerian War turned the colonial question into 'a major theme and element of radicalization' for French student leaders.[124] In 1958, the ascent of a more radical faction within the ranks of the National Union of French Students meant that the body took a prominent role in

---

Aligned Movement: Genesis, Organization and Politics (1927–1992), trans. Alex Skinner (Leiden: Brill, 2019), 42–83.

[118] Paget, *Patriotic Betrayal*, 144 and 153–4.
[119] Chandra Bhal Tripathi, 'The Student Movement in Indonesia', *The Student* 1, no. 6 (October 1957): 8.
[120] Isaac Omolo and Crawford Young, 'Colonialism and the University in Africa', *The Student* 2, no. 10 (1958): 1–5; Lovemore Mutambanengwe, 'The First Pan-African Students Conference', *The Student* 2, no. 10 (1958): 6–7.
[121] 'Should National Unions Be "Political"?', 8
[122] W. E. Abrahamson [Willie Abraham], 'Ghana Students and Politics', *The Student* 1, no. 6 (March 1957): 12.
[123] Fischer, 'L'Unef et l'Union internationale des étudiants', 90.
[124] Alain Monchablon, 'L'apogée d'un mouvement syndical (1944–1962)', in *Cent ans de mouvements d'étudiants*, ed. Legois et al., 79.

French campaigns against the ongoing war in Algeria.[125] By 1960, the National Union of French Students maintained direct relations with Algerian students and organized a major demonstration against the war's continuation.[126]

The evolution of Franco–Algerian student ties can be seen within a wider international context. In 1955, Algerian students had founded the *Union Générale des Étudiants Musulmans Algériens* (UGEMA) and soon engaged with international networks, including the student conference at Bandung. In its quest for support from Africa, Asia and the Middle East, the ISC endorsed its actions – a stance that already became evident at an ISC council meeting in Ceylon in 1956.[127] Moreover, in 1958, the ISC held a special session in London on student problems in Algeria. In this context, it defined UGEMA as 'a National Union of Students with a wide range of syndicalist activity on behalf of its members'.[128] The portrayal of UGEMA as a student, rather than political, organization was vital, as it enabled the ISC to treat the suppression of UGEMA as 'student matter' and issue pronouncements that denounced the actions of the French authorities. The case shows how a cause such as Algerian independence – often seen within the context of the 'long Sixties' – can also be integrated into an earlier history of European student internationalism and its engagement with politics.[129]

Conclusion

Student activism is often viewed through the lens of political and social protest. At the international level, such forms did indeed exist well before the 1960s, as illustrated by the role of communist students and the involvement of university students in anti-colonial campaigns. This chapter has noted, however, that another prominent strand of student internationalism before 1960 cast itself as 'apolitical', emphasizing cooperation, aid and expertise. Such ventures were aimed at supporting students through practical efforts and by working with other actors within the international order, including the League of Nations and the UN. The boundaries between protest and 'apolitical' work were blurrier than student leaders were willing to admit: student organizations engaged with political questions at several levels, even when they did not acknowledge it. This point is worth noting as it also allows us to connect the work of the more limited 'student internationals' of the earlier period to the more radical forms of student activism of the 1960s.

As this chapter has highlighted, the First World War was not necessarily a rupture. Instead, it changed the contexts in which older organizations – notably the WSCF

---

[125] Louis Vos has even described it as 'the main centre for the entire resistance movement against the war in Algeria': Vos, 'Student Movements and Political Activism', 291.
[126] Monchablon, 'L'apogée d'un mouvement syndical', 80
[127] Paget, *Patriotic Betrayal*, 162–3.
[128] Research and Information Commission of the ISC, *Report on Higher Education and Culture in Algeria* (Leiden: RIC, 1959), 5.
[129] For a consideration of transnational activism on Algeria and other 'Third World' issues in a 1960s context, see Robert Gildea, James Mark and Niek Pas, 'European Radicals and the "Third World"', *Cultural and Social History* 8, no. 4 (2011): 449–71.

– operated, and it triggered the creation of new bodies. Moreover, the presence of substantial communist and anti-colonial strands within the world of student internationalism clearly preceded the era of Cold War and decolonization. This observation connects with a wider point – namely that research on internationalism is well suited to questioning existing periodizations.

Moreover, student internationalism highlights the fluidity of internationalism, as young people moved in and out of positions and stances. While some individuals stayed within organizations well beyond their student days – serving as student officials – the general feature of student organizations was that, because of their connection to a particular stage in the educational cycle, they were subject to frequent renewal. In this respect, generational shifts were even more prominent than within other international organizations. It is therefore all the more striking that in terms of concerns and rhetoric, a range of common threads can be observed. The transient nature of university life also offers intriguing paths for further research. In particular, it raises the question whether individuals who had acquired a taste of internationalism continued or terminated their internationalist commitments after they had graduated from university – and from the student organizations they had been involved in.

10

Vegetables of the world unite!

Grassroots internationalization of disabled citizens in the post-war period

Monika Baár

Approximately 15 per cent of the world's population is estimated to have a form of disability: they constitute the world's largest minority.[1] Moreover, family members, carers and the environment are also affected by their condition. Precise numbers prove difficult to estimate because definitions and categorizations are constantly evolving and shifting. Because of the volume and the societal significance of the issue, it may appear surprising that 'disability internationalism' (a phrase coined for the purposes of this chapter) has remained a virtually unstudied field and has yet to be written into the canon of internationalism.[2] Little attention has so far been paid to this topic for a variety of reasons. A crucial one is that the process of internationalization itself commenced at a relatively late stage: until the 1970s and in several cases even well beyond that period, the majority of persons with disabilities had lived in isolation and segregation – whether because they were confined to institutionalized settings or because of the physical and attitudinal barriers which prevented them from leaving their homes and contributing to societal life in the first place. Legislation, policies and decision making were typically confined to the national or municipal-local level.

Even in those instances when a certain degree of internationalization could be observed prior to the 1970s – for example, in the case of deaf and blind people – these were not grassroots initiatives, but organizations intended *for* disabled people which were managed by experts and policymakers. Characterized by a charitable mentality, and by the perception of disability as a 'personal deficit', leaders of these organizations usually took it for granted that disabled people, regardless of the type and severity of their condition, were not in the position to make decisions about their own fate, so these needed to be taken on their behalf.

---

[1] The author acknowledges the support of the ERC Consolidator Grant *Rethinking Disability* contract nr. 648115 and the support of the Brocher Foundation in the form of a residential fellowship for writing this chapter.
[2] The available literature is written nearly exclusively from an anglophone perspective and as such cannot provide an adequate framework for the study of Europe.

By contrast, the emerging grassroots organizations, which were inspired by and often revealed parallels with other social movements – be they the women's movement, youth movement or gay liberation – started to 'talk back' by claiming agency for themselves and asserting that they were best qualified to make decisions about their own needs, and proposing ideas about how to eliminate the obstacles (whether physical or social) that stood in the way of equality with their able-bodied counterparts. These organizations were formed *of* and run by disabled people themselves. In the course of this politicization and internationalization, members of the disabled community started to question the 'cripple' or 'abnormal' status assigned to them by society and gradually started to perceive themselves as a collective body of people. This resulted in enhanced social visibility and a new form of self-confidence, which made it possible for disability activists on many occasions to contest the expertise of medical professionals and policymakers. As shall be outlined later in the chapter, these developments led to the redefinition of disability from being a merely medical category into a social concept and from being a charitable matter into an issue of human rights and, in some cases, even as an identity which can be a source of pride. This development allowed for the emergence of new international networks in addition to the already-existing medical-professional ones.

A major barrier in the way of writing the history of grassroots disability internationalism is practical in nature: the dearth of available sources. Grassroots initiatives typically emerge in the informal sphere, leaving behind only a limited amount of documentation and often none at all, which makes the reconstruction of their early histories difficult. Typically, relevant information can only be traced in 'grey materials': leaflets, pamphlets and newsletters which did not make it into archival collections, but are stored in the cellars and attics of activists and as such have limited accessibility and are vulnerable to destruction. Existing literature on the topic is not only extremely limited, but it nearly exclusively focuses on developments in the Anglo-American world. Often – however inadvertently – these studies take it for granted that developments in Britain and North America were invariably pioneering and as such must have served as models to be reiterated in other parts of Europe and the rest of the world. As this chapter will demonstrate, such instances definitely existed. However, upon closer study a more complex overall picture emerges. This reveals the prominent role and the 'connected status' of non-Anglophone activists and organizations from continental Europe and from the 'peripheries'.

One reason for initiatives in continental Europe was that the first disability organizations were typically formed of veterans and hence their presence was particularly strong in the countries which were seriously hit by the war. Here expertise in the field of rehabilitation was particularly necessary, and this need motivated the establishment of international networks. Although these were not yet bottom-up organizations, the contacts developed in this way could form the basis of genuinely grassroots initiatives at a later stage. Another example is the Nordic countries' leading role in the institutionalization of international networks of organizations intended initially *for*, but later also *of*, people with cognitive disabilities and their families. One potential circumstance that could trigger this activism may have been the stark contrast between the famously generous nature of the Nordic welfare states and the often astonishingly bad treatment to which especially people with serious disabilities were subjected: such a discrepancy could even prove harmful for the image of these countries.

Moreover, in the majority of the cases it may not even be meaningful to trace the origins of an idea or initiative, because activism and internationalization evolved in polycentric ways. Reactions to the 'Zeitgeist' could result in the expression of similar ideas and in similar developments across different parts of Europe and even globally. But even when intentions were shared, the process of internationalization could trigger tensions: the broader its scope, the larger is the number of the involved organizations and individuals; the more difficult it became to reach consensual decisions. Such cleavages could arise about ideological issues, priorities and even practicalities. Often, one single formula was not sufficient, particularly when the scope of European activism expanded into a global one. The fundamental principles of the disability movement: independence, 'rights not charity' and equal opportunities did not translate easily (if at all) to non-Western environments. It was at that stage that the implicit assumption hitherto shared by representatives of the disability movement – that the desires and needs of disabled people were universal – needed to be questioned. 'Identity politics', something that formed the core of the 'Western' disability movement, often clashed with the perceptions of activists elsewhere, who typically lobbied for project funding to support the local communities, rather than for more abstract rights. Moreover, aside from the ideological issues, technical matters also caused complications. One of those was related to communication: not everyone was ready to accept that English should be the sole means of communication in international meetings and correspondence.

This chapter argues that by moving beyond the 'usual suspects' and embarking on the study of the somewhat 'unusual suspect' of disability activism has potential to complicate and nuance both received knowledge about the history of internationalism and about our perception of the post-war period in Europe, including the Cold War and its aftermath. The pursuance of this topic also aligns with recent calls for diversifying existing research on the forging of international connections, which has so far primarily focused on the internationalism of liberal elites. Furthermore, because this research weaves initiatives and developments at the individual, local and national levels into the international context, it aligns with the recent historiographical shift which has been described as 'history in between'.[3] Studying disability internationalism adds a fresh perspective on the contribution of individuals who are typically qualified as 'recipients' of internationalism, but who have claimed themselves the expertise which is drawn not from medical or administrative knowledge but from the lived experience. It also helps recent ambitions to geographically de-centre the history of internationalism.[4] While the main sites of international legislation are certainly located in New York, Geneva and Brussels, *the steps* that lead to the realization of new law-making often happen at different sites. All in all, the study of 'disability internationalism' contests

---

[3] A. Antic, J. Conterio, and D. Vargha, 'Conclusion: Beyond Liberal Internationalism', *Contemporary European History* 25, no. 2 (2016): 361.

[4] Ibid., 365.

binary divisions and monolithic views on expert versus lay knowledge, top-down and bottom-up action, the formal and the informal sphere.

Studying disability internationalism may help us rethink established labels and categorizations in the field. In that context, it represents a somewhat porous and often chameleon-like variant of internationalism which escapes straightforward categorizations. In many cases, this type of internationalism forms part of a social movement. In others it constitutes part of medical internationalism. This ambiguity is to a large extent due to the fact that while disability is a condition that connects people across borders, it is also an extremely heterogeneous condition: some people are born with it, while others acquire the condition during the course of their life. It may be permanent or temporary. It can manifest as a physical or cognitive condition, arising from a range of factors – genetics, accident, external circumstances or advancing age. Often, people with such divergent conditions have nothing much in common other than the label of 'disability'. Some internationalization projects revolve around one single-impairment type, such as Down syndrome and autism, while others are cross-disability initiatives involving a broader or a full spectrum of the condition. Whereas some 'internationalists' demonstratively reject the notion that disability is a medical condition – for example, sign language users who consider themselves to form part of a linguistic minority and others, such as AIDS activists, frame their condition as an 'illness identity'. While bonds of solidarity, a *Schicksaalgenossenschaft* frequently emerged among these groups in the process of internationalization, it should not be denied that conflict and factions likewise frequently occurred. For example, people with physical disabilities often tended to distance themselves from those with cognitive or mental disabilities, a phenomenon which is usually referred to as 'horizontal hostility'.[5]

Moreover, disability could be combined with additional identities. For example, in some countries, gay and lesbian disability groups also came into being. They often experienced double marginalization or exclusion: they felt that while the disability movement was dominated by heteronormative tendencies, the gay and lesbian movement was dominated by ableist tendencies. Forming a network of their own within either these communities was however not necessarily useful because of the small size of their groups.[6] Such shared experiences fostered internationalization and motivated the organization of the European Conference on Homosexuality and Disability, held in Uddel, the Netherlands in 1991.

Yet, it is precisely this ambiguity and multifariousness which may allow for adding new nuances to received knowledge on the history of internationalism.

Disability internationalism also provides an excellent platform to study the interaction between activities undertaken at the local, national and international levels. It reminds us that the national framework is neither irrelevant nor can it be discarded: many initiatives first evolve at the national level (often simultaneously) and

[5] Eli Clare, *Exile and Pride: Disability, Queerness and Liberation* (Durham, NC: Duke University Press, 2015), 92.
[6] See Nina Little's MA thesis, 'Minority Consciousness Gone Mad?' Exclusion, Inclusion and Self-Organization of Disabled LGBTI People in the Dutch and British LGBT+ and Disability Movements in the Late Twentieth Century' (Institute for History, Leiden, 2019)

the specificities of respective welfare states also hold relevance. At the same time, by constituting a shared experience which connects people across the world, irrespective of the region and political system in which they live, the adoption of transnational and international perspectives on the study of disability is not an option but a must.

This chapter outlines the emergence of disability internationalism in the second half of the twentieth century, first and foremost in the European context, but also paying attention to regional specificities and global entanglements. It reveals that internationalization has been a gradual process, and certainly not a teleological one: it was characterized by conflicts and detours, and the changing nature of the concept of disability has required the constant redefinition of its remit. At times it was characterized by certain shorter periods when an unusual density of activities could be observed. Typically, semantic shifts in disability-related terminologies in different languages provide a good indication of when those 'compressed periods' occurred. From this point of view, the 1970s were significant because it was in this decade that disability became problematized as a social and legal matter, while in the 1980s the International Year of Disabled Persons (1981) and the subsequent International Decade of Disabled Persons (1993–2003) accelerated and intensified activities at the grassroots level. The topic provides new angles on the role of citizens' initiatives in the process of European integration by revealing how their lobbying contributed to a ground-breaking development on the global scale: the integration of disability into the framework of human rights, which culminated in the adoption of the United Nations Convention on the Rights of Persons with Disabilities (UNCRPD) in 2006. Moreover, the study of disability internationalism promises to provide fresh perspectives on the rising influence of non-state actors and impact of the proliferation of NGOs in the second half of the twentieth century. Last but not least, it may help us ponder at what stage and with what consequences grassroots organizations transformed into formalized institutions and how that process, which typically involves the acceptance of certain superimposed expectations and a great deal of bureaucratization, changes their very nature.

Legacies of the war

The most gruelling legacy of the Second World War for disabled people was *Aktion Gnadentod* (Action Merciful Death), or *Aktion T4*, in the course of which altogether approximately 210,000 individuals with intellectual or psychological disabilities in the German Reich and a further 80,000 in occupied Poland and the Soviet Union were murdered through deliberate medication overdose, poisoning or systematic starvation.[7] An initiative which evolved into an early instance of disability internationalism in a religious setting, and has been referred to as 'a kind of inverse reflection to Nazism

---

[7] The literature on this topic is enormous. A suitable point of departure is Michael Burleigh, *Death and Deliverance: 'Euthanasia' in Germany c. 1900-1945* (Cambridge: Cambridge University Press, 1994).

and an anti-fascist alternative to concentration camps',[8] was the Camphill movement founded by the Austrian Jewish paediatrician Karl König. Compelled to seek refuge in Scotland after the Anschluss and inspired by Rudolf Steiner's anthroposophy and the ideas of the Welsh utopian socialist Robert Owen, König established a life-sharing community model in which abled-bodied people lived together initially with severely disabled children and later also with adults in a spiritually curative environment.[9] Representatives of the Camphill movement considered the status of disability as a meaningful one and disabled individuals as capable of fully contributing to society. König believed that spiritual courage can help to make the 'mountain of handicap' irrelevant: in a supportive and sympathetic environment even those with a learning disability could develop self-confidence. Moreover, he viewed disabled children as social refugees who had been expelled from society in a similar way that he had been forced out of his homeland. The initiative quickly spread throughout the world, at present there exist over one hundred communities in twenty countries.

A further instance of religious disability internationalism was the progressive Catholic *fraternité catholique des maladies*, founded by father Henri François in France in 1942. The first initiative in France was quickly followed by numerous autonomous groups in Western Europe and in Latin America and they have been in existence ever since. From the late 1960s onwards, many of these fraternities became influenced by the spirit of the Vatican II synod and liberation theology. They were run by priests and layman who often themselves had a disability, and while performing an evangelizing role, they were open to every denomination and even to atheists. The fraternities sought to liberate themselves from what they considered the paternalism of healthy people and they encouraged their membership to fight for disability rights and legislative changes in their respective countries. The various fraternities which were originally dispersed in different countries today operate in coordination and are known as the Intercontinental Christian Fraternity of People with Disabilities.[10]

Yet another community which grew out of religious roots is the initially Catholic and subsequently ecumenical *L'Arche*.[11] It was started in France in 1964, in Trosly-Breuil, a small village north of Paris, by the philosopher and religious leader Jan Varnier, who invited two people with intellectual disabilities to leave their institution and live with him. From this micro-community, a global movement emerged: in 2019, it involved 149 communities in 38 countries across the world. Like in the case of Christian fraternities, the unexpected expansion also necessitated a greater degree of coordination, which was realized by the establishment of an International Board.

---

[8] Dagmar Herzog, *Unlearning Eugenics: Sexuality, Politics and Reproduction in Post-Nazi Europe* (Wisconsin, MA: University of Wisconsin Press, 2018), 88.
[9] For an analysis, see Dan McKanan, *Touching the World: Christian Communities Transforming Society* (Collegeville, MN: Liturgical Press, 2007).
[10] Gildas Brégain, 'An Entangled Perspective on Disability History: The Disability Protests in Argentina, Brazil and Spain, 1968-1982', in *The Imperfect Historian: Disability Histories in Europe*, ed. A. Klein, P. Verstraete and S. Barsch (Frankfurt am Main: Peter Lang, 2013), T. D'Argenlieu, *La fraternité catholique des malades* (Bourges, 1953).
[11] Jean Varnier, *The Challenge of L'Arche* (London: Darton, Longman & Todd 1982); Frances Young, *Encounter with Mystery: Reflections on L'Arche and Living with Disability* (London: Darton, Longman & Todd, 1997).

The novelty of *L'Arche*'s approach is that it went beyond traditional models of care and charity and created communities which are simultaneously protective and stimulating. It considers people with intellectual disabilities not as clients or patients but as companions who can undertake work and therapeutic and leisure activities in dignity.

Apart from resulting in the murder of a hundred thousand of disabled adults and children, the war also disabled millions of soldiers and civilians. Of them, the ex-servicemen's assertion that they had sacrificed their health 'on the altar of the fatherland' could be utilized to forge a new form of agency: they were not satisfied with the promise of mere survival and did not shy away from voicing their dissatisfaction with their conditions. Another group to assert their agency in a special way were people whose disability occurred in the course of industrial accidents – in a similar manner to the veterans, they were in the position to claim that they had sacrificed their able bodies in the service of their employers. Insurance companies and welfare states typically handled them as a separate category. By contrast, civilians, whose condition was neither due to war nor to accident, were treated as a burden that was draining the resources of the state. The relationship between these different types of groups was not always harmonious, particularly when they needed to compete for limited resources.

Disabled veterans – whose first experience of 'internationalization' often commenced on the front – and victims of work accidents could also use their 'comparative advantage' for forging international contacts: theirs was the first organization that connected national or local ones at the international level. Fédération Internationale des Mutilés, des Invalids du Travail et des Invalides Civics (FIMITIC) was established in 1953 as an umbrella association connecting already-existing national organizations.[12] Associations for blind and deaf people which had come into being well before their equivalents for other types of impairment were next in the line to internationalize. The World Council for the Welfare of the Blind was established in 1949, while the World Federation of the Deaf was founded in 1951, and both of them regularly organized congresses, some of which took place in Eastern Europe. These were, however, organizations intended *for* blind people without including them in management and leadership. In 1964, a grassroots attempt was undertaken to turn World Council for the Welfare of the Blind into an organization *of* blind people by advancing the proposition that at least 50 per cent of the leadership should be comprised of blind people themselves. This was however rejected by the leadership and, as a result, a group seceded and formed an alternative platform, International Federation of the Blind (IFB). These two organizations then merged into the World Blind Union in 1984 during IFB's conference in Saudi Arabia.

Sport events provided a prominent site for internationalization. In 1952, the International Stoke Mandeville Wheelchair Sports Federation was formed to cater for the sporting interests of tetraplegic and paraplegic athletes, and it initiated the first Paralympic Games that was held in Rome in 1960.[13] Under the aegis of the World

---

[12] Despite its crucial role, there exists virtually no academic literature on the history of FIMITIC. A small pamphlet published by the organization dating back to 1977, *The FIMITIC's Social and Socio-Political Programme*, gives a short overview.

[13] The first event to be officially called Paralympics was held in Tokyo in 1964. The Rome games initially ran under the title Ninth International Stoke Mandeville Games; it was then designated as the first Paralympics with retroactive effect.

Veterans Federation, International Sports Organization for the Disabled (ISOD) was formed in 1964 with twelve participating countries, and it acted as an umbrella organization that sought to unite participants with different types of disabilities, from both veteran and civilian groups.[14] The first Winter Paralympic Games were held in Sweden in 1976. Deaf people also have their own tradition of organizing international sports games; the first such event – today known as Deaflympics – was organized in Paris in 1924, while the inaugural Winter Deaflympics was held in Austria in 1949, with the exclusive participation of male participants.

Professionals, parents, grassroots: The remaking of mental retardation

As has been hinted earlier, isolation and segregation belonged to the fundamental experiences of persons with disabilities for a very long time. Their status was considered to hold relevance for social policy and charity, in line with the general assumption that they were in fact eternal children and decisions needed to be taken on their behalf. Although international contacts did occur between medical personnel and policymakers – for example, in the form of conferences and visits – such contacts between disabled people themselves were at first largely unheard of and even unthinkable. While the status of persons with any type of impairment carried a stigma with it, this was especially the case for people with mental and intellectual disabilities. They constituted 'a hidden society' confined to an indefinitely prolonged childhood, whose situation was deplorable even in the world's most coveted welfare states. This situation was recognized by the (progressive) members of the scientific-medical community, by parents and families, in addition to the representatives of the concerned groups.

At the grassroots level, unsurprisingly, parents were the first 'agents' to initiate change by forming organizations that brought these issues out of the private, family sphere to the public realm and then aligned themselves with professionals to solicit help from the state. Parents' organizations in the Nordic countries evolved out of the paradox that while these countries fashioned themselves as norm entrepreneurs in welfare matters, they neglected the needs of disabled people, particularly if they were not in employment. Like in several other countries, the inhuman and unacceptable conditions in institutions and boarding schools caring for children and adults with intellectual disabilities became disclosed with methods ranging from undercover journalism to full-fledged documentary films. As is often the case with grassroots organizations, a well-known public figure may find himself in a good position to give impetus to sparking a 'movement'. This happened in Norway in the 1960s when Arne Skouen, a film director with an autistic daughter, demanded 'Justice for the Disabled' and criticized the Norwegian state for violating human rights. He compared conditions in institutions to concentration camps, which led to two legal cases: a defamation case

---

[14] For a comprehensive account of the Paralympic games, see Steve Bailey, *Athlete First: A History of the Paralymics Movement* (Chichester: Wiley and Sons, 2008).

against him and an investigation on the conditions of institutions. The outcome of the investigation was that while Skouen exaggerated his claims, living conditions in institutionalized settings were definitely unacceptable.[15]

Parents' struggles yielded significant results: the principle of normalization, that is, that the living conditions of those with disabilities should become as close as possible to 'regular' life (rhythm of life, choices, provisions) became increasingly accepted as a desideratum: 'If an equality viewpoint is not acknowledged, there is a risk of ending simply in sentimental pity, in theories of overprotection, in group-discrimination or something else.'[16] Nordic parental groups easily connected across borders because of the absence of the language barrier, but similar problems elsewhere triggered similar responses. For example, the Greek Panhellenic Union of Parents and Guardians of Unadjusted Children was confronted with identical problems and as a nonprofessional voluntary association it contributed to the 'politicization of the private' from the grassroots level in late twentieth-century Greece.[17]

The 'remaking' of mental retardation[18] required the dissociation from the earlier notions of degeneration and eugenics and framing it as an issue of rights and social integration – the latter of which required special educational opportunities. This transformation provided the foundations for the emergence of international self-advocacy. The rights of people with intellectual and developmental disabilities were taken up by the International Association for the Scientific Study of Intellectual and Developmental Disabilities (IASSIDD), an organization which was born out of three international congresses held in London, Vienna and Copenhagen in 1960, 1961 and 1964, respectively. The International Association and its constitution were formalized at the 1964 Congress. Another important association that contributed to the coming into being of new international legislation was the International League of Societies for the Mentally Handicapped (today Inclusion International), which was established in 1960 during the World Mental Health Year and which operated in collaboration with experts, parents and volunteers. Moreover, a symposium organized in Stockholm in 1967 on legal aspects addressed the role that parents associations can play in ensuring that new legal provisions would be fully implemented. It also pointed to the 'limits' of internationally imposed norms: political cultures and welfare provision differed from country to country, so no single 'winning formula' could be proposed. Instead, a variety of methods were suggested, including (1) the creation of a favourable public opinion; (2) active dialogue with public authorities and members of the practising professions; (3) appeals to members of legislative bodies; (4) appeals to the courts, where feasible; (5) the nomination of parents on Boards of Control by the responsible authority,

---

[15] Rannveig Traustadóttir, Borgunn Ytterhus, Snæfrídur Thóra Egilson, and Berit Berg (eds.), *Childhood and Disability in the Nordic Countries: Being, Becoming, Belonging* (London: Palgrave, 2015), 30.; see also Jan Tøssebro, 'Scandinavian Disability Policy: From Deinstitutionalization to Non-discrimination and Beyond', *Alter* 10, no. 2 (2016): 111–23, Marie Sepulchre, 'Tensions and Unity in the Struggle for Citizenship: Swedish Disability Rights Activists Claim: Full Citizenship!', *Disability & Society* 33, no. 4 (2018): 539–61.

[16] Tøssebro, 'Scandinavian Disability Policy', 3.

[17] Despo Kritsotaki, 'Turning Private Concerns into Public Issues: Mental Retardation and the Parents' Movement in Post-War Greece, c. 1950-80', *Journal of Social History* 49, no. 4 (2016): 990.

[18] Ibid.

agency or ministry concerned.¹⁹ Both IASSIDD and the League played crucial roles in placing the issue onto the UN's agenda. To that end, at its Jerusalem conference of 1968 the League formerly passed the Declaration on the General and Special Rights of Mentally Retarded Persons, which directly influenced the 1971 UN Declaration on the Rights of Mentally Retarded Persons.

A new dynamic in these discussions occurred when some (elite) representatives of the groups with intellectual and learning disabilities, surely also inspired by the spirit of the student movement of 1968, started to 'talk back' to what they considered to be the misrepresentation of their cause by professional and even parents' organizations. The most significant instance of such counter-initiatives was *People First*, which had its origins in Sweden and in the United States. It was the reaction of a group of young people with intellectual disabilities to the well-meaning, but in their view patronizing, impact of parents' organizations which were formed across Europe and the world. They no longer found the Swedish parents' organizations' motto, 'We speak for them', acceptable because they wanted to *speak for themselves*. They prepared a list of changes that they wanted in their services. Similar groups formed in the Britain, Canada, New Zealand and many other countries including one in 1974 in the United States. Here, one member, whose name and person had fallen into oblivion, grew tired of being called 'retarded' and burst out declaring, 'We are people first', and hence, the name of the self-advocacy movement was spontaneously born. One of the significant achievements of the People First movement has been the creation of an easy language variant in several languages. In Sweden, the idea to publish easy-to-read texts was first proposed in 1968 by the Swedish National Agency for Education. The first journal in simple language was published in 1984 and since then *8Sidor* appears on a weekly basis and contains eight pages (hence the title). The initiative gained recognition at regional and international meetings and became 'Europeanized' when in 1998 the first European guidelines were established and in 2009 Inclusion International adopted it.²⁰ Easy language – understandable and accessible information – is considered a political issue, because it dismantles barriers which are created by difficult and inaccessible language. On the other hand, it is not intended to be patronizing; this is why one of the remarkable recommendations in the European guidelines is not to use the familiar form ('dutzen') in these texts.²¹

The social model of disability and the emergence of a human rights-based framework

As we have seen, the emergence of self-advocacy groups had been preceded and accompanied by a host of developments which led to the redefinition of disability

---

[19] Symposium, 'Legal Aspects of Mental Retardation, Stockholm, 1967, Conclusion', Section II/2, pages 7–8, https://mn.gov/mnddc/parallels2/pdf/60s/67/67-ILS-ILS.pdf
[20] Gudrun Kellermann, 'Die Rolle der Leichten Sprache aus wissenschaftlicher Sicht', https://www.zedis-ev-hochschule-hh.de/files/kellermann_08042013.pdf
[21] Ibid.

from being an exclusively medical concept into a social category and from a status of 'burden' on the state into a condition which offered the possibility of active citizenship. According to this new understanding, disability could no longer be merely considered a personal 'defect' in need of rehabilitation but was perceived as a collective issue of a marginalized community struggling for equality. As the old, medical model of disability was gradually replaced by the social one, attention shifted away from the individual's impairment to the discriminatory social attitudes and physical barriers that prevented disabled people from participating fully in the community. The upsurge in disability activism led to a new, rights-based approach which required an entirely new way of thinking: rather than just ensuring the mere survival of disabled people, it acknowledges that they are entitled to a quality of life. Instead of being objects, patients, eternal children, they became subjects, active agents in their own fate. Grassroots movements started to 'talk back' to the mainstream of society by refusing the 'abnormal' and 'crippled' label. This process of politicization went hand in hand with the recognition that disability can become the basis of a social movement and a social identity. Like other social movements, the disability movement was characterized by a paradox: on the one hand, it was fighting for equalization and integration, and such claims for recognition implied the abolition of differentiation. On the other hand, it sought to obtain parity of participation and made claims for redistribution, and this presupposed that disability is a distinct movement and identity. This 'bivalent' character of the social movement – emphasizing integration versus emphasizing difference – led to a certain tension in citizenship claims.[22]

The world's most significant cross-disability organization, Disabled People's International (DPI), owes its existence to a scandal at the 1980 Winnipeg World Congress of Rehabilitation International, a traditional organization of medical and rehabilitation experts founded in 1922. The tension that emerged during this conference provides a good illustration of changing perceptions. It was during that meeting that Swedish delegates recommended amending the organization's constitution in such a way that at least 50 per cent of the delegates should be a person with disabilities. This amendment was rejected, much to the irritation of many participants who seceded the meeting and organized an alternative one, at which they decided to form a separate world coalition of persons with disabilities. This ambition was realized at the 1981 inaugural meeting of DPI in Singapore. In its draft constitution – which was modelled after the ILO's constitution– DPI complimented Rehabilitation International 'for making possible the vehicle for the formulation of the world coalition' and in that way contributing to acquiring a voice of their own.[23] Due to an unexpected turn of events, it became possible for Henry Enns, one of the founding members, to attend the United Nations Advisory Committee meeting for the International Year of Disabled Persons in Vienna held in August 1981 and to contribute to the drafting of the World Program of Action Concerning Disabled Persons (WPA) as well as to publicize DPI's philosophy.[24]

[22] Nancy Fraser, 'From Redistribution to Recognition? Dilemmas of Justice in a "Post-Socialist" Age', *New Left Review* 212 (1995): 68–93.
[23] Diane Driedger, *The Last Civil Rights Movement: Disabled People's International* (London, Hurst & Co., 1989), 36.
[24] Ibid., 43–5.

The history of DPI provides a remarkable instance for the study of internationalization because it reveals that the trajectories, interests and opportunities of European internationalists at times converge, but on other occasions conflict with those of non-European internationalists. DPI was compelled to set certain priorities: for example, it devised a development programme which only included developing regions. This was understandable given the scarce resources, but on the other hand it did not reflect on the fact that even in Europe disabled people constituted the poorest of the poor. Moreover, the existence of an array of disability-related organizations in Europe initially weakened the motivation to collaborate with DPI. Especially the leaders of FIMTIC, which had a consultative status with the UN's affiliated organizations, were reluctant to collaborate at the outset. Differences in ideology also caused frictions: members from 'Western regions' prioritized debates about identity politics, much to the dismay of members from developing regions who wanted concrete action and financial support. Notions of equal opportunity and full participation and demands for justice rather than charity did not necessarily resonate in their local environments. They were also disappointed by DPI's attitude: it did not raise funds itself; rather, it sought to provide contacts, so that disability organizations can find their own funding for their projects.[25] Moreover, fundraising itself proved difficult, as funds were usually controlled either by governments or charities. In order to be able to compete for funding, the disability organizations were compelled to exploit stereotypes of pity and helplessness – the very stereotypes they were seeking to counter with their activities.

Developments in the 1970s and early 1980s, which led to a breakthrough in disability legislation at the UN level, also made their mark within the European community, albeit somewhat slowly. In 1980, the Disability Intergroup of the European Parliament was established, one of the earliest intergroups in the history of the Parliament. Initially, the focus was on market integration, and this was stimulated by two Community Action Programmes for Disabled People: HELIOS I (1988–91) and II (1993–6). These initiatives and policy measures intended to help disabled people mentioned earlier, but it was not before long that the motto 'nothing about us without us' entered discourses within the European community.

A crucial concept which provided the main rationale for the establishment of the European Network of Independent Living (ENIL) in 1989 was *independent living*. It entails that disabled people, if they so wish, should be able to lead a life which does not make them subject to paternalistic tutelage, but enables them to exercise their autonomy. In addition to the accessibility of the environment, at the core of the concept is the notion of individualized *personal assistance* which increases independence and equal opportunities.

The origins of the independent living movement reach back to a student initiative at Berkeley in 1972 and, as such, provide a good instance of the transnational character of international disability activism. In this year, a group of disabled students moved out of the Berkeley campus to the local community and created an Independent Living Center. That the concept could take firm roots in Europe was to a large extent due to Adolf Ratzka, a German polio survivor who moved to Berkeley after he had not

[25] Ibid., 67.

been able to find an accessible and affordable place to pursue his studies in his native country. The experience at Berkeley changed his life, as he put it: 'I was catapulted from the vegetable existence of a German hospital to the hotbed of flower-power activism'.[26] It was at an international conference on housing in Gothenburg that the Norwegian Bente Skansgard, paralysed due to a car accident in her youth, met Ratzka in 1981, who by this time was living in Sweden. Three years later, she organized the first conference on independent living in Scandinavia and the Stockholm cooperative for independent living was formed – a pilot project for personal assistance for twenty-two people.[27] While the concept was becoming a reality in Sweden and Norway, European-wide awareness was still lacking. In April 1989, seventy-two disabled persons from twenty European countries convened at a conference in Strasbourg with the intention to spread the independent living approach throughout Europe, where residential segregation of disabled people was still very much the norm. It was at this meeting that the decision was undertaken to establish an informal network and this is how ENIL came into being.

Grassroots international initiatives also proved crucial in pushing for new European legislation, and the act of 'pushing' could at times be rather spectacular. On 3 December 1993, the newly opened European Parliament building in Brussels was witness to a rather unusual scene: 440 disabled people from all over Europe entered the huge debating chamber, and 72 of them took the floor and gave short talks about their experiences of segregation, discrimination and abuse. The occasion was the first Day of Disabled Persons and the unusual guests came to affirm their human rights under the European Convention.[28] As the masterminds of this event, British activist Rachel Hurt and Arthur Verney, at that time president of the British Deaf Association later recalled, the event was rather difficult to organize: on two previous occasions, Hurst's request to use the building was turned down by the Parliament's gatekeepers. So they had to turn to direct action. As she recalled,

> I got in the heavy mob from Northern France. I made contact with Disabled People's International in France and they sent half-a-dozen fierce young men in large wheelchairs, with posters. The Parliament went completely egg-shaped and refused to allow them into the building with their posters. So I said, 'Why not? This is a place of democracy and we are entitled to come in.' Faced by concerted lobbying, the questors capitulated. We found out later that the reason they had said no in the first place was because they thought we were going to pee on their seats![29]

It was on the recommendation of activists from different countries to include a specific non-discrimination clause when the Maastricht Treaty of 1992 (the founding treaty of the European Union (EU)) came up for revision. This eventually happened in 1996,

---

[26] See https://www.independentliving.org/docs5/time.html
[27] Today this is the Stockholm Independent Living Institute.
[28] 'Rachel Hurst: Activist/Campaigner', in *Defying Disability: The Lives and Legacies of Nine Disabled Leaders*, ed. Mary Wilkinson (London: Jessica Kingsley Publishers, 2009), 58.
[29] Ibid., 60–1.

with the introduction of article 13 to the Amsterdam Treaty.[30] The year 1999 saw the establishment of the International Disability Alliance (IDA) as a network of global and, since 2007, regional organizations of persons with disabilities (DPOs) and their families. The organization has five regional sections, among them a European one, which represents 350 organizations in 50 countries. The main objective of IDA is to ensure the implementation of the UNCRPD worldwide.

Impairment-specific international organizations

In addition to these umbrella organizations with a European or global mandate, the number of single-impairment organizations has been greatly increasing over the last three decades. One reason for this proliferation may be that paradoxically, the more 'universal' and inclusive the definition and perception of disability has become internationally with the adoption of the UNCRPD; the less attention can be paid to the specificities of particular types of disability in specific situations. Even within Europe, the problems that need addressing may be entirely different in Switzerland than in Serbia. In this context, it is worth noting that while many of these organizations collaborate with the institutions of the European Union, their mandate typically extends to the entire continent and not merely to EU countries. Listing all of these associations would go beyond the remit of this chapter; however, introducing three of them briefly may offer an insight into their dynamics. The Brussels-based Autism Europe, which was set up in 1983 by parents groups, has risen to prominence because of the huge increase in the diagnosis of autism in recent decades (whether because of better diagnostic facilities or because of changing definitions of the condition): seven million people are estimated to be affected by autism in Europe.[31] The main objective of the organization is awareness-raising and the promotion of the rights of those living with autism. In doing so, the association is compelled to navigate between divergent approaches to autism. Representatives of the neurodiversity movement believe that neurodiversity is as crucial for the human race as is biodiversity for nature. At its extreme, autism can therefore be understood as a natural human variation of the human genome and not a pathological disorder that would require cure or treatment.[32] This approach may have a 'normalizing effect', but the 'romanticization' of autism downplays the problems associated with it, and it may also lead to reluctance among parents to seek treatment for their children. To a certain degree, the organization embraces the principle of neurodiversity, but it simultaneously advocates for better care and educational opportunities for autistic people.

While more and more people are becoming diagnosed with autism, fewer and fewer children with Down syndrome are being born in Europe as a result of prenatal screening.

---

[30] Deborah Mabbett, 'The Development of Rights-Based Social Policy in the European Union: The Example of Disability Rights', *Journal of Common Market Studies* 33, no. 1 (2005): 106.
[31] https://www.autismeurope.org/who-we-are/mission-vision-values/
[32] Jim Sinclair, *Don't Mourn for Us*, 1993, See also *Autonomy, the Critical Journal of Interdisciplinary Autism Studies* 1, no. 1 (2012): 1-5.

The European Down Syndrome Association is the continental representative of Down Syndrome International, an organization which was founded in 1993.[33] It is mainly run by parents and caregivers as a human rights advocacy organization with the aim of spreading information and contributing to the de-stigmatization of the condition. It is operated on the principle that the capabilities of persons with Down syndrome should take precedence over their limitations. Somewhat similarly to the dilemma of autism advocates, members of the organization need to navigate between the assumption that 'there is much richness in life with an extra chromosome', and hence the syndrome is not a tragic divergence of proper human function, and the realization that having a family member with a Down syndrome is often experienced as a lifelong burden. The association has recently led highly successful campaigns on World Autism Day (2 April) that encouraged people to wear mismatched socks on that day to raise awareness. Yet, the case of international autism activism once again reveals that developments at the national level cannot be overlooked. Currently, abortion rates of pregnancies that test positive are around 90 per cent in the UK, 98 per cent in Denmark and 100 per cent in Iceland. It is not surprising therefore that in 2017 Iceland's president was criticized for his 'progressive hypocrisy' for posing with mismatched socks in social media while 'modern eugenics' is supported in his country.

The emergence of grassroots organizations of (former) mental health patients followed a somewhat different trajectory from that of those with physical disabilities. This group was often stigmatized even within some segments of the disability movement. Groups were initiated by survivors of psychiatry who were subject to involuntary institutionalization, forced treatment and abuse. The invention of modern psychiatric drugs provided an important impetus for de-institutionalization. Nevertheless, many people experienced the involuntary used of drugs not as a form of cure but as a form of control. Paradoxically, both those who have advocated the better accessibility of drugs and those who pointed to the misuses have accommodated their plight as a human right issue. The idea to establish a network of users and survivors of psychiatry first arose in 1991, during a conference in Mexico. In 1999, the organization was formalized with a secretariat in Denmark and continued to operate under various names. The Center for the Human Rights of Users and Survivors of Psychiatry (CHRUSP) was established in the final stage of the negotiation of the CRPD (2006). The European section of the global organization, ENUSP, defines itself as a pan-European disease-specific organization.

The majority of these organizations, even if at their outset they were flexible and informal grassroots networks, today operate as NGOs or international NGOs (INGOs). This is also in alignment with the UNCRPD in 2006, the acceptance of which was hailed as an achievement 'giving voice' to disabled persons. However, the convention's sole emphasis on 'strategic leadership in human rights advocacy' and awareness-raising has become a target of criticism: abstract claims of empowerment do not replace service provision and can hardly help people whose situation demands immediate intervention. Moreover, the formalization of status led to a high degree of bureaucratization and the imposition of straightjacket models and 'predetermined scripts', which often went in parallel with the need to relinquish their grassroots status. The expectation of self-sufficiency, a crucial buzzword of policy, in certain situations

[33] The association's archived newsletters can be accessed here: http://www.edsa.eu/historyarchives/

may amount to nothing less than the relinquishing of any collective responsibility towards the vulnerable members of society.[34]

Last but not least, cultural organizations promoting 'disability art' have also seen a degree of internationalization recently, although some early instances can also be observed. For example, the Association of Foot and Mouth Painting Artists of the World (AFMPA) was established in 1957 in Lichtenstein, as a self-help group, a 'democratic cooperative'. Its first director, Arnulf Erich Stegmann was a polio victim. Members had the opportunity to exhibit their work in several museums and exhibition halls, the first two exhibitions took place in 1981 in the Town Hall of Madrid and in the UN's Headquarters in Geneva. AFMPA grew into a global organization with regional sections, and the main activity of the contributing artists is the production of Christmas cards. Operating as a for-profit organization, in recent years it attracted criticism because of the aggressive marketing strategies and because it was established that the artists themselves received only a minuscule portion of the profit. In addition to the existence of separate associations of disabled artists, another trend has been the emergence of a 'disability scene' within the mainstream art circuits. For example, Disability Arts International, which was created in 2013 by the British Council as part of an EU initiative, promotes disabled artists in collaboration with Greek, Dutch, Italian, German and Swedish theatres.[35]

How can the study of the internationalization of disability organizations and disability activism complicate existing mainstream knowledge on the history of internationalism? For one thing, it encourages us to pay more attention to the multifarious spatial dimensions and patterns of internationalism both within and outside Europe. The dynamics of disability activism could follow different trajectories: at times they grew out of a single initiative, and at other times from bi-or multilateral cooperation that can easily be located in time and space, but more frequently it involved a polycentric process. While initially the main ideals of disability activism appeared to be self-evident, once the movement expanded onto the global stage, it became clear that despite being a universal condition, it meant many things to many people.

In light of the pivotal role that the notion of expertise plays in histories of internationalism, the concept of disability can contribute to changing implicit assumptions about the clear delineations of expert knowledge. This chapter has revealed an intriguing relationship between medical experts operating as activists or advocates, parents claiming expertise as activists or advocates and people with disabilities emphasizing their own expertise and asserting their right to speak for themselves. Put differently, it has demonstrated that identities of experts, activists and 'recipients' are uniquely fluid and fraught. Last but not least, by hinting at the connections between the disability movement and other internationalisms, such as the gay and lesbian movement, the chapter has also outlined a methodological desideratum for future research: the need to pay more attention to those overlaps by putting on an intersectional lens in historical studies of internationalism.

---

[34] Stephen Meyers, 'Civil Society as Megaphone or Echo Chamber? Voice in the International Disability Rights Movement', *International Journal of Politics, Culture and Society* 27, no. 4 (2014): 461.
[35] http://www.disabilityartsinternational.org/creative-europe-announcement/

11

'A writer deserves to be paid for his work'

American progressive writers, foreign royalties and the limits of Soviet internationalism in the mid-to-late 1950s

Kristy Ironside

By the mid-twentieth century, the Soviet Union was one of the world's most unrepentant literary pirates. Like the Tsarist government before it, the Soviet government did not sign the 1886 Berne Convention for the Protection of Literary and Artistic Works, the first major international agreement on copyright. In that rejection, they were far from alone: widespread resistance to Berne, including on the part of major world powers like the United States, was one reason the United Nations Educational, Scientific, and Cultural Organization (UNESCO) developed the Universal Copyright Convention (UCC). More importantly, in the wake of the Second World War and in the context of the burgeoning Cold War, UNESCO sought a new approach to copyright that removed barriers to the free exchange of ideas and knowledge, a means of creating mutual understanding between nations and promoting world peace.[1] Unlike Berne, which required its signatories to provide minimum standards of protection to foreign authors with regard to the length of copyright and moral rights, among other protections, the UCC acknowledged the existence of diverging copyright practices and revolved around the principle of reciprocity: the agreement required signatories to provide 'national treatment' to foreign authors – in other words, the same copyright protections and benefits they provided to their own authors, including royalties. Although it was invited to do so, the Soviet Union did not help draft the UCC and did not sign the resulting 1952 agreement, leaving it one of the few countries to remain outside both international copyright systems for another twenty years.

The Soviet Union's rejection of Berne and the UCC stemmed, in part, from ideological principles that supposedly made its domestic copyright system incompatible with these international agreements. Soviet copyright law was not based on the 'bourgeois' notion of intellectual property. Rather, as legal experts emphasized, it took into consideration

---

[1] See UNESCO, 'Constitution of the United Nations Educational, Scientific and Cultural Organization', *Basic Texts 2018 edition* (Paris, 30 October–14 November 2017) (Paris: UNESCO, 2018), 5-6.

'the interests of the government and the people on the one hand, and the author on the other'; however, 'in the Soviet Union, there is not and cannot be a contradiction between these interests.'[2] Under the Copyright Act of 1928, which set the contours for the Soviet Republics' own regulations and remained relatively unchanged into the Khrushchev era, the Soviet author had the exclusive right to reproduce and distribute her work, as well as the right to derive 'material gains' (*imushchestvennye vygody*) from it in the form of royalties (*gonorary*), a right her heirs also enjoyed for fifteen years after her death.[3] She could not enter into an exploitative, 'antagonistic' relationship with her publisher, who could not treat her work as a commodity to profit from, for the Soviet press was merely an instrument for transmitting her work to the public or 'an organisation that fulfils the national affair of the communist education and enlightenment of workers by means of publishing ideologically solid, principled, and truthful works of literature, science, and art'.[4]

Foreign authors enjoyed no such rights on Soviet soil. The 1928 act explicitly denied them copyright protections in the absence of bilateral agreements with their home countries for any works that did not first appear in the Soviet Union.[5] It was not until 1967 that the Soviet Union signed such an agreement, and it was with one of its own satellite states, the Hungarian People's Republic. Complicating matters further, under the principle of 'freedom of translation', it was not considered a violation of an author's rights, Soviet or foreign, to translate a work into any minority language of the multi-ethnic Soviet Union without her consent.[6] Finally, the ruble was non-convertible and foreign royalties had to be paid in scarce hard currency (*valiuta*) that was earmarked primarily for industrial imports. Remaining non-signatories to the international conventions, and dragging its feet on signing bilateral agreements, allowed the Soviet government to conserve on hard currency and promote its vision of cultural revolution.

For a brief moment, however, the Soviet Union seemed poised to change course. In the wake of Stalin's death in 1953, the country experienced a cultural thaw and took a renewed interest in socialist internationalism after years of 'anti-cosmopolitanism'.[7] It joined UNESCO in 1954. Culture was identified as an important tool for building peace and understanding between the communist and capitalist camps in the Cold War and solidarity within the international socialist community.[8] After the October

---

[2] 'Predislovie', *Avtorskoe pravo na literaturnye proizvedeniia; sbornik ofitsial'nykh materialov*, ed. L. M. Azov and S. A. Shatsillo (Moskva: Gosudarstvennoe izdatel'stvo iuridicheskoi literatury, 1953), 3.
[3] See Articles 7, 9 and 15 of 'Osnovy avtorskogo pravo', *Avtorskoe pravo na literaturnye proizvedeniia*, 10.
[4] 'Predislovie', *Avtorskoe pravo na literaturnye proizvedeniia*, 3.
[5] Ibid., 8.
[6] See Article 9a of 'Osnovy avtorskogo pravo', *Avtorskoe pravo na literaturnye proizvedeniia*, 10.
[7] On the cultural thaw and the exchanges as a return to internationalism, see Eleonory Gilburd, 'The Revival of Soviet Internationalism in the Mid-to-Late 1950s', in *The Thaw: Soviet Society and Culture during the 1950s and 1960s*, ed. Denis Kozlov and Eleonory Gilburd (Toronto: University of Toronto Press, 2006), 362–401.
[8] On cultural exchanges as a move towards peace and understanding between the Soviet Union and the United States in particular, see Yale Richmond, *Cultural Exchange and the Cold War: Raising the Iron Curtain* (University Park: Pennsylvania State University Press, 2003), 14–15. On the use of culture to forge an international community in the 'Second World' of socialist states, see Kiril

1955 meeting of the 'Big Four' foreign ministers in Geneva, the Soviet Union embraced official cultural exchanges with the capitalist West. As Eleonory Gilburd has noted, it did not wait for the formal exchanges to begin: exhibits and festivals of Western culture, as well as dramatically increased publication of Western literature, commenced immediately.[9] These developments inspired hope that the Soviet Union might finally set aside its objections and join the international copyright order. Yet, it quickly became clear that nothing had changed on the copyright front: the Soviet government signed neither Berne nor the UCC, Soviet publishers engaged in literary piracy on an even larger scale, and foreign writers received inconsistent ex gratia royalty payments, if at all, as the cultural exchange negotiations proceeded and the resulting agreements were implemented in the late 1950s.[10] In the meantime, the Soviet Union continued to use a 'back door' strategy to protect its works in Western countries by giving exclusive rights to a trusted foreign publisher or intermediary, and even aggressively defended Soviet cultural producers against breaches of their intellectual property rights abroad under the very 'bourgeois' copyright laws it otherwise rejected.[11]

This seeming hypocrisy garnered scathing criticism in the Anglo-American world and prompted several highly publicized efforts on the part of officials, lawyers, activists and writers to pressure the Soviet government to address the issue, all of which were rebuffed.[12] Soviet authorities stubbornly defended their copyright practices in the face of these criticisms, pointing out that, as the 'the most reading people in the world' (*samyi chitaushchii narod v mire*), the financial obligations of any international copyright agreement were unduly burdensome on the Soviet Union. When the American journalist and peace activist Norman Cousins suggested a copyright agreement that would 'erase past debts' but require future royalty payment commitments on the part of the Soviet Union during his 1963 meeting with Khrushchev, the latter reportedly exploded at him: 'What kind of a deal is this? You get all the benefits, and what do we get?'[13] Khrushchev complained that while Soviet readers devoured millions of copies of Hemingway, Faulkner and Twain, Americans were interested in only a handful of the Russian 'classics' but not in contemporary Soviet writers. 'But we would be glad to

---

Kunakhovich, 'Ties That Bind, Ties That Divide: Second World Cultural Exchange at the Grassroots', in *Socialist Internationalism in the Cold War Exploring the Second World*, ed. Austin Jersild and Patryk Babiracki (Cham: Palgrave Macmillan, 2016), 136.

[9] Gilburd, 'The Revival of Socialist Internationalism', 364.

[10] Copyright came up in the 1955 Geneva talks that led to the cultural exchange agreements. The Western powers initially requested that the Soviet Union 'accord more adequate protection to Western industrial property rights and copyrights'. The Soviet delegates objected, and it was ultimately left out of the agreements. See *The Geneva Meeting of Foreign Ministers, October 22-November 16, 1955* (Washington, DC: Department of State Publications, 1955), 259.

[11] Kiril Tomoff has highlighted the use of this strategy in the Soviet Union's cultural confrontations with the West in the early Cold War. See Kiril Tomoff, *Virtuosi Abroad: Soviet Music and Imperial Competition During the Early Cold War, 1945–1958* (Ithaca: Cornell University Press, 2015), 21–2.

[12] The most famous of these was the failed lawsuit brought by the estate of Sir Arthur Conan Doyle for 'unjust enrichment' from the unauthorized use of the character of Sherlock Holmes, a test balloon for what might be accomplished through Soviet domestic courts. See Harold J. Berman, 'Sherlock Holmes in Moscow', *Harvard Law School Bulletin* 11, no. 4 (February 1960): 29–36.

[13] Norman Cousins, *The Improbable Triumvirate: John F. Kennedy, Pope John, Nikita Khrushchev* (New York: W. W. Norton & Company, 1972), 103.

talk to you about developing something approaching parity in our literary exchange', Khrushchev indicated, 'once that is done, we can consider the copyright problem.'[14]

While complaints about lost profits and appeals to 'fairness' expressed by 'bourgeois' authors, publishers and governments could be rejected on ideological and state-interest grounds, those of the so-called 'progressive writers' (*progressivnye pisateli*) – writers supportive of the Soviet Union in the Western capitalist world who belonged to the Communist Party, or who had socialist sympathies, and were often persecuted for their views – could be less easily dismissed. Within the Soviet Union, they were praised for their important contributions to the international socialist cause, raising awareness of the injustices of capitalism in their home countries, and for their activism in pursuit of world peace. However, they were no more legally entitled to royalties for the publication of their works in the Soviet Union than their 'bourgeois' counterparts. Amid anti-communist boycotts and blacklists in McCarthy-era America, foreign royalties took on increased significance in their incomes; as a result, they, too, lodged bitter complaints against the Soviet publishing industry's practices and the Soviet government's intransigence on the royalty issue. By the mid-to-late 1950s, a loose but dogged group of American progressive writers had coalesced around this issue, pressing Soviet cultural authorities to meet their ethical, if not their legal, commitments to them as intellectual workers engaged in a common international socialist struggle.

The Khrushchev government's continued refusal to join the international copyright conventions or otherwise standardize foreign royalty payments called into question the sincerity of its commitment to international cooperation, undermining its efforts to portray itself as a leader in the global pursuit of peace and mutual understanding – not only in the minds of its foes but also in the minds of some of its allies, as this chapter shows. Soviet cultural authorities were keenly aware of this: publicly, they invoked a vision of international cultural collaboration that transcended such mundane and 'bourgeois' considerations as financial compensation; privately, they acknowledged that the Soviet Union's failure to pay regular royalties risked alienating many progressive writers as key supporters. This chapter takes as a case study the American writer-activist Howard Fast and his allies within the Soviet cultural elite, Boris Izakov and Boris Polevoy. As it shows, Izakov and Polevoy mobilized the economic plight of Fast and his fellow progressive writers in their efforts to convince the Soviet government of the benefits of embracing the international copyright order, an argument that did not gain traction. The Soviet government's failure to pay the royalties he believed he was owed, in turn, contributed to Fast's growing disillusionment with the Soviet Union and the Communist Party.

'A faithful friend of the Soviet Union'

Howard Fast was perhaps the quintessential 'progressive writer' in the Soviet understanding of the term: a brave, beleaguered writer, who was persecuted, suppressed

---

[14] Ibid., 104.

and thrown in jail for his efforts to spread the truth.[15] A New Yorker of working-class Jewish heritage, Fast became interested in communism at a young age and in the Soviet Union after Nazi Germany attacked it in 1941.[16] He joined the Communist Party of the United States of America (CPUSA) in 1943. His writings from the 1940s to the 1950s addressed contemporary and historical injustices: his most well-known work from this period is undoubtedly *Spartacus*, his novel about a slave revolt which went on to be the basis of the famous Hollywood film. Fast began writing it in prison, where he spent three months on contempt charges after being summoned before the House Un-American Activities Committee (HUAC) in 1950 and refusing to name names. He emerged from prison to discover that he was 'no longer a writer who had full and normal access to the American public', as he later put it.[17] His books were ordered to be removed from libraries and were no longer reviewed by the mainstream press, he was banned from speaking on university campuses, and he was blacklisted by commercial publishers. He self-published *Spartacus* in 1951.[18] The following year, using his personal savings, Fast founded Blue Heron Press, which became the sole American publisher of his work until 1956. The press quickly slid into insolvency, leaving Fast constantly concerned about his finances and dependent upon foreign royalties as income.[19]

Because of the professional and financial hardships associated with being blacklisted in America, Fast took great interest in the popularity of his work in the Soviet Union and in the prospect of receiving Soviet royalties. He had good reason to believe these were substantial. Since coming to the Soviet Union's attention in the late 1940s, Fast's reputation there had skyrocketed. In a 'bourgeois' literary scene purportedly characterized by 'decadence and disintegration', Fast was praised as 'the most significant figure in the younger generation of (American) writers', as the Soviet expert on English-language literature, Aleksandr Anikst, argued in a 1948 public lecture.[20] Fast was a 'writer-warrior' (*pisatel'-borets*) struggling for 'peace, democracy, and social progress', Anikst contended.[21] A Soviet handbook on his work called Fast 'a faithful friend of the Soviet Union': he was quoted as saying that 'the paradise you have built in the Soviet Union will be praised in countless songs and written of in countless legends'.[22] Fast enjoyed international fame, but, the handbook emphasized, his works were especially popular in the Soviet Union, where they had been published thirty-six times to date in twelve languages, excluding English, for a total of 13,859,000 copies.[23]

---

[15] On the Soviet definition of a 'progressive' writer, see Deming Brown, *Soviet Attitudes Toward American Writing* (Princeton: Princeton University Press, 1962), 272.

[16] Gerald Sorin, *Howard Fast: Life and Literature in the Left Lane* (Bloomington: Indiana University Press, 2012), 53.

[17] Howard Fast, *The Naked God: The Writer and the Communist Party* (New York: Praeger, 1957), 114.

[18] Fast funded the publication of the book by selling copies in advance in late 1951. See Philip Deery, *Red Apple: Communism and McCarthyism in Cold War New York* (New York: Fordham University Press, 2014), 47–8.

[19] Deery, *Red Apple*, 48.

[20] Aleksandr Abramovich Anikst, *Progressivnyi amerikanskii pisatel' Govard Fast; stennogramma publichnoi lektsii prochitannoi v Moskve* (Moskva: Pravda, 1948), 5–6.

[21] Ibid., 7.

[22] I. M. Levidova, *Progressivnye pisateli stran kapitalizma: Govard Fast* (Moskva: Vsesoiuzny gosudarstvennaia biblioteka inostrannoi literatury, 1953), 10.

[23] Ibid., 9.

Fast's extraordinary popularity in the Soviet Union has been attributed to the Soviet government's aggressive promotion of him and to its broader financial backing of the international left-wing literary movement. As Rossen Djagalov notes, his notoriety puzzled Western visitors to the Soviet Union like the American scholar of Slavic literature Deming Brown, who, during a 1956 visit, was surprised to find Fast's name 'on everyone's lips'.[24] Yet, Djagalov maintains that 'Kremlin gold', in both the literal sense of money and in the figurative sense of bestowing prestige, only goes so far as an explanation: he suggests that Fast never received royalties from the Soviet Union for the publication of any of the 2.5 million copies of his books published there (a claim I will dispute later in the chapter, as have other scholars), and he was already a bestselling author in a number of countries outside the Soviet bloc before his work was published there.[25] At the same time, as Gerald Sorin emphasizes in his biography of the author, Fast's work from the socialist phase in his career was 'panned or ignored' at home.[26] It was, Sorin writes, 'mostly flat, one-dimensional, distorted by ideology, and simply uninteresting to those outside leftist circles'.[27]

While Fast struggled to reach an audience and make a living as a writer in the United States, he was a respected and bestselling author in the Soviet Union, as cultural authorities there repeatedly reminded him in their correspondence. They bemoaned the fact that Fast could not come to the Soviet Union to see for himself: he was invited there on several occasions but could not travel abroad because the State Department refused to give him a passport.[28] In 1953, he was awarded the Stalin International Peace Prize, which came with a gold medal and a prize of USD 25,000; unable to come to Moscow, he accepted it at a reception in New York. In 1954, Fast was offered an all-expenses-paid trip to attend the Second Congress of Soviet Writers as a guest of

---

[24] Rossen Djagalov, '"I Don't Boast About It, but I'm the Most Widely Read Author of This Century": Howard Fast and International Leftist Literary Culture, ca. Mid-Twentieth Century', *Anthropology of East Europe Review* 27, no. 2 (2009): 40; Brown, 282.

[25] Djagalov, 44. Scholars are divided on the issue of how much Fast actually received. In his memoirs, written decades after his break with the Soviet Union and after he had reinvented himself as a successful screenwriter, Fast mentions only his Stalin prize when it comes to money, writing that he donated the medal but kept the prize money because 'considering the hundreds of thousands of my books printed in the Soviet Union, for which no royalties had ever been paid, the $25,000 aroused no guilts for undeserved gratitudes'. See Howard Fast, *Being Red: A Memoir* (Armonk: M.E. Sharpe, 1994), 318. Djagalov seems to take this statement at face value. Philip Deery estimates that Fast only collected around 5 per cent of the 2 million roubles (USD 500,000) owed to him in royalties by the Soviet Union. See Phillip Deery, 'Finding His Kronstadt: Howard Fast, 1956, and American Communism', *Australian Journal of Politics and History* 58, no. 2 (2012): 197. This figure is based upon Fast's claim, which will be discussed in detail later in this chapter, that Boris Izakov promised him this amount was being held for him by Soviet authorities. Gerald Sorin, on the other hand, suggests that Fast received substantial royalties from the USSR, which paid him 'handsomely, even if irregularly ... while Fast was occasionally strapped for cash because payments from the Soviet Union arrived erratically, he was financially secure'. According to Sorin, between 1951 and 1956 Fast received $20,000 in royalties from the Soviet Union for the publication of his novel *The Last Frontier* alone. Fast liked to 'moan and groan about the blacklist reducing him to "devastating poverty" and "near-bankruptcy"' but he was 'really talking only about the drastically undercapitalized Blue Heron Press'. See Sorin, 242, 297–8.

[26] Sorin, 4.

[27] Sorin, 6.

[28] 'Passport Denied to Fast, Novelist', *The New York Times*, 8 November 1950, 2.

honour.[29] He could not attend for the same reason. In a letter to Fast, Boris Polevoy, then secretary of the presidium of the Union of Soviet Writers, lamented the author's absence but informed him that, when he had mentioned Fast's work during his speech at the Congress, he was met with 'a burst of loud and long-sustained applause', which, he emphasized, 'was not for me but for you and all those American writers who continue to create great humanistic literature in difficult circumstances'.[30]

Fast not only never managed to see the 'paradise' that was the Soviet Union, but was unable to claim any royalties for the publication of his work there in roubles in person. Although royalties were sometimes paid to foreign authors in local currencies via wire transfers, Soviet authorities preferred in-country payments in roubles for two reasons. First, since the 1920s, the Soviet Union had used these payments to curry favour with visiting authors, whom it put up in luxurious accommodations in Moscow and presented a wad of cash 'royalties' upon arrival to be spent there.[31] Second, given the government's perpetual scarcity of hard currency, payment in roubles was cheaper and less complicated. In rare cases, Soviet royalties were paid in a combination of roubles and foreign currencies.[32] In all cases, the payment of any royalties to foreign authors was the exception rather than the rule.

In the absence of international copyright agreements, the Soviet Union's financial relationship to foreign authors was characterized by inconsistent, informal and personalized, rather than routine, formal and institutionalized transactions. As Eleonory Gilburd has shown, Soviet publishers were not constrained by international copyright law, but they were 'constrained by its spirit'. They cultivated patronage relations with individual authors and, though they could in principle publish whatever they liked without permission or compensation, 'they did so with great circumspection' because it irritated Western writers, who expressed 'endless' complaints about it.[33] Yet, as she goes on, any royalties that were paid to these authors were granted in exchange for loyalty, monetary payments were less entitlements than favours, and all payments were technically 'exceptions' made on a case-by-case basis after negotiations between the Foreign Commission of the Writers' Union and the Cultural Department of the Central Committee of the Communist Party.[34] Representatives of the Foreign Commission 'acted as "brokers", couching their petitions in the customary, and therefore compelling, language of help and support', emphasizing writers' poverty, mistreatment by capitalist

---

[29] Howard Fast Papers (thereafter Fast Papers), University of Pennsylvania: Kislak Center for Special Collections, Rare Books and Manuscripts, Box 13, Folder 2, Letter from Aleksandr Fadeev and Boris Polevoy, 20 October 1954.

[30] Fast Papers, Box 13, Folder 2, Letter to Fast from Polevoy, 2 November 1954.

[31] For example, the French writer André Malraux, who, in his later role as minister of cultural affairs would be extremely critical of the Soviet Union's failure to standardize its copyright relations, spent three months in the Soviet Union in 1934, where he and his wife 'lived nicely' on the royalties from his book *La Condition Humaine*, so nicely that his wife was able to afford to buy a fur coat. See Herbert R. Lottman, *Left Bank: Writers, Artists, and Politics from the Popular Front to the Cold War* (Chicago: University of Chicago Press, 1982), 64.

[32] See, for example, the royalties negotiated for French writer Roger Vailland, in roubles and in hard currency, when he visited the Soviet Union in May 1956: RGANI, f. 5, op. 36, d. 18, l. 43.

[33] Eleonory Gilburd, *To See Paris and Die: The Soviet Lives of Western Culture* (Cambridge: The Belknap Press of Harvard University Press, 2018), 112.

[34] Ibid., 113.

publishers and the high price they paid for their principles. As Gilburd argues, 'money came as compensation for progressive views rather than literature', and was intended to be 'a credit that would bind recipients to Soviet benefactors'.³⁵

Although they did not sign contracts with foreign authors or send them regular statements regarding print runs, sales and royalties earned, Soviet patrons often sent their foreign clients occasional reports on their works' performance in the Soviet book market. This cultivated loyalty and gratitude, especially in those who struggled to publish at home, but also inadvertently imparted the impression that royalties were steadily accruing to them in the Soviet Union. One of Howard Fast's most important sources for this information was Boris Izakov, a former foreign correspondent for *Pravda* in the UK, one of Fast's translators and an influential member of the Writers' Union. Though the two men met each other in person only once in New York in 1955, they exchanged frequent and warm letters prior to Fast's split with the Communist Party in 1957 and considered each other friends. Izakov kept Fast apprised of print runs, performances and reactions to his work; he also became one of Fast's most important advocates and a 'broker' for his financial interests in the Soviet Union.

Fast frequently raised the issue of royalties with Izakov and other cultural authorities in response to glowing reports about the success of his work in the Soviet Union. In a typical exchange, on 31 December 1954, Izakov informed Fast that his play 'Thirty Pieces of Silver' had been published in a literary magazine and as a book, and had been produced in ninety-eight theatres across the country, all 650,000 copies of the literary magazine *Roman gazeta* that had featured his story 'The Passion of Sacco and Vanzetti' had sold out, and his new novel *Silas Timberman* was soon to be published in serialized form in the thick journal *Novyi Mir*.³⁶ Fast responded that it gave him 'great joy ... to read of the treatment of my work in your country', all the more so since '"The Passion of Sacco and Vanzetti" was not reviewed in a single bourgeois journal in all of the United States, and, indeed, was sold in many commercial book stores from under the counter with fear and trepidation but also with sincerity and courage'.³⁷ He then quickly changed the subject to royalties, suggesting that Izakov 'might be instrumental in seeing that some of my royalties for the sale of books in your country were forwarded here'. He emphasized: 'that would be a very good thing, and something I would deeply appreciate, for our need, as you may imagine, is quite great.' He asked that the money be sent from a Soviet bank account in New York.³⁸

In another example, in August 1955, Pavel Chuvikov, the head of the Foreign Literature Press, the Soviet Union's main press for literature in translation, sent Fast three copies of the Russian translation of his novel *Silas Timberman* as a courtesy, informing him that it 'had been greeted by Soviet readers with great interest'.³⁹ In response, Fast thanked him for the books, wished Chuvikov great success with the novel and expressed his hope that Soviet readers would enjoy it. Once again, he brought up the question of royalties, pointing out that 'recently, we read in *The New York Times*

---

[35] Ibid.
[36] Fast Papers, Box 13, Folder 1. Letter to Fast from Izakov and Golysheva, 31 December 1954.
[37] Fast Papers, Box 13, Folder 1. Letter from Fast to Izakov, 9 March 1955.
[38] Ibid.
[39] Fast Papers, Box 13, Folder 5. Letter from Chuvikov to Fast, 20 August 1955.

that Soviet publishers would be paying regular royalties at request of foreign authors. If that is so, could this letter be considered such a formal request . . . [and] could the royalties be paid to me in American currency?'[40]

Fast was referring to an interview Chuvikov had recently given, in which he was quoted as saying that the Foreign Literature Press planned to double publications of American authors and they would be paid royalties at a rate of 900 roubles per author's sheet (twenty-two typewritten pages) in roubles or the author's own currency, 'depending on his wish'.[41] The interview sparked rumours that the Soviet Union was about to join the UCC, for it appeared just days before the convention was scheduled to go into effect and the rate listed reflected that paid to Soviet authors for reprints of their work, seemingly abiding by its reciprocity principle.[42] However, in the months that followed, the Soviet government made no moves to join the UCC. No money came to Fast either, for he repeated his request to Chuvikov on 24 May 1956: 'I am curious to know whether any arrangements have yet been made for transmission of royalties to writers such as myself. I mentioned this in a previous letter to you and am very hopeful that something can be done about it. I think you will understand how important this could be to democratic American writers.'[43] He did not receive a reply.

'The most elementary right of compensation'

Soviet cultural authorities typically responded to royalty inquiries such as Fast's with radio silence; however, behind the scenes, some expressed urgent anxieties about them. As they were well aware, the Soviet Union's failure to pay regular royalties contributed to the country's image problem abroad, especially in America. Progressive writers had emphasized this to them when they had met in person during a 1955 visit by a Soviet journalists' delegation to New York, one goal of which was to find more effective ways to transmit Soviet propaganda to American audiences.[44] In his final report and recommendations, Boris Polevoy, who had headed up the delegation, drew a direct link between the unresolved copyright issue and the Soviet Union's negative image in America, as Rósa Magnúsdóttir has noted. Polevoy emphasized that, in addition to publishing its own books in America, the Soviet Union could counter 'negative narratives' about it by simply paying royalties to American progressive writers.[45]

By mid-1956, some of this anxiety could be traced to a damning open letter that was circulating among the American left and among Soviet cultural elites. It was written by another American progressive writer, Albert Maltz, a contemporary and comrade of

---

[40] Fast Papers, Box 13, Folder 5. Letter from Fast to Chuvikov, 26 September 1955.
[41] Welles Hangen, 'Soviet Due to Pay Authors Abroad: Official Says Foreign Writers May Ask', *The New York Times*, 14 September 1955, 33.
[42] Ibid.
[43] Fast Papers, Box 13, Folder 5. Letter from Fast to Chuvikov, 24 May 1956.
[44] Rósa Magnúsdóttir, *Keeping Up Appearances: How the Soviet State Failed to Control Popular Attitudes toward the United States of America* (PhD dissertation, University of North Carolina, Chapel Hill, 2006), 176.
[45] See footnote 10 in Ibid., 187.

Howard Fast's. Like Fast, Maltz had been subpoenaed by the HUAC and imprisoned, and was currently blacklisted. Also like Fast, Maltz was regularly published in the Soviet Union and his plays had been widely staged there since the 1930s.[46] Maltz first sent his complaint anonymously to the All-Union Society for Cultural Relations with Foreign Countries (*Vsesoiuznoe obshchestvo kul'turnoi sviazi s zagranitsei*, VOKS), the organization charged with promoting contacts between Soviet and foreign cultural producers. At some point before 1 June 1956, the letter was translated into Russian and fell into Boris Polevoy's hands. It was also published in the June 1956 issue of the American left-wing literary journal *Masses and Mainstream*, this time in Maltz's own name.[47]

Maltz addressed his criticism to Aleksandr Anikst, who had recently published an article in which he argued that the massive number of American books now being published and read in the Soviet Union was clear proof that 'there exists all of the necessary prerequisites for the growth and strengthening of cultural and spiritual ties between our peoples'.[48] Maltz also praised the Soviet Union's 'immense publishing program' and commitment to cultural exchange, arguing that '[it] is one of the vital paths by which people of different nations can learn to know and respect each other. Moreover, in a world longing for peace, mutual knowledge and respect are indispensable cornerstones for coexistence'. Yet, he went on, 'there is one area of the relationship between cultural institutions in your country and American writers, (and perhaps with all foreign writers), that remains highly unsatisfactory ... your publishers issue books, your theatres produce plays, and your literary journals print stories without entering into normal, accepted relations with the authors of those works.'[49] Maltz wondered if it was simply the case that the Soviet Union was unaware of 'normal' publishing practices elsewhere, even other socialist countries: (1) the publisher advised the author of his desire to translate a book and offered terms; (2) a mutually acceptable contract was signed by both parties; (3) copies of the work were forwarded to the author upon publication; (4) reviews were sent to the author on request; (5) statements of book sales and royalty payments were sent to the author at regular intervals; and (6) letters sent by the author to the publisher were answered within a reasonable period of time (a subtle but obvious criticism of Soviet cultural authorities' tendency to flatly ignore royalty payment requests).[50] This procedure was, Maltz claimed, 'universally accepted as just. It is based upon the obvious principle that an author owns his own work and that others may not make use of it without his permission, or in a manner not agreeable to him.' Royalties were important, but only one part of 'the principle of respect for an

---

[46] Inna Mikhailovna Levidova, *Progressivnye pisateli stran kapitalizma: Al'bert Mal'tz* (Moskva: Vsesoiuz. gos. b-ka inostr. literatury, 1954), 12. See also: Brown, 274–5.
[47] Albert Maltz, 'Attention: Soviet Publishers; An Open Letter', *Masses and Mainstream* 9, no. 5 (June 1956): 40–2. For the Russian translation, see Rossisskii gosudarstvennyi arkhiv noveishei istorii (thereafter RGANI), f. 5, op. 36, d. 18, l. 49–50. It is unclear what, if any, role Howard Fast played in the publication of this article, but he was on the editorial board of *Masses and Mainstream*, and he certainly approved of the article's message.
[48] Alexander [sic] Anikst, 'American Books and Soviet Readers', *New World Review* 4, no. 3 (March 1956): 18–20.
[49] Maltz, 'Attention: Soviet Publishers', 40.
[50] Ibid., 40–1.

author's work'. Maltz could accept that, when the Soviet Union was the only socialist country in the world and when it was under attack by foreign nations, its cultural relations with those nations should also be 'irregular'.[51] But a different situation now existed and 'the time has come for cultural institutions in the USSR to establish more normal relations with foreign authors, and to effect a thorough-going change in their procedures'.[52]

In an appeal to the Central Committee on 1 June, Boris Polevoy, who was by then the chairman of the Writer's Union, called the open letter 'in essence, a cry from the soul and, although the author wishes to remain anonymous, it is obvious he is a friend of the Soviet Union'.[53] He lamented that the Soviet Union's rejection of international copyright law not only undermined its authority among foreign writers, especially since some other countries within the socialist camp had joined the conventions, but also gave rise to harmful 'anti-Soviet myths' that foreign authors who were paid royalties received enormous sums in an 'extremely ambiguous and last-minute way' (this was no 'myth', but exactly what happened).[54] He reiterated that when he had met with 'our best and most faithful friends', including Howard Fast and Albert Maltz, during the journalist delegation's visit to the United States, they had pleaded with him to make the Soviet government aware of the problem and pay American writers. But this was not enough in Polevoy's view: 'having observed the situation on the ground, the Soviet government's failure to join Berne brings enormous damage to our country in the eyes of all progressive intellectuals', he argued, 'they often say to us, "you are a socialist country, with a constitution that measures the worth of an individual by his labour service, and at the same time you do not observe the most elementary right of compensation for intellectual labour, as is observed by every other capitalist country"'.[55]

In the wake of Polevoy's plea to the Central Committee, and after Boris Izakov made further inquiries on Fast's behalf, the Soviet government finally loosened its purse strings and paid Howard Fast.[56] He acknowledged receiving an unspecified sum of royalties from the Soviet Union in a letter to Izakov in late September. He wrote: 'I think you will be pleased to know that I recently got some royalties and that they were well needed and will be, I hope, wisely used. I think I can say that this is a great deal due to your efforts and to the efforts of Polevoy. And indeed, I am most grateful.' Echoing Maltz's open letter, he then asked for 'some sort of statement or royalty sheet so that I might know where the royalties are coming from and for what period of time. This is fairly important.'[57]

However, by the fall of 1956, Soviet central authorities were rapidly losing patience with Fast and his Soviet allies' grumbling – like all foreign authors, Fast was, in fact, owed nothing under the law. In a November 1956 letter to the undersecretary of the Communist Party, Boris Izakov, who was by then head of the Writer's Union's Committee

[51] Ibid., 42.
[52] Ibid.
[53] RGANI, f. 5, op. 36, d. 18, l. 46.
[54] Ibid.
[55] RGANI, f. 5, op. 36, d. 18, l. 47.
[56] See Fast Papers, Box 13, Folder 1, Letter from Izakov to Fast, circa summer 1956.
[57] Fast papers, Box 13, Folder 1. Letter from Fast to Izakov, 20 September 1956.

on Foreign Writers, defended himself against the charge that *he* was responsible for Fast's grousing, having allegedly informed the author that a huge sum of Soviet royalties was soon coming his way.[58] The Soviet diplomat Ilya Chernyshev had reported back to Moscow that Fast was going around New York saying that the Soviets owed him 2 million roubles; and 'Chernyshev felt the need to add that "if Izakov really told him [. . .] then he accomplished nothing but harm with his chatter"'.[59] Izakov refuted the accusation that he had put that sum into Fast's head. He had met Fast in person only once, during the 1955 journalists' visit, he emphasized, and, during that conversation, Fast had indeed asked many questions about royalties but, 'due to the irregularity of our settlements with foreign authors, we were forced to give evasive answers'.[60]

Regardless of who said what, Izakov argued that the present arrangement, in which foreign writers received extra-legal payments on an ad hoc basis, was far from satisfactory. In his opinion, 'instead of spreading unverified rumours, our diplomats should have long ago pressed the need to reform financial settlements with foreign authors'.[61] The absence of any law regulating foreign royalties led to 'lots of misunderstandings, unpleasantness and, in the final score, sets many foreign authors against us'. Even when royalties were paid, it was often after long delays and 'after [writers] have had time to make demands, and only under pressure'. Even when foreign authors received the money, many were left with 'a negative impression'. As evidence, he pointed to Albert Maltz's open letter. Izakov concluded that 'even if we cannot muster the hard currency to adhere to the Universal Copyright Convention, we should still do something, take some measures'.[62] He proposed putting together a special commission composed of cultural, legal and economic authorities and coming up with an action plan within three weeks.[63] The Central Committee scheduled a discussion of the issue for the new year.[64] By then, Howard Fast's royalty grievances would be cast in a totally different light.

'The honor is hollow'

At the Twentieth Party Congress in February 1956, Khrushchev delivered his 'secret' speech denouncing Stalin's crimes. Howard Fast read a copy of it in the office of the American communist newspaper *The Daily Worker* in June.[65] After months of

---

[58] RGANI, f. 5, op. 36, d. 18, l. 96.
[59] In the letter, it is written as '[. . .]' without specifying what Izakov is alleged to have said to Fast, but from the context, it is clear that it refers to the sum of royalties Fast believed he was owed.
[60] Fast remembered their conversation differently. During a television interview after the split, he claimed that, during the 1955 journalists' visit to the United States, Boris Izakov had explicitly told him that he had 'on deposit in the Soviet Union two million rubles. . . . He felt, at the time he spoke to me, that the money would be obtainable in the near future.' See 'The Only Honorable Thing a Communist Can Do; Howard Fast interviewed by Martin Agronsky', *The Progressive* (March 1958): 37.
[61] RGANI, f. 5, op. 36, d. 18, l. 97.
[62] RGANI, f. 5, op. 36, d. 18, l. 97.
[63] RGANI, f. 5, op. 36, d. 18, l. 98.
[64] RGANI, f. 5, op. 36, d. 18, l. 99.
[65] Deery, 'Finding His Kronstadt', 185.

inactivity and rumours that he had quit the party, he publicly confirmed this in an interview with *The New York Times* on 1 February 1957, in which he listed the speech's revelations about the purges and about anti-Semitism in the Soviet Union among his reasons.[66] One month later, in the communist journal *Mainstream*, he elaborated on his decision, lambasting the Soviet Union as 'socialism without morality' and criticizing its restrictions on artistic freedom.[67] Sorin argues that it took Fast so long to announce the split because he initially believed that a period of self-examination and healthy changes was beginning in the Soviet Union.[68] Fast wrote that he was not a person who was 'easily unconvinced', and it took 'months of thought, reading and discussion to make up my mind finally'.[69]

As demonstrated earlier, Fast continued to correspond with his Soviet colleagues and press his case for being paid royalties after he became aware of the speech's contents. If, earlier, he had been more cautious and supplicatory when making these requests, he now spoke in much blunter terms. In an undated letter, most likely from October 1956, he sent his complaint over Izakov's and Polevoy's heads to the minister of culture, himself, Nikolai Mikhailov:

> I desire to state directly to you my feelings concerning plays of mine produced in the Soviet Union. By now, there is a long history of such productions ... from all that I have heard, they were very successful. ... The point at issue now is that I have received no royalty payment whatsoever for any of these productions. My own feeling is that this is harmful and incorrect far beyond my own personal need. At this point, I wish to state that your Foreign Language Publishing House has accorded me the same recognition that is given to Soviet writers and has paid royalties to me on the many books of mine that they have published in the Soviet Union. I am asking for the same equality of treatment in connection with my plays. It is a cardinal principle of international literature that a writer deserves to be paid for his work, and by and large that principle is honored by nations large and small, whether or not they have exchange copyright agreements. Otherwise, a writer is grieved that his work has been appropriated by a unilateral exercise of power. Never have I refused publication for any of my work in Russian, and I always felt honored by such publication. But the honor is hollow unless the writer is treated with dignity and respect. His work is his way of life, and for that way of life, he must have sustenance.[70]

Fast requested that Soviet authorities not only address his concerns but 'examine the question in terms of all non-Soviet writers. This can be another step toward better relations and more understanding with other nations.'

---

[66] See Fast, *Being Red*, 353; Harry Schwartz, 'Reds Renounced by Howard Fast: Writer Traces Party Break to Khrushchev Speech', *The New York Times*, 1 February 1957, 1, 4.
[67] Howard Fast, 'My Decision', *Mainstream* (March 1957): 29–38.
[68] Sorin, 303.
[69] Fast, *The Naked God*, 98.
[70] Fast Papers, Box 13, Folder 6. Copy of a letter from Fast to Mikhailov, circa October 1956.

Fast does not appear to have received a response from Mikhailov. However, in his memoirs, Fast claims that, around that time, he received a letter from a cultural attaché at the Soviet embassy in Washington DC explaining that the Soviet Union intended to give him a lump sum of almost USD 600,000 for past royalties, payable in February 1957.[71] He recalled wondering if the Soviet government did not yet know that he had left the party or if the money was a bribe for his silence about Stalin's crimes; moreover, 'how did I know that my books had earned this money? Where were the royalty statements?' While some of his friends argued that he had rightfully earned this money, his wife disagreed, and 'I became convinced that she was right. If I took that money, I would be silenced and obligated, and I had decided that I would never again be silenced or obligated or disciplined'. Fast and his wife 'licked our lips at the thought of that avalanche of money pouring into our almost empty bank account, and then, as I recall it, we burst into laughter. What a gesture! Six hundred thousand dollars down the drain.' Fast rejected the offer, explaining that he had resigned from the Communist Party, and that 'I intended in the future to write about the Soviet Union as I pleased'. The royalty payments, he claimed, were never sent, and 'if they had been, they would have been returned'.[72]

In *The Naked God*, Fast's rambling reflections on his reasons for leaving the Communist Party and severing ties with the Soviet Union, written in the immediate wake of the split, he emphasizes the tyrannical nature of the party, which demanded the writer's obedience and discipline and which forced him to choose between it and his 'growth and achievement' as a writer.[73] He does not cite his royalty grievances. Fast does, however, repeatedly return to the issue of money. He complains bitterly about the economic consequences of being blacklisted in America, lamenting that 'at great cost and financial loss, I had to publish my own books. From comparative wealth and success, I was reduced to a struggle for literary existence.'[74] He donated thousands of dollars to the party, financed the publication of communist writers and drained his family's savings, only to be 'accused of enriching myself'.[75]

Moreover, this principled poverty was not expected of communists in the Soviet Union, where the party leader enjoyed 'fat material rewards', Fast argued, and had 'but to lift a finger and have his every want satisfied'.[76] Soviet writers were similarly well-compensated, as Fast was aware. Back in 1955, when Fast had complained in person to the Soviet journalist delegation about unpaid royalties and about the financial hardships he endured as a blacklisted author in America, he had entered into a telling exchange with Soviet delegates. According to Boris Izakov, after listening to his complaints, Fast's Soviet interlocutors informed him that 'authors are fully provided for (*obespechennym*) in the USSR'.[77] Fast jokingly wondered aloud if he would also be

---

[71] Fast, *Being Red*, 352–3. As of 1950, the official exchange rate was 4 roubles for USD 1; therefore, USD 600,000 was 2,400,000 roubles, slightly more than what Fast argued he was owed.
[72] Ibid., 353. I was unable to find this letter among Howard Fast's papers.
[73] Fast, *The Naked God*, 107–8.
[74] Ibid., 115.
[75] Ibid., 22.
[76] Ibid., 96.
[77] RGANI, f. 5, op. 36, d. 18, l. 97.

'provided for' were he to move to there, and if he would be better off than Anatoly Sofronov, the former chairman of the Writers' Union and another member of the delegation. 'We jokingly answered in the affirmative,' Izakov wrote. As he became disillusioned with the Soviet Union, Fast concluded that his freedom was more valuable than his financial security.[78]

Conclusion

The conflict between Soviet authorities and American progressive writers over unpaid royalties reveals a clash of understandings of the benefits of, and priorities associated with, internationalism in the context of the Cold War. As Nikita Khrushchev told the National Press club at the beginning of his 1959 visit to America, the Soviet Union was committed to cultural exchange as a means to 'know and understand one another better' and build 'trust and peaceful cooperation'.[79] However, it expected cultural exchange to go hand in hand with economic exchange: indeed, as Khrushchev emphasized in the same speech, the Soviet Union was 'prepared to do everything we can for the expansion of world trade'. Khrushchev argued that 'Trade is like a barometer. It shows the trend in political development whether clouds are gathering as before a storm or whether it will be fair and fine. We sincerely hope the barometer will always point to 'Fair', and this, we are deeply convinced, requires all-around expansion of international trade'.[80] Soviet political authorities were thus reluctant to waste precious hard currency earmarked for foreign trade on paying royalties, even to progressive writers whose activism on behalf of the international communist movement was officially portrayed as invaluable. Moreover, when it came to such royalty payments, as Gilburd notes, 'the Central Committee preferred unwritten rules and personal dependencies to formalised agreements'.[81]

Soviet cultural authorities were left to defend the contradiction between this stance and the Soviet Union's dramatic increase in publication of foreign literature under the banner of improved relations with the West and the promotion of peace and mutual understanding. When they did not remain mute on the subject (as they often did), they typically portrayed cultural exchange as divorced from economic exchange, as exemplified by Aleksandr Anikst's article that had so irked Albert Maltz by saying nothing about the consequences of the Soviet Union's newfound interest in American writers' work for the same writers' intellectual property rights. American progressive

---

[78] At least, this was how he publicly presented it in interviews given after the split, in which he emphasized that he had walked away from substantial sums of royalties owed to him there. See 'The Only Honorable Thing a Communist Can Do', 37, and Deery, *Red Apple*, 71.

[79] 'N. S. Khrushchev Meets Journalists at the National Press Club', *Khrushchev in America: Full Texts of the Speeches Made by N. S. Khrushchev, Chairman of the Council of Ministers of the USSR on His Tour of the United States 15–27 September 1959* (New York: Crosscurrents Press, 1960), 22.

[80] Ibid., 25. On the Soviet government's eagerness to engage in foreign trade and its global economic ambitions, see Oscar Sanchez-Sibony, *Red Globalization: The Political Economy of the Soviet Cold War from Stalin to Khrushchev* (New York: Cambridge University Press, 2014).

[81] Gilburd, *To See Paris and Die*, 113.

writers found this uncoupling of cultural and economic exchange hard to reconcile with the economic sacrifices they made to support the Communist Party and the Soviet Union in McCarthy-era America. Moreover, as communists, Soviet leaders were supposed to abhor labour exploitation; in both Albert Maltz's and Howard Fast's eyes, they should have paid progressive writers what was ethically owed to them as producers of an international socialist literature that transcended borders, regardless of formal copyright agreements. Otherwise, the Soviet Union was not engaged in cultural exchange, but appropriation.

The oft-made argument that the Soviet Union simply could not afford to join the international copyright conventions or otherwise standardize the payment of royalties also rang increasingly hollow. If, in the immediate post-revolutionary period, the Soviet Union was economically embattled, it was by its own admission no longer a poor and developing country but a prosperous world superpower by the mid-twentieth century. In his memoirs, Howard Fast wrote that he had received many requests to republish his work from developing countries and by groups too poor to pay royalties, and 'never did I allow this to stand in the way of publication'. The Soviet Union was a different story, and, decades after falling out of its good graces, he still chafed at the transactional nature of their relationship: at the peak of its investment in his work, it was publishing his novel *Freedom Road* by the millions of copies, making it the 'most widely printed and most read book of the twentieth century', but it immediately stopped publication and 'wiped my name from their literary courses and journals once I announced my resignation from the Communist Party'.[82]

It is unclear what, if any, role Howard Fast's acrimonious and embarrassing split with the Communist Party and the Soviet Union played in the Soviet government's and cultural elite's thinking about joining the international copyright conventions or otherwise standardizing royalty payments to progressive authors after 1957. It is clear, however, that their economic plight was not a major consideration behind the Soviet government's decision to finally join the UCC and begin paying regular royalties to foreign authors beginning in the early to mid-1970s. To the Soviet government's frustration, the copyright issue stood in the way of realizing its desire to expand foreign trade relations, especially with the United States, whose political and business leaders balked at the Soviet Union's lack of formal respect for foreign intellectual property.[83] The desire for trade opportunities hovered in the background of the Brezhnev government's decision to finally accede to the UCC, though the move was officially portrayed as 'serv[ing] above all the interests of international cultural cooperation'.[84]

Although it was not a primary cause of it, the Soviet government's failure to pay regular royalties contributed to left-wing writers' disappointment in the first socialist state, as the case of Howard Fast demonstrates. They held onto their royalty grievances

[82] Fast, *Being Red*, 85.
[83] See, for example, Senator Hubert Humphrey's comments on the Soviet Union's lack of respect for copyright during his visit with Soviet leaders: GARF, f. 5446, op. 210, d. 1452, l. 42.
[84] M. M. Boguslavskii, *Uchastie SSSR v mezhdunarodnoi okhrane avtorskikh prav* (Moskva: Iuridicheskaia literatura, 1974), 7.

long after they had lost faith in the Soviet Union. After years of following the travails of Soviet dissident authors, a plight he knew all too well, in 1972, on the cusp of the Soviet Union's accession to the UCC, Albert Maltz demanded that his 'uncollected' royalties go to the reportedly blacklisted and impoverished author Aleksandr Solzhenitsyn, a widely publicized move that inspired other Western authors to do the same with their 'unpaid' Soviet royalties.[85] Soviet cultural authorities were surely left wondering if it would not have been easier to have paid up twenty years ago.

---

[85] See 'The Citizen Writer in Retrospect; Albert Maltz interviewed by Joel Gardner, Vol. II', *The Oral History Project of the University of California Los Angeles* (UCLA: Los Angeles, 1983), 983–9. See also: George Gent, 'Maltz Offers Funds to Solzhenitsyn', *The New York Times*, 11 December 1972, 50; George Gent, 'Two More Offer Aid to Solzhenitsyn', *The Globe and Mail*, 22 December 1972, 13.

12

Antagonistic internationalists

Catholic activists and the UN system after 1945

David Brydan

In 1952, the head of the International Federation of Catholic Men, Jean le Cour Grandmaison, wrote an article on the relationship between Catholics and the new international system built around the United Nations (UN). The principle of international cooperation, he argued, was now self-evident. 'Peace, war, liberty, prosperity are, from this time forward, world affairs.'[1] And as a result there was a clear necessity for 'international or supranational institutions capable of translating into action this solidarity of the world's peoples in confronting the questions which are vital to all'. But while the principle of international cooperation was lauded, the article was far less positive about the 'structure, methods, spirit and activity' of the UN as it had developed over the preceding six years. Like other post-war Catholic activists, Grandmaison lamented the 'error', 'failures' and 'defects' of the UN and its specialized agencies. Such defects, he felt, were rooted in the organization's secularism and the absence of Christian values among its leadership. 'It is no secret', he wrote, 'that the U.N. was born in an atmosphere of religious neutrality and that several of its directors, not the least influential, have more or less materialist viewpoints'. For these reasons, Grandmaison acknowledged, many Catholics felt deeply antagonistic towards the UN system. But he argued that with effort and commitment, international organizations could be reformed. In order to make that happen, Catholics had a duty to support both international cooperation in general and the work of the UN and its agencies in particular.

It was this duty, Grandmaison felt, that explained the rapid recent development of a group of Catholic NGOs known at the time as International Catholic Organizations (ICOs), whose raison d'etre was 'to ensure the indispensable participation of Catholics in international activity'. The essential duty of ICOs, he argued, was to 'sow the seed of the Gospel in the work of world reconstruction undertaken by the U.N. and its

---

[1] American Catholic History Research Center and University Archives, Washington, DC (ACUA), US Conference of Catholic Bishops Office of the General Secretary (USCCB), series 1, box 51, folder 18.

specialized agencies'.² It was a task in which they were often strikingly successful. As this chapter will show, ICOs and the activists who led them played an active role in the development of internationalist ideas in the post-war era and were deeply involved in the work of the UN and its specialized agencies. But they also reflected the profound ambivalence of many Catholics towards post-war internationalism – enthusiastic advocates of the ideals and language of international cooperation, but often deeply distrustful of international organizations in practice. 'Sowing the seeds of the gospel in the work of world reconstruction' was a core task of post-war Catholic internationalism, but one driven as much by antagonism towards international organizations as by a positive embrace of internationalist ideals.

The immediate post-war period witnessed an explosion of international Catholic activism, manifested most visibly in the work of ICOs. The kind of lay Catholic internationalism they represented was not a new phenomenon. Most ICOs had emerged during the interwar period, with some tracing their origins back to the nineteenth century or earlier, and in that sense they were part of the wider emergence of international society from the mid-nineteenth century.³ But these organizations, and Catholic internationalism more generally, reached the peak of their influence in the aftermath of the Second World War.⁴ By the mid-1960s, there were almost forty ICOs recognized by the Vatican, claiming to represent millions of Catholics worldwide.⁵ They included organizations representing specific groups, like the students' and intellectuals' organization Pax Romana; organizations in particular fields of activity such as social work or migration; and campaigning and humanitarian organizations such as Caritas.

Their attitudes and activities demonstrate the profound influence of religious ideas, organizations and values on the history of post-war internationalism and international organizations. Studies of the post-1945 era often focus on secular developments and ideas, from human rights and technology, to planning and atomic power. More recently, historians have begun to challenge these secular narratives, exploring, for example, the influence of Christian ideas and thinkers in the development of human rights, or the role of the Vatican in European reconstruction and integration.⁶ The history of ICOs offers new perspectives on these developments. Firstly, it highlights the diversity of Catholic internationalism as a phenomenon which incorporated the Vatican and the church hierarchy, but which was often driven by the overlooked work of lay

---

² Ibid.
³ Vincent Viane, 'Nineteenth-Century Catholic Internationalism and Its Predecessors', in *Religious Internationals in the Modern World*, ed. Abigail Green and Vincent Viane (Basingstoke: Palgrave Macmillan, 2012), 82–110.
⁴ On the history of Catholic internationalism, see Vincent Viane, 'International History, Religious History, Catholic History: Perspectives for Cross-Fertilization (1830-1914)', *European History Quarterly* 38, no. 4 (2008): 578–607; Giuliana Chamedes, *A Twentieth-Century Crusade: The Vatican's Battle to Remake Christian Europe* (Cambridge, MA: Harvard University Press, 2019). See also Carmen Mangion's chapter in this volume.
⁵ La Conferencia de las Organizaciones Internacionales Católicas y el Comité Permanente de los Congresos Internacionales para el Apostolado de los Laicos, eds, *Los católicos en la vida internacional* (Madrid: Vicentius Tena, 1960).
⁶ Wolfram Kaiser, *Christian Democracy and the Origins of European Union* (Cambridge: Cambridge University Press, 2007); Samuel Moyn, *Christian Human Rights* (Philadelphia: University of Pennsylvania Press, 2015).

activists, both elites and 'ordinary' Catholics from a wide range of backgrounds and professions. In particular, it foregrounds the role of women and women's organizations in international debates. Secondly, it shows how Catholics succeeded in influencing the UN and other post-war international organizations, forming transatlantic alliances of NGOs, activists, church officials and Catholic-majority states to promote Catholic policies and values on the world stage. Finally, it shows how the history of post-war internationalism was not driven solely by the efforts of Anglo-American liberal internationalists who still dominate much of the scholarship, but by organizations and individuals with often profoundly illiberal values whose international work was driven as much by their fear of and hostility towards international organizations as by their embrace of stereotypically internationalist values.

This chapter will begin with an overview of post-war Catholic internationalism and its relationship with the UN. It will then use two post-war controversies involving Catholics and the WHO as case studies to explore the impact of ICOs and Catholic activists on the UN system. The WHO sat at the conjunction of a series of issues which were regarded as crucial for post-war Catholic activists – development, maternal and infant health, rural health, venereal diseases and, above all, population and birth control. As such, it became the focus of intensive Catholic lobbying, led by ICOs. And by the mid-1950s, it was the case study which Catholic internationalists such as Grandmaison were pointing to as evidence of the 'extremely encouraging' influence that ICOs could exert over the work of international organizations.[7]

The first controversy concerned the recognition of the international Catholic nursing organization by the WHO, which became a focus for conflict between Catholic activists and leading international health experts. At the heart of this debate were divergent views over the nature of international expertise. Secular international health leaders viewed the question as a purely technical or scientific one, whereas Catholic activists argued that only religious health workers could provide the moral expertise which was required to truly address international health problems. The second issue concerned proposals for WHO involvement in international birth control and family planning, plans which met fierce and coordinated resistance from Catholic lay activists, ecclesiastical bodies and statesmen. Their success in ultimately blocking the WHO's work in the field was widely held up as an example of the influence that Catholics could exert on the international stage.

These case studies also provide a new perspective on the role of Europe and Europeans in post-war internationalism. Catholic internationalism was dominated by a familiar transatlantic alliance of North Americans and Western Europeans until the 1960s. And in the context of the Cold War, much of the work of ICOs was driven by anti-communism and a defence of the perceived values of the Christian West. But the global dimensions of the Catholic faith and the unusual alliances which developed over issues such as birth control meant that European Catholics often saw secular Europeans as the greatest threat to Catholic values on the international stage, instead seeking alliances with Catholics and other faith communities from beyond Europe to promote their vision of world order.

[7] ACUA, USCCB, series 1, box 51, folder 18.

ICOs and the United Nations

Many Catholics were enthusiastic supporters of the new post-war international system built around the UN, and of Catholic participation within it. The Spanish Catholic intellectual Carlos Santamaría, who worked with a range of ICOs and secular international organizations, argued in 1949 that participating in international congresses, conferences and organizations was 'at the same time the most human and the most Christian work that can be carried out today'. It was the world's Catholics, he argued, thanks to their sense of citizenship and their consciousness of the universality of humankind, who were 'best prepared for international collaboration'.[8] For Santamaría, this collaboration needed to take the form of both international cooperation between Catholics and active Catholic participation in secular international institutions. But he was careful to distinguish this model of Catholic internationalism from its secular counterparts, particularly on the left. During the early stages of the Cold War, Catholic internationalism still revolved around the anti-communism which had defined it in the interwar period, and by the long-running political battle between Catholics and the secular left.[9] For Santamaría, embracing international cooperation should not mean undermining the diversity among nations or imposing a form of 'Catholic Kominform', but merely recognizing the primacy of the 'essential' sentiment of humanity over the 'accidental' sentiment of nationality.[10]

As Jean le Cour Grandmaison had advocated, Catholic engagement with post-war internationalism was often focused on countering the perceived anti-religious and anti-Catholic elements latent within the UN system. UNICEF, for example, was seen by many Catholic internationalists as potentially the most important and effective specialized agency, at its best mirroring the 'spirit and practice of charity' embodied by religious NGOs working in the field of child welfare.[11] But it was also seen as vulnerable to 'infiltration' by groups such as the International Planned Parenthood Federation, which advocated birth control, or the World Federation of United Nations Associations, which many Catholic activists feared had been infiltrated by communists.[12] On the ground, its technical assistance programmes were dominated by non-religious NGOs which, their Catholic counterparts feared, genuinely believed that religion was divisive and had the lobbying and organizational skills to successfully embed their beliefs within UNICEF's structures.[13] UN agencies like UNICEF thus became central to the work of post-war Catholic internationalists, a vehicle for developing Catholic projects and defending Catholic interests. And within these organizations, battles over representation, legitimacy and influence often played out over the minutiae of

---

[8] Carlos Santamaría, 'Notas para un dialogo', *Documentos: Conversaciones Católicas Internacionales* 3 (1949): 87–101.
[9] On the history of Catholic internationalism and anti-communism, see Chamedes, *A Twentieth-Century Crusade*.
[10] Ibid.
[11] 'Resolution in Regard to the International Children's Emergency Fund', 4 November 1947, ACUA, USCCB, Series 1, Box 51, folder 15.
[12] NCWC Office for UN Affairs, 10 May 1954, ACUA, USCCB, series 1, box 51, folder 20.
[13] NCWC Office for UN Affairs, 'Meeting of the International Catholic Organizations Representatives', 20 October 1958, ACUA, USCCB, series 1, box 51, folder 22.

bureaucratic rules and procedures, or debates about the makeup of international committees.

Catholic engagement with post-war international organizations was channelled through new structures designed to coordinate relationships with the UN and its specialized agencies. Catholic influence over the UN was exerted in three different ways. The first way was the Vatican's efforts to both monitor the work of international organizations, and where possible to influence them through direct lobbying and the mobilization and coordination of Catholics on a national level. The Vatican enjoyed observer status with a number of international organizations and UN agencies, and regularly sent official delegates to international conferences and events. The second was through national church hierarchies, particularly in the United States as the country which dominated the post-war Western system. At the heart of these efforts was the US bishops' organization, the National Catholic Welfare Conference (NCWC). The NCWC had its origins in efforts to coordinate the activities of American Catholics during the First World War. It comprised the annual meeting of American bishops, and a permanent secretariat which included departments of social action and lay organizations. NCWC officials were involved with the creation United Nations in various ways, and in 1946 the organization established a UN Office in New York.[14] According to its director Catherine Schaefer, the office was designed to 'integrate Catholic principles into the formal action and atmosphere of the United Nations and of international life, and to inform Catholics of developments to which these principles might be applied'.[15]

The third strand were ICOs. Like the Vatican they sought to mobilize their members to influence policy and governments within their specific fields. But they also sought to coordinate among themselves. The origins of these efforts lay in the creation of the Conference of International Catholic Organizations in 1927, which had brought together the directors of eleven ICOs and which had worked closely with the League of Nations up until the outbreak of the Second World War.[16] In 1950, the conference opened an ICO Information Centre in Geneva (*Centre d'Information des Organisations Internationales Catholiques*), the counterpart of the NCWC's New York office, to monitor the work of international organizations based there.[17] And in 1951, it established a permanent secretariat based in Fribourg, Switzerland. By 1953, over 10 per cent of the NGOs granted official status with the UN were ICOs, including organizations representing Catholic intellectuals and students, social workers, migration experts, journalists and workers.[18] ICOs worked closely with both the Vatican and with national church hierarchies in their efforts to influence the work of international organizations.

[14] On the NCWC and the UN, see Joseph S. Rossi, *Uncharted Territory: The American Catholic Church at the United Nations, 1946-1972* (Washington, DC: The Catholic University of America Press, 2006).
[15] Ibid., 26. For more on Schaefer, see Joseph S. Rossi, '"The Status of Women": Two American Catholic Women at the UN, 1947-1972', *The Catholic Historical Review* 93, no. 2 (2007): 300–24.
[16] Conferencia de las Organizaciones Internacionales Católicos, *Los católicos en la vida internacional: misión de la O.I.C.* (Madrid: Artes Gráficas Iberoamericanas, 1967), 16–18.
[17] ACUA, USCCB, series 1, box 74, folder 17.
[18] Rossi, *Uncharted Territory*, 80.

The activities of ICOs after 1945 could not be separated from their Cold War context. In the immediate post-war era, Catholic internationalism was dominated by North American and Western European actors. It 'thought' globally in the sense that it was interested in what was going on in the rest of the world, and thanks to the global scale of the Catholic Church it could draw on ideas and activists from Asia, Africa or Latin America. But until the 1960s it was an internationalism primarily of and within the Cold War West. ICOs and Catholic activists declared that their work with the UN and its specialized agencies was about promoting 'spiritual' ideas and values on the international stage. But such values were not necessarily neutral or universal. Rather, in the context of the early Cold War, they were often conceived and presented specifically as the values of Western civilization, of the Christian West or the *Abendland*.[19] Many ICOs and Catholic activists were driven as much by their anti-communism as by their philanthropic or religious mission, and their work was inextricably bound up with the political projects of Cold War Western states. Interwar Catholic internationalism, whether pursued by the Vatican or by lay elites, had been driven by a militant anti-communism which often drew Catholics into alliances with fascists and the far right.[20] By pursuing humanitarian action after 1945 focused on the 'victims of communism' and the defence of a spiritually rooted vision of Western civilization, ICOs helped to forge the transnational ties which underpinned the Cold War Western bloc, as well as disseminating a popular understanding of the West as a spiritual community united by its shared Christian heritage. The challenge for Catholic activists at the UN was to defend these values against both the communist powers and other forms of secular materialism which they feared were becoming increasingly influential in Western society.

Perhaps the clearest example of the success of their efforts was in work of the WHO. As well as the relevance of its work to ICOs and Catholic activists, it was also the organization where many Catholics felt the UN's secularist bias was most evident. As the founder of the ICO Information Centre in Geneva and leading activist in the International Union of Catholic Women's Leagues, Jadwiga de Romer,[21] argued in 1950, the WHO offered 'a deplorable picture from the standpoint of Catholic interests', its Executive Committee apparently dominated by atheists and freemasons.[22] For de Romer, this was in no small part due to the 'anti-Catholic attitude' of the WHO's director general Brock Chisholm, who was something of a bogeyman for Catholic internationalists of the era. The Vatican shared this interest in the work of the WHO, as well as concerns about the 'strong anti-Catholic bias' of its leadership.[23]

[19] On post-war Catholics and the idea of the *Abendland*, see Udi Greenberg, *The Weimar Century: German Émigrés and the Ideological Foundations of the Cold War* (Princeton, NJ: Princeton University Press, 2014), ch. 3; Vanessa Conze, 'Facing the Future Backwards: "Abendland" as an Anti-liberal Idea of Europe in Germany between the First World War and the 1960s', in *Anti-liberal Europe: A Neglected Story of Europeanization*, ed. Dieter Gosenwinkel (New York: Berghahn, 2015), 72–90; Rosario Forlenza, 'The Politics of *Abendland*: Christian Democracy and the Idea of Europe after the Second World War', *Contemporary European History* 26, no. 2 (2017): 261–86.
[20] Giuliana Chamedes, 'The Vatican, Nazi-Fascism, and the Making of Transnational Anti-Communism in the 1930s', *Journal of Contemporary History* 51, no. 2 (2015): 261–90.
[21] Sometimes known as Hedwige de Romer.
[22] 'World Health Organization and Catholics', de Romer to NCWC, 3 March 1950, ACUA, USCCB, series 1, box 56, folder 19.
[23] Archbishop of Laodicea to Paul Tanner, 25 May 1949, ACUA, USCCB, series 1, box 56, folder 19.

Catholic nurses and moral expertise

One of the major sources of tension between Catholics and the WHO during the period was the debate over whether or not to grant consultative status to the international Catholic nursing association, the *Comité International Catholique des Infirmières et Assistantes Médico-Sociales* (CICIAMS). Although the issue appeared to be an obscure one, it had significant practical consequences for the organizations and activists involved; NGOs with consultative status received subsidies and enjoyed opportunities to work on WHO projects and committees. But it also reflected a fundamental disagreement between Catholics and their secular counterparts over the work of the UN's specialized agencies and the nature of international expertise. For many Catholic activists, the problems inherent within the UN system stemmed from a narrowly technical view of international problems which could only be resolved by adopting a more expansive understanding of expertise combining both technical and ethical dimensions.

CICIAMS had been formed in the 1930s as the group representing Catholic nurses and social workers, organizing international conferences, study trips and publications. Although it had global ambitions and extended its reach to North and South America, the majority of its member organizations were in Western Europe.[24] Its leading activists were often experienced international figures who were also active within other ICOs and secular international organizations. They shared the same enthusiasm for international cooperation of many of their co-religionists, as well as their antagonism towards the UN and its specialized agencies. Addressing the CICIAMS annual conference in 1949, one delegate denounced UN organizations for not respecting 'the laws of moral life' and forgetting that 'man has moral value', calling on Catholics to intervene in organizations like the WHO to make clear that they are 'not the master of the world, but that they must be at the service of the world'.[25] CICIAMS had originally lobbied for recognition by the WHO in 1946, but was rejected on the grounds that there should only be one affiliated group for each medical profession, and that nurses were represented by the 'neutral' International Council of Nurses (ICN). Although CICIAMS was an active member of the ICN executive board, its relationship with its secular counterpart was complicated, with CICIAMS members consistently lobbying the organization to adopt a more 'spiritual' and 'religious' approach to nursing.[26]

The WHOs decision was partly driven by practical concerns that admitting CICIAMS would open the gates to a flood of other religious and sectional NGOs. But it also reflected a deep-seated belief among its leadership about the purely technical nature of the organization's work. Most of the WHO's founders and early leaders had long-standing experience of international health work. Many had worked with or for the WHO's predecessor, the League of Nations Health Organization, which had been beset by the political tension which hamstrung the League in the 1930s. When

---

[24] *CICIAMS News: Bulletin of the International Catholic Committee for Nurses and Medico-Social Assistants* 2 (1983): 7–18.
[25] María Rosa Cardenal, 'Impresiones del Congreso Internacional de Enfermeras y Asistentas médico-sociales en Amsterdam', *Salus Infirmorum* 9 (1949): 22–3.
[26] Ibid.

it came to establishing a new post-war health organization, therefore, their priority was to cordon it off as far as possible from political debates, and to protect its status as a purely technical, apolitical body.[27] That meant refusing to engage with any of the national, religious or geopolitical controversies of the immediate post-war years, and when it came to questions like the criteria for NGO affiliation, that only technical considerations should be taken into account. Admitting a religious group when the nursing profession was already represented by the ICN, WHO leaders felt, would represent an unjustifiable concession to sectional, sectarian interests.[28]

But Catholic nurses and other Catholic activists saw the question very differently. For them, viewing international health as a purely technical field overlooked the vital ethical components of healthcare in general, and of nursing in particular. The WHO's conception of nursing, a group of Spanish Catholic nurses argued, was 'too materialist', and it needed to be reminded that 'man is composed of body and soul, and only by attending to both can the nurse fulfil her mission'.[29] As Jadwiga de Romer described it, 'the nurse the more so because of her more technical and professional qualifications, enters into the intimacy of the life of individuals and families and from this fact she should inspire confidence and correspond to the mentality of the sick.'[30] If the WHO refused to recognize Catholic nurses, it would be incapable of winning the support and trust of the world's Catholics, and would be left with a partial and incomplete understanding of the major health challenges of the era. 'If the WHO', de Romer argued, 'understands that the nurse to whom one entrusts delicate problems relating to the beginning of life or to its last moments, must inspire the confidence placed in her and in the accomplishments of her functions, the confidence of Catholic women could be won.'[31] Fundamentally, many Catholics suspected, the refusal to recognize CICIAMS was driven by the secular prejudice of the WHO's leadership, which was exploiting the language of technical expertise to discriminate against their religion.

These arguments about the ethical and technical dimensions of health expertise crystalliszd around a debate over human rights and sterilization.[32] In 1949, the UN Human Rights Commission had asked the WHO to contribute to its work on provisions against mutilation and scientific experimentation. When the WHO consulted on the question with its affiliated NGOs, the ICN submitted a report on behalf of the nursing profession which suggested that medical procedures might be needed to prevent the spread of diseases, even in certain cases where patients didn't consent.[33] There were also suggestions made during the debate that exceptions might be necessary

---

[27] David Brydan, *Franco's Internationalists: Social Experts and Spain's Search for Legitimacy* (Oxford: Oxford University Press, 2019), ch. 2.
[28] Untitled Report, 26 January 1950, ACUA, USCCB, series 1, box 56, folder 19.
[29] 'CICIAMS', *Firmes*, 15 (July 1956), 19.
[30] De Romer, 'The Conversation with Dr. Hafezi of the World Health Organization', 13 May 1949, ACUA, USCCB, series 1, box 56, folder 19.
[31] Ibid.
[32] On debates about Catholicism and sterilization prior to 1945, see Marius Turda and Aaron Gillete, *Latin Eugenics in Comparative Perspective* (London: Bloomsbury, 2014), ch. 4.
[33] World Health Organization Executive Board, 'Proposed Rewording of Article 7 of the International Covenant of Human Rights', 30 December 1949, ACUA, USCCB, Series 1, Box 56, folder 19.

to allow the sterilization or castration of dangerous sex offenders. These arguments were bitterly opposed by CICIAMS and by the International Union of Catholic Womens' Leagues, and were eventually rejected by the relevant WHO committee.[34] But as Jadwige de Romer reported to her NCWC colleagues, the episode reflected the fundamental limitations of an organization which refused to accept the relevance of ethical expertise in its work. 'Whatever the medical qualifications of its distinguished members', she reported to ICO leaders, 'there was evident a real helplessness before ethical or philosophical concepts.'[35]

The argument about a distinct ethical or moral form of health expertise, however, ran up against the practical difficulties which Catholic internationalists faced in identifying Catholic experts. Much of the work of ICOs concerning the UN and its specialized agencies, and particularly of the ICO Information Centre in Geneva, involved 'counting heads' – identifying Catholic experts who could be relied upon to defend and uphold religious values. A committee of ICOs working in the field of health was set up in 1950, for example, with the aim of 'instilling Catholic thought' in the WHO by lobbying national governments to appoint Catholic delegates and by identifying Catholic experts across various medical fields in each country.[36] But often, activists lamented, the Catholic delegates who were involved with the WHO failed to defend Catholic values, such as the delegates from the Philippines and Brazil who voted against the recognition of CICIAMS. The struggle, then, was to identify and promote Catholic experts who would reliably prioritize the interests and policies of the church ahead of any competing professional or technical demands. Such figures were variously described in ICO correspondence as experts 'who can be counted on to defend Catholic principles', 'Catholics as Catholics' or even 'accredited Catholics'.[37]

Sometimes the most supportive experts were not even Catholics at all, but members of other faiths. The Iranian doctor who was the liaison between the WHO and health NGOs, explained de Romer, 'as an Iranian faithful to Allah, has probably more understanding for our Christian convictions than western secularism'.[38] In her report on one of the early WHO debates over CICIAMS in 1950, de Romer also argued that the Turkish delegate Dr Tok 'showed the most Christian (evangelique) spirit of all in stating to the President of Catholic Nurses and to myself that he thought a nurse could accomplish her mission with zeal only if she is prompted by religion'.[39] For Catholic activists, the dividing lines over this controversy, as with so many other post-war international issues, were not simply between Christians and non-Christians,

---

[34] NCWC News Service, 'World Health Group Rejects Legal Sterilization Upon Protest of Catholic Nurses', 2 June 1950, ACUA, USCCB, Series 1, Box 56, folder 19.
[35] De Romer letter, 31 January 1950, ACUA, USCCB, series 1, box 56, folder 19.
[36] 'Meeting of International Catholic Organizations Interested in Health Problems', 30 April 1950, ACUA, USCCB, series 1, box 56, folder 19.
[37] De Romer, 'Memorandum from the Information Center of the International Catholic Organizations', 2 April 1952, ACUA, USCCB, series 1, box 56, folder 20.
[38] De Romer, 'The Conversation with Dr. Hafezi of the World Health Organization', 13 May 1949, ACUA, USCCB, series 1, box 56, folder 19.
[39] De Romer, 'World Health Organization and Catholics', 20 March 1950, ACUA, USCCB, series 1, box 56, folder 19.

or between the Western and non-Western worlds, but between spiritual and religious values on the one hand and 'materialism' on the other. On the international stage, transatlantic Catholic internationalists often felt they had more in common with Muslims or people of other faiths than with their secular rivals in the West.

Although apparently a minor issue, CICIAMS recognition became a major front in Catholic efforts to instil Catholic thought within the WHO. It was an effort led by ICOs and by the ICO Information Centre in Geneva, but one which also involved both national governments and the church. Indeed, the Vatican declared itself 'deeply interested' in the question of CICIAMS recognition as early as 1949, discussing the matter regularly with ICOs and asking the NCWC to lobby the US government on the issue.[40] Every World Health Conference between 1949 and 1953 witnessed a row over the question, which was finally resolved in CICIAMS' favour in 1953 when the World Health Assembly agreed to accept the principle of plurality in the recognition of NGOs. The influence of Catholic lobbying efforts was evident in the words of Brock Chisholm, who complained that he had been forced to change his mind on the issue because 'outside pressures and corridor intrigues multiplied to a surprising degree . . . they had degenerated into direct attacks against WHO in the press, in public meetings even within Parliamentary Assemblies. . . . [The] WHO was accused of discrimination against a religious sect.'[41] But Catholic activists had their eyes on an even greater controversy. At the same time as the CICIAMS debate was taking place, a wider battle was being waged over the WHO's approach to birth control.

'The insidious efforts of the family planners'

Population, particularly the dangers posed by overpopulation, were among the chief concerns of the UN and its specialized agencies in the post-war years. As historians such as Alison Bashford and Matthew Connelly have shown, the issue of global population, both its size and distribution, had been an ongoing concern of international organizations and networks from the start of the twentieth century, standing at the nexus of debates about food, nutrition, health, migration and eugenics.[42] The postwar era witnessed renewed fears that peace, order and reconstruction would be undermined by a population explosion, which would have a particularly harmful impact on developing states. A number of different international agencies were involved in population debates, working through the UN Population Division to coordinate their work. Many leading international experts, including Brock Chisholm

[40] Archbishop of Laodicea to Paul Tanner, 25 May 1949, ACUA, USCCB, series 1, box 56, folder 19.
[41] Information Center for International Catholic Organizations, 'WHO Executive Council – Discussion of NGO Status', 9 April 1953, ACUA, USCCB, series 1, box 56, folder 20.
[42] Alison Bashford, 'Population, Geopolitics, and International Organizations in the Mid Twentieth Century', *Journal of World History* 19, no. 3 (2008): 327–48; Matthew Connelly, *Fatal Misconception: The Struggle to Control World Population* (Cambridge, MA: Belknap Press, 2008). On the wider history of global population policies and ideas, see Alison Bashford, *Global Population: History, Geopolitics, and Life on Earth* (New York: Columbia University Press, 2014); Heinrich Hartmann and Corinna R. Unger, eds, *A World of Populations: Transnational Perspectives on Demography in the Twentieth Century* (New York: Berghahn Books, 2014).

at the WHO, had ambitious hopes for a globally coordinated programme of population control which would include family planning advice and contraception.[43]

These international efforts were supported by states such as India and Ceylon, which saw overpopulation as their overriding development challenge and sought international support to address it. In 1951, India requested that the WHO send experts to advise on potential family planning programmes. The result was a proposal for the WHO to lead a pilot study in India on the effectiveness of the rhythm method of birth control.[44] At the same time, Ceylon, the WHO Regional Committee for Southeast Asia and the UN Population Division all formally requested that the WHO begin to systematically study the health aspects of population questions.[45] Chisholm and other leading WHO experts regarded these as relatively modest proposals, but ones which could potentially be scaled up in the future. For Chisholm, indeed, 'over-population' was *the* major health problem for the post-war world, and one which the global community had so far failed to face up to.[46]

But right from the start they met concerted opposition from the Catholic Church and from Catholic activists. The ICO Information Centre in Geneva had established a committee of ICOs to discuss ways to influence the WHO and raise awareness of the dangers of certain WHO policies in 1950. From 1951, the committee, which included leaders from CICIAMS, the Caritas health branch Salubritas, and the international secretariats of Catholic doctors and pharmacists, became central to efforts to mobilize Catholic activists around the world against the WHO's plans.[47] Jadwiga de Romer and the ICO Information Centre closely followed debates within the WHO in Geneva and produced regular reports which were circulated among ICOs and church bodies around the world.

CICIAMS was particularly vocal in its concerns, arguing that the rhythm method trial in India would inevitably be extended to other countries, and would mean nurses being forced to 'cooperate in illicit acts'.[48] Indeed, the arguments underpinning the birth control controversy mirrored the debate about CICIAMS membership. One of the chief criticisms Catholic activists made was that family planning and population was not fundamentally a medical question, and that by engaging with it the WHO was reaching beyond its legitimate area of expertise. When the WHO's expert committee on maternity care proposed integrating problems associated with family planning into their work in 1952, the ICO Information Centre denounced the decision as an

---

[43] Information about these plans, and details about the birth control debate within the WHO which is explored in the rest of this section, can be found in Connelly, *Fatal Misconception*, ch. 4.

[44] The 'rhythm method' is a natural form of family planning which involves tracking the menstrual cycle and abstaining from sex when a woman is most likely to conceive.

[45] NCWC Office for UN Affairs, 'Confidential Notes', 21 November 1951, ACUA, USCCB, series 1, box 56, folder 20.

[46] NCWC Office for UN Affairs, 'Summary of Press Conference held by Dr. Chisholm', 3 April 1952, ACUA, USCCB, series 1, box 56, folder 20.

[47] 'Meeting of International Catholic Organizations Interested in Health Problems', 30 April 1950, ACUA, USCCB, series 1, box 56, folder 19. Further related material from the Committee in folder 20.

[48] NCWC Office for UN Affairs, 'Memorandum – Birth Control Projects in India – From the Catholic Nurses' Association of Canada', 18 February 1952, ACUA, USCCB, series 1, box 56, folder 20.

'invasion of the "medico-cracy"', an unjustified encroachment of doctors and their advisers 'outside the specified domain of medicine'.⁴⁹

The NCWC's UN office in New York was also actively involved in the struggle, and particularly in highlighting the role of Planned Parenthood in the WHO's plans. The office closely monitored the work of Planned Parenthood within the UN and its specialized agencies, distributing regular updates and copies of the Planned Parenthood bulletin to ICOs, and monitoring delegates at international population conferences who were linked to Planned Parenthood or their ideas. It particularly sought to emphasize the fact that one of the WHO experts sent as a consultant to the Indian Ministry of Health in 1951 was Abraham Stone, the vice president of the Planned Parenthood Federation of America and director of the Margaret Sanger Research Bureau in New York.⁵⁰ His presence stoked Catholic fears that the Indian project was a trojan horse for a global Planned Parenthood programme, and was heavily publicized in the Catholic press.

Indeed, this was a very public controversy played out across the press and the airwaves. Brock Chisholm was an accomplished media operator, regularly defending the WHO's plans at press conferences and on radio broadcasts. He particularly went out of his way to address religious concerns about the Indian rhythm method study. In October 1951, he told a press conference that 'no religious objections have been expressed', to the project and that 'the rhythm method apparently does not conflict with Moslem or Hindu teachings'.⁵¹ A few months later, in response to Catholic objections, he issued a statement through the UN press bureau presenting the programme as a response to the threat to India's food supplies caused by rapid population growth, arguing that the rhythm method 'does not under clearly specified circumstances conflict with the teaching of the Roman Catholic Church', and citing recent comments from Pius XII about the right of families to limit the size of their families through natural means if justified by medical, economic or social reasons.⁵² This prompted an angry response from Catholics around the world, including the archbishop of Chicago who denounced 'the insidious efforts of the family planners to harmonize their nefarious work with Catholic teaching'.⁵³

The NCWC issued regular press releases in response to Chisholm's claims, and provided information for articles syndicated in newspapers across the world attacking the WHO's plans. These materials particularly emphasized the opposition which the programme faced from Indian Catholics. The fact that India's government had directly requested the WHO's support was one of the chief obstacles Western Catholics faced in opposing the family planning programme. Indeed, India was a consistent advocate of family planning across the UN system in ways which were often awkward for Catholic activists and Catholic-majority states. In 1954, for instance, Indian diplomats used the UN

---

[49] Information Center of the International Catholic Organizations memorandum, 5 March 1952, ACUA, USCCB, series 1, box 56, folder 20.
[50] NCWC News Service, 'U.S. Birth Control Leader to Advise Indian Government', 29 October 1951, ACUA, USCCB, series 1, box 56, folder 20.
[51] 'Birth Control Experiment to Be Carried on in India', *New York Times*, 30 October 1951, 18.
[52] UN Press and Publications Bureau, 'WHO Director-General Points Out That Family Planning Does Not Conflict with Roman Catholicism', 17 January 1952, ACUA, USCCB, series 1, box 56, folder 20.
[53] Archbishop Casey to Monsignor Carroll, 12 February 1952, ACUA, USCCB, series 1, box 56, folder 20.

Trusteeship Council to argue that Belgium should introduce birth control programmes in the Ruanda Urundi colony in order to boost its development.[54] Indian Catholics, however, offered an important counterweight to the arguments made in favour of the WHO's work. In response to the argument that family planning was vital to address India's projected food and nutrition crisis, the NCWC quoted the (Italian-born) archbishop of Madras' assertion that 'it is not family planning especially as advanced by birth-controllers, that will save India from its economic anguish, but agricultural and industrial planning'.[55] And against Chisholm's claim that the rhythm method was compatible with Muslim and Hindu teachings, the Canadian Catholic nursing association (who were particularly exercised by the nefarious international activities of their compatriot) cited a statement from Indian bishops that 'not only the Catholic Church, but also the tradition of India has always upheld the sacred character of family life'.[56] In the post-war era, transatlantic Catholic activists understood that, for their arguments to gain international traction, they had to demonstrate support from beyond the West.

The key moment in the WHO's debate about birth control came at the Fifth World Health Assembly held in the summer of 1952.[57] In advance of the assembly, a concerted programme of action was put together by the ICO Information Centre in Geneva, the NCWC in the United States, and the Vatican. Together they sought to ensure that as many Catholics as possible were appointed to national delegations at the conference, that delegates from key states were lobbied on the issue, and that sympathetic delegates were given points to raise. As a result of these efforts the conference witnessed a strong rearguard action from the delegates of both European states such as Belgium and Ireland, and Latin American states such as Cuba. This included threats that these countries would be forced to withdraw from the WHO if motions in favour of birth and population control were passed.[58] At a time when the organization had already been severely weakened by the withdrawal of the Soviet Union and other socialist states, this was a threat which carried real weight. The votes were ultimately deadlocked, forcing the WHO leadership to cancel its India project and to reject plans to collaborate with the UN Population Commission.

This decision marked the complete withdrawal of the WHO from the question of population and birth control, and it was not until 1968 that the World Health Assembly was able to formally endorse family planning.[59] It represented a major blow for those seeking to coordinate a global population control policy through the UN. A similar process was playing itself out in other specialized agencies, and the seminal 1954 Population Conference in Rome was ultimately scaled down to a purely academic event without any major policy debate or outcome.[60] Catholic internationalists, it

---

[54] NCWC Office for UN Affairs, 'United Nations Newsnotes', April 1954, ACUA, USCCB, series 1, box 51, folder 18.
[55] NCWC News Service, 'U.S. Birth Control Leader to Advise Indian Government', 29 October 1951, ACUA, USCCB, series 1, box 56, folder 20.
[56] NCWC Office for UN Affairs, 'Memorandum – Birth Control Projects in India – From the Catholic Nurses' Association of Canada', 18 February 1952, ACUA, USCCB, series 1, box 56, folder 20.
[57] The events of the assembly are described in detail in Connelly, *Fatal Misconception*, 147–53.
[58] Information Center of the International Catholic Organizations memo, 'Fifth Session of the World Health Assembly', 16 June 1952, ACUA, USCCB, series 1, box 56, folder 20.
[59] Alison Bashford, 'Population, Geopolitics, and International Organizations'.
[60] Connelly, *Fatal Misconception*, 150–2.

seemed, were more than justified in holding up the WHO's change of policy as evidence of the real impact Catholics could have by coordinating their work across borders and engaging with international organizations and issues.

* * *

The history of Catholic internationalism and ICOs highlights the complex and multifaced nature of the so-called 'liberal world order' which emerged after 1945. This was not a system shaped straightforwardly by commitments to international cooperation, liberal democracy, anti-fascism, modernity, planning, technological development or any of the other forces which are commonly ascribed to it. Rather, it was one plagued by conflict between competing actors, all trying to mould international structures and organizations into their preferred image. Catholic internationalists were particularly clear-eyed about this struggle. For them, international organizations were the site of a straightforward contest between Christian values on the one hand, and the forces of atheism and materialism on the other, most obviously represented by communists but also to a greater or lesser extent by secular international experts, European social democrats or developing world governments. Catholic activists were enthusiastic about international cooperation in principle, but antagonistic towards the UN and its specialized agencies in practice. For them, international cooperation inevitably involved conflict over divergent ideas and interests. Sometimes these conflicts led to the triumph of 'liberal' ideas, policies of institutions. But at other times they did not.

The geography of Catholic internationalism also highlights the precarious dominance which Western Europeans and North Americans still enjoyed over post-war international organizations and networks. ICOs adopted a global rhetoric but were not genuinely global in either composition or outlook. They were dominated by activists from France, Switzerland, Italy, Germany and the United States, and were preoccupied with defending 'Western' interests and values. The global scope of the church and the Catholic community became important when it could be mobilized within the UN and its specialized agencies, as in the case of Latin American states at the WHO. And Catholic internationalists were able to boost their influence by making common cause with other faith communities against European secularism.

But the period of international influence enjoyed by Catholic internationalists was relatively short-lived, and from the 1960s it had begun to lose both its coherence and its force. Decolonization and the growing assertiveness of Third World states in international organizations challenged Catholic influence. With the arrival of newly independent Asian and African states into UN agencies from the 1950s, for example, Catholics activists could no longer rely on a bloc of Western European and Latin American countries to defend their interests. Social and political changes in the West boosted the number and status of secular NGOs. Perhaps most important were the changes within the church and the global Catholic community itself – including Vatican II and the growing influence of Catholics from the Global South. International Catholic opinion, always more diverse than the apparent unity over birth control suggested, became increasingly fragmented. Although ICOs and Catholic activists continued to advocate for 'spiritual' values on the international stage, what this meant in practice became increasingly open to debate.

Part IV

Europe in a global context

13

Internationalists in flight?

Tourism, propaganda and the making of Air France's global empire[1]

Jessica Lynne Pearson

Most histories of twentieth-century internationalism have focused on the role that formal political institutions have played in uniting the globe.[2] But if the League of Nations and the United Nations (UN) loom large in these narratives, we must also consider the ways that other forms of internationalism have brought people together across national boundaries; internationalism was as much a lived experience as it was a catalyst for the creation of organizations like the UN and the League. Indeed, social and professional communities, cultural associations, economic markets, aid and development schemes, and tourism and transportation networks also operated as agents or vehicles of internationalism, building crucial connections between Europe and the world at large.[3]

Over the course of the twentieth century, these different currents of internationalism also engaged, overlapped and collided with European empires in innumerable ways. While the League of Nations had served as a conservative force in a world of empires, after 1945 the UN quickly became a central forum for anti-colonial activism. As new states joined the organization – almost all former colonies – the UN assumed an increasingly global character, and international public opinion about empire grew

---

[1] The author would like to thank the editors, as well as Ernesto Capello, Rachel Kantrowitz, Crystal Moten, Katrina Phillips, Kate Thomas and Macalester African Studies colleagues for their extremely helpful feedback on earlier drafts of this chapter.
[2] See, for example, Mark Mazower, *Governing the World: The History of an Idea, 1815 to the Present* (London: Penguin, 2013); and Simon Jackson and Alanna O'Malley, *The Institution of International Order: From the League of Nations to the United Nations* (London: Routledge, 2018).
[3] See Akira Iriye, *Cultural Internationalism and World Order* (Baltimore: Johns Hopkins University Press, 2010); and Glenda Sluga and Patricia Clavin, eds, *Internationalisms: A Twentieth-Century History* (Cambridge: Cambridge University Press, 2016). For an excellent exploration of the myriad ways that European tourism has operated as a form of internationalism, see ed. Eric G. E. Zuelow, *Touring Beyond the Nation: A Transnational Approach to European Tourism History*, (Surrey: Ashgate Publishing Limited, 2011). For another approach to analysing the intersections between internationalism and travel, see Richard Ivan Jobs, *Backpack Ambassadors: How Youth Travel Integrated Europe* (Chicago: University of Chicago Press, 2017).

progressively hostile with each passing year.⁴ Among other tactics to combat this growing opposition to colonial rule, colonial authorities would capitalize on the global tourism industry to cast their empires in a more favourable light.⁵ The French, in particular, took advantage of their rapidly expanding commercial air travel sector to promote post-war colonial reforms to an international audience.⁶ Using Air France's vast print media operation, French officials made the case that aeroplanes were revolutionizing the very nature of colonial rule, connecting the empire to the broader world in new and innovative ways.⁷ In doing so, they seized an opportunity to use one form of internationalism to mitigate the perceived threat posed by another, all the while masking enduring inequality in France's overseas territories.

From 1918 until the collapse of France's overseas empire in the 1950s and 1960s, aeroplanes played an essential role in linking French territories in Africa, the Caribbean, South America and Southeast Asia to the rest of the world.⁸ During this period, Air France – the country's national airline – encouraged tourists to explore the most far-flung corners of the French empire, from Guadeloupe to the French establishments in India, and from Brazzaville to Saigon. Although much of Air France's marketing was directed at French citizens, encouraging them to take vacations in the empire rather than ski trips to northern Italy, the messages contained in Air France's publications were also intended for a wider international audience. At stake in these efforts to promote colonial tourism were not just the economic benefits that came with increasing traffic to and from the empire, but also a need to legitimize the French empire and to establish a central role for France in the broader international system.

The aeroplane in the 1930s was a powerful symbol of modernity, one capable of fundamentally transforming France's place in the world. In 1936, French author (and

---

4   On the League of Nations and the preservation of European colonialism, see Susan Pedersen, *The Guardians: The League of Nations and the Crisis of Empire* (New York: Oxford University Press, 2015). On the United Nations and the role that it has played in the process of decolonization, see Jessica Lynne Pearson, 'Defending Empire at the United Nations: The Politics of International Colonial Oversight in the Era of Decolonisation', *The Journal of Imperial and Commonwealth History* 45, no. 3 (2017): 525–49; Yassin El-Ayoutey, *The United Nations and Decolonization: The Role of Afro-Asia* (The Hague: Martinus Nijhoff, 1971); and Vrushali Patil, *Negotiating Decolonization in the United Nations: Politics of Space, Identity, and International Community* (New York: Routledge, 2008).
5   Andrew Wigley, 'Against the Wind: The Role of Belgian Colonial Tourism Marketing in Resisting Pressure to Decolonise from Africa', *Journal of Tourism History* 7, no. 3 (2015): 193–209.
6   On the history of French colonial propaganda, see Tony Chafer and Amanda Sackur, eds, *Promoting the Colonial Idea: Propaganda and Visions of Empire in France* (Basingstoke: Palgrave, 2002).
7   *Air France revue* was published under the 'auspices of the General Commissariat for Tourism with the support of the Ministries of Foreign Affairs and Overseas France, [and] the General Secretariat for Civil and Commercial Aviation', and thus served as a platform not only for the airline but for the French administration as well. See *Air France revue*, 'Outre-Mer', Spring 1950. Note: all translations from French sources are my own.
8   While trains, cars and ships also played a key role in the expansion of colonial rule, the aeroplane offered an opportunity for an even more immediate connection between the empire and the metropole. On the history of colonial tourism and the automobile in the French empire, for example, see Archives Nationales de la France d'Outre-Mer (hereafter ANOM), Agence économique de la France d'outre-mer (AGEFOM) 388, Charles Duvelle, 'L'automobile au service du tourisme africain', *Marchés coloniaux* 215 (24 December 1949): 2272–4; and ANOM, AGEFOM 388, Pierre Quesnel, 'En automobile à travers le continent noir', *Union française*, 10 January 1947, 5. On African tourism by ship, see ANOM, AGEFOM 388, 'Un voyage en A.O.F.'

later Nazi collaborator) Paul Morand contributed a short piece to *Air France revue,* the airline's in-flight magazine. The article, entitled 'Air and Politics', described the ways that the aeroplane would shape broader geopolitical relations in the twentieth century. 'Railroads follow a zigzag pattern, like experience', he explained, 'whereas airplanes fly straight like thoughts. The sea and rivers, the fords and hills, have constrained people within traditional approaches to politics. The air is free, it instantly allows for all possible combinations.'[9] Morand's views were widely shared, and many of his compatriots – from all sides of the political spectrum – also considered the aeroplane to be an important vehicle for political and social change.[10]

This chapter interrogates the intersection between aeroplanes, politics and society in an era of growing internationalism and anti-colonialism. It asks: What role would global air travel play in reimagining 'Greater France' in the twentieth century and in what ways did promotional travel materials serve as a critical propaganda opportunity for the French empire at a moment when colonial administrators conceived of internationalism as one of the most significant threats to the empire? How did Air France's publications respond to international critics, who claimed that colonial governments were underdeveloping their colonies and condemning their inhabitants to lives of inescapable political, social and economic inequality? And finally, how did the global political landscape of the 1940s and 1950s transform staunch imperialists into reluctant internationalists, as colonial officials found themselves forced to confront a decolonizing and democratizing world?

Global tourism, this chapter argues, offered French administrators a chance to showcase what they saw as the achievements of post-war colonial development, as well as an opportunity to promote the political, social and cultural rapprochement between France and its empire to an international audience. More crucially, in an era when many colonial officials viewed the presence of foreigners in the empire as a threat, tourism offered a way to carefully mediate how international outsiders engaged with Europe's overseas territories. As new transportation infrastructure in the twentieth century linked colonial empires to a swiftly coalescing global society, economic and political imperatives dictated a certain degree of openness between those empires and the rest of the world. In this context, French officials who had long thought about the world through an imperial lens, suddenly found themselves needing to also think internationally. Glossing over chronic underdevelopment, deeply entrenched segregation and growing political unrest, they used marketing for tourists to display to the world a vision of a unified French empire that was modern, alluring and accessible.[11]

---

[9] Paul Morand, 'Air et politique', *Air France revue,* Spring 1936, 7.
[10] On the broader history of the aircraft industry in France, see Herrick Chapman, *State Capitalism and Working-Class Radicalism in the French Aircraft Industry* (Berkeley: University of California Press, 1991). For another example of the way that infrastructure has facilitated the imagining of a new political entity, see the *Making Europe* project, https://www.makingeurope.eu (accessed 23 April 2020).
[11] On the persistence of segregation in 1950s French Africa, see, for example, Gilbert Houlet, *Les guides bleus illustrés: Brazzaville, Léopoldville, Pointe-Noire* (Paris: Librairie Hachette, 1958) and Marcel Soret, *Démographie et problèmes urbains en A.E.F.: Poto-Poto, Bacongo, Dolisie* (Montpellier: Imprimerie Charité, 1954).

Global travellers in the empire

Historians of tourism generally agree that 'modern' tourism in Europe was born in the mid-eighteenth century, when wealthy young men travelled from England to the continent on what became known as the 'Grand Tour'. As Eric G. E. Zuelow has succinctly noted, 'Mobility is not new'. But, he argues, while certain aspects of what we know as tourism today date as far back as the Greeks and the Romans, there are other features that are decisively linked to historical developments of the last two and a half centuries. Technological innovations like the steamship and the train created new possibilities for travel in the nineteenth century, and the growing availability of travel opportunities for the bourgeoisie saw the concurrent growth of the travel guide industry. Thomas Cook popularized the now-commonplace concept of the 'packaged tour' and the growing availability of postcards and inexpensive souvenirs allowed travellers to relay their experiences to friends and family back home.[12]

Like those men who embarked on the 'Grand Tour' of Europe, 'tourists' in this story were still most certainly people of means. Even with the relative democratization of air travel in the late 1930s and early 1940s, the cost of a plane ticket remained outside the realm of possibility for the average citizen. A ticket to Africa, Asia or the Caribbean was – as it remains today – a costly voyage for someone travelling from Europe. Indeed, air travel generally, whether to a nearby destination or a far-flung locale, was a luxury that far exceeded the available income of most aspiring vacationers. In 1922, French airline companies transported only 9,502 passengers. As routes expanded and aircraft technology became more reliable – and more comfortable – the number of passengers increased exponentially. By 1938, the number of passengers transported by Air France over the course of that year had risen to 104,424.[13] Despite this rapid growth, however, the ability to travel abroad for leisure still remained accessible only to an economically privileged group.

It is also worth noting the striking absence in Air France's advertising of tourists travelling *from* the colonies. While some Indigenous elites from the empire may have had the means to vacation in metropolitan France – or in Europe beyond the Hexagon – these publications focused almost exclusively on white tourists travelling from Europe and the United States. Both *Air France revue* and *Échos de l'air* (*Echoes of the Air*) – the airline's monthly bulletin – are conspicuously silent on the ways that people of colour engaged in the global tourism industry as travellers themselves. While these publications depict white travellers as sightseers, colonial populations were portrayed as sightseeing opportunities, rather than actors in their own right.

Although the number of people who were actually able to visit the empire remained limited, 'tourists' in this chapter include not only those who actually made the voyage to France's overseas territories but also *would-be* travellers to the colonies. Featured articles about travel in French-ruled Indochina and advertisements for weekend

---

[12] Eric G. E. Zuelow, *A History of Modern Tourism* (New York: Palgrave Macmillan, 2016). On the history of the 'Grand Tour', see Jeremy Black, *The British Abroad: The Grand Tour in the Eighteenth Century* (New York: St. Martin's Press, 1992). On the history of Cook's tours, see Piers Brendon, *Thomas Cook: 150 Years of Popular Travel* (London: Secker and Warburg, 1991).

[13] Musée Air France, http://www.airfrancesaga.com/en/content/history (accessed 23 April 2020).

getaways in Dakar aimed to reach not only people who would actually travel to these places but also those who might *think* about it, however briefly. Readers who spent a few seconds considering what it might be like to fly to Brazzaville or French Polynesia as they perused an issue of *Air France revue* at a newsstand in Zürich or New York are just as much a part of this story as those who actually went. As vital as it was for Air France to generate air traffic on new routes to the colonies, equally important was its mission of shaping how people worldwide thought about France's global presence.

The process of generating international interest in travel to the colonies was a protracted one, and required significant intervention on the part of the state. In the interwar years, colonial tourism was still in its infancy and the French government devoted a great deal of funding and effort to drawing foreign travellers to the empire.[14] While the 1931 Colonial Exhibition in Paris had roused much domestic and international curiosity about the colonies, travel between Europe and the empire remained uncomfortably long and prohibitively expensive. Colonial administrators, moreover, admitted that tourism infrastructure in much of the empire remained woefully inadequate.[15] Over the course of the 1930s, France's premier travel club, the Touring club de France, made a number of voyages to France's overseas colonies. These trips aimed to give members a personal experience of travelling to the empire, but also operated as reconnaissance missions, allowing participants to scout out the strengths and weaknesses of tourist accommodations and services in order to offer advice and suggestions on how they could be improved.[16]

The evolution of tourism in France's overseas colonies between the wars varied drastically from territory to territory. In Indochina, a thriving tourist industry was emerging, which included the construction of luxury hotels and resorts – largely at the expense of brutally mistreated indigenous labourers.[17] Algeria, with its proximity to Europe and large settler population, offered its own charms: Roman ruins, skiing, hiking and Mediterranean beaches.[18] In sub-Saharan Africa, tourism was less developed, but

---

[14] For a broader history of tourism in twentieth-century France, with a focus on the metropole, see Ellen Furlough, 'Making Mass Vacations: Tourism and Consumer Culture in France, 1930s to 1970s', *Comparative Studies in Society and History* 40, no. 2 (April 1998): 247–86. Also see Stephen L. Harp, *Marketing Michelin: Advertising and Cultural Identity in Twentieth-Century France* (Baltimore: Johns Hopkins University Press, 2001). On the origins of colonial tourism in the French empire, see Charles Duvelle, 'Le tourisme: facteur de développement économique et social dans nos territoires d'outremer', *France outremer* 31, no. 283 (May 1953): 21–4. On the push to expand colonial tourism in the 1930s, see ANOM, AGEFOM 388, 'Pendant l'escale du "Maréchal Lyautey" à Casablanca, M. Delmas, président du S.I.T.A.O.F. est reçu par le Syndicat d'initiative et prononce une allocution en faveur du tourisme en A.O.F.', *A.O.F. Magazine* (August 1938); and ANOM, AGEFOM 388, Globe Trotter: Bureau de voyages et de tourisme, 'Projet pour l'organisation et le développement du tourisme en A.O.F.', 1938.

[15] On the 1931 Paris Colonial Exhibition, see Ellen Furlough, 'Une leçon des choses: Tourism, Empire, and the Nation in Interwar France', *French Historical Studies* 25, no. 3 (Summer 2002): 441–73; and Patricia A. Morton, *Hybrid Modernities: Architecture and Representation at the 1931 Colonial Exhibition, Paris* (Cambridge: MIT Press, 2003).

[16] See ANOM, AGEFOM 607, 'Tourisme: Le Touring club de France', 1943–1944.

[17] See Aline Demay, *Tourism and Colonization in Indochina* (Newcastle-upon-Thyne: Cambridge Scholars Publishing, 2015); and Eric T. Jennings, *Imperial Heights: Dalat and the Making and Undoing of French Indochina* (Berkeley: University of California Press, 2011).

[18] See Colette Zytnicki, '"Faire l'Algérie agréable": Tourisme et colonisation en Algérie des années 1870 à 1962', *Le Mouvement social* 242 (January–March 2013): 97–114. On the conservation of Roman

presented important opportunities for expansion. There, the focus was on hunting and nature tourism, along with an ethnographic-style exploration of African folklore and culture. This brand of tourism, according to Sophie Dulucq, would ultimately lead to the 'patrimonialization' and 'commodification' of local African cultures and traditions, as travellers sought to discover the 'authentic' and 'eternal' Africa.[19]

In the early twentieth century, the majority of European tourists to the French empire came from metropolitan France. Already by the 1920s and 1930s, however, efforts to promote tourism in the empire had taken on an internationalist orientation.[20] In 1927, the French administration in Indochina created both a tourism office and a propaganda service to promote tourism there, especially to foreign travellers.[21] In 1938, the First International Congress on African Tourism was held in Costermanville, in the Belgian Congo.[22] Early discussions of internationalism and African tourism focused on the development of the Alger-Le Cap trans-African highway and on the harmonization of customs procedures and border crossings. Journalists who wrote about the conference emphasized the importance of international collaboration, especially between colonial powers in Africa. According to one article in *Le monde colonial illustré*:

> The usefulness of these international meetings cannot be contested, as it is necessary to pursue the organization of Africa methodically across the entirety of the continent. A colonial voyage generally encompasses a number of territories belonging to different powers and it is thus indispensable that both governments and tourism organizations keep in close contact in order to work together and in the same spirit.[23]

In 1947, in the wake of the war, the Second International Congress on African Tourism was held in Algiers. The conference had originally been scheduled for 1940, but was postponed because of the war.[24] During this period, however, Vichy officials nonetheless explored ways to increase international tourism in the colonies.[25] Efforts in the late 1930s and early 1940s focused not only on supporting the economic goals

---

ruins in Algeria for the purposes of heritage tourism, see ANOM, 81 F 1699, Gouvernement général de l'Algérie (Direction de l'intérieur et des beaux-arts), Assemblée de l'Union française, 'Discussion d'une proposition tendant à inviter le gouvernement à assurer la conservation des ruines de Tipasa', 1950.

[19] On colonial tourism in francophone Africa, see Sophie Dulucq, '"Découvrir l'âme africaine": les temps obscurs du tourisme culturel en Afrique coloniale française (années 1920-années 1950)', *Cahiers d'études africaines* 40, no. 193/194 (2009): 27–48.

[20] ANOM, AGEFOM 388, Syndicat d'initiative et de tourisme de l'Afrique occidentale française, Dakar, 8 July 1938. On the internationalization of French tourism more generally, see ANOM, AGEFOM 388, Bulletin hebdomadaire d'information du Centre national d'expansion du tourisme, du thermalisme et du climatisme, 2ème année – no. 47, Paris, 4 March 1938.

[21] ANOM, AGEFOM 607, 'Résumé des rapports du Conseil supérieur des colonies', no date.

[22] ANOM, AGEFOM 388, 'Le tourisme en Afrique', *Revue la porte océane* 25 (May 1947): 13–15.

[23] Jean-Claude Bertaux, 'Le deuxième Congrès international du tourisme africain', *Le monde colonial illustré* XVI (1939).

[24] *Deuxième Congrès International du Tourisme Africain, Alger, 1947* (Paris: Les presses de l'imprimerie Chaix, 1947).

[25] ANOM, AGEFOM 607, 'Étude d'ordre général sur le tourisme aux colonies', 1940.

of the French tourist industry but also on providing an opportunity for the world to experience what French officials referred to as 'our black Africa'.²⁶ Travel-related propaganda provided the French administration with a crucial opportunity to promote its colonial 'achievements' to a global audience.

Building global connections: Air France between the wars

Despite these efforts to expand colonial tourism, travel within the French empire remained constrained by limited transportation options and long travel times.²⁷ The aeroplane offered an innovative means to overcome these obstacles.²⁸ The advent of commercial air travel linked France more closely to its colonies, while simultaneously connecting the rest of the world to the French empire. Air travel offered new prospects for tourism as well as an opportunity to think about colonial politics in a new way. Over the course of the 1930s *Air France revue* filled its pages with new travel experiences afforded by the ever-expanding air routes from France to Africa, Indochina and the Caribbean, and those that united the empire and the rest of the world. *Échos de l'air* likewise celebrated the new possibilities for easily accessible colonial tourism.

No single national airline existed in the 1910s and 1920s in France, and air routes were served by a number of companies that would ultimately consolidate in 1933 under the banner of 'Air France'.²⁹ The first French airline, la Compagnie générale transaérienne, flew between Paris, Belgium and Switzerland. Another airline, Lignes Latécoère, pioneered routes from France to Morocco (1919) and Tunisia (1925). In 1927, Latécoère began a new route from Toulouse to Dakar, opening up French sub-Saharan Africa to air travel for the first time. In 1928, the airline added a flight from Marseille to Algiers, and, finally, in 1931, Air Orient inaugurated service between France and Indochina.³⁰ During the 1930s, after the launch of Air France, these routes connected France and its empire to other key locations across the globe: London, Hong Kong, Lisbon, Natal, Santiago, Buenos Aires and Barcelona.³¹ Throughout this period, Air France actively supported the government's efforts to promote tourism in the empire, and the airline's publications celebrated the role that aeroplanes could

---

[26] ANOM, AGEFOM 388, Syndicat d'initiative et de tourisme de l'Afrique occidentale française, Dakar, 8 July 1938, 1.
[27] ANOM, AGEFOM 388, 'Le tourisme en Afrique occidentale française: ce que nous dit M. Marius Moutet', *L'œuvre*, 7 August 1937. Also see ANOM, AGEFOM 388, 'Rapport sur le tourisme en Afrique occidentale française', *Croisière de la revue générale des sciences*, 1.
[28] ANOM, AGEFOM 388, 'Le tourisme en A.O.F.'; and ANOM, AGEFOM 388, Marcel Griaule, 'Afrique française', Téléfrance: Service international d'articles et de photographies, 1. On the broader history of air travel, see Kenneth Hudson and Julian Pettifer, *Diamonds in the Sky: A Social History of Air Travel* (London: The Bodley Head, Ltd., 1979).
[29] http://www.airfrancelasaga.com/en/content/history.
[30] 'Quelques dates dans l'histoire d'Air France et des transports aériens mondiaux', in *Air France revue*, 'Afrique', Fall 1949, 111. On the expansion of Air France's network, also see *Air France revue*, Spring 1935, 26.
[31] *Échos de l'air*, March 1938, 11–12.

play both in France's 'civilizing mission' and in the internationalization of colonial tourism.[32]

In 1939, in one of its first features on air travel to the colonies, *Air France revue* published a story of two adventure travellers, Georges Mesnil and Pierre La Chapelle, who found themselves stranded in French-ruled Mauritania. While friends had warned them of the dangers of such a daring trip, the two men assured them that they had once landed in Paris during a blizzard, and surely a flight along the West African coast could be no more difficult. In flight, however, a harrowing sandstorm throws them off course. After blindly landing their plane in the desert, the two men emerge from the aircraft to find themselves greeted by a young boy named Mokhtar, who introduces himself in French and assures the two men that they are in friendly territory. Mokhtar eagerly guides Mesnil and La Chapelle to his village where their request for him to accompany them in their aeroplane to the nearest airstrip provokes great consternation among his family members. Mokhtar, for his part, refuses, shakes his head and hands, and with terror in his voice, exclaims: 'Me, me, me, get in there? Oh! No way, no way, no chance!' The two pilots trick him into boarding the plane and safely reach their destination with Mokhtar's direction. When they thank him with a generous handful of cash and offer to rent him a camel to make the return trip home, he thanks them, returns the money, and states proudly that he would rather fly with them in their 'bird' to Saint Louis, Senegal. Drawing on the racist trope of the 'backwards' African waiting to be enlightened by European science and technology, this story aimed to demonstrate that French innovation and 'civilization' had the ability to triumph over even the most reluctant audiences.[33]

If the aeroplane was capable of contributing to France's *mission civilisatrice* and of bringing a particularly French conception of modernity to the empire, it was also uniquely positioned to connect the empire to the broader world. According to authors who wrote for Air France's publications, the aeroplane had created an unprecedented opportunity for foreign travellers to become acquainted with *la plus grande France*. Everyone, according to *Air France revue*, needed to make the pilgrimage to French Africa at least once in their lifetime:

> One cannot not go. This voyage is just as essential for the citizen of the universe in the twentieth century as the trip to Paris was for Europeans in the eighteenth, and it is imperative to make the journey *by plane*. To deprive oneself of this glimpse of magic and history would be a sacrilege, an insult to human enthusiasm and reason.

While the primary goal of this journey was a sense of personal fulfilment, it also offered the traveller an important lesson about the role that the French had played in 'civilizing' the colonized world. Drawing on stereotypes of a savage Africa, one article explained: 'We have defined the ideal of peace and order that is necessary to implement

---

[32] On the history of the concept of the 'civilizing mission' in the French empire, see Alice Conklin, *A Mission to Civilize: The Republican Idea of Empire in France and West Africa, 1895-1930* (Stanford, CA: Stanford University Press, 1997).

[33] Jacques Zimmerman, 'Le passager', *Air France revue*, Summer 1935, 20-2, 34.

when a place becomes ours. Where blindness, paralysis, vermin, morass, crime, and injustice once reigned, now order and thought can triumph.' If the aim of this voyage was to give the world a chance to experience Africa, it also offered an occasion to combat 'misinformation' about France's mission there. The same author writes: 'There are . . . imbeciles who wonder what France has done for the Arab people! The flight over this easy and tame land will combat this ignorance and blasphemy.'[34]

Indeed, France's civilizing mission was something that French officials had long claimed set their colonizing efforts apart from other empires. While more limited in reach than the British Empire, the French could paint their own overseas project as one more closely connected to the quest for modernity, hygiene and rationality. Indeed, Air France's publications also served as an important venue for criticizing the practices of colonial rule in other empires. In 1938, for example, French bureaucrat Francisque Vial made the long voyage from France to Indochina by air, with stops along the way in the Levant, India and Thailand. Over the course of several issues of *Échos de l'air*, Vial published a series of articles entitled 'Letter from Indochina' in which he narrated his experiences in these different stopovers.[35] In the final instalment, Vial spares no criticism of Britain's colonial capitals. Leaving India on the final day of his journey, he writes: 'I couldn't wait to take off . . . to flee Calcutta. What I saw yesterday, from the airport to the hotel, was a horrible and stinking suburb, swarming with vermin and poverty.' When he finally crosses the border from Thailand into Indochina, he is relieved to finally find signs of modern French society:

> From our cabin, this land appears to be methodically, rationally – even 'Cartesianly' – cultivated. We have just crossed the border from Siam and penetrated into Indochina. This methodical exploitation of rice cultivation is the *œuvre* of France. The active and industrious intelligence of the West has brought discipline and order to the inexhaustible and chaotic richness of the enormity that is Asia.[36]

While articles like those penned by Vial served the French government's political agenda, they also emphasized the unique travel experiences that the empire could hold for foreign travellers. The French empire, according to Air France's promotional materials, offered tourists from across the globe an opportunity to experience history in a different way, and to be enchanted by a world so foreign from their own. In the 1930s, many of these publications focused on travel to North Africa, which was rapidly becoming connected to Europe by a vast network of air routes.[37] Round-trip tickets to

---

[34] Pierre Weiss, 'L'Afrique aux portes de Paris', *Air France revue*, Summer 1936, 11–12.
[35] Francisque Vial, 'Lettre d'Indochine', in the June, July, August and September issues of *Échos de l'air*. On Vial's mission to Indochina, see Guy Caplat, '122. VIAL (Francisque, Jules)', *L'Inspection générale de l'instruction publique au XXe siècle. Dictionnaire biographique des inspecteurs généraux et des inspecteurs de l'Académie de Paris, 1914-1939* (Paris: Institut national de recherche pédagogique, 1997), 497–501.
[36] Francisque Vial, 'Lettre d'Indochine', September 1938, 6–7. For another perspective on tourism and air travel to Indochina, see Henry Bontoux, 'L'inauguration du tourisme aérien en Indochine: De la rivière de Saigon aux douves d'Angkor-Vat, *Extrême-Orient: Revue indochinoise illustrée, organe official du Bureau du tourisme en Indochine*, May 1929.
[37] 'En deux coups d'ailes', *Air France revue*, Winter 1936–1937, 22–3.

Figure 13.1 1948 Air France poster. Artist: B. Villemot. Reproduced with permission from Musée Air France.

North Africa were affordable compared to their sub-Saharan counterparts. In 1938, a ticket from Marseille to Algiers cost a little less than 1,500 francs, while a ticket from Marseille to Dakar would set a traveller back by almost 10,000 francs.[38] The ability to travel quickly from France to North Africa made it a natural destination for short holiday trips. In December of 1938, *Échos de l'air* dedicated an issue to 'Christmas in Morocco', noting that this was 'once just a dream for those whose jobs kept them at the office or the factory, and who only enjoyed limited leisure time during the holidays'. Thanks to daily air service to North Africa now offered by Air France, one could leave France the night before and by the next morning have 'left behind the cold, the rain, the mist, and maybe even the snow, to find [oneself] in a sun-soaked land, rich with a thousand seductions, in the heart of a country . . . that juxtaposed aspects of the Middle Ages and Modern Life'.[39]

---

[38] 'Nouveaux tarifs au départ de la France', *Échos de l'air*, February 1938, 15.
[39] 'Noël au Maroc', *Échos de l'air*, December 1938, 1–2.

Although most of the tourists using these routes were French, Air France's publications went out of their way to emphasize foreign travellers' satisfaction with the company's empire service. An article about travel to Tunisia begins with a review from a satisfied client, a representative of the American airline Transcontinental, who claimed to have 'never made such an agreeable journey'. The author continues:

> The planes that fly from Marseille to Tunis are extremely comfortable and quiet. The stop-over in Ajaccio is made even more agreeable by the small restaurant there that provides the passengers with an excellent meal.... I wrote to my company to tell them how pleased I was with the trip, because I knew they would be as happy about it as I am.[40]

Another article chronicling one traveller's trip from Accra to London on Air France was subtitled: 'Travel notes from an entirely satisfied British passenger', who assured his readers that he was in no way connected to Air France or Aéromaritime.[41]

By foregrounding these global voices, Air France was highlighting the role that internationalism played in its broader agenda. Indeed, in the course of the two decades that followed the First World War, Air France had developed a vast global network capable of linking both the metropole and the empire to the furthest reaches of the earth. Travel destinations that were once completely beyond the reach of middle-class vacationers now seemed to lie within the realm of possibility. And for the many more people worldwide who couldn't afford to actually make the journey to France's overseas territories, Air France's wide-reaching media offered an unprecedented opportunity to introduce the French empire and its *mission civilisatrice* to a global audience. Thanks to these publications' extensive coverage of colonial tourism, ordinary people could now 'experience' travel to France's territories overseas without ever setting foot outside their own front door. Several years hence, as the Second World War was drawing to a close, this global travel network would become an even more critical publicity tool as the French empire found itself facing an increasingly sceptical international audience.

Flying the French Union

The Second World War brought far-reaching changes to the structure of France's overseas empire. After six years of fighting – which drew heavily on resources and labour from the colonies – politicians and officials from across the French-controlled world gathered to map out a new kind of political entity.[42] The 'French Union', as the empire would now be called, was to be based on a relationship of equality and mutual support between the colony and metropole, rather than on the basis of inequality and

---

[40] 'Parmi tant de merveilles: Tunisie', *Échos de l'air*, April 1938, 1.
[41] W. G. H. Blake, 'D'Accra à Londres par Aéromaritime et Air France: notes de voyage d'un passager britannique entièrement satisfait', *Échos de l'air*, April 1938, 9.
[42] See Ruth Ginio, *French Colonialism Unmasked: The Vichy Years in French West Africa* (Lincoln, NE: University of Nebraska Press, 2006); and Eric Jennings, *Free French Africa in World War II: The African Resistance* (Cambridge: Cambridge University Press, 2015).

exploitation that had so long characterized European imperial rule.[43] These lofty goals, however, were difficult to realize in practice, and over the course of the 1940s and 1950s the French colonial administration found itself facing mounting anti-colonialism, both within the empire and from new international organizations. As a growing number of newly independent states joined the UN, attention turned to the persistently unequal economic, social and cultural policies of the organization's 'administering members'. Throughout the late 1940s and early 1950s, French officials bemoaned what they perceived as the dramatic expansion of the UN's power of oversight over colonial territories.[44] While they grappled with this apparent threat posed by the UN, French officials also faced growing agitation from within the empire, from the railway strikes along the Dakar-Niger railway line in the late 1940s to the growing popularity of the National Liberation Front (FLN) in French-controlled Algeria.[45]

In response to these local and international political developments, the French administration searched for new opportunities to rebrand France's empire. The tourism industry offered a unique opportunity to combat intensifying anti-colonialism at home and abroad. If promotional travel materials were in part about generating new interest in travel to the colonies, they also focused on educating a wide international audience about the scope and significance of post-war colonial reforms. Over the course of the late 1940s and early 1950s, Air France's publications focused less on the practical aspects of travelling to France's overseas territories, and instead dedicated more space to celebrating political cooperation and economic development projects within the French Union. Publications like *Air France revue* and *Échos de l'air* also emphasized the social and cultural connections that were being forged between the empire's diverse components, as well as the myriad technological advancements that the French claimed to be bringing to their overseas territories.

In 1949 and 1950, *Air France revue* released two special issues, respectively entitled 'Africa' and 'Overseas France'. The following year *Échos de l'air* published a similar special issue entitled 'The French Union'.[46] Each of these three publications celebrated the deep connections between France and its overseas territories, as well as the role that France had played – with the help of aircraft technology – in driving economic development in French territories in Africa, the Caribbean, Southeast Asia and the Pacific. These special issues papered over rampant discrimination and inequality in the empire, while still drawing on racist colonial stereotypes to make their case for the value of ongoing French rule.

---

[43] Frederick Cooper, *Citizenship Between Empire and Nation: Remaking France and French Africa, 1945-1960* (Princeton, NJ: Princeton University Press, 2014). Also see ANOM, AGEFOM 406, 'Éléments d'une politique d'Union française'.

[44] See Jessica Lynne Pearson, *The Colonial Politics of Global Health: France and the United Nations in Postwar Africa* (Cambridge: Harvard University Press, 2018).

[45] On the Dakar-Niger Railway strike, see Frederick Cooper, '"Our Strike": Equality, Anticolonial Politics, and the 1947-48 Railway Strike in French West Africa', *Journal of African History* 36 (1996): 81–118. On the FLN in Algeria, see Matthew Connelly, *A Diplomatic Revolution: Algeria's Fight for Independence and the Origins of the Post-Cold War Era* (New York: Oxford University Press, 2002); and Alistair Horne, *A Savage War of Peace: Algeria, 1954–1962* (New York: Viking Press, 1977).

[46] See *Air France revue*, 'Afrique', Fall 1949; *Air France revue*, 'Outre-Mer', Spring 1950; and Air France, *Échos de l'air*, September 1951.

In the 'Africa' special issue of *Air France revue*, the editors of the magazine begin their story in Paris, which, as 'the capital of the French Union', was an apparently 'natural' starting point for an issue about Africa. The magazine's introductory article begins with an imagined conversation between two men. The first says: 'Hello there, old bushman, what are you doing in Paris? I thought you would be in Africa, in the land of chevrotains and mandrills, of hippopotamuses and crocodiles.' His interlocutor replies: 'But I am in Africa, my friend, Africa in Paris. I can't take one step in this capital without believing myself to be somewhere on the black continent.' Hot on the trail of Africa in Paris, the two men hop on the *métro*, alighting first at Rue Monge. Gazing towards the Paris Mosque, the African guide notes the eager Parisians who have come to pursue Arabic-language training, as well as the Muslims and non-Muslims enjoying both the hammam and the library. Paris, according to the guide, is in many ways a more centrally located home base for African Muslims. It is easier, he explains, for a mechanic living in Auteil to start on a pilgrimage to Mecca than it is for a Moroccan peasant living deep in the Atlas Mountains.[47]

As the two men head in the direction of the *quartier latin*, the guide points out the assorted African eateries that dot the Parisian streetscape. Their next stops include the university – a favourite hangout for West African students – and an antique shop near Raspail, whose dusty shelves are crammed with African pottery. Next, they make a detour to the Vincennes zoo, where monkeys brought by plane from Central Africa are now on view. Last, at Pyramides, they visit the souk at the Avenue de l'Opéra. While items like the masks, bananas and colourful fabrics that fill the market stalls are the most visible signs of Africa in the metropole, the guide explains, even more significant are the people and what they represent. Africans in Paris, he contends, 'speak the purest French', and the mélange of races in these neighbourhoods is the 'very essence of the French Union'.[48] From Paris, the magazine takes the reader to different locations in French Africa: from Algeria to French West Africa and French Equatorial Africa to Togo, Cameroon, Madagascar and Réunion. In each of these settings, the magazine's writers celebrate both the cultural connections and a shared sense of purpose among Africans and the French. An article about French West Africa, for example, minimizes the role that Gorée Island played as a slave port in earlier centuries, focusing instead on the political reforms that led to the creation of the French Union.[49]

The following year, in 1950, *Air France revue* published another special issue to continue its exploration of 'Overseas France'. This issue, like the preceding one on Africa, was clearly intended to reach readers abroad. Instead of providing practical travel information, the issue reads more like a primer on French colonial reform. More than four years after the creation of the French Union – whose basic contours would have already been familiar to the average French person – the magazine aimed to educate a global public about France's changing relationship to its empire. The

---

[47] Jean-Jacques Brissac, 'L'Afrique à Paris: Voyage sans billet', *Air France revue*, 'Afrique', Fall 1949, 11.
[48] Ibid., 15.
[49] Jean Flavien, 'Interview de M. le gouverneur général Béchard', *Air France revue*, 'Afrique', Fall 1949, 152.

introduction to the issue, for example, defines both 'Overseas France' and the 'French Union':

> *Overseas France* is a geographic expression that designates the countries of the world today where France is officially present, where its representatives assume the duties and the rights of direction, counsel, control, or trusteeship.
>
> *The French Union* is a recently created entity of public and international statute grouping together those peoples currently represented by the new political assembly headquartered in Versailles and created by our most recent constitution, that of 27 October 1946.[50]

According to the article, the French government intended to guide the peoples of the French Union with 'its heart and with reason', rather than to 'command' them. Over the course of almost 200 pages, the contributors to the magazine celebrated the cultural and spiritual similarities between metropolitan French people and the inhabitants of France's overseas territories. In an article entitled 'Elegant Women of the French Union', for example, Jean-Jacques Brissac celebrated the shared virtues of women across the empire, and – perhaps even more noteworthy – across different ethnic identities. Women throughout the Union could identify with each other as 'mothers, lovers ... and flirts'. These women 'resemble each other like sisters', he argued, sharing the same love for fashion and luxury. Indeed, Brissac claimed, one could spot a Senegalese woman sporting a shirt cut in a way that was very 'Saint-Germain-de-Près' just as easily as one could spot a Parisian woman dressed in the 'Pagoda' sleeves of a Vietnamese dress. The article featured large photographs of women from different regions of the French Union, with captions like: 'Aïcha: the Algerian woman unveiled, for once', and 'Latia: the Bedouin woman with the Mona Lisa smile'. All of these women, the article argued, merited the title of *parisienne,* or Parisian woman.[51]

Beyond their celebration of a shared political, social and sartorial culture, each of these issues also highlighted the role that the French had played in stimulating economic development in Africa. At the core of the new French Union, its champions argued, was the economic modernization of France's overseas territories. The aeroplane, according to the union's most enthusiastic proponents, was the quintessential agent of development, opening up new markets for African goods and facilitating travel for European investors. In the 1949 'Africa' issue of *Air France revue*, the African guide points out the myriad products that had made their way to France from the continent: cacao, palm oil, meat, diamonds, etc. He notes: 'Africa is everywhere in Paris, in every street, every shop, every home.'[52] Turning the reader away from France's long history of economic exploitation, the issue celebrated the mutual aid that emerged from economic cooperation between France and its African territories. Africa provided a source of raw materials, while France invested in Africa's economic development through the Monnet

---

[50] 'La France d'outre-mer – L'Union française', *Air France revue*, 'Outre-Mer', Spring 1950, 7.
[51] Jean-Jacques Brissac, 'Élégantes de l'Union française', *Air France revue*, 'Outre-Mer', Spring 1950, 9.
[52] Brissac, 'L'Afrique à Paris: Voyage sans billet', 18.

Plan and the Investment Fund for Economic and Social Development (FIDES).[53] With the support of these funds, the magazine claimed, French investors had revolutionized agriculture, animal husbandry, forestry, mining and industry on the continent.[54]

Aeroplanes played a crucial part in these post-war economic development plans. Algeria, one article explained, 'has found in the airplane the ideal means to profit from its agricultural resources, especially perishable items like produce that can be consumed in Paris just a few hours after being harvested.' In places like Morocco where the physical terrain presented obstacles to development, the aeroplane offered a way to (literally) overcome the mountainous landscape, 'offering to the tourist the picturesque riches of Casablanca, Meknès, Rabat, Fez, Taja, Marrakech, and to the businessman all of the commercial and industrial opportunities of a country in full evolution.'[55] Thanks to the aeroplane, the author noted, Africa would benefit from the same level of economic modernization that Europe had undergone in an earlier era: 'It's been some time already since there ceased to exist any peasants in the Danube ... with Air France's airplanes, soon there will also cease to be any peasants in the Congo.'[56]

In each of these articles, *Air France revue*'s authors sought to dispel what many French officials believed were myths about the French Union that were being propagated at the UN, and within the global community more broadly.[57] While certainly many French people would also have encountered these magazines in flight, their intended audience was unmistakably an international one. These publications highlighted the social, political and cultural cohesion of the French Union, as well as the seemingly unbreakable economic bonds between the metropole and France' overseas territories. By showcasing France's extensive modernization efforts, *Air France revue*'s writers were combatting global accusations that colonial governments – even reformed ones – were condemning their constituents to lives of poverty, ignorance and starvation.[58]

* * *

In the post-1945 era, internationalism and imperialism intersected in novel and often unforeseen ways. The movement towards greater international oversight of colonial rule clashed with French efforts to build a closer union between empire and metropole. The French administration, as a result, needed to promote its rebranded 'French Union' not only to its own constituents but also to an international public that was increasingly attuned to the inner workings of European empires. In this context, some French officials enthusiastically embraced global tourism as one form of internationalism that could actually serve France's imperial interests. Their efforts to promote a shiny

---

[53] 'Les portes de la civilisation', *Air France revue*, 'Outre-Mer', Spring 1950, 43.
[54] 'Richesses terrestres', *Air France revue*, 'Afrique', Fall 1949, 52.
[55] 'Air France en Afrique du Nord', *Air France revue*, 'Afrique', Fall 1949, 132.
[56] M. Cornut-Gentille, 'Vocation de l'Afrique équatoriale française', *Air France revue*, 'Afrique', Fall 1949, 168.
[57] ANOM, 2 G 50 (124), AOF, Direction du Cabinet, 'Synthèse périodique d'informations no. 2, annexe: Les politiques française et britannique dans l'Ouest africain', March–April 1950, 99.
[58] On anti-colonial critiques at the UN, see The National Archives (TNA), Kew, CO 936/162, United Nations General Assembly, Eighth Session, 'Report on Debate'; CO 936/164, 'Communist Exploitation of Anti-Colonialism and Nationalism in Africa'; and CO 936/164, 'Anti-Colonialism'.

new vision of France's empire to a global audience illuminate the extent to which the 'colonial question' had become internationalized, and their use of tourist publications to combat anti-colonialism speaks to the myriad currents of internationalism that shaped how Europeans engaged with the wider world in the post-war era. If the advent of air travel had fundamentally transformed colonial tourism, the concurrent expansion of promotional tourist publications similarly revolutionized the way the French depicted their empire to the rest of the world. As they attempted to safeguard colonial rule in an era when – for the first time in history – European empires found themselves facing an overwhelmingly anti-colonial majority on the world stage, French colonial officials reluctantly recast themselves as internationalists, ready to welcome the modern global traveller to their reformed colonial empire. That is, at least on paper.

14

Even better than the real thing?

The United States, the TVA and the development of the Mekong

Vincent Lagendijk

In 1941, British internationalist Julian Huxley, the world-renowned evolutionary biologist who would later become the first director of the United Nations Educational, Scientific and Cultural Organization (UNESCO), travelled through the United States. On his US tour, he became fascinated by the Tennessee Valley Authority (TVA) and decided to author a short book on his impressions. At the time, the TVA was relatively new, set up only in 1933 as part of Roosevelt's New Deal. It sought to uplift the backward American South through a system of dams in the Tennessee river valley combined with several socio-economic programmes. According to Huxley, it was the outstanding example of 'democratic planning', as within the TVA's 'enlightened social policy [. . .] everything is done by persuasion'.[1] He added that 'TVA ideas and methods are helping to guide the growth of new planning agencies [. . .] ; studies are being made of how a set-up of general TVA type could be adapted to serve as an international instead of a national agency'.[2] Huxley was thinking not only about reconstructing post-war Europe but also the Global South.

As Huxley already hinted at in 1943, the TVA came to be seen as a model at the international level after the Second World War. In post-war decades, the TVA gained further global popularity, establishing itself as a strong brand in the development 'industry'. International organizations (IOs) appropriated it as a template while the TVA itself institutionalized parts of its technical assistance activities. Wrapping this in a consumerist metaphor, esteemed development economist Albert O. Hirschman went as far to compare the TVA to Coca Cola, as many post-colonial leaders were in search of 'the real thing' when developing their own river valleys:

> Although obviously two river valley development schemes will differ vastly more from one another than two Coca Cola bottling plants, the impression was created,

---

[1] Julian Huxley, *TVA: Adventure in Planning* (London: The Architectural Press, 1943), 55 and 31.
[2] Ibid., 135.

by the appeal to the 'TVA model', that clear sailing lay ahead for the proposed schemes. To be acceptable, it seems, a project must often be billed as a pure replica of a successful venture in an advanced country.[3]

In that light, it hardly comes as a surprise that the TVA became an instrument of foreign policy as well. Starting with Truman's Point IV programme in 1949, the US foreign development apparatus took it as a main example, and the Tennessee Valley became a standard stopover for foreign dignitaries visiting the United States.[4] For long the history of the TVA and its global post-1945 influence has been conceived as such and dominated by a US-centred approach. David Ekbladh has convincingly conceptualized the TVA as the synecdochical project that defined the 'American mission' to democratize and develop the world along liberal lines.[5] With Europe in shambles looking to reconstruct and a growing number of newly independent nations hoping to develop after 1945, the United States seemed the place to look for models. Whereas the primacy of the formerly European great powers was declining, the vast country across the Atlantic emerged out of the Second World War as the most technologically advanced and arguably most potent superpower. Both countries from the Global South and war-torn European countries looked to the United States for inspiration and know-how. Forged in the smithy of New Deal America, the TVA became a sword in the hands of developers in post-war decades, while the United States eagerly embraced it as a model development project infused with allegedly democratic Western ideals.

Arguably the best example of this 'American mission' was a 1965 presidential pledge. In order to mitigate tensions in South-East Asia resulting from the Vietnam War, US president Lyndon B. Johnson proposed to use the TVA as a template to utilize the River Mekong. Delivering a televised speech in April of that year, he promised no less than a billion dollars for developing the river, extending this support to the Soviet Union, China and North Vietnam. This should be seen as an attempt to initiate a programme of economic development of South-East Asian countries and an alternative pathway to reach a peaceful settlement with North Vietnam and the other parties with vested interest in the conflict.[6] In comparing the Mekong to the TVA, Johnson was anything but modest: 'The vast Mekong River can provide food and water and power on a scale to dwarf even our own TVA.'[7] In other words, to stay close to Hirschman's metaphor, the TVA on the Mekong thus promised to be even better than the real thing.

---

[3] Albert O. Hirschman, *Development Projects Observed* (Washington, DC: Brookings Institution Press, 1967), 21.
[4] Sönke Kunkel, *Empire of Pictures: Global Media and the 1960s Remaking of American Foreign Policy* (New York and Oxford: Berghahn, 2016), 86–9.
[5] David Ekbladh, *The Great American Mission: Modernization and the Construction of an American World Order* (Princeton: Princeton University Press, 2010).
[6] Lyndon B. Johnson, *The Vantage Point: Perspectives of the Presidency, 1963-1969* (New York: Holt, Rinehart and Winston, 1971), 132.
[7] 'President Lyndon B. Johnson's Address at Johns Hopkins University: "Peace Without Conquest", April 7, 1965', in *Public Papers of the Presidents of the United States: Lyndon B. Johnson, 1965*, vol. 1 (Washington, DC: Government Printing Office, 1966), 394–9, http://www.lbjlib.utexas.edu/johnson/archives.hom/speeches.hom/650407.asp.

This chapter claims that this US effort, though unilateral in intent, led to a more pronounced internationalist effort. Internationalism is commonly defined as the further and closer cooperation between nations in order to achieve peace, or the development of a world community.[8] Here the role of the United States partially filled the vacuum left by the European powers in South-East Asia. But it shared the limelight with IOs, as part of internationalist efforts. Traced back to the sixteenth century and emerging in varieties due to different ideologies and eras, internationalism has long been regarded a defunct political ideology or concept unworthy of study (or both), as it seems hardly compatible with the more realist outlook of international relations of scholars since E. H. Carr.[9] Instrumental in the emergence of transnational history, Akira Iriye also shed new light on the concept of internationalism. He defined it as 'an idea, a movement, or an institution that seeks to reformulate the nature of relations among nations through cross-national cooperation and interchange', tying it to transnational efforts surpassing the national.[10] At the same time, scholars adhering to this new perception of internationalism seem more 'sensitive to cultural analyses and with expertise in the history of imperialism and transnationalism as well as nationalism'.[11] Recent scholarship has further advanced the notion of internationalism, somewhat deploring the conceptual vagueness of terms like 'transnationalism' and 'internationalism', and lambasting the focus its manifestations from a liberal, intentionally and often teleological point of view.[12]

While claimed to be quintessentially American, the TVA built upon European and colonial experiences, and was part of global exchanges on dam-building and river development. This chapter should be seen as following in those footsteps. Presented as an overtly American project, by contemporaries but also historians in retrospect, this chapter argued that the Mekong's development was in fact strongly internationalist in nature. South-East Asia was not Americanized through the application of the TVA model, but that model was further internationalized by wide range of actors. And before making a splash on the international scene, ideas about development, including the TVA, were affected by experiences in European colonies as well as Central and Eastern Europe.

The chapter thus claims that US attempt to forge a TVA for the Mekong can be regarded a type of internationalism. It seeks to provide an alternative perspective on

---

[8] Soyang Park, 'Internationalisms', in *The Palgrave Dictionary of Transnational History*, ed. Akira Iriye and Pierre-Yves Saunier (Basingstoke: Palgrave Macmillan, 2009), 586; Cornelia Navari, *Internationalism and the State in the Twentieth Century* (London and New York: Routledge, 2000), 1. Also see Mark Mazower, *Governing the World: The History of an Idea* (New York: Penguin Press, 2012), chap. 1.

[9] Carr divided between 'realism' and 'utopianism', regarding internationalism part of the latter category. Edward Hallet Carr, *The Twenty Years' Crisis, 1919-1939: An Introduction to the Study of International Relations* (London: Macmillan, 1939), 6–9.

[10] Akira Iriye, *Cultural Internationalism and World Order* (Baltimore: Johns Hopkins University Press, 1997), 3; Akira Iriye, *Global Interdependence: The World after 1945* (Berkeley: University of California Press, 2014), 9–11.

[11] Glenda Sluga and Patricia Clavin, 'Rethinking the History of Internationalism', in *Internationalisms*, ed. Glenda Sluga and Patricia Clavin (Cambridge: Cambridge University Press, 2016), 4.

[12] Jessica Reinisch, 'Introduction: Agents of Internationalism', *Contemporary European History* 25, no. 2 (May 2016): 195–8.

the existing historiography of this Mekong episode. Current scholarship fits the bill of what Jessica Reinisch characterized as the 'transnationalism canon': a body of literature which 'has been written exclusively from the perspective of Western, usually Anglo-American, actors and members of the liberal international elite, or has used them as a yardstick for studying transnational phenomena in the rest of the world'.[13] The TVA became one of the most well-known acronyms after the Second World War, acting as an inspiration for many, not least for the many (unknown) technicians and experts from all over the globe. US agencies, including the TVA itself, played an active role in spreading these engineering ideals that were perceived to be tied to democratic principles.

Yet at the same time, post-war developmentalist internationalism cannot be reduced to just the United States. European ideas also profoundly influenced this vector. The aim of this chapter therefore is to show the internationalist agency in what largely has been conceived as an American project. In doing so, this chapter sees the TVA and the Mekong as part of several overlapping forms of international cooperation and attempts at community-building. In addition, the US effort to boost Mekong development resulted in stronger internationalist tendencies, but hardly all of them intentional. Johnson's initiative was not intended as a multilateral effort, but nevertheless could only bear some success by latching on to existing international cooperation. Not only was the TVA-inspired Mekong development supported by a wide range of internationally minded actors who had been working on the Mekong prior to US involvement, including the United Nations and the World Bank, but the TVA itself was also part of a wider stream of ideas about regional rejuvenation, water management and dam-building. These included European projects of river management and socio-economic development.

Both the interwar American TVA and the Mekong project were driven by experts and conceptions of technologically infused development. Internationalism in this story does not only entail political activities but in line with Antic et al. also includes 'interrogating the border between technical and political', for example by taking scientific and expert networks into account, while not seeing IOs as monoliths.[14] In line with what historians of technology as well as science and technology scholars have been doing for long, this chapter does not regard Mekong development schemes as purely technical either, and applies Gabrielle Hecht's concept of technopolitics, capturing 'the hybrid forms of power embedded in technological artifacts, systems, and practices'.[15]

This chapter first charts how the TVA came about in connection to wider discussions on river development and dam-building. In a second step, it reviews how ideas stemming from the TVA became part of international discussions on development aid after the Second World War. The main emphasis is on the roles played by the UN and World Bank, bringing notions from the TVA into the spawning international development community. In the last section, the chapter examines plans

[13] Ibid., 196.
[14] Ana Antic, Johanna Conterio, and Dora Vargha, 'Conclusion: Beyond Liberal Internationalism', *Contemporary European History* 25, no. 2 (May 2016): 359–60.
[15] Gabrielle Hecht, 'Introduction', in *Entangled Geographies: Empire and Technopolitics in the Global Cold War*, ed. Gabrielle Hecht (Cambridge, MA: The MIT Press, 2011), 3.

for developing the Mekong River. Initiated by a set of internationally minded actors, the United States joined in 1965. Although intending to forge a unilateral non-military 'front', it had to rely upon the existing internationalist community, and in the end actually strengthened this. The chapters end with a concluding section, which also examines the changing internationalist scene for dam-building.

An international TVA

The TVA was established in 1933 as a New Deal institute aiming to develop backward American southern states along the Tennessee Valley. Turning an often destructive river into a productive force, the TVA built a series of dams to curb flooding and improve river navigation, but most of all to produce electric power. The New Deal body also initiated programmes to combat erosion, agricultural training programmes and social schemes to uplift the rural South. Underpinning the TVA were Rooseveltian ideas not only on planning and nature conservation but also on public intervention.[16] As powerful private electricity utilities refused to serve the countryside, the TVA exemplified the president's notion of public power by stimulating rural electrification.[17] Though the TVA's rise to fame (at least in planning and development circles) would come after 1945, its dams and activities attracted visitors from the start. A 1943 staff memo reported that '[f]oreign and domestic visitors din into our ears the wonders of our achievement'.[18]

At the same time, the TVA is always seen as part of a more international trend of river development and dam-building. Regional newspapers envisioned the Tennessee Valley to become the New Deal version of the German Ruhr Valley.[19] The 1920s saw the erection of single large dams on the Rivers Dnieper (Soviet Union), Colorado and Columbia (the United States), and in the Japanese imperial sphere of influence.[20] Not only was the Ruhr seen as a paradigmatic model for the TVA, many European countries pursued their own water-related projects. In 1933, a public body was set

---

[16] Sarah Phillips, *This Land, This Nation: Conservation, Rural America, and the New Deal* (New York: Cambridge University Press, 2007), 21–3, 30–2.
[17] Thomas K. McCraw, *TVA and the Power Fight, 1933-1939* (Philadelphia: Lippincott, 1971).
[18] Harry S Truman Library and Archive, Independence, MS (hereafter HST), Gordon R. Clapp Papers (1933-1963), Box 2: Tennessee Valley Authority, Folder Staff Meetings – Notes T.V.A., Notes for Staff Meeting – January 11, 1945. On this, also see David Ekbladh, 'Depression Development: The Interwar Origins of a Global US Modernization Agenda', in *Internationalism, Imperialism and the Formation of the Contemporary World*, Palgrave Macmillan Transnational History Series (Cham: Palgrave Macmillan, 2018), 147–63.
[19] See, for example, 'Vast American "Ruhr" Seen for Shoals Are Under Roosevelt', *The Florence Times*, 9 May 1933.
[20] Anne D. Rassweiler, *The Generation of Power: The History of Dneprostroi* (New York: Oxford University Press, 1988); A. F. Yakovlev, 'The V. I. Lenin Dnieper Hydroelectric Station, One of the Earliest Undertakings of Communist Labor', *Hydrotechnical Construction* 3, no. 11 (November 1969): 993–6; Donald Worster, *Rivers of Empire: Water, Aridity, and the Growth of the American West* (New York: Oxford University Press, 1985), 269–71; Aaron Stephen Moore, '"The Yalu River Era of Developing Asia": Japanese Expertise, Colonial Power, and the Construction of Sup'ung Dam', *The Journal of Asian Studies* 72, no. 1 (18 March 2013): 115–39.

up to oversee the development of the River Rhône in France, bearing a great deal of similarity to the TVA.[21]

This seems to indicate the TVA was one example in 1930s experimentation with policies and water-related projects, and the exchange of such ideas.[22] The latter was facilitated by experts consulting in various places around the world. US engineer George Davidson was sent out to China, India, Egypt and Italy in 1875 to seek inspiration for remaking the American West. He would be pivotal in transferring Indian hydraulic knowledge to the Golden State.[23] Hugh Lincoln Cooper, architect of the key TVA dam at Muscle Shoals, was the primary engineer of the vast Dnieprostroi dam. Completed in 1932, this dam was a vital part of Stalin's five-year programme, earning Cooper the prestigious Order of the Red Banner of Labour.[24] Back home, both supporters and opponents made frequent comparisons between TVA and Soviet planning. A popular journal wrote that '[t]he world has seen nothing like [the TVA] before, except in the case of Russia's five-year plans'.[25] This, on the one hand, shows that exchanges with the Soviet Union were still taking place and that colonial as well as European examples left an imprint on the TVA as well.

IOs played a role, too, in setting up this global dam-building community. In 1931, the International Labour Organization (ILO) proposed to coordinate international cooperation on public work projects to stimulate employment.[26] The League of Nations supported this call, which subsequently started to make a survey of ongoing of public works. Though initially restricted to European countries, it was extended to include the United States as well. The inventory regarded the TVA '[o]ne of the most important ventures of the present [US] Administration', and also noted that the federal government made substantial investments in dams aimed at controlling floods, irrigation purposes and electricity generation.[27] ILO's efforts and publications further helped to view New Deal policies including the TVA, as part of a global pool of potential answers to unemployment and underdevelopment.[28] In addition, the 1936 World Power Conference was organized in the US capital, bringing together technicians working

---

[21] Sara B. Pritchard, *Confluence: The Nature of Technology and the Remaking of the Rhône* (Cambridge, MA: Harvard University Press, 2011); Alexandre Giandou, *La Compagnie nationale du Rhône: 1933-1998. Histoire d'un partenaire régional de l'état* (Grenoble: Presses universitaires de Grenoble, 1999).

[22] On these exchanges, see Kiran Klaus Patel, *The New Deal: A Global History* (Princeton, NJ: Princeton University Press, 2016); Daniel Rodgers, *Atlantic Crossings: Social Politics in a Progressive Age* (Cambridge, MA: Belknap Press of Harvard University Press, 1998); Liesbeth van de Grift, Stefan Couperus, and Vincent Lagendijk, 'Experimental Spaces: A Decentered Approach to Planning in High Modernity', *Journal of Modern European History* 13, no. 4 (2015): 476–81.

[23] Worster, *Rivers of Empire*, 147–8; Jessica B. Teisch, *Engineering Nature: Water, Development and the Global Spread of American Environmental Expertise* (Chapel Hill: University of North Carolina Press, 2011), 28–33.

[24] Harold Dorn, 'Hugh Lincoln Cooper and the First Détente', *Technology and Culture* 20, no. 2 (April 1979): 322–47.

[25] Paul Hutchinson, 'Revolution by Electricity', *Scribner's Magazine*, October 1934, 135.

[26] Communications and Transit Organization, 'Circular Concerning Programmes of Important Public Works' (Geneva: League of Nations, 1931), 1.

[27] Organization for Communications and Transit, 'Enquiry on National Public Works' (Geneva: League of Nations, 31 October 1934), 115.

[28] One such publication was Herman Finer, *The T.V.A.: Lessons for International Application* (Montreal: International Labour Office, 1944).

on energy issues. They spent considerable time on New Deal projects, including the TVA. Apart from discussing them, study tours helped to further advertise New Deal achievements as a three-week tour brought participants to the Hoover Dam, finishing off at the TVA before returning to the nation's capital.[29]

After the Second World War, the TVA's role as a template would gain further importance. Much in line with Huxley's conclusion, a wartime study on the TVA argued that '[t]he T.V.A., after its first ten years, came to be looked upon both as a model and as a preliminary to wider developments elsewhere'.[30] He saw the potential of developing the Danube along TVA lines.[31] Again in line with international cooperation, the TVA proved highly compatible with an emerging discourse on development that strongly valued universal solutions that were rooted in technical and scientific expertise. Reinisch has argued that this insistence on technical expertise can be regarded a vector of internationalism as well.[32] At the same time, new IOs established themselves as clearinghouses and conveyor belts of ideas on development and reconstruction. The TVA became an alleged proven model in their development tool box.[33]

The new United Nations Organization (UN) was a key node in this evolution. When announcing the UN's first development assistance programme in 1949, Secretary General Trygve Lie indicated the TVA as a best practice to follow by Asian, African and Latin American countries. He hoped the next twenty years would see 'the development of many T.V.A.'s in many parts of the world'.[34] The relationship between UN and TVA was further deepened at the 1949 UN Scientific Conference on the Conservation and Utilization of Resources (UNSCCUR). The TVA figured prominently throughout the whole conference. A trip to the Tennessee Valley was one of the official excursions, several TVA staffers spoke at the venue, and frequent references were made both during the opening and the closing session. One participant spoke about the TVA as 'one of the most inspiring events of the Conference'.[35] UNSCCUR proved to be a meeting

---

[29] *Transactions: Third World Power Conference*, vol. 1 (Washington, DC: US Government Printing Office, 1938), 32, 109.

[30] Finer, *The T.V.A.*, i.

[31] Vincent Lagendijk, 'Divided Development: Post-War Ideas on River Utilisation and Their Influence on the Development of the Danube', *The International History Review* 37, no. 1 (1 January 2015): 84.

[32] Reinisch, 'Introduction', 103.

[33] For more on this period and context, see Donna Mehos and Suzanne Moon, 'The Uses of Portability: Circulating Experts in the Technopolitics of Cold War and Decolonization', in *Entangled Geographies: Empire and Technopolitics in the Global Cold War*, ed. Gabrielle Hecht (Cambridge, MA: The MIT Press, 2011), 43–74; Daniel Speich Chassé, 'Der Blick von Lake Success: Das Entwicklungsdenken der frühen UNO als "lokales Wissen"', in *Entwicklungswelten: Globalgeschichte der Entwicklungszusammenarbeit*, ed. Hubertus Büschel and Daniel Speich Chassé (Frankfurt: Campus Verlag, 2009), 143–74; Daniel Speich Chassé, 'Technical Internationalism and Economic Development at the Founding Moment of the UN System', in *International Organizations and Development, 1945-1990*, ed. Marc Frey, Sönke Kunkel, and Corinna R. Unger (Palgrave Macmillan, 2014); Jessica Reinisch, 'Internationalism in Relief: The Birth (and Death) of UNRRA', *Past & Present* 210, no. Supplement 6 (January 2011): 258–89.

[34] Trygve Lie, 'Needs for More UN Economic Development Projects – From an Address at the University of Chattanooga, June 6, 1949', in *Public Papers of the Secretaries-General of the United Nations*, vol. 1: Trygve Lie, 1946-1953 (New York: Columbia University Press, 1969), 197–200.

[35] 'Review of the Conference: A Symposium on Future Lines of Study and Directions for Progress', in *Proceedings of the United Nations Scientific Conference on the Conservation and Utilization of*

place for international experts on river development and dam-building, forming an international community of river development experts for years to come.

The World Bank also had a considerable influx of TVA experience, particularly since several key staff members were (former) TVA employees. One such was Alexander D. Spottswood, who was chief Transport and Industrial Economics Division (1937–44) at the TVA before being instrumental in setting up the Bank's engineering department. He would, among other things, make a survey of the Damodar Valley in India, modelled along the lines of the TVA.[36] Another example was Donald D. Fowler, one of the first forty employees of the Bank in 1946. He had held several high bureaucratic positions at the TVA in its planning division but also as a personnel recruiter and deputy secretary.[37] Both the UN and the World Bank would be rallying points for international cooperation in the field of development and proved to be important assets in transferring Western ideas on development.

Whereas during interwar years European developments seemed on par with the United States, this changed drastically after the Second World War. For one, European countries came out of the war looking at the United States for financial assistance and technological know-how. The World Bank was founded in 1944 as the International Bank for Reconstruction and Development, and initially intended for Europe's reconstruction.[38] But soon after the Bank was outspent by the Marshall Plan, it moved into the development business and turned towards the Global South. Michele Alacevich recently spotlighted how European reconstruction was decoupled from the development mission. Yet at the same time, European experiences left strong marks on theories of socio-economic development, in particular those of Britain and Central and Eastern Europe.[39] Many developmental ideas were built upon European (and European colonial) experience, with many former colonial officers moving into the new development IOs.[40] Apart from links with colonial and interwar eras, early post-war development thinking rejuvenated the 'dormant subject of economic growth' of classic European economists like Smith, Mill, Marx, Schumpeter and, more recent, Simon Kuznets.[41] Among other elements, they brought the notion of development as

---

Resources, Volume I: Plenary Meetings, by UN Department of Economic Affairs (Lake Success, New York: United Nations, 1951), 408.

[36] Roscoe C. Martin, 'TVA and International Technical Assistance: A Report to the Board of Directors and the General Manager' (Syracuse, NY, December 1970); General Raymond Wheeler, interview by Robert Oliver, 14 July 1961, 1–2, Oral Histories, Fonds 44, World Bank Group Archives; Aelred Joseph Gray and David A. Johnson, *The TVA Regional Planning and Development Program: The Transformation of an Institution and Its Mission* (Aldershot: Ashgate Publishing, Ltd., 2005), 42.

[37] Adam Bernstein, 'Donald D. Fowler, World Bank Executive', *The Washington Post*, 18 April 2013, 206, http://articles.washingtonpost.com/2013-04-18/local/38641096_1_gujarat-state-spas-vad odara.

[38] Michele Alacevich, *The Political Economy of the World Bank: The Early Years* (Stanford: Stanford Economics and Finance, 2009), 2.

[39] Michele Alacevich, 'Planning Peace: The European Roots of the Post-War Global Development Challenge', *Past & Present* 239, no. 1 (1 May 2018): 221–3.

[40] See for example Joseph M. Hodge, 'British Colonial Expertise, Post-Colonial Careering and the Early History of International Development', *Journal of Modern European History* 8, no. 1 (15 April 2010): 24–46.

[41] Robert Dorfman, 'Review Article: Economic Development from the Beginning to Rostow', *Journal of Economic Literature* 29, no. 2 (June 1991): 581.

a series of stages in a linear way.[42] For economists like Lewis, capital accumulation, combined with technological innovation and knowledge, should lead to the creation of surplus. But often, argued Lewis, backward countries cannot create such surpluses by themselves and hence the import of capital, goods and expertise is required.[43] Lewis was hardly alone, and was supported by economists such as Ragnar Nurkse and Paul Rodan-Rosenstein. All generally insisted on strong state guidance and extensive capital injections.[44]

Whereas Lewis took his cue from experiences in Britain, Egypt, India and Jamaica, the Polish-born Rosenstein-Rodan took Central and Eastern European countries as his example.[45] These countries struggled with labour surplus from the vast agrarian sector – he used the term 'economically backward' to describe this.[46] He saw two potential routes towards industrialization: one where these countries adhere to the international division of labour and the other where the 'Russian' route of autarky is tried – though not necessarily under communism.[47] In any case, Rosenstein proposed that states should coordinate and plan, and act as a guarantor of investments.[48] Apart from taking a strict economic perspective on the issue of development, Rosenstein-Rodan frames the uplifting of the 'economically backward areas of the world [. . .] the most important task facing us in the making of the peace'.[49] His ideas did not just influence developmental thinking; Rosenstein-Rodan became part of the machinery as the assistant director of the Economic Department at the World Bank (1947–53).

Issues of peace and stability also reappeared in the work of Nurkse. Like Rosenstein-Rodan, he emphasized how international economic coordination and helping 'backward' countries would contribute to a more stable and peaceful world. The Estonian Nurkse was one of the League of Nations' most foremost economists,

[42] Gilbert Rist, *The History of Development: From Western Origins to Global Faith* (London: Zed Books, 1997), 40–3.
[43] When combined with productivity increase, the adverse effects on inflation remain fairly limited, claimed Lewis. See W. Arthur Lewis, 'Economic Development with Unlimited Supplies of Labour', *The Manchester School* 22, no. 2 (1954): 420, 439–40.
[44] Frederick Cooper and Randall Packard, 'Introduction', in *International Development and the Social Sciences: Essays on the History and Politics of Knowledge*, ed. Frederick Cooper and Randall Packard (Berkeley, CA: University of California Press, 1997), 13; Michael R. Carter, 'Intellectual Openings and Policy Closures: Disequilibria in Contemporary Development Economics', in *International Development and the Social Sciences: Essays on the History and Politics of Knowledge*, ed. Frederick Cooper and Randall Packard (Berkeley, CA: University of California Press, 1997), 120–1. Also see Ragnar Nurkse, 'International Monetary Policy and the Search for Economic Stability', *The American Economic Review* 37, no. 2 (1947): 569–80; Lewis, 'Economic'; P. N. Rosenstein-Rodan, 'Problems of Industrialisation of Eastern and South-Eastern Europe', *The Economic Journal* 53, no. 210/211 (1 June 1943): 202–11.
[45] Also see Alacevich, 'Planning Peace', 228–9.
[46] He was not the first economist to problematize the agricultural character of the eastern 'half' of Europe. During Interwar years, French economist Francis Delaisi came to a similar conclusion, making a distinction between 'horse-drawn' and 'horse-powered' Europe. See Francis Delaisi, *Les Deux Europes* (Paris: Payot, 1929).
[47] Rosenstein-Rodan, 'Problems', 203–4.
[48] Karla Hoff, 'Beyond Rosenstein-Rodan: The Modern Theory of Underdevelopment Traps' (The World Bank, 10 April 2000), http://documents.worldbank.org/curated/en/2000/04/3357887/beyond-rosenstein-rodan-modern-theory-underdevelopment-traps.
[49] P. N. Rosenstein-Rodan, 'The International Development of Economically Backward Areas', *International Affairs (Royal Institute of International Affairs 1944-*, 20, no. 2 (1 April 1944): 159.

and co-authored key publications on the transition from war to peace.[50] After the Second World War, he advocated strong state-interference in economic and financial affairs, while bearing in mind international policy adjustments on trade and monetary policy.[51] With that, he placed his hopes on financial and technical assistance from new multilateral organizations, specifically the UN and the World Bank. The conceptions of Rosenstein and Nurkse seemed to combine economic and technical aspects, blended with a form of internationalist idealism, tying economic and financial stability to peace. The aspect of attaining peace also reappeared in TVA-related discourses, as well as within IOs working in the field of development.

The TVA and the Mekong project

Similar notions returned in the discourse regarding the TVA on the Mekong. By the time the Johnson Administration gained an interest in the Mekong's development, international cooperation had been under way since 1955. Sparked by the disintegration of European empires in Asia, the River Mekong had become the focal point for socio-economic improvement of the riparian nations. Regional actors, relatively benign Western powers and IOs set up what became known as the so-called Mekong project. A key agency was the UN Economic Commission for Asia and the Far East (ECAFE). As part of its work on flood control, it instigated an initial survey of the river, conducted by the US Bureau of Reclamation in 1955. It also built upon a French colonial framework, focused on international river navigation on the river.[52] Appropriating ideas from the TVA, ECAFE issued a manual for river development, authored by Indian engineer Kanwar Sain. The manual recognized the American agency as the best example of comprehensive planning with unified control, coordinating the development of land and other resources with the river.[53] In that, the international community had embraced the TVA as a model, without directly relying upon a US intermediary.

Following this initial phase, ECAFE sponsored a study tour of an international group of experts in 1957. They reported that '[t]he Mekong is a majestic river' and once 'developed, this river could easily rank with Southeast Asia's greatest natural resources. Wise conservation and utilization of its waters will contribute more towards improving human welfare in this area than any other single undertaking.'[54] International

---

[50] League of Nations and Financial Economic and Transit Department, *The Transition from War to Peace Economy* (Geneva: League of Nations, 1943).

[51] Nurkse, 'International Monetary Policy'; Patricia Clavin, *Securing the World Economy: The Reinvention of the League of Nations, 1920-1946* (Oxford: Oxford University Press, 2013), 308.

[52] M. Bidault, Ministre des Affaires Étrangères, à M. Varet, Secrétaire Général du Comité interministériel pour l'Indocine, D.N° 659, Paris, 4 July 1947, in France Ministère des affaires étrangères, *Documents diplomatiques Français: 1947 – Tome II (1er juillet–31 Décembre)* (Brussels: Peter Lang, 2009).

[53] UNECAFE, *Manual of River Basin Planning*, Multiple Purpose River Basin Development 1 (Bangkok: United Nations, 1955), 8.

[54] United Nations, 'Programme of Studies and Investigations for Comprehensive Development of the Lower Mekong River Basin: Report of United Nations Survey Mission, 19 November 1957–23 January 1958' (New York: United Nations, 1958), 6.

cooperation was subsequently institutionalized in 1957 as the Committee for Co-ordination of Investigations of the Lower Mekong Basin, or Mekong Committee, composed of Cambodia, Laos, Thailand and South Vietnam. Communist China and Burma declined participation.

Despite the absence of communist nations, the Mekong Committee received extensive international support. Australia and Canada supported the Mekong efforts through the Colombo Plan, to be used for producing more accurate maps of the Lower Mekong Basin. The Japanese government dispatched a reconnaissance team in 1959 to study several Mekong tributaries. Assistance also came in kind: Iran provided fuel while New Zealand provided four jet crafts for river exploration. These support pledges underwrite the truly global (i.e. not limited to the Western world) involvement and optimism, making the Mekong project an example of post-1945 internationalist efforts.[55] With that help, the Mekong Committee presented three major river projects in 1958. Situated on the main river, all three were expensive and challenging dam projects.

No surprise then that the Mekong Committee also pursued less ambitious projects on tributary rivers. One prime site surveyed by the Japanese reconnaissance team was Nam Ngum, north of the Laotian capital Vientiane. Work by the Japanese firm Nippon Koei indicated that Nam Ngum dam could provide both electricity and irrigation. It would become the Mekong Committee's most prominent pilot project, but also a long and tensed process, spanning a period from 1959 until its dedication in 1971. To acquire funding, the Committee first supported a Laotian request to the World Bank in 1962.[56] Laos aspired the dam to be an integral piece in their modernization programme. To the Mekong Committee's disappointment, the Bank negatively assessed the project in 1963. While recognizing Nam Ngum as the Mekong Committee's best project thus far, the World Bank did see 'sufficient justification for embarking on the construction of the project'.[57] The World Bank also saw Nam Ngum as politically 'tricky', with Laos practically in a state of civil war split between a neutralist government and a communist insurgency, and both sides sponsored by the superpowers.[58] Despite this rejection, both the Mekong Committee and the Laotian government continued to lobby the Bank.[59]

While US involvement for the Mekong endeavour is often highlighted in the literature, Washington's role was not a prominent one at this stage.[60] And this was purposefully. In 1957, State Department had advised against becoming too involved in

[55] UN Document E/CN.11/475, 24 February 1958: Report of the Committee for Co-ordination of Investigation of the Lower Mekong Basin, 2.
[56] The World Bank Group Archives, Washington, DC (hereafter: WBGA), 182920B, Laos – Nam Ngum Multipurpose Project, Letter CHS to Cargil, 26 October 1962, 'Possible International Bank Mission to Laos and Nam Ngum Project'.
[57] WBGA, 182920B, Letter Michael L. Lejeune (ass director, Department of Operations, Far East) to Phouangphet Phanareth (Sec of State for Finance, Laos), 14 May 1963.
[58] Odd Arne Westad, *The Global Cold War: Third World Interventions and the Making of Our Times* (Cambridge: Cambridge University Press, 2005), 128 and 189.
[59] WBGA, 182920B, Memorandum by Arthur Karasz to Files, 5 September 1963, 'Laos'.
[60] See, for example, David Ekbladh, '"Mr. TVA": Grass-Roots Development, David Lilienthal, and the Rise and Fall of the Tennessee Valley Authority as a Symbol for U.S. Overseas Development, 1933-1973', *Diplomatic History* 26, no. 3 (2002): 335–74; Brian VanDeMark, *Into the Quagmire: Lyndon Johnson and the Escalation of the Vietnam War* (New York and Oxford: Oxford University

the Mekong project, arguing that '[a]ntagonism toward regional cooperation is deep-seated, especially in Cambodia, and premature United States action could, therefore, be counterproductive'.[61] Neither did the United States expect much from the Mekong scheme, and had in mind 'nothing even remotely comparable to a Tennessee Valley Authority'.[62] Though endorsing the Mekong Committee's efforts because of its potential (political) significance, the United States hardly played an active role.[63]

But Johnson's 1965 speech entailed a considerable shift in policy and framed the Mekong project as an extension of US foreign policy – and this is also how scholars have depicted it. Yet the White House could not ignore the existing international groundwork, nor could it do without the help of IOs to be able to have some success. The Johnson Administration hoped to forge a more peaceful front of economic development in the region, get North Vietnam involved and improve domestic support for its Southeast Asian policy.[64] But LBJ's hopes were feeble as Hanoi responded with conditions: end the bombing raids against the North and a complete military withdrawal from South Vietnam.[65] Not complying with these wishes, Washington remained persistent supporting the Mekong's development. US officials therefore started to exert pressure on the Mekong Committee and the UN, bringing the World Bank into the fold as well. What was intended as a unilateral effort now became a development front in the escalating Vietnam War requiring an internationalist underpinning. The White House asked Eugene Black, former World Bank president (1949–63), to broker between the various parties. Black hoped the Mekong Committee could transform itself an agency more akin to the TVA, 'a Mekong Development Authority'.[66] Now having to rely upon the existing web of international relations made the Johnson Administration into an example of reluctant internationalism. At the same time, it made the Mekong venture an internationalist project where war acted as a catalyst, and a patchwork of overlapping, if not competing, internationalist perceptions came about.

This patchwork consisted of the United States, but also the continuous support of the higher echelons of the UN, including Secretary-General U Thant, and ECAFE's secretary general U Nyun, as well as the leadership of the United Nations Development Programme (UNDP).[67] But it would also include the World Bank.

Press, 1995), 123–5; Michael Adas, *Dominance by Design: Technological Imperatives and America's Civilizing Mission* (Cambridge, MA: Belknap Press of Harvard University Press, 2006), 330.

[61] National Archives of the Unites States, College Park, MA (hereafter: NARA), Record Group 59, Office of Southeast Asian Affairs, Records Relating to Cambodia and Vietnam, 1953-1958, Entry# UD 51, Box 4, Folder Briefings 1957, 'Development of the Lower Mekong River Basin', 4/8/57, by J. A. Mendenhall and C.H. Price, p. 2.

[62] Ibidem.

[63] NARA, RG 59, Box 1, Entry P 161, Classified Report of United States Delegation to the 18th Session, Economic Commission on Asia and the Far East, Tokyo, 6–8 March 1962, by Philip M. Klutznick, Chairman of the Delegation, 19 March 1962.

[64] Dror Yuravlivker, '"Peace without Conquest": Lyndon Johnson's Speech of April 7, 1965', *Presidential Studies Quarterly* 36, no. 3 (2006): 468.

[65] VanDeMark, *Into the Quagmire*, 123–4.

[66] United Nations Organisation Archives, New York City (hereafter: UNARMS), S-0200-2-1, 'Notes on Meeting held at United Nations Headquarters at 9 a.m. on Monday 19 April 1965'.

[67] WBGA, 182920B, Off Mem A.D. Spottswood to Gordon Street, June 8, 1964, 'Nam Ngum Project – Laos'.

Reluctant to fund Nam Ngum, their position changed once the United States announced in May 1965 that it would pay 40 per cent of Nam Ngum's construction, provided that other countries provided the remainder in the form of grants – including Denmark and the Netherlands.[68] Otherwise European involvement was rather limited and indirect. The Bank hence agreed to take on the role of administrating the grants and supervise the construction process. In the meantime, and despite the civil strife, the Mekong Committee claimed it had secured support for the dam of all Laotian parties – the neutralists, the communists and the royalists – embraced Nam Ngum as a 'nation building' project, and thus would not interfere with its construction.[69]

The signing of the agreement for Nam Ngum came with exuberance. Laos saw it as a huge step forward for human improvement, and even World Bank officials lauded the strength of the 'Mekong spirit'.[70] Underlining the change of heart, Johnson said in 1967 that US aid had morphed 'from *American* programs to build Asia to *world* programs to build Asia', mainly through the World Bank and new Asian Development Bank, suggesting that Washington had come to accept the internationalist reality.[71]

But Nam Ngum's construction in the end was hampered by civil strife. While the dam site was left untouched, various armed hostilities affected nearby military installations and scared the construction workers.[72] Yet the dam was completed on schedule in 1971. One internationalist outcome was a power line from Nam Ngum in Laos to Thailand, two countries without official diplomatic relations nor physical connections (the first bridge was put up in 1994). It transferred electricity generated at Nam Ngum into Thailand. Perhaps the *international* outcome of this effort was best exemplified by a sign put up underneath the power cables crossing the Thai-Laotian border. The sign lauded the UN's contribution by adorning their well-known logo at the top, but also the role of the so-called Mekong Committee, and the help of the Western world as crucial supporters and donors to the Mekong project as a whole. While stressing the UN's and the Mekong Committee's role, it effectively ignored the US impulse for Nam Ngum and made it part of the internationalist tendencies buttressing the Mekong effort altogether.

---

[68] WBGA, Folder 1881467, A1995-181, Box # 2, 182920B, Laos – Nam Ngum Multipurpose Project (United Nations Mekong) (UNDP) Correspondence II, Telegram Spottswood to Goodman, 12 May 1965.

[69] WBGA, 182920B, Memo of Melmoth to Files, 19 January 1965, 'Visit of U Nyun, Secretary General, ECAFE'.

[70] WBGA, 182924B, Letter Arthur Goldschmidt (Director for Special Fund Operations, Dep of Econ and Soc Affairs, UN) to Peter Cargill (Director of Operations, Far East, WB), 8 April 1966.

[71] Emphasis in the original. 'Special Message to the Congress Proposing a U.S. Contribution to the 'Special Funds' of the Asian Development Bank', 26 September 1967, in United States et al., *Public Papers of the Presidents of the United States, Lyndon B. Johnson: Containing the Public Messages, Speeches, and Statements of the President* (Washington, DC: U.S. Government Printing Office, 1965), 860–4.

[72] See, for example, UNARMS, S-200-02-04: Nam Ngum Project – General Correspondence and Memoranda (1014), telegram UPI-41 (Laos), 25 July 1969, and WBGA, 12923B, A19950181, Laos – UN Mekong Nam Ngum Project Administration 1969- I, Memo from Gibbs to Files, 'Laos – Nam Ngum', 8 August 1969.

Conclusions

Often taken as *the* post-war development project, the TVA never was solely an American invention. It always was part of more global conversations on development and river utilization. The Soviet Union prominently engaged in erecting large dams, and in France similar endeavours were planned. When the Depression hit hard, European countries committed to public works and government-led planning, assisted by IOs. After the Second World War, the European primacy in global politics waned. This is also observable in the Mekong endeavour; while European expertise and experience play a role at the beginning, the explicit involvement of European governments is quite limited. Across the Atlantic, the United States emerged out of the war as arguably the most potent actor on the international stage, as the main supplier of capital and technical know-how. The TVA found a niche in the latter.

IOs played a key role in popularizing interwar TVA ideas, and their development ideologies were grounded in European (Central and Eastern Europe) and colonial experience alike. Initially intended for European reconstruction, this quickly reoriented towards the Global South. This is also how the River Mekong came into the crosshairs of developmental thinking. Here the regional initially took the lead, supported by IOs, while the United States remained interested yet at arm's length. This changed rather abruptly in 1965.

In his announcement to provide a billion dollars for the common development of the Mekong – including to communist countries such as North Vietnam and China – President Johnson also suggested that the TVA would be eclipsed by the Mekong's potential. This episode has received strong emphasis in development literature and studies of US foreign relations. While taking its cue from the TVA, which in turn was influenced by colonial and European experiences, the Mekong project did not necessarily only evolve around direct US involvement. Indeed, while supporting the Mekong efforts through technical assistance, Washington initially refused to be politically tied to the project. Its stance changed with the escalation of the Vietnam War, but Johnson's peace-through-development suggestion was rejected almost immediately. The Mekong Committee, the institutional arm of this river development endeavour, was supported by a diverse international group of countries as well as the United Nations. Internationalist tendencies thus proved to be strong. The international community of the Mekong was so strong that US involvement, while intended to be unilateral, had to rely upon these forces in order to have some tangible results.

Interestingly enough, this turned the Johnson Administration into a vector of 'reluctant internationalism' – not intending to rely upon the international community but seeing no other way to reap benefits, which materialized in the Nam Ngum dam. Its involvement brought the Mekong Committee its first major success, and also brought aboard the World Bank, which through its 'good offices' helped play a role in fostering a development project in a troubled region. In addition, Johnson's initiative came about in response to the expansion of the Vietnam War, making war the catalyst of this rejuvenation of the Mekong internationalist venture. This makes the

US involvement akin to what Antic et al. label the 'dark' force of internationalism.[73] Washington's involvement did not have liberal-internationalist aims at the forefront. Instead, it sought to help legitimize its military intervention in Vietnam.

The further history of the Mekong's development proves that internationalism is neither stable nor always perceived to be a positive force. For one, the alleged Mekong Spirit faltered over the course of the 1970s. With the communists taking over in Cambodia, it no longer responded to the Mekong Committee's invitations.[74] For another, the early 1970s also saw the emergence of profound international actions in the realm of the environment and conservation. Alternative visions to the large-scale reworking of rivers had always existed, insisting on smaller-scale development and what were labelled as 'appropriate technologies'.[75] With the UN picking up the issue of environmental change at the Stockholm Conference of 1972, the development regime slowly underwent a change.

Hence a new internationalist tendency emerged in the shape of internationally oriented opposition to dam-building, correlating with 'increasing grassroots mobilization and growing numbers of nongovernmental advocacy organizations in domestic civil societies'.[76] This greatly amplified the power to influence decision making on dams. One example was the NGO International Rivers Network (IRN). Formed in 1987, the IRN brought together a group of activists that started to publish a bulletin entitled 'International Dams Newsletter' in 1985, at the occasion of Hoover Dam's fiftieth birthday.[77] Due to the increased pressures, the World Bank eventually withdrew its support for several projects, the most prestigious one probably being the Narmada River scheme. The main bone of contention was the displacement of people due to the dams, which was estimated to be between 39,700 to 205,000 people. Arguably, the biggest success of the anti-dam movement was the creation of a new institution that operates as an interface between proponents and opponents, the World Commission on Dams (WCD). The WCD was established following a workshop in Gland, Switzerland, in 1997, and participants concluded that the differences between 'builders' and activists appeared insurmountable and needed a constructive platform.[78]

---

[73] For more on 'dark' versions of internationalism, in contrast to its often default form of liberal internationalism, see Antic, Conterio, and Vargha, 'Conclusion', 365; Kiran Klaus Patel and Sven Reichardt, 'The Dark Side of Transnationalism: Social Engineering and Nazism, 1930s-40s', *Journal of Contemporary History* 51, no. 1 (11 January 2016): 3–21.

[74] 'Mekong Talks Called Off', *Bangkok Post*, 19 October 1975.

[75] Stephen J. Macekura, *Of Limits and Growth: The Rise of Global Sustainable Development in the Twentieth Century*, Global and International History (New York: Cambridge University Press, 2015), chap. 4. On small-scale development ideas, some of which also stemmed from TVA, see E. F. Schumacher, *Small Is Beautiful: Economics as If People Mattered* (New York: HarperPerennial, 1989); Daniel Immerwahr, *Thinking Small: The United States and the Lure of Community Development* (Cambridge, MA: Harvard University Press, 2015).

[76] Sanjeev Khagram, *Dams and Development: Transnational Struggles for Water and Power* (Ithaca, NY: Cornell University Press, 2004), 190.

[77] Guro Aandahl, 'Technocratic Dreams and Troublesome Beneficiaries: The Sardar Sarovar (Narmada) Project in Gujarat' (Submitted, University of Oslo, Faculty of Social Sciences, 2010), 87.

[78] World Commission on Dams, *Dams and Development: A New Framework for Decision-Making* (London: Earthscan Publications, 2000), 104, 21.

It again shows how internationalist tendencies remain key in the dam-building and development discussions, but hardly as stable entities. The TVA, usefully framed as a US model only, played a key part in this international community. While initially regarded as an international inspiration, the subsequent model of development is now under strong pressure from newly emerging international communities. Due to this new movement, while Southeast Asian countries, and Laos in particular, still aspire to dam the river, it is hardly likely that a dammed and developed Mekong River will ever be perceived to be 'better than the real thing'.

Afterword

On the chances and challenges of populating internationalism

Kiran Klaus Patel

Some forty years ago, in 1980, Charles S. Maier published a devastating critique of the state of the art in the history of international relations. Once the pivot for the rise of history to become an academic discipline in its own right, the history of international relations had turned into a 'stepchild'. Unabashedly old-fashioned methods, narrowly cast inquiries and parochial perspectives guided the debates. Maier, a specialist in European history, was particularly disdainful of American diplomatic history as merely 'marking time', but in those days similar criticism was also voiced in Europe.[1]

International history has come a long way since then, and today the theme of internationalism is much more than just a 'whisper in narratives of the past'.[2] In fact, the field is now one of the most thriving domains of historical inquiry. Certainly, globalization and the tectonic changes in the international system have become processes too big to ignore. But innovation in historiography also helps to explain the new hype. Possibly the most important reason in this respect lies in the field's fundamental reorientation beyond the concerns and approaches once associated with a traditionalist form of diplomatic history. Its boundaries have become ever fuzzier, with inroads, synergies and overlaps, as well as new bifurcations, vis-à-vis cultural, imperial, global and environmental history along with the history of emotions, to name but a few. Forty, and even twenty years ago, books with (sub)titles such as *The Emotions of Internationalism* and *The Emotional Strategies of the Équipe Mitterrand*

---

[1] Charles S. Maier, 'Marking Time: The Historiography of International Relations', in *The Past Before Us: Contemporary Historical Writing in the United States*, ed. Michael G. Kammen (Ithaca: Cornell University Press, 1980), 355–87, quote 355; see, for example, also 'Responses to Charles S. Maier, "Marking Time: The Historiography of International Relations"', *Diplomatic History* 5 (1981): 353–82; Patrick Finney, 'Still 'Marking Time'? Text, Discourse and Truth in International History', *Review of International Studies* 27 (2001): 291–308; on the debates in Europe during the 1980s and 1990s, see the comprehensive surveys in: Wilfried Loth and Jürgen Osterhammel, eds, *Internationale Geschichte. Themen – Ergebnisse – Aussichten* (Munich: Oldenbourg, 2000); as one of the most recent references to the debate to Maier's intervention, Erez Manela, 'International Society as a Historical Subject', *Diplomatic History* 44 (2020): 184–209.

[2] Glenda Sluga and Patricia Clavin, 'Rethinking the History of Internationalism', in *Internationalisms: A Twentieth-Century History*, ed. Glenda Sluga and Patricia Clavin (Cambridge: Cambridge University Press, 2017), 3–14, quote 3.

would hardly have been conceivable,[3] and domains such as the history of development – today a major branch of international history – were mostly uncharted.[4] The title of a recent stocktaking exercise in Italian sums up the state of the art: 'Una storia, tante storie', probably best translated as 'One (hi)story, many (hi)stories'.[5]

The present volume is part of this movement and helps to push the boundaries in interesting new ways. The contributions highlight the diversity and ubiquity of European actors who populated the international sphere and propagated their respective visions and ideas. In so doing, the book seeks to examine their background, the constellations they were part of and the outcome of these interactions. In what follows, I will first highlight three of its key concerns, and findings that I find particularly noteworthy (I). I will then briefly lay out two ideas that might help to develop the book's agenda of paying more attention to the internationalists themselves, examining the subject through the lens and lives of specific people (II), before summarizing my findings (III).

I

Rediscovering Europe

Over the past decades, research has stressed the need to overcome Eurocentrism. The new interest in international and global history since the 1990s often went hand in hand with sidestepping Europe as an empirical field of observation. Given how long phenomena and processes primarily located in or associated with Europe have stood in the limelight of research, and have defined the very notion of the international, this development was long overdue. Consequently, many studies over the past twenty years have assessed global links revolving around other actors and geographies than those

---

[3] See, for example, Ilaria Scaglia, *The Emotions of Internationalism: Feeling International Cooperation in the Alps in the Interwar Period* (Oxford: Oxford University Press, 2019); Frederike Schotters, *Frankreich und das Ende des Kalten Krieges. Gefühlsstrategien der équipe Mitterrand 1981–1990* (Berlin: De Gruyter, 2019); Miguel Bandeira Jerónimo and José Pedro Monteiro, eds, *Internationalism, Imperialism and the Formation of the Contemporary World: The Pasts of the Present* (Basingstoke: Palgrave Macmillan, 2018).

[4] See, for example, Sara Lorenzini, *Global Development: A Cold War History* (Princeton: Princeton University Press, 2019); Stephen J. Macekura and Erez Manela, eds, *The Development Century: A Global History* (Cambridge: Cambridge University Press, 2018); Marc Frey, Sönke Kunkel and Corinna Unger, eds, *International Organizations and Development, 1945–1990* (Basingstoke: Palgrave Macmillan, 2014).

[5] Mariele Merlati and Daniela Vignati, eds, *Una storia, tante storie. Studi di storia internazionale* (Milano: FrancoAngeli, 2019); as other recent exercises of stocktaking see, for example, Giulia Bentivoglio and Antonio Varsori, eds, *Realtà e immagine della politica esterna italiana* (Milano: FrancoAngeli, 2017); Mario del Pero and Guido Formigoni, 'Storia internazionale, transnazionale, globale: una discussione', *Ricerche di Storia Politica* 19, no. 3 (2016): 263–393 (special issue); Pierre Grosser, 'Etat de littérature. L'histoire des relations internationales aujourd'hui', *Critique internationale* 65 (2014): 173–200; Barbara Haider-Wilson, William D. Godsey and Wolfgang Mueller, eds, *International History in Theory and Practice* (Vienna: Verlag der Österreichischen Akademie der Wissenschaften, 2017); Jost Dülffer and Wilfried Loth, eds, *Dimensionen internationaler Geschichte* (Munich: Oldenbourg, 2012); Robert Frank, ed., *Pour l'histoire des relations internationales* (Paris: Presses Universitaires de France, 2012).

associated with Europe, and rightly so.[6] Having said that, this move sometimes created imbalances and false dichotomies. Such work was prone to ignore Europe's ongoing role in world affairs. Moreover, its tendency to conflate anglophone actors with Europe and the West more broadly glossed over Europe's internal diversity. Against the backdrop of these shortcomings, we now witness renewed attention to Europe, but a different Europe than before. The interest in Europeans' role (from both East and West) in drilling loopholes into the Cold War Iron Curtain is only one example of how recent work has reinserted their actorship into a larger historiographical debate.[7] In a similar vein, this book seeks to reinstate European actors into the picture. But it does not hark back to an old understanding that puts diplomacy at the centre of internationalism; instead, it situates European internationalists within a global landscape and, through this process, tries to understand how internationalists have contributed to the making of Europe – not just through various forms of cooperation but also by competing with each other over which vision would dominate and consequently be identified as 'European' within and beyond its shores. This rightly implies seeing European internationalists in their diversity, beyond lumping them together into a single epistemically, culturally and politically homogenous group – as post-colonial and global studies sometimes tend to do.

Beyond that, some of the chapters provide astute analyses of how nominally 'international' endeavours were actually European. Although bearing the banner of internationalism, they were in fact driven by European agendas, epistemes and actors. As Heidi Tworek demonstrates, the International Telegraph Union became a central puzzle piece in the global communication infrastructure that institutionalized linguistic hierarchies between Europe and the rest of the world – and privileged some European languages over others. In a similar vein, Basic English epitomizes a specific British imperial version of Western and European liberal internationalism, as Valeska Huber convincingly argues. And, as Elidor Mëhilli underscores, socialist internationalism helped to turn the radio station of a small, often-overlooked European country into a global voice of communism. What this demonstrates is that Europeans were highly effective in cloaking their specific concerns as international, and that it is extremely productive and necessary to probe and deconstruct such claims.

This does not imply that non-European actors were mere powerless objects in the international arena. Discussing Jawaharlal Nehru, Valeska Huber briefly mentions

---

[6] See, for example, Torsten Weber, *Embracing 'Asia' in China and Japan: Asianism Discourse and the Contest for Hegemony, 1912–1933* (Basingstoke: Palgrave Macmillan, 2018); Pedro Iacobelli, Danton Leary and Shinnosuke Takahashi, eds, *Transnational Japan as History: Empire, Migration, and Social Movements* (Basingstoke: Palgrave Macmillan, 2016); Tim Harper and Sunil Amrith, eds, *Sites of Asian Interaction: Ideas, Networks and Mobility* (Cambridge: Cambridge University Press, 2014); Madeleine Herren, ed, *Networking the International System: Global Histories of International Organizations* (Berlin: Springer, 2014); Cemil Aydin, *The Politics of Anti-Westernism in Asia: Visions of World Order in Pan-Islamic and Pan-Asian Thought* (New York: Columbia University Press, 2007).

[7] See, for example, Lars Stöcker, *Bridging the Baltic Sea: Networks of Resistance and Opposition during the Cold War Era* (Lanham, MD: Lexington Books, 2017); Oliver Bange and Poul Villaume, eds, *The Long Détente: Changing Concepts of Security and Cooperation in Europe, 1950s–1980s* (Budapest: CEU Press, 2017); Simo Mikkonen and Pia Koivunen, eds, *Beyond the Divide: Entangled Histories of Cold War Europe* (New York: Berghahn, 2015).

that non-European actors sometimes sought to use European ideas for their own, very different ends. Vincent Lagendijk highlights one of the twentieth century's many instances in which European primacy in global affairs withered away, as the United States emerged as the main player on the international stage (although its approach remained grounded in European and colonial experiences). Beyond that, actors from the Global South deserve special attention; for the focus of this book, it is particularly interesting to see how they interacted with 'Europeanisms' that were dressed up as 'internationalisms'. Obviously, one way of rejecting European claims was to propose other 'isms', such as Pan-Africanism or Pan-Asianism, as explicit alternatives. But the European rhetoric of the international also opened an option for non-Europeans to challenge the meaning of the respective 'international' on its own terms. The International Labour Organization (ILO) is an excellent example: while it originally had a strong European bias with regard to its ideational mooring, institutional scaffolding and personnel, the interwar years already saw interesting developments, with actors, for instance, in Latin America striving to redesign it according to their own needs. From being a form of Europeanism in disguise, ILO internationalism expanded into new directions, and its allegedly global appeal made this development all the more logical.[8] Recent work on UNESCO's programmes points in a similar direction, seeing an agenda originally shaped by specifically European understandings of culture and heritage incrementally gravitating in new directions. Here again, non-Europeans played interesting roles. For instance, the Ethiopian government and its experts embraced existing Western notions in the World Heritage programme during the 1960s and 1970s, while also employing them to support nationalist ends.[9] In the Universal History of Humanity programme, in contrast, UNESCO member states from the Global South had been pushing for a less Eurocentric approach since the 1960s.[10] In UNESCO's World Heritage List negotiations, actors from the Global South were less prominent in the development of visions of heritage dissociated from Eurocentric notions; here it was mostly Europeans and Americans who argued that Eurocentrism had to be overcome.[11] Obviously, none of these examples implies that internationalism became 'truly' international. It was simply different mixes and blends of ideas that now shaped UNESCO's agenda. These examples show the diversity of constellations and dynamics, the need to de-naturalize notions of Europe and to critically assess Europeanist claims and their alternatives.

And, as a final thought on the relationship between Europe and internationalism: interestingly, the European Union and its predecessors since the 1950s hardly feature in this collection. They crop up in Monika Baár's chapter on disability internationalism and make a quick cameo appearance in the book's introduction. But otherwise, this

---

[8] Guy Fiti Sinclair, *To Reform the World: International Organizations and the Making of Modern States* (Oxford: Oxford University Press, 2017).
[9] Marie Huber, 'Ethiopia and the Beginnings of the UNESCO World Heritage Progamme 1960-1980' (unpubl. PhD thesis, Humboldt University, Berlin, 2017).
[10] Chloé Maurel, 'L'UNESCO: un âge d'or de l'aide au développement par l'éducation (1945–1975)', *Cahiers d'histoire: revue d'histoire critique* 108 (2009): 145–70.
[11] Aurélie Elisa Gfeller, 'Negotiating the Meaning of Global Heritage: "Cultural Landscapes" in the UNESCO World Heritage Convention, 1972-92', *Journal of Global History* 8 (2013): 483–503.

forum and the men and women who populated it play no role whatsoever. Even Baár does not give the EU the pride of place, but puts it in the context of other international organizations. It is futile to speculate why this form of European internationalism does not figure more prominently in the specific set of case studies assembled in this book. But it is a stark reminder that the EU's rise to become the foremost, and on many issues even dominant forum of international organization in Europe is quite recent. In my own work, I have argued that this process only started for Western Europe during the 1970s and 1980s, and for other parts of the continent obviously even more recently.[12] The findings of this collection seem to point into a similar direction. This again underscores the multiplicity of internationalisms in Europe, and the added value in explicitly studying the European or internationalist rhetoric of internationalists – including the question of what such terms implied or hid, and how they were subject to change over time.

Diversifying internationalism

A second historiographical current to which the chapters in this collection contribute is a more nuanced understanding of internationalism, beyond its liberal-democratic variants. This development is highly welcome, and it is probably useful to put it in a wider historiographical context. It was only for a comparably short period that research concentrated on internationalism as a liberal, anti-nationalist project. For most of the twentieth century, even this form of internationalism remained on the margins of scholarly enquiry. Instead, historical scholarship was preoccupied with the role of states and their foreign policies, often undergirded by what political scientists would call 'realist' notions of the world. Realists have never shied away from analysing the ways in which dictators, autocrats and other opponents of liberalism have projected power internationally, with Adolf Hitler and Joseph Stalin as prime examples. Research of that kind was essential for diplomatic history. It is only since the 1990s that a new historiographical trend started to break the dominance of state-centred approaches, with their tendency to see the international as a mere function of national interests. At the epistemological level, this was a move beyond realism informed by the cultural turn in the humanities and the social sciences. In history, it expressed itself in new research questions and the rise of transnational history. Quickly turning into a fashion, transnational history sought to capture a past that transcended the bounds of nations.[13] Its initial impulse to focus on liberal and possibly also anti-nationalist forms of internationalism, for instance in the work of Akira Iriye as one of its pioneers, must thus be seen against the backdrop of the diplomatic history mainstream of the time.[14] Scholars of this branch tended to perceive the prism of the nation state as a conceptual prison. Hence the emphasis on pacifists, feminists, anti-imperialists and

---

[12] Kiran Klaus Patel, *Project Europe: A History* (Cambridge: Cambridge University Press, 2020).
[13] See, for example, Kiran Klaus Patel, 'An Emperor without Clothes? The Debate about Transnational History Twenty-Five Years On', *histoire@politique*, 26 (2015), online: http://www.histoire-politique.fr/index.php?numero=26&rub=pistes&item=32 (last accessed 1 May 2020).
[14] See, most importantly, Akira Iriye, *Global Community: The Role of International Organizations in the Making of the Contemporary World* (Berkeley: University of California Press, 2004).

other groupings and their organizations, which tend to be associated with liberal brands of internationalism. Moreover, research on liberal internationalism often tried to overcome deterministic and teleological accounts, particularly for the pre- and the interwar years, since both phases ended with a lethal crisis of liberal transborder engagement. This concern, for instance, explains the interest in the League of Nations shown by transnational history since the late 1990s.[15] This historiographical context as well as the political and cultural climate in a new era of globalization at the end of the Cold War help to explain the emphatic tone of some publications particularly during the first wave of transnational research during the 1990s and early 2000s. Put differently: breaking away from orthodox diplomatic history created its own biases.

But as David Brydan and Jessica Reinisch rightly argue, liberal internationalism is no longer the only or main historiographical concern, and the 'Reluctant Internationalists' project mentioned in the book's introduction has clearly contributed to this development.[16] Over the past twenty years, scholars have worked hard to disassociate 'international' from a narrow definition focusing on liberal forms of cross-border links. They have widened the panorama of ideological and institutional currents under study. Utopian illusions of a rediscovered transnational past paving the way for a better future have long evaporated. Less benign forms of internationalism have attracted a lot of attention over the past two decades, with fascist internationalism recently generating vibrant debate. This trend has injected new life into research on fascism more broadly, where the dominant comparative approach had become somewhat sterile before the transnational turn.[17] And fascist internationalism is only one example of how broadly the debate has impacted wider historiographical contexts; similar things can be said for research on socialist internationalism.[18]

Today, many historians would agree with Glenda Sluga and Patricia Clavin who recently argued that 'categorisations of internationalism as either good or bad should

---

[15] See as a signal and first summary of new research on the League in the mid-2000s, Susan Pedersen, 'Back to the League of Nations', *American Historical Review* 112 (2007): 1091–117; as two of the latest publications on the League, which provide evidence on the continuous interest in this topic, Haakon A. Ikonomou and Karen Gram-Skjoldager, eds, *The League of Nations: Perspectives from the Present* (Aarhus: Aarhus University Press, 2019); Simon Jackson and Alanna O'Malley, eds, *The Institution of International Order: From the League of Nations to the United Nations* (London: Routledge, 2018).

[16] Also see Jessica Reinisch, 'Introduction: Agents of Internationalism', *Contemporary European History* 25 (2016): 195–205.

[17] See as an overview by a leading expert in the field Madeleine Herren, 'Fascist Internationalism', in: *Internationalisms*, eds. Sluga and Clavin, 191–212, though quite a number of contributions have again been published since her chapter came out.

[18] See, as a few examples, Talbot C. Imlay, *The Practice of Socialist Internationalism: European Socialists and International Politics, 1914-1960* (Oxford: Oxford University Press, 2018); Patryk Babiracki and Austin Jersild, eds, *Socialist Internationalism in the Cold War: Exploring the Second World* (Basingstoke: Palgrave Macmillan, 2016); Daniel Laqua, 'Democratic Politics and the League of Nations: The Labour and Socialist International as a Protagonist of Interwar Internationalism', *Contemporary European History* 24 (2015): 175–92; Brigitte Studer, *The Transnational World of the Cominternians* (Basingstoke: Palgrave Macmillan, 2015); Oscar Sanchez-Sibony, *Red Globalization: The Political Economy of the Soviet Cold War from Stalin to Khrushchev* (Cambridge: Cambridge University Press, 2014); Austin Jersild, *The Sino-Soviet Alliance: An International History* (Chapel Hill, NC: University of North Carolina Press, 2014).

be abandoned once and for all'.[19] The same holds true for the recent claim by Sluga and Philippa Hetherington about the 'interrelation between and the mutual dependence of liberal and illiberal internationalisms since 1880'.[20] Against this backdrop, the complex interplay between state stakeholders and internationalism has attracted new attention, too,[21] as has the blend of older, aristocratic forms of internationalism with the rightist politics of the 1930s, as epitomized by those sections of European nobility that volunteered as go-betweens for Hitler.[22] There is also fascinating new research on the relationship between internationalism and imperialism,[23] while some time ago Tara Zahra proposed 'national indifference' as a category of analysis.[24] Forms of internationalism that defy simple political categories have also been added to the picture, such as scientific internationalism, which often fashioned itself as neutral.[25] Law, long ignored by most historians, has re-entered the picture as means of formulating and negotiating, consolidating and challenging internationalisms. The League of Nations and the history of human rights provide two examples of how an interest in matters international has fostered new interdisciplinary connections with legal scholars. Martti Koskenniemi has become a household name for many international historians of the contemporary era,[26] helping to transcend disciplinary boundaries that long seemed harder than the 'steel-hard casing' in Max Weber's famous description of modern rationality.

Several of the contributions to this volume add further nuance to the picture, underlining the diversity of internationalist efforts even during a period as short as the twentieth century. While missionaries have long been studied as international actors (whole fields of Early Modern History would be non-existent without them, and long library shelves empty), this volume reveals the level of differentiation the literature has now achieved. For instance, David Brydan's and Carmen M. Mangion's analyses of Catholic activists underscore the diversity of Catholic internationalism, as well as

---

[19] Sluga and Clavin, 'Rethinking the History of Internationalism', 10.
[20] Philippa Hetherington and Glenda Sluga, eds, 'Liberal and Illiberal Internationalisms', *Journal of World History* 31 (2020): 1–262 (special issue), quote: 1; see, for example, also Ana Antic, Johanna Conterio and Dora Vargha, 'Conclusion: Beyond Liberal Internationalism', *Contemporary European History* 25 (2016): 359–71.
[21] See, for example, Glenda Sluga, *Internationalism in the Age of Nationalism* (Philadelphia: University of Philadelphia Press, 2013).
[22] Karina Urbach, *Go-Betweens for Hitler* (Oxford: Oxford University Press, 2015); on conservative and aristocratic internationalism, see, for example, Charlie Laderman, 'Conservative Internationalism: An Overview', *Orbis* 62 (2018): 6–21; another example is the 'vernacular international', in which ideas of Heimat were shared transnationally, see Maiken Umbach, 'The Vernacular International: Heimat, Modernism and the Global Market in Early Twentieth-Century Germany', *National Identities* 4 (2002): 45–68.
[23] For example, Jerónimo and Monteiro, *Internationalism, Imperialism and the Formation of the Contemporary World*.
[24] Tara Zahra, 'Imagined Non-Communities: National Indifference as a Category of Analysis', *Slavic Review* 91 (2010): 93–119.
[25] See, for example, Rebecka Lettevall, Geert Somsen and Sven Widmalm, eds, *Neutrality in Twentieth-Century Europe: Intersections of Science, Culture, and Politics after the First World War* (London: Routledge, 2012); John Krige, 'Atoms for Peace, Scientific Internationalism, and Scientific Intelligence', *Osiris* 21 (2006): 161–81.
[26] Martti Koskenniemi, *The Gentle Civilizer of Nations: The Rise and Fall of International Law 1870–1960* (Cambridge: Cambridge University Press, 2004).

religion's continuously important role in Europe's twentieth century.[27] Daniel Laqua has a similar claim for student activists, who were neither apolitical nor predominantly left. Others in this volume expand the definition of internationalism into new directions, such as Jessica Pearson, who uses Air France's promotional literature to assess how international air travel was used to reimagine 'Greater France', or Kristy Ironside with her analysis of how Soviet internationalism came in conflict with the international copyright regime.

Beyond sheer expansion of the list of internationalisms, various chapters show that the majority of internationalisms remained ephemeral. '-Isms' frequently and quickly turned into '-wasms' – such as Esperanto in revolutionary Russia or the project of Basic English. But obviously this eventual fate was not clear from the outset, relativizing the standard interpretation according to which Europe's twentieth century witnessed an epic struggle between three grand ideologies of international appeal – liberal democracy, fascism and communism. In fact, there were many more. And throughout most of the century, it was not clear which of them would dominate – nor that the main stage was reserved for just these three contenders. Much more work is needed to see whether these various '-isms' can be organized in a typology of sorts and to discern trends, chronologies and particularly powerful groups of actors. This is clearly an agenda for the future which would further deepen the impact of the history of internationalism(s) on broader historiographical themes and threads.

And, as a final thought in this context: in our own times, the fate of liberal internationalism seems less certain than ever since the 1940s. The triumphalism against which Mark Mazower pitched his argument about Europe as the 'Dark Continent' is now itself part of history.[28] Some might even look back at the internationalist post-Cold War moment with a quantum of nostalgia. Having said this, the new threats to democracy and a liberal order make research on alternative forms of internationalism, the diversity of movements, their conflicts and forms of global disconnection all the more pressing.

Bringing people back in

In their introduction, David Brydan and Jessica Reinisch argue that it is time to pay more attention to the lived experiences of internationalists, and thus to move beyond unpopulated characterizations of internationalist ideas, organizations and processes. Indeed, internationalist thinking has long been a concern of intellectual historians and diplomatic history has always been interested in the role of the institutions facilitating and shaping international exchange. By contrast, the people involved in the various registers of internationalism have attracted less attention to date. This applies especially to those actors below (and alongside!) the level of the Adenauers, Brezhnevs and Churchills – and the other dominant state actors from earlier and later times who have always been central for diplomatic historians of the traditional blend. This holds

---

[27] See, for example, also, Abigail Green, 'Religious Internationalisms', Sluga and Clavin, *Internationalisms*, 17–37.

[28] Mark Mazower, *Dark Continent: Europe's Twentieth Century* (London: Allen Lane, 1998).

particularly true for those involved in the 'inner mechanisms' of internationalism – the secretariats of international organizations, the key congresses and other, less formalized and institutionalized groupings and gatherings for whom internationalism was a lived experience that has to be studied at local and micro levels. Potentially, this expansion of focus can go as far as including all those upon whom internationalism impacted in their daily lives, but the authors in this volume are wise enough to adopt a slightly less expansive definition and concentrate mostly on what the editors call actors and agents of internationalism.

Doing so reflects the way many scholars conceptualize the international these days. Even if an internationalism developed stable institutional structures crystalizing in a formal organization, one should not overemphasize the consistency of such efforts. Many such organizations, including the League of Nations and the ILO, resembled more 'force fields' than monolithic actors with clear-cut structures, a consistent agenda and coercive powers. In Sandrine Kott's words, they are 'not so much *actors* in global governance as they are *sites* of internationalization'.[29] If the organizations are not the actors, but serve mainly as planks and platforms, as forums and facilitators for divergent ambitions and activities, it is obviously the people within them who deserve more attention. Again, this is not a plea to concentrate on 'great men' and the top tier of policymakers, but rather to create space for activists, experts, philanthropists and cultural protagonists alongside government officials, bureaucrats, diplomats and national representatives.[30] The focus then also goes beyond the insular examination of international negotiations that is so typical of a certain brand of international history. Instead the very practice of internationalism on the ground stands at the centre of scholarly attention.

Doing so is not easy. The official material produced by internationalists and their organizations often mixes excessive dullness with a good dose of self-celebration. This holds true for more formal international organizations and NGOs alike. In archival material, institutions also regularly dominate over internationalists. Even the most marginal form of internationalism has created an image of itself. It is these images that structure the sources we have, and they often provide the grammar with which internationalisms are studied. It therefore often proves difficult to step out of these narrative trails. The challenge is all the harder since documents of the kind described earlier are often comparably easily available. At the same time, it can be much more difficult to generate sources that provide different insights, such as personal papers, memoirs and documents that enable external perspectives on a form of internationalism. The job of combining and triangulating as many perspectives as possible, and thus to read sources against the archival grain, is time-consuming. It

---

[29] Sandrine Kott, 'Toward a Social History of International Organisations: The ILO and the Internationalisation of Western Social Expertise (1919–1949)', in *Internationalism, Imperialism and the Formation of the Contemporary World*, ed. Jerónimo and Monteiro, 33–57, quote 34; for the League of Nations as a 'force field': Susan Pedersen, *The Guardians: The League of Nations and the Crisis of Empire* (Oxford: Oxford University Press, 2015), 5; with an approach inspired by this work for the EU: Patel, *Project Europe*.

[30] This is also the approach of Miguel Bandeira Jerónimo and José Pedro Monteiro, 'Pasts to Be Unveiled: The Interconnections Between the International and the Imperial', in *Internationalism, Imperialism and the Formation of the Contemporary World*, ed. Jerónimo and Monteiro, 1–29, here 8.

often hinges on a good research budget to travel to faraway destinations and mastery of several languages. Moreover, it is full of cul-de-sacs, and academic kudos for going the extra mile remains rare. The search for a non-triumphalist tone and analytical distance therefore continue to be a challenge.

Still, there are several productive ways to shed light on the internationalists themselves. For instance, Carmen M. Mangion uses oral narratives to move beyond official decision making. Kornelija Ajlec also works with reports, interviews and other sources of information from refugees and relief workers in her analysis of Yugoslav camps in Italy and Egypt. Similar things can be said of Sławomir Łotysz's contribution on the history of the first Czechoslovak penicillin factory, which relies on archival evidence including Nobel laureate Ernst Boris Chain's personal papers. Such sources can provide us with deep insights into the motives and perceptions of those who shaped and experienced internationalism, and thus transcend a focus on the institutional side of internationalism that dominates existing research. While such sources often allow for a much better assessment of institutional dynamics and their eventual results, they also often nudge research towards examining institutional processes instead of actual practices, which makes it necessary to read archival documents both *against* and *along* the archival grain. While I have already sketched what I mean by reading against the grain, the latter can take inspiration from Ann Laura Stoler, who has stressed the need to study colonial archives as subject, not just as a source. Rumours, shifting and contested knowledge, and future imaginings along with other issues that bring past actors to life then gain more attention.[31] What Stoler has argued for the colonial archive can easily be transposed to the (European) internationalist archive, just as in general Europeanists still have much to learn from global historians and anthropologists.

This point ties in with a call to pay more attention to what the editors call the 'software of communication'. In general, we need to create more space for the practical conditions facilitating or impeding internationalism. As Brigid O'Keeffe and others show, language clearly matters. In most cases, internationalist projects hinged on communication across linguistic divides, which created new links, but at times also unexpected barriers, as well as in- and outgroups. Gayatri Chakravorty Spivak's 'Can the Subaltern Speak', a classic of post-colonial thought, carries important implications for the history of internationalism.[32] Her intervention can be seen as a plea to recover the agency of marginal voices as best as the historical archive allows, while also making visible the incompleteness of their representation. Spivak's work is illuminating both at profound anthropological and epistemological levels, but also at the mundane level of linguistic skills that might mute some, provide opportunities for others, and lead to (productive) misunderstandings that deserve to be studied in their own right.

Beyond language and communication, the whole sphere of internationalism's 'nuts and bolts' needs to be analysed further. Max Weber reminded us that economic

---

[31] Ann Laura Stoler, *Along the Archival Grain: Epistemic Anxieties and Colonial Common Sense* (Princeton: Princeton University Press, 2009).

[32] Gayatri Chakravorty Spivak, 'Can the Subaltern Speak?', in *Imperialism: Critical Concepts in Historical Studies*, ed. Peter J. Cain (London: Routledge, 2001), vol. III, 171–219. See as a fascinating attempt to transfer post-colonial studies to a different field (which can be inspiring for international history) Julian Go, *Postcolonial Thought and Social Theory* (Oxford: Oxford University Press, 2016).

independence giving people flexibility and security (the more precise German word is *Abkömmlichkeit*) may or may not define the role of professional politicians.³³ Similar things hold true for internationalists. Travel costs were a major reason why Latin Americans were less present at the Geneva-based League of Nations than Europeans, and location clearly mattered. Beyond money, travel connections and technical standards, passports and spouses, visas and vaccinations, many other things impacted the itineraries and trajectories of internationalists, too.³⁴ These 'nuts and bolts' clearly deserve more attention. Giving them that will help international history to move further away from a concern with either lofty ideas or 'realist' perspectives, to a set of factors that defined the parameters of internationalism and the lives of internationalists to a larger extent than is visible in most research.

II

Given the challenges of expanding research to internationalists and their travails, I will now elaborate on two perspectives that might help to further elucidate the daily practice of internationalism: for one, by shedding more light on people who were involved in several internationalisms simultaneously or successively and thus researching the dynamics resulting from these constellations; for the other, by examining constellations in which internationalists of several brands were interacting with each other on the ground. These are merely two examples, to which others could easily be added. They both draw inspiration from the book's chapters. They underline the importance of this volume's agenda; at the same time, this section seeks to open space for further discussion.

Multi-internationalists

Given the proclivity of most research in the field to follow the archival grain in a straightforward fashion, internationalists often only crop up in the one ideational or institutional context under study. Interestingly, however, many internationalists were busy on several fronts and thus defy easy categorization into one or other branch of internationalism. The Belgian author, bibliographer, entrepreneur, lawyer, peace activist, theosophist and visionary (the list itself speaks volumes, and could be expanded further) Paul Otlet (1868–1944) is a good example. In 1895, Otlet was one of the co-founders of the International Institute of Bibliography, which set out to establish new European standards for the organization and communication of documentation. The Universal Decimal Classification system Otlet developed is sometimes called a

---

[33] Max Weber, *Gesammelte politische Schriften*, ed. Johannes Winckelmann, 5th edn (Tübingen: Mohr, 1988).

[34] On some of these issues, also see Kiran Klaus Patel and Wolfram Kaiser, 'Continuity and Change in European Cooperation during the Twentieth Century', *Contemporary European History* 27 (2018): 165–82 and the wider special issue the text is part of. And, from a very different perspective, Nancy Green, 'The Trials of Transnationalism: It's Not as Easy as It Looks', *Journal of Modern History* 89 (2017): 851–74.

forerunner of the World Wide Web.³⁵ But creating an internationalism of knowledge by means of bibliography and documentation was not Otlet's only concern. He was also one of the founders of the Union of International Associations (UIA). Established in 1907, the UIA had the goal of uniting the existing documentary services of international organizations, but also covering international life in general.³⁶ Otlet also developed ideas for a world capital – conveniently to be situated in Brussels, where he lived. In this context, he collaborated with architects such as Le Corbusier to push for this agenda and raised funds from the Carnegie Endowment for International Peace and other bodies.³⁷ Like several of Otlet's projects, this came to naught. However, the UIA exists to this day, and its *Yearbook of International Organizations* continues to be the prime source of statistical information on NGOs. During the interwar years, Otlet and the UIA also helped to set up the so-called International University, which did not live up to his hopes of becoming a permanent institution, but played an important role in education internationalism – and the internationalization of education – at the time.³⁸ From an intellectual vantage point, Otlet is a perfect example of a tendency described earlier: cloaking Eurocentrism and a European focus more generally under the (dis)guise of internationalism. And like many internationalists, he pushed a very national agenda, in which his beloved Brussel and Belgium served as central node of international order. More important for the argument here, Otlet was a hatcher of internationalisms and a perfect example of why examining projects and institutions in isolation can be utterly misleading.

Otlet was not alone, and the deep fissures in the political history of the first half of the twentieth century did not keep actors from being involved in various forms of internationalism. Otlet pursed several internationalisms simultaneously; others are better known for doing so successively, with the Frenchman Jean Monnet (1888–1979) as an excellent example. Originating from a family of well-to-do cognac merchants, Monnet became a global traveller for his father's business at a young age. During the First World War, he worked for the Allied Maritime Transport Council, an agency coordinating shipping for the allied powers. After the war, at the age of thirty-one, he became Deputy Secretary General of the League of Nations. Monnet helped coordinate Allied armaments production and procurement during the Second World War before becoming the *éminence grise* of European integration from the late 1940s onwards.³⁹ Eleven years younger than Monnet, Belgian Paul-Henri Spaak began with a brilliant career at the national level. After 1945, he served as president of the first United Nations

---

[35] Alex Wright, *Cataloging the World: Paul Otlet and the Birth of the Information Age* (Oxford: Oxford University Press, 2014).

[36] Daniel Laqua, Wouter Van Acker and Christophe Verbruggen, eds, *International Organizations and Global Civil Society: Histories of the Union of International Associations* (London: Bloomsbury, 2019).

[37] Wouter Van Acker and Geert Somsen, 'A Tale of Two World Capitals: The Internationalisms of Pieter Eijkman and Paul Otlet', *Revue belge de philologie et d'histoire* 90 (2012): 1389–409.

[38] Daniel Laqua, 'Educating Internationalists: The Context, Role and Legacies of the UIA's "International University"', in *International Organizations and Global Civil Society*, ed. Laqua, Wouter Acker and Verbruggen, 53–72.

[39] See, for example, Klaus Schwabe, *Jean Monnet: Frankreich, die Deutschen und die Einigung Europas* (Baden-Baden: Nomos, 2016); Frederic J. Fransen, *The Supranational Politics of Jean Monnet: Ideas and Origins of the European Community* (Westport, CT: Greenwood Press, 2001).

General Assembly and, a few years later, as president of the Consultative Assembly of the Council of Europe, before becoming president of the Parliamentary Assembly of the European Coal and Steel Community (the oldest predecessor of today's EU) in 1952. As if this was not enough, he later served as Secretary General of NATO.[40] There was hardly a form of top-notch post-1945 Western internationalism in Europe in which Spaak was not involved. While links and learning processes between forums have attracted some attention in relation to Monnet and Spaak, there is still much room to investigate such connections.

For people simultaneously involved in several internationalisms, the relevance of *Abkömmlichkeit* was amplified, since international commitments often offered no source of revenues. And while some, like Otlet, lived internationalisms from where they sat, others had to hunt for them around the globe. Nationalism, racism, and war were not just abstract, intellectual reasons for people to become involved in internationalism. Circumstances sometimes pushed people into a continuous involvement in internationalism. Ludwik Rajchman, born into an upper-middle-class family of Christianized Jews in 1881, grew up in Warsaw when it was part of the Russian Empire. After studying medicine in Krakow, postdoctoral studies in Paris and a short stint back in Krakow (he was banned from the Russian-occupied part of Poland), he set up a life in London during the First World War, sharing his time between a bacteriological laboratory and lobbying for Polish independence. After 1918, he continued his bright career first in Warsaw, then for the League of Nations in Geneva, for which he travelled extensively, for instance to China. Known for his staunch anti-fascism, he was ousted from the League in 1938. Finding himself without a job, he reconnected with his Chinese contacts, helped the Chinese government purchase weapons from the Americans and soon resettled to France. After the German invasion, he fled to the United States and worked there on humanitarian issues, but also advised the nationalist Chinese government on questions of development. Rajchman then got involved in UNRRA, and when this agency declared that it would soon end its relief activities, he called for a new body supporting children in need throughout the world. This was the starting point for UNICEF, as whose chairman he served until 1950.[41] Rajchman thus moved from one internationalism to the other, inventing UNICEF along the way. His internationalist *tour du monde* ended happily: ultimately, he retired to the French chateau he had purchased shortly before the German invasion. Needless to say that others were less fortunate: Oswald Stein, a leading Czech ILO representative, died under mysterious circumstances in 1943. The Swede Dag Hammarskjöld helped set up the Marshall Plan organization OEEC in 1947–8 but passed away under even more dubious circumstances than Stein – as serving UN secretary general – in an aeroplane crash in Africa in 1961.[42]

[40] Paul-Henri Spaak, *The Continuing Battle: Memoirs of a European, 1936–1966* (London: Weidenfeld & Nicholson, 1971).
[41] Marta A. Balinska, *For the Good of Humanity: Ludwik Rajchman, Medical Statesman* (Budapest: Central European University Press, 1998).
[42] On Stein, see Sandrine Kott, 'Organizing World Peace: The International Labour Organisation from the Second World War to the Cold War', in *Seeking Peace in the Wake of War: Europe, 1943–1947*, ed. Stefan-Ludwig Hoffmann, Sandrine Kott, Peter Romijn and Olivier Wieviorka (Amsterdam:

While twentieth-century societal norms created a certain proclivity between white middle-class men with means and internationalism, the spectrum was obviously much broader. Internationalism is about families, not just about individuals – a point to which I will return later. Women have always played defining roles in internationalism. Marthe Boël, a Belgian feminist, worked as a nurse during the First World War. In 1919, she established the *Association des ex-prisonnières politiques de Siegburg*, a correspondence network of former POWs who had been held in the German city of Siegburg during the war. She also became a prominent member of the *Union belge pour la Société des Nations*, the national section of the League of Nations association. In 1936, she was elected president of the International Council of Women.[43] Widad Akrawi was born into a secular Kurdish family in Iraq in 1969. As a Danish-Kurdish human rights defender and peace activist, she served on the executive committee of Amnesty International; in 2007, she co-founded Defend International as an NGO fighting human rights violations. She is also involved in a whole range of other internationalist activities.[44] A third example is Tamara Bunke, also to underscore that not all female international activism falls into the category of peaceful, liberal-democratic engagement. Born to German communist exiles in Buenos Aires in 1937, her family moved to the GDR in 1952. Later, Bunke became an activist in communist Cuba, before joining Che Guevara's fight in various Latin American revolutionary movements. Aged twenty-nine, 'Tania the Guerrilla' died in an ambush while crossing the Rio Grande in 1967.[45]

Class, race, gender and also age – as well as access to internationalism's nuts and bolts as mentioned earlier – were important factors shaping (multi-)internationalist biographies. It has often been argued that in the case of Monnet, his Allied Maritime Transport Council and League of Nation experiences had a tremendous impact on how he thought and acted in the Western European context post-1945. But beyond individual cases, we still know little about how 'multi-internationalism' fired and shaped the people's lives and the international order more generally.

Societies of internationalists

The second dimension brings up childhood memories. I hope readers will bear with me if I get personal for a few lines: my parents spent ten years in Ghana, starting in 1963. They then relocated to Germany, my mother's country of origin, living some three kilometres away from my maternal grandparents. My father, born in India and raised in East Africa, was not the only exception to what then became a predominantly German local life. During their time in Kumasi, Ghana's second

---

Amsterdam University Press, 2015), 297–314, here 307; on Hammarskjöld, see Susan Williams, *Who Killed Hammarskjold?: The UN, the Cold War and White Supremacy in Africa* (New York: Columbia University Press, 2011).

[43] Eliane Gubin, 'De Kerchove de Denterghem Marthe (1877–1956), épouse Boël', in *Dictionnaire des femmes belges. XIXᵉ et XXᵉ siècles*, ed. Eliane Gubin, Catherine Jacques, Valérie Piette and Jan Puissant (Brussels: Racine, 2006), 163–6.

[44] https://widad.org/about-widad-akreyi/ (last accessed 1 May 2020).

[45] Gerd Koenen, *Traumpfade der Weltrevolution. Das Guevara-Projekt* (Cologne: Kiepenheuer & Witsch Verlag, 2008).

largest city, my parents acquired a very international circle of friends: Indian agricultural scientists and Pakistani doctors, a British-trained Spanish nurse and a French technician, Ghanaian GPs, a Swiss industrialist and a Yugoslav bacteriologist, Lebanese traders and business families, Irish Methodists and Dutch Catholic priests. Many of them were mixed couples, at odds with the racial order and gender roles prevalent in Europe during the first two post-war decades. During the 1970s, as living conditions in Ghana deteriorated and societies in the West liberalized, some of these families stayed in Ghana. Many migrated back to their countries of origin (often the home country of the European partner) or on to other parts of the globe. But they remained connected to their friends from the time in Ghana via letters, calls and occasional visits.

The internationalisms that brought them together in the West African country during the 1960s and 1970s were highly diverse. Ghanaians doctors were frequently funded by the Ghana Cocoa Marketing Board, a government-controlled institution which today is the world's second largest producer of the commodity. For a short period after the country's early independence in 1957, cocoa made Ghana affluent, and some of the revenues were used to send bright students to European universities. Some of these young men (yes, men, again reflecting gender conventions of the time) returned to Ghana with European spouses, at least among my parents' friends. This form of internationalism intersected with direct and indirect Western development aid (for some time, my father was paid by the Ghanaian Ministry of Education but when the cedi, the Ghanaian currency, faltered, he received a top-up from the British government),[46] with Christian missions, Lebanese and Swabian transnational business, and several other forms of internationalist engagement.

Moving from my parents' circle of friends to more illustrious members of Ghanaian society of the time, Pan-Africanist W. E. B. Du Bois, who spent the last two years of his life in Ghana, springs to mind. One of the last pictures shows him in 1963, on the occasion of his ninety-fifth birthday, together with Ghana's first post-independence president Kwame Nkrumah and Nkrumah's wife Fathia, who was of Coptic Egyptian background. Other prominent Ghanaians epitomized imperial legacies, for instance Peggy Cripps-Appiah, a children's author and daughter of the British politician Sir Stafford Cripps. She met her future husband, the pan-African activist and politician Joe Appiah, in the early 1950s in England through her work in an organization fighting racism; at the time, he was the president of the West African Students' Union. When they got married in 1953, the news made headlines in both Ghana and Great Britain; their son Anthony Appiah later became a very prominent philosopher. But not all internationalism was liberal: for several years during the 1960s, Hanna Reitsch, Hitler's star pilot, lived in Ghana and helped to build the country's aviation sector. During the post-war decades, she never quite understood why she should not wear the Iron Cross the Third Reich had awarded her.[47]

---

[46] Heidi G. Frontani and Lauren C. Taylor, 'Development through Civic Service: The Peace Corps and National Service Programmes in Ghana', *Progress in Development Studies* 9 (2009): 87–99.

[47] See, for example, 'Für Hitler flog sie durch die Hölle', *Spiegel*, 29 March 2012; Hanna Reitsch, *Das Unzerstörbare in meinem Leben*, 7th edn (Munich: Herbig, 1992).

All this is meant to illustrate a lacuna in our research that is closely related to my first point: most studies still focus on one specific form of internationalism and the actors who stood for it, and not on how various and diverse internationalisms intersected and interacted on the ground. Admittedly, Ghana at the time was a particularly exciting laboratory for internationalists of all sorts: in 1963, for instance, Nkrumah invited Soviet volunteers to his country – alongside the American Peace Corps, the Canadian international development organization CUSO and its British homologue VSO. He thought pitching one form of international engagement against the other was a 'brilliant ideological coup'.[48] So it would be wrong to confuse the confluence of internationalists with a harmonious community. In the racist language of the time, some said that Cripps-Appiah 'had gone bush'; her views on race and international engagement were fundamentally different from Reitsch's. Yet both lived their lives in ways that would have been much more difficult to realize in Europe at the time, and what the one meant for the other is just one of the questions that have remained neglected.

Research continues to rely too heavily and too one-sidedly on the files of international organizations. This creates an ever longer list of segregated internationalisms, since official files tend to tidy up the messy and fascinating reality actors were creating and facing on the ground. Zooming in on internationalists in their daily lives – from their work to the quarters they lived in, to the church services they attended, the kindergartens they sent their children to and the parties they enjoyed – would help us move beyond a purely nominalist emphasis on the multifarious '-isms'. It would bring out more clearly how internationalists learned from and impeded each other, how their work led to new synergies and other dynamics, and what the ultimate role of all things international was in comparison to other factors. Methodologically, this implies a greater use of private papers, personal letters, memoirs and interviews. This could help to shed new light on places like Kumasi and Accra as global sites of internationalism with a strong European whiff, while keeping in mind the complexity of documentary records particularly for Africa's post-colonial archive.[49] Other examples of concrete sites that deserve our attention are the Latin American cities where, after 1945, Jewish and other European refugees had to rub shoulders with former SS men, members of the Croatian Ustaše and others who had used the 'ratline' escape routes. In Europe, cities such as Brussels, Geneva, London and Paris would be excellent examples to analyse such dynamics – given that Belgium alone was the seat of up to one-third of all international organizations before 1914.[50] Of course, studies that read primary sources against the institutional and instead along the individual grain only make sense if they do leave the local level to recontextualize internationalist dynamics with

---

[48] Quoted in Elizabeth Cobbs-Hoffman, *All You Need Is Love: The Peace Corps and the Spirit of the 1960s* (Cambridge, MA: Harvard University Press, 1998), quote 162.

[49] Jean Allman, 'Phantoms of the Archive: Kwame Nkrumah, a Nazi Pilot Named Hanna, and the Contingencies of Postcolonial History-Writing', *American Historical Review* 118 (2013): 104–29.

[50] An inspiration for such work could be Michael Goebel, *Anti-Imperial Metropolis: Interwar Paris and the Seeds of Third World Nationalism* (Cambridge: Cambridge University Press, 2015), though also he concentrates on only one form of internationalism, in this case anti-colonial activism; also see Marc Matera's *Black London: The Imperial Metropolis and Decolonization in the Twentieth Century* (Berkeley: University of California Press, 2015).

wider processes and issues. In this book, chapters such as the one by Brigid O'Keeffe already go some way to show how different forms of internationalism intersected, and Jo Laycock also stresses the shared commitment to rational planning of various relief organizations in Soviet Armenia. But there is ample scope for more.

III

To conclude: this book provides impressive evidence that historiography on internationalism and internationalists is far from just marking time. Europeanists contribute to global conversations without resorting to the 'methodological grumpiness' that only a few years ago the aforementioned Charles S. Maier saw as a typical response to 'global history' from the diplomatic and international history fraternity.[51] Most Europeanists do not see Europe as the world's centre, but underline the continuous need to discuss the role of European actors in international and global affairs. By disaggregating the black box 'European' into smaller, more meaningful categories, such research adds to global conversations, and the same is also true of assessing the specific roots of Eurocentric ideas, institutions and persons populating the international stage. Other recent contributions to international history have pursued complementary agendas, for instance highlighting the spatial dimension of internationalism or the impact of internationalist preoccupations beyond their specific bubbles. Such agendas do not compete with each other; together, they help to nuance our understanding of internationalists and their activities.

Almost ten years ago, David Armitage argued that the 'hegemony of national history is over'.[52] This judgement is probably truer now than it was then. Having left the moorings of narrow normative and teleological approaches, international history has become one of the fields driving this process. Yet the group of scholars involved in researching European internationalism is still modest in size. A social network analysis of those active in the international community of scholars doing international history will be easy pickings for future historians of knowledge, and will show many links and overlaps. Multi-internationalism – in this case meaning researchers living international lives and studying a variety of internationalisms – would quickly emerge as a lived experience. But for all the talk about internationalizing research, multi-internationalists continue to be a minority. This makes the kind of research perspective proposed in this book more vulnerable than we sometimes tend to admit to ourselves.

The latter point also reflects the world we are living in today. In spring 2020, many may wonder if the heyday of internationalism is over, with neo-nationalist politics and criticism of globalization mushrooming across the globe and COVID-19 reducing

---

[51] Charles S. Maier, 'Dis/Relocating America: Approaches to Global History in the United States', *International History in Theory and Practice*, ed. Haider-Wilson, Godsey and Mueller, 315–31, quote 329.

[52] Martine van Ittersum and Jaap Jacobs, 'Are We All Global Historians Now? An Interview with David Armitage', *Itinerario* 36 (2012): 7–28, quote 16.

transnational movement to an extent hardly imaginable just a few months – in fact, weeks – before these lines were penned.

Some might fear that global trends will entail or trigger the demise of international history. Such tendencies are indeed visible in many countries, where historians are no longer free to speak their mind, curtailed by nationalist political elites and their (neo-)nationalist historiographical agendas. Elsewhere, there is less need to be pessimistic. International historians in and beyond Europe have long stressed the fragility of any form of international engagement and started to study processes of disengagement, disconnection and, in our concrete case, de-Europeanization. Hegel (who, by the way, died in a pandemic, just like Max Weber) noted that 'the owl of Minerva only spreads its wings with the falling of dusk' – meaning that philosophy only comes to understand a historical condition after the events have taken place. As much as one might hope politically for a resurgence of liberal internationalism, its crisis in our times does not necessarily reflect the situation of a historiography in a state like Minerva's owl. Instead, international history is needed more than ever, and it has developed a toolbox of approaches that is rich enough to tackle the challenges.

Select bibliography

Antic, Ana, Johanna Conterio and Dora Vargha, 'Conclusion: Beyond Liberal Internationalism', *Contemporary European History* 25, no. 2 (2016): 359–71.
Applebaum, Rachel, *Empire of Friends: Soviet Power and Socialist Internationalism*. Ithaca: Cornell University Press, 2019.
Brydan, David, *Franco's Internationalists: Social Experts and Spain's Search for Legitimacy*. Oxford: Oxford University Press, 2019.
Chamedes, Giuliana, *A Twentieth-Century Crusade: The Vatican's Battle to Remake Christian Europe*. Cambridge, MA: Harvard University Press, 2019.
Frey, Marc, Sönke Kunkel and Corinna Unger (eds), *International Organizations and Development, 1945–1990*. Basingstoke: Palgrave Macmillan, 2014.
Geyer, Martin H., and Johannes Paulmann (eds), *The Mechanics of Internationalism: Culture, Society, and Politics from the 1840s to the First World War*. Oxford: Oxford University Press, 2001.
Goebel, Michael, *Anti-Imperial Metropolis: Interwar Paris and the Seeds of Third World Nationalism*. Cambridge: Cambridge University Press, 2015.
Green, Abigail, and Vincent Viaene (eds), *Religious Internationals in the Modern World: Globalization and Faith Communities since 1750*. Basingstoke: Palgrave Macmillan, 2012.
Herren, Madeleine (ed.), *Networking the International System: Global Histories of International Organizations*. Cham: Springer, 2014.
Hetherington, Philippa, and Glenda Sluga (eds), 'Liberal and Illiberal Internationalisms', *Journal of World History* 31, no. 1 (2020): 1–262 (special issue).
Huber, Valeska and Jürgen Osterhammel (eds), *Global Publics: Their Power and Their Limits*. Oxford: Oxford University Press, 2020.
Ikonomou, Haakon A., and Karen Gram-Skjoldager (eds), *The League of Nations: Perspectives from the Present*. Aarhus: Aarhus University Press, 2019.
Imlay, Talbot C., *The Practice of Socialist Internationalism: European Socialists and International Politics, 1914–1960*. Oxford: Oxford University Press, 2018.
Iriye, Akira, *Cultural Internationalism and World Order*. Baltimore: Johns Hopkins University Press, 1997.
Iriye, Akira, *Global Community: The Role of International Organizations in the Making of the Contemporary World*. Berkeley: University of California Press, 2004.
Jackson, Simon and Alanna O'Malley (eds), *The Institution of International Order: From the League of Nations to the United Nations*. Abingdon: Routledge, 2018.
Jerónimo, Miguel Bandeira and José Pedro Monteiro (eds), *Internationalism, Imperialism and the Formation of the Contemporary World: The Pasts of the Present*. Basingstoke: Palgrave Macmillan, 2018.
Kott, Sandrine and Kiran Klaus Patel (eds), *Nazism Across Borders: The Social Policies of the Third Reich and Their Global Appeal*. Oxford: Oxford University Press, 2018.
Laqua, Daniel, Wouter Van Acker and Christophe Verbruggen (eds), *International Organizations and Global Civil Society: Histories of the Union of International Associations*. London: Bloomsbury, 2019.

Manela, Erez, *The Wilsonian Moment: Self-Determination and the International Origins of Anticolonial Nationalism*. Oxford: Oxford University Press, 2007.

Matera, Mark, *Black London: The Imperial Metropolis and Decolonization in the Twentieth Century*. Oakland: University of California Press, 2015.

Mazower, Mark, *Governing the World: The Rise and Fall of an Idea*. London: Penguin, 2012.

Mëhilli, Elidor, *From Stalin to Mao: Albania and the Socialist World*. Ithaca, NY: Cornell University Press, 2017.

Mikkonen, Simo, and Pia Koivunen (eds), *Beyond the Divide: Entangled Histories of Cold War Europe*. New York: Berghahn, 2015.

O'Keeffe, Brigid, 'An International Language for an Empire of Humanity: L.L. Zamenhof and the Imperial Russian Origins of Esperanto', *East European Jewish Affairs* 49, no. 1 (2019): 1–19.

Patel, Kiran Klaus, *Project Europe: A History*. Cambridge: Cambridge University Press, 2020.

Patel, Kiran Klaus, and Sven Reichardt, 'The Dark Side of Transnationalism: Social Engineering and Nazism, 1930s-40s', *Journal of Contemporary History* 51, no. 1 (2016): 3–21.

Pearson, Jessica Lynne, *The Colonial Politics of Global Health: France and the United Nations in Postwar Africa*. Cambridge, MA: Harvard University Press, 2018.

Pedersen, Susan, *The Guardians: The League of Nations and the Crisis of Empire*. Oxford: Oxford University Press, 2015.

Reinisch, Jessica, 'Introduction: Agents of Internationalism', *Contemporary European History* 25, no. 2 (2016): 195–205.

Rosenboim, Or, *The Emergence of Globalism: Visions of World Order in Britain and the United States, 1939–1950*. Princeton: Princeton University Press, 2017.

Scaglia, Ilaria, *The Emotions of Internationalism: Feeling International Cooperation in the Alps in the Interwar Period*. Oxford: Oxford University Press, 2019.

Sluga, Glenda, *Internationalism in the Age of Nationalism*. Philadelphia: University of Pennsylvania Press, 2015.

Sluga, Glenda, and Patricia Clavin (eds), *Internationalisms: A Twentieth-Century History*. Cambridge: Cambridge University Press, 2017.

Tworek, Heidi J. S., *News from Germany: The Competition to Control World Communications, 1900–1945*. Cambridge, MA: Harvard University Press, 2019.

Zahra, Tara, 'Imagined Non-Communities: National Indifference as a Category of Analysis', *Slavic Review* 69, no. 1 (2010): 93–119.

Index

Africa   29, 80, 111 n.27, 123, 145, 177–80, 228, 231–46, 275–8
Akrawi, Widad   276
Albania   11–12, 68–85
Algeria   175, 179–80, 235, 242–5
Algerian National Liberation Front   242
All-Union Society for Cultural Relations with Foreign Countries (VOKS, *Vsesoiuznoe obshchestvo kul'turnoi sviazi s zagranitsei*)   207
American Relief Administration (ARA)   90, 96 n.36
Armenia   12, 89–104, 279
Armenian General Benevolent Union (AGBU)   93, 99, 101 n.66
Armenian National Delegation (AND)   89 n.4, 92, 98–9, 101

Basic English   11, 51–67, 265, 270
Belarus   144, 150–1, 154, 155–6
Belgium   43–5, 227, 237, 273–4, 276, 278
Berlin   24, 71
Boël, Marthe   276
Bolshevik   18, 20–1, 23–30, 32–3, 99
Brazil   41, 85, 135, 223
Breslau, Boris   21–2
Brezhnev, Leonid   213, 270
British Broadcasting Corporation (BBC)   63, 69 n.3, 74, 82
Brussels   48, 194, 195, 274
Bunke, Tamara   276
Burma   178, 257

Caritas   216, 225
Catholicism   12, 124–39, 173, 215–28
Center for the Human Rights of Users and Survivors of Psychiatry (CHRUSP)   196
Central Commission for the Navigation of the Rhine (CCNR)   39
Central Intelligence Agency (CIA)   49, 73, 150–1, 174

Central Refugees Board (CRB)   109–13, 115–18, 120–2
Chain, Ernst B.   145–6, 152–6, 272
China   5, 12, 63, 68, 79–84, 166, 169, 178, 248, 252, 257, 260, 275
Chinese (language)   31, 36–7, 46, 50, 56
Chisholm, Brock   220, 224–7
Churchill, Winston   64–6, 270
Cold War   5, 9, 69, 120, 140, 145, 170, 173–6, 178–9, 199–9, 212, 217–18, 220, 265
Comité International Catholique des Infirmières et Assistantes Médico-Sociales (CICIAMS)   221–5
Communist International (Comintern)   5, 7, 12, 17–18, 23–32
Communist Party of the Soviet Union (CPSU)   30, 204, 208
Communist Party of the United States of America (CPUSA)   202, 205, 208, 211, 213
Communist University for the Toilers of the East   30
Conference of Latin American Bishops (CELAM)   128, 133
COVID-19   2, 279
Cuba   175, 227, 276
Czechoslovakia   12, 75, 140–57, 171, 272, 275
Czechoslovak People's Party (*Československá Strana Lidová*, ČSL)   152

decolonization   8–9, 80–1, 163, 178–9, 181, 228, 232 n.4
Denmark   196, 259
de Romer, Jadwige   220, 222–3, 225
disability   12, 182–97
Disabled People's International (DPI)   192–3
Down syndrome   185, 195–6

Egypt   12, 82, 105–23, 252, 255, 272
Esperanto   11, 17–32, 36, 49, 53, 55–6, 270
Ethiopia   266
European Student Relief (ESU)   165–71
European Union (EU)   1, 194–5, 197, 266–7, 275

family planning   122, 217, 224–8
Fast, Howard   12, 201–14
Fédération Internationale des Mutiles, des Invalids du Travail et des Invalides Civics (FIMITIC)   188
First World War   20, 89, 180, 219, 274–6
France   9, 13, 19, 168, 187, 194, 228, 230–46, 252, 260, 270, 275
French Union   241–5
Friedman, William F.   33, 33 n.1, 37 nn.18, 21, 38, 38 n.23, 41 nn.38, 40, 42, 42 nn.44–6, 44, 44 n.51, 45 n.54, 46 nn.59, 61, 47 nn.63, 66, 68, 48–50

Geneva   24, 154, 169, 197, 200, 219–20, 223–5, 227, 273, 275, 278
German Democratic Republic (GDR)   84, 276
Germany   4, 84, 146, 166–7, 276
Ghana   179, 276–8
Greece   72–4, 82, 101, 105, 115, 190, 197

Hitler, Adolf   32 n.65, 267, 269 n.22, 277 n.47
Hoover, Herbert   145
Hoover Dam   253, 261
House of Un-American Activities Committee   202, 207
Hoxha, Enver   70, 73, 78–9, 82
Hungary   77, 171, 175, 199
Huxley, Julian   51, 247, 253

India   30, 35, 51, 63–4, 67, 166, 178–9, 225–7, 232, 239, 252, 254–6, 276
International Association for the Scientific Study of Intellectual and Developmental Disabilities (IASSIDD)   190–1
International Auxiliary Language Association (IALA)   55, 59

International Catholics Organisations (ICOs)   215–28
International Council of Nurses (ICN)   221–2
International Decade of Disabled Persons   186
International Federation of the Blind (IFB)   188
International Federation of University Women   162
International Institute of Bibliography   273
International Labour Organisation (ILO)   192, 252, 266, 271, 275
International Refugee Organisation (IRO)   120
International Rivers Network (IRN)   261
International Sports Organisation for the Disabled (ISOD)   189
International Student Conference (ISC)   174–6, 178–80
International Telegraph Union (ITU, from 1932 the International Telecommunication Union)   11, 33–5, 37–50, 265
International Union of Students (IUS)   170, 172–4, 176, 178
International Year of Disabled Persons   186, 192
International Young Catholic Students (JECI, *Jeunnesse Étudiante Catholique Internationale*)   173
Investment Fund for Economic and Social Development (FIDES, *Fonds d'Investissement pour le Développement Economique et Social*   245
Iron Curtain   68, 74 n.28, 77 n.42, 84, 154, 199, 265
Italy   4, 12, 25, 38, 68, 70–1, 73–6, 105–23, 132 n.40, 143 n.11, 144–5, 150, 197, 227, 252, 272

Johnson, Lyndon B.   248, 256, 258–60

Khrushchev, Nikita   77–81, 199–201, 209, 212

Laos   257, 259, 262
L'Arche   187–8

Index

Lausanne Treaty   92–3, 101
League of Nations (LON)   8, 12, 54, 58, 90, 92, 104, 162, 165, 167, 169, 172, 219, 231, 252, 255, 268–9, 271, 273–6
League of Nations Health Organization (LNHO)   221
Lenin, Vladimir Ilyich Ulyanov   5 n.11, 17, 25, 29 n.50, 32, 95, 251 n.20
liberation theology   124, 128, 136, 138–9, 187
London   41–2, 48, 62, 82, 120, 147, 169, 180, 190, 241, 275
Lord Mayor's Fund for Armenian Refugees (LMF)   90, 93–4, 97–9, 101, 103

McGeachy, Mary   166–7
Maltz, Albert   206, 208, 212, 214
Mao Zedong   5 n.13, 18 n.2, 76 n.35, 79, 84 n.71
Marxism-Leninism   21, 31, 79, 80, 83, 84, 128 n.21, 136
Mekong river   247–62
Middle East Relief and Refugee Administration (MERRA)   109, 112–16, 118, 120–1
missionaries   12, 91, 95, 124–39, 164, 269
Monnet, Jean   244, 274–5
Morse code   35, 37, 39, 41–2, 46–7
Moscow   17, 20, 22–3, 26, 29, 31, 75–8, 98–100, 203–4

Nansen, Fridtjof   89 n.4, 90, 90 n.8, 92, 94 n.25, 97, 97 n.44, 98, 99, 100 n.58, 102, 102 n.67
Nansen passports   92
National Catholic Welfare Conference (NCWC)   218 nn.12–13, 219, 223–7
National Socialism   4 n.10, 11, 171, 172, 186, 261 n.73
Nazi   4, 12, 71, 74, 114, 118, 142, 147, 148, 172 n.69, 202, 220 n.20, 233, 278 n.49
Nazism, see National Socialism
Near East Relief (NER)   90, 93–101, 103
Nehru, Jawaharlal   51, 64, 67, 178, 265
Netherlands   61, 185, 259
Neurath, Otto   60, 66

New Deal   13, 247–8, 251–3
New Economic Policy (NEP)   29, 95
New International Economic Order   9
New York   55, 57, 103, 169, 184, 203, 205–6, 209, 219, 226, 235
North Atlantic Treaty Organisation (NATO)   1, 275
Norway   30, 189, 194

Office of Strategic Services (OSS)   115
Ogden, Charles Kay   52, 56, 59–61, 65–6
Otlet, Paul   273–5
Ottoman Empire   35, 40, 83, 89–92, 95, 98, 107, 111

Pan-Africanism   9, 177–9, 266, 277
Pan-Asianism   265 n.6, 266
Paris   9, 18, 24, 38, 43, 55, 57, 72, 92, 99, 169, 177–8, 187, 189, 204, 212, 235, 237–9, 243–5, 252, 255, 275, 278
Paris Peace Conference   72, 92, 99 n.55, see also Treaty of Versailles
Pax Romana   167, 172–3, 216
penicillin   12, 140, 142–57, 272
People's Commissariat of Enlightenment (Narkompros)   22–3, 28
Peru   12, 124–6, 129–39
Planned Parenthood   218, 226
Plojhar, Josef   152–3
Poland   84, 140 n.1, 143, 143 n.11, 144, 144 n.16, 146 n.23, 150–1, 154–6, 186, 275
Polevoy, Boris   201, 204, 206–8, 210
Portugal   85 n.76, 174

Radio Free Europe / Radio Liberty (RFE)   69, 75, 77, 77 n.44, 79 n.49, 82 n.62
Rajchman, Ludwik   275
Ransome, Arthur   23 n.26, 24
Red Cross   115, 146
refugees   6, 10, 12, 89–94, 97–102, 104, 105–23, 166, 187, 272, 278
Richards, Ivor Armstrong   51, 56, 59–60, 62–6
Roosevelt, Franklin Delano   64, 247, 251
Rouse, Ruth   164–6, 171
Russian Revolution   18, 21, 25, 80

Sadoul, Jacques   23, 24
St Petersburg/Petrograd   17, 20, 41
Save the Children   99 n.52, 101, 101 n.65, 138
Second Vatican Council   127–8, 139
Second World War   3–4, 9, 12–13, 49, 53, 63–4, 66, 83, 107, 109 n.17, 121, 123, 162 n.9, 167, 170, 172, 186, 198, 216, 219–20, 241, 247–8, 250, 253–4, 256, 260, 274, 275 n.42
Spain   27, 84, 132 n.40, 173–4, 187 n.10, 222 n.27
Stalin, Josef   5 nn.11, 13, 18 n.2, 25, 25 n.32, 32 n.65, 73, 73 n.26, 76 n.35, 77–80, 84, 110, 156, 170, 199, 203, 203 n.25, 209, 211, 212 n.80, 252, 267, 268 n.18
Sweden   163, 189, 191, 194
Switzerland   30, 38, 84, 164, 167, 172, 195, 219, 228, 237, 261

Tennessee Valley Authority (TVA)   13, 247–54, 255–8, 260
Tito, Josip Broz   73, 116–19
tourism   13, 231–8, 241–2, 245–6
Transcaucasian Federation   95–6, 98, 100
Treaty of Versailles   55
Turkey   30, 58–9, 67, 82, 98

Ukraine   93 n.21, 144, 150, 154, 154 n.56, 156
Union Générale des Étudiants Musulmans Algériens (UGEMA)   180
Union of International Organisations   274
Union of Soviet Socialist Republics (USSR)   5, 10–11, 18 nn.2, 4, 30–1, 59, 68–9, 71 n.11, 75–6, 79–80, 82, 90–1, 93, 97–9, 102–4, 144, 154, 170, 174, 176, 186, 198–214, 227, 248, 251–2, 260
United Nations (UN)   1, 7–9 n.24, 13, 106 n.7, 121, 141, 144 n.14, 163 n.12, 167, 175, 191–3, 215–28, 231–2, 242 n.44, 245 n.58, 247, 250, 253–4, 256, 258–61, 268, 274–5
United Nations Convention on the Rights of Persons with Disabilities (UNCRPD)   186, 195–6

United Nations Development Programme (UNDP)   258–9
United Nations Educational, Scientific and Cultural Organization (UNESCO)   51, 63, 65, 98, 198–9, 247, 266
United Nations Relief and Rehabilitation Administration (UNRRA)   7, 12, 106 n.7, 107 n.12, 111, 112 n.38, 114 n.46, 115–16, 118, 120–2, 140–4, 146–53, 155–7, 167, 253 n.33, 275
United Nations Scientific Conference on the Conservation and Utilization of Resources (UNSCCUR)   253
Universal Copyright Convention   198, 200, 213
US State Department   154, 174, 203, 257

Vatican   13, 74, 82, 127, 127 n.17, 128 n.19, 130 n.31, 139, 173 n.80, 187, 216, 219–20, 224, 228
Vietnam   178, 244, 248, 257–61

Weber, Max   269, 272, 273 n.33, 280
Wells, H. G.   51, 57, 62, 64
World Bank   250, 254–61
World Commission on Dams (WCD)   261
World Health Organisation (WHO)   9, 141, 146 n.22, 152, 154–6, 217, 220–7
World Program of Action Concerning Disabled Persons (WPA)   192
World's Student Christian Federation (WCSF)   163–8, 177, 180
World Student Association (RME, *Rassemblement Mondial des Étudiants*)   168–9, 178

Yugoslavia   12, 68, 70, 73–4, 78, 82, 106 n.6, 107, 110–12, 115–22, 143–4, 149, 154–6, 166
Yugoslav Communist Party (CPY)   109, 115–17, 120–1
Yugoslav National Liberation Army (YNLA)   105, 108, 111 n.27, 118

Zamenhof, Ludwig   19, 36

www.ingramcontent.com/pod-product-compliance
Lightning Source LLC
Chambersburg PA
CBHW072125290426
44111CB00012B/1784